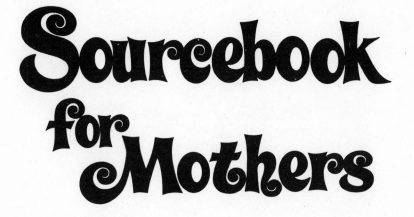

Sourcebook for Mothers

*A COMPILATION OF READINGS,
BANQUET IDEAS, TOASTS, POEMS,
SEED THOUGHTS, DEVOTIONAL
TALKS, PLAYS, DIALOGS*

by ELEANOR DOAN

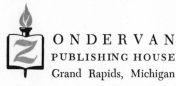
ONDERVAN
PUBLISHING HOUSE
Grand Rapids, Michigan

To Cynthia's Mother* and to mine . . .
whose lives were a tribute to womanhood
in their devotion to the Lord Jesus whom
they loved and served, and in whose presence
they are now rejoicing.

*See "Letter to Cynthia," page 197

ACKNOWLEDGMENTS

Grateful acknowledgment is made to the following publishers and authors for permission to use the copyrighted selections in this book:

Jeanne Allen for "Today's Christian Leaders Had Mothers Who" and "Mother's Tasks—A to Z" from *Christian Mother*.

AMERICAN TRACT SOCIETY, Oradel, New Jersey, to reprint "A Mother's Calling to Make and to Mend" by Raymond L. Cox and "I'm the Only Mother My Children Will Ever Have" by Ruth Vaughn.

ASSOCIATED CHURCH PRESS for the poem by Blaise Levai.

BEACON HILL PRESS of Kansas City, Missouri, for "Come Into the Living Room," "Home" and "Yesterday" from *In Favor with God and Man* by Kathryn Blackburn Peck; "What a Home Should Have," "A Devotional Reading" and "I'm Glad Today" from *Together With God* by Elizabeth B. Jones.

William M. Bower for permission to use four poems by Helen Frazee-Bower: "A Mother Dedicates Her Children" which appeared in *King's Business*, and "A Mother's Request," "Young Mother" and "A Mother's Prayer" from *Garments of Praise* by Helen Frazee-Bower.

Ruth Bowker for "A 'Thank-You' to Grandma."

Helen Good Brenneman for "To My Daughters: A Spiritual Will and Testament" from *Christian Living*.

CHICAGO TRIBUNE for the poem "A Father's Prayer," reprinted in *Moody Monthly*.

CHRISTIAN HERALD for "Five Cornerstones of a Good Home" by Mrs. Daniel Poling, a paragraph by Miriam Philips Platig, the poem "Where's Mother?" by Marie W. Musselwhite, and the tableau "Mothers of the Bible" by Jane Kirk Huntley.

CHRISTIAN LIFE PUBLICATIONS, Wheaton, Illinois, for "An Adored Mother" by Carolyn Beaucamp and quoted by Flo Price.

THE CHRISTIAN MOTHER for "Resolutions for Parents," Copyright by Standard Publishing.

Myrtle M. Clemmer for the poem, "Mother" by Allen A. Stockdale, published in *Reveille*, June 1939 by Cornelius Publications, Indianapolis, Indiana.

DAVID C. COOK for "A Mother's Wishes on Her Day" by Ruth Pierce, reprinted by permission from *Sunday Digest*. Copyright 1967 by David C. Cook Publishing Co., Elgin, Illinois.

COVENANTER WITNESS for "What a Real Home Is" by Edward Purinton.

June Lord Crabtree for "Parables for Mothers," adapted from a writing by Temple Baily. Copyright 1952 by Standard Publishing.

CRUSADER for the play, "The Weavers."

DECISION for permission to use two quotations by Sherwood E. Wirt from "The Real Mother's Day," Copyright 1965, and for a quotation by Clifford Barrows. Copyright 1962.

DEFENDER for the poem "Mother—Daughter of a King" by Dr. May H. Clutter.

Dr. Russell V. DeLong for "The Ten Commandments for Fathers."

DOUBLEDAY AND COMPANY, INC., for "Mother O'Mine" by Rudyard Kipling from *Rudyard Kipling's Verse: Definitive Edition*. Reprinted by permission of Mrs. George Bambridge and Doubleday & Company, Inc.

DROKE HOUSE for six quotations from *The Quotable Billy Graham* edited by Cort R. Flint and the staff of *Quote*.

Louise B. Eavey for "A Mother's Dedication." Copyright 1956 by *Sunday School Times*.

Katherine Edelman for the poem, "Mother's Love."

EVANGELICAL PUBLISHERS for the poem "The Prayer of Martha" by Annie Johnson Flint. Reproduced by permission Evangelical Publishers, Toronto, Canada.

Helen Kitchell Evans for the poem "My Grandmother" from *Mother's and Father's Day Program Book No. 10*. Copyright 1956 by Standard Publishing.

Geraldine Everett Gohn for the poem "Blessed Event."

First Church of Christ, Scientist, Maywood, Illinois, for permission to reprint the poem "Hymn for a Household" by Daniel Henderson from *1000 Quotable Poems*. Copyright by Harper and Row.

Alvey E. Ford for the poems "My Daddy" and "My Mummy."

Margaret Freeman for "God's Love" and "A Thank You Prayer." Copyright by Standard Publishing 1956 and 1958.

Vivian Gunderson for "Jochebed, a Bible Mother," "A Mother's Secret and Great Faith," "Where's Mother," "The Mothers Consult," "Getting Paid," and "Robbed of Mother."

Carol Clark Hagelin for the poem "Always Onward" by Grace Stoner Clark. Copyright by Standard Publishing, 1954.

Inez Hallan for "Women of the Bible" from *Child Evangelism*. Copyright 1966.

HALLMARK CARDS, INCORPORATED for the poem "What Is a Mother?" Copyright Hallmark Cards, Incorporated. Reprinted by permission.

HARPER AND ROW for "A Mother Understands" from *The Best of Studdert Kennedy*. Copyright 1929 by Harper and Brothers; "So Long as There are Homes" from *Light of the Years* by Grace Noll Crowell. Copyright 1936 by Harper and Brothers. "Mothers" from *Songs of Faith* by Grace Noll Crowell. Copyright 1939 by Harper and Brothers. "Hands" from *Facing the Stars* by Grace Noll Crowell. Copyright 1941 by Harper and Brothers. All reprinted by permission of Harper and Row, Publishers, Incorporated.

Paul Harvey, News Commentator, and the American Broadcasting Company for "What Are Fathers Made Of?" Copyright 1963 by General Features Corp.

THE HENRY F. HENRICHS PUBLICATIONS, INC., for the following materials reprinted from *Sunshine Magazine*: "Things that Honestly Thrilled Me" by Mrs. N. J. Cline; "Life" by Elizabeth Giles Donaldson, "New Shoes" by Marian Kennedy, "My Mother's Hands" by Hugh W. Phillips, "The Unseen" by William Arthur Ward, "A Woman's Wish," "Grandmothers of America," "No Place Like It," "Job Tickets."

Esther B. Heins for the poem "For My Mother" from *Mirror of Christ*.

J. Edgar Hoover for the essay "What Is a Good Home," printed in *Link* by the National Sunday School Association.

HOUGHTON MIFFLIN CO., for two poems by Henry Wadsworth Longfellow: "From the Children's Hour" and "Weariness."

Barbara A. Jones for the poem "Haven" from *Christian Living*.

KING'S BUSINESS for "A Mother's Prayer" by Mrs. Willard M. Aldrich, "A Tribute to a Daughter"

Reprinted by permission of Harper & Row, Publishers.

Grace Watkins for the poem "The Challenge."

Margaret Widdemer for the poem "The Watcher," from *Cross Currents,* published by Harcourt, Brace and World, Inc.

Lon Woodrum for the poem "I Had a Christian Mother."

WORLD VISION MAGAZINE for "I Must Make the Time Count" by Larry Ward. Copyright by World Vision.

ZONDERVAN PUBLISHING HOUSE for selections from *Sermon Outlines on the Home* by Al Bryant; *Heart to Heart Talks with Mothers* by Ann Hoek; *Poems That Bless* and *Short Talks for Banquets* by Louis Paul Lehman, Jr.; *Devotional Programs for Women's Groups* by Lora Lee Parrott; *Book of Favorite Poems* by John Peterson; *Mother-Daughter Banquets* by Grace Ramquist; *Points for Parents* by Martin P. Simon; "Mother's Day Beatitudes" by William Stidger; *Listen Mothers* by Charles F. Weigle; also for portions of James taken from *The Berkeley Version of the Holy Bible* by Gerrit Verkuyl.

Diligent effort has been made to locate the original source of all copyrighted materials in this book and to secure permission for their inclusion. If such acknowledgments have been inadvertently omitted, the compiler and publisher would appreciate receiving full information so that proper credit may be given in future editions.

MOTHERS ARE SPECIAL

Mothers are very special.

They are special because each one is the most loved person in the life of some individual. People everywhere share a common bond in paying tribute to Mother. Except for Christmas, Mother's Day is the most popular special day of the year.

On this particular day loving thoughts of Mother well up in the hearts of individuals young and old, rich and poor, strong and frail. It is a time for remembering Mother with the heart! Remembering her patience and understanding, selflessness and love, her disciplines and guidance, her encouragements and training, her soft voice reading a Bible story or teaching a prayer, the quiet comfort of sorrows shared and confidences that were always kept, times of happiness for achievements great and small, tears of joy for the unexpected hug of appreciation and kisses flavored with peanut butter and jelly, her laughter in shared joys, her tears when there were hurts, the burdens borne with faith in God and her prayers in time of discouragement and trials.

Mother's Day is special not only for the natural mothers, but for those who have been mothers in every sense of the word except in childbearing. Ofttimes they deserve tribute far above that for the natural mothers because they have borne the responsibilities of child rearing and character molding when those who gave birth turned their backs on their offspring.

Because mothers are so very special, the need for appropriate materials honoring them prompted the request for the compilation of a family book spotlighting Mother. For too long there had been too little material available for this noble purpose.

This book wraps up all the needs for Mother's Day materials and other occasions honoring mothers, from a recitation by a little child, a sermon from the pulpit, nostalgic reading by grandma, gifts to make for Mother, toasts and talks for banquets, to plays and a tribute to the best loved member of the family. This is an idea book, a reference book, a program book, a book of inspiration, a scrapbook, a book of poetry and a sourcebook.

Because of the close family relationships mothers cherish, and the importance of each family member, there are portions of the book devoted to the home, parents, family, children, daughters, sons, grandparents, and, of course, father.

This book reaches across the cultural and age spans of mothers: working mothers, old-fashioned mothers, lonely mothers, poor mothers, Christian mothers, young mothers, old mothers. And it purposes to honor each of them, including your mother and mine . . . because mothers are special.

Eleanor Doan
Glendale, California

CONTENTS

WAYS TO OBSERVE MOTHER'S DAY

Mother's Day can be observed anywhere—at home, Sunday school, in church, clubs, organizations,. school, rest homes, hospitals—and in many different ways—from the making of a greeting card to a special program. Wherever and whatever the observance, the day should be one of joy and happiness. It should be one involving every individual in the group whether he be young or old, for each shares a common bond in paying tribute to Mother.

There are many and varied ways to observe Mother's Day.

Social Affairs: banquets, teas, breakfasts, brunches, coffee hours, parties, etc.

Home Observances: dinner, surprise party, family program, family reunion, etc.

Contests: "Mothers, Queens for One Day"; letters about "What Mother Means to Me"; poems or essays on "Mother's Love," etc.

Programs: by children or youth, Sunday school departments, clubs, organizations, etc.

Projects: visiting shut-in mothers in rest homes, sanitoriums, hospitals, etc.; adopting mothers who may be alone, "mothers" who have no children; writing letters to mothers who may be lonely (whose children are away, not living, sick, in the Armed Services, etc.).

Church Services: special programs, music, sermons, recognitions, etc.

Community: Contests with newspaper, radio and TV assistance; programs; visitation projects to honor all "shut-in" mothers, etc.

Special recognitions for Mothers can be varied:

Mothers with birthdays on Mother's Day.

Oldest mother, grandmother, great grandmother, etc.

Youngest mother, grandmother, great grandmother, etc.

Newest mother, grandmother, great grandmother, etc.

Mother with most children living.

Mother with most children present.

Mother with most relatives present.

Mothers of twins, triplets, etc., present.

Twin or triplet mothers present.

Most generation of mothers present.

Missionary mothers.

Mothers of missionaries.

Mothers with children born on Mother's Day.

Mothers of service men.

Mothers may be presented with flowers, plants, buttons, tags, candy, booklets, letters, cards, gifts, etc.

Tributes may be paid to deceased mothers with gifts given in her memory, such as flowers or plants for the church or church's shut-ins; plantings for community parks; books for the library of the Sunday school, rest home, church organizations or community.

Mother's Day in the Sunday school and Church.

In the Sunday school and church, this special day should be utilized fully to unite with the home in Christian Education. Whatever observances there are should contribute to growth, not merely entertainment, of all members of the church and home.

In the Sunday school

Pupils may assist with all the preparations such as arranging an interest center with flowers (one for each mother), placed around an open Bible. A guest-book may be placed on a table near the door for each mother to sign as she enters. During the fellowship period each pupil may introduce his mother, then join together in singing "Happy Wel-come" to the tune, *Happy Birthday* (see page 256). Mothers of each class or grade may be recognized, also mothers having birthdays on their special day. The spe-cial program may include a piano duet by a mother and daughter or instru-mental music by a mother and son, etc. Selected passages of Scripture which re-fer to mothers may be read (see page 102). Children might read letters or poems which they have written to honor their mothers. Recitations or plays may be given by the children.

During the time when children are in classes, mothers can enjoy a "Coffee Hour" with a special devotional talk by a well-known mother.

At Church

Music selected may include hymns written by mothers, duets or trios by mothers, instrumental solos by mothers, etc.

Recognition may be one or more of the foregoing ideas.

Special features might include the ded-ication of children, reading of a winning essay or poem on "Mother's Love," "What Mother Means to Me," "My Mother Is Best of All," etc. (See sug-gestions under "Children and Mother's Day.")

Sermon topics appropriate to the day might be "The Real Mother's Day," "Thank God for Mothers," "Faith of Our Mothers," "A Mother's Touch," "Mothers are Special," "The Priceless Name of Mother," "Godly Mothers," and topics from Sermon Seed Thoughts, page 206.

Children and Mother's Day

There is much that children can do to make Mother's Day meaningful, not only on that day, but in preparation for it.

Invitations for mothers to special af-fairs may be made by children.

Gifts may be made also (see page 262), including extra gifts for mothers in rest homes, hospitals, etc.

Letters, essays, poems, etc., may be written. Here are two, both written by third-graders.

My Mother

My Mother's special you shall see.
She always says that she loves me.
I have lots of brothers and sisters too,
But Mommy likes me best, that's true.

My Mother Is Best of All

My Mother is best of all,
In summer, spring, winter and fall.
She gives me the best of food each day,
And after that she will let me play.
She is very patient with the things I do,
And she loves me best out of each one of
    you.

Acrostics may be worked out by the children using the words MOTHER and GRANDMOTHER.

Recitations, songs, duets, etc., may be learned to use at school, Sunday school, or at home.

Girls may write essays on "The Kind of Mother I Would Like to Be," "The Influence of Mothers I Have Known" (grandmother, a friend's mother, a Christian mother—perhaps their Sunday school teacher—a step-mother, a career mother, a missionary mother, a praying mother, etc.).

Boys may enjoy writing out a list of "Because I Love You" promises for the next month. These might include: "Mow the grass without grumbling," "Abide by the TV rules," "Run one errand each day," etc.

On Mother's Day at home children might prepare breakfast or dinner, make the beds, do the dishes, clean the house, etc. They may plan various ways to honor all the mothers present with a program, gifts, flowers, poems, essays, music.

Other Ideas

Many other ideas may be worked out by using the various portions of this book as resource materials to make Mother's Day meaningful to all family members and to all groups where this special day is observed.

MOTHER

Mother, Home and Heaven

It has been said that the three most loved words in the English language are mother, home and heaven.

Mother is a wonderful word. It takes a great deal of wisdom and courage to be a mother. It also takes time. Time to wash faces, to brush little girls' hair, patch jeans, keep a house clean and inviting, nourishing meals planned and prepared, clothes washed, ironed and mended.

Yes, it takes time.

How alert, how active these children of ours are! It takes time to discover what goes on inside the heads and hearts of boys and girls. How receptive they are to things of the Spirit! How difficult they are at times, too, and how inadequate we often feel in dealing with them!

It takes patience and understanding, too, to be a mother. If there is any prayer that I have prayed with great frequency, it is the plea to my understanding heavenly Father to grant me patience.

Yes, much is required of mother.

While we are busy with preparations for dinner, while putting the finishing touches to a birthday cake, or perhaps in the darkness of the night during a wakeful hour, the realization sweeps over us suddenly and poignantly that these children of ours will not be children in our homes always. There will come a tomorrow—much sooner than we realize—when our homes will no longer ring with the carefree laughter of our children. If there are standards of living to set up, a family altar to establish, truths to impart, love for God and loyalty to the church to instill, or prayers to be prayed for our boys and girls, we must do it today in our homes!

The Bible is full of references to heaven. We need not be ignorant of the home that awaits us in eternity. If it has been some time since you have read John's description of heaven as God gave him the revelation, or if you have never read it, open your Bible right now and read Revelation 21 and 22. Of course, the truly glorious part of heaven will be His presence.

Recently a neighbor, an avowed agnostic, said to me when we were discussing the hereafter and eternity, "Eternity? Who wants to live forever? Perish the thought of having to spend an eternity with my mother. My father was an atheist, my mother a———(and she named a liberal denomination). I am the result of that kind of a home . . . ."

Obviously for her the words mother, home and heaven were not loved.

Are these three words of love for you?

Will they be words the memories and thoughts of which will be happy and pleasing to your children?

HELEN KOOIMAN

Mother

I know not where in all this world I'd
    find
    Another half so precious or so dear,
Or one whose love would hold so firm
    and kind
    Throughout the changing fortunes of
    each year.
In all my life I can not hope to pay
    That priceless debt of faithful loyalty;
I asked no sweeter bondage than to stay
    A debtor to her precious love for me.
For it I'd yield the honor men confer,
    For it I'd give all wealth and eminence.

And all I have I humbly offer her—
  My deepest love and truest reverence.
I know none other I could so enshrine
  Within my heart, save her—that
  mother mine.

M.P. LITTLE

Mother

Her love outlasts all human love:
Her faith endures the longest, hardest
  test;
Her grace and patience through a life-
  time prove
That she's a friend, the noblest and the
  best.

AUTHOR UNKNOWN

Hallowed Name of Mother

The dying words of Henry Clay were,
"Mother, mother, mother." Then he
went to join the one who had loved him
next to his God.

O, the hallowed name of mother;
  How we lisp it o'er, and o'er,
While we're drifting in time's ocean,
  Drifting toward the golden shore,
In the Christian's home in glory,
  Out across death's silent goal—
We shall meet her—we shall greet her—
  In the homeland of the soul.

E.W.C.

A Mother's Heart

A Mother's heart is a many-faceted
thing.

First of all, it must be like a cheery,
constantly glowing hearth to which the
members of her family can always come
to warm themselves, and from which
they can go comforted with their faith in
themselves renewed.

But it must also be a cool and placid
lake in the midst of family storm and
stress. It must be calm and undisturbed,
a source of constancy, guidance, humor
and reason . . .

It must be gentle and soft, yielding
and giving and ready to receive, always

touched and delighted by the dear foolish gifts of feathers and dandelions and
school drawings and lumpy pot holders
that her children bring her . . . moved,
too, and understanding of all their
secrets and confidings, whatever their
age. It must be tender and pliant, yes,
before all these things . . . but oh, it
must be strong!

It must, in fact, be sturdy and strong
to withstand the many blows it will receive. The disappointments and things
that might otherwise tear it apart, for
they are the lot of every mother, no
matter how hard she has tried, or how
fine her children may be . . .

Above all a mother's heart must be a
bridge upon which people are continually crossing to find and reach and understand each other. A bridge between
brothers and sisters, husbands and in-
laws, fathers and sons. Somewhere there
in the center it stands, not always
steady, but enduring nonetheless . . . supporting the whole living structure of the
family.

And so a mother's heart must be everything . . . warm and rosy, yet cool and
calm . . . gentle and tender, yet dependable and strong. And though it can't be
all of these things all of the time (else
mothers would be saints) it manages, by
some miracle, to be most of these things
a great deal of the time.

MARJORIE HOLMES

Mother

True, I was yours before you even saw
  me,
You loved me when I had not known
  the light,
Your tender thought was waiting for my
  coming
And boy or girl, no matter, all was right.

Your love was calm and true when I was
  crying,
A soothing peace was waiting at your
  breast;
Your touch was like a fairy's, full of
  magic
And all your words came lulling me to
  rest.

You lived for me and by your understanding,
Kept open court of justice for my rights;
No faults of mine could make you turn
against me,
You trusted me and prayed through
tempting nights.

You loved me, served me, watched me,
precious Mother,
Rejoicing more than I when good things
came,
And where I failed to reach some high
endeavor
You seemed to feel as if you were to
blame.

And then the Lord promoted you in
glory,
Released you to a life forever new,
But I have followed after you in spirit—
And in my prayers I love to talk to you.

ALLEN A. STOCKDALE

Just Mother

She could not paint, nor write, nor
rhyme,
Nor leave her footprints on the sands of
time
As some famous women do;
Just simple things of life she knew,
Like putting little ones to bed
And listening while their prayers were
said.

She wasn't learned in chemistry,
Law, science, or philosophy;
She could not speak her thoughts aloud
In eloquence, before a crowd;
But hers a tranquil atmosphere
That brought a bit of heaven here.

She was no singer; neither blessed
With any special loveliness
To bring applause or passing fame;
No headlines ever blazed her name,
But oh, she was a shining light
To us, who loved her day and night!

Her home, her kingdom . . . she, its
queen;
Her rule was honest, loving, clean;

Impartial, just, and loyal to each
And everyone she sought to teach.
Her name? Of course there is no other
In all the world so sweet
. . . just Mother!

MAY ALLREAD BAKER

A Mother's Creed

I believe in little children
And in the Great Creator of this bit of
art.
I believe in the desire of every child
To do what is basically good and right.
It is my duty as a mother to help my
child
Accomplish this good by whatever
means
Is necessary.

I believe in love . . .
I think every child, young or old needs
love.
It therefore becomes my privilege to
give him
The gift of love and understanding,
Withholding none.

I believe in faith . . .
The faith of a little child who questions
not
The wisdom of the Heavenly Father;
I know I must help my child keep that
faith
Throughout life's day.

I believe in hope . . .
I see in my child the hope of the world.
In him and through him this great uni-
verse
Must become a better place to live;
Perhaps not because of any measure
Of his greatness, but because of the
abundance
Of his kindness and his thoughtfulness
Toward others.

I believe I cannot create, direct, or show
By example how life can be lived at
its best
Without the help of the Father above
. . .

His is the power, the kingdom, and the
  glory.
But I believe that because God has en-
  trusted
To my care a little child,
Because He has placed this child's tiny
  hand
In my own, He will grant me a mother's
  love,
Her faith, her hope, her wisdom.

And I believe that He will teach me
How to use these virtues
If I seek each hour of the day
His blessing for us both,
Mother . . . and child.

PHYLLIS MICHAEL

An Adored Mother

She mended a doll
  and the washing waited.
The dust lay thick
  while a fish hook was baited.

When Injuns attacked
  her dinner burned up.
She provided a bed
  for a straying pup.

A two-year-old helped
  with the cookie dough,
The ironing dried out
  while she romped in the snow.

Her neighbors whispered
  to one another,
But the children laughed
  and adored their mother.

CAROLYN BEAUCAMP

An Ideal Mother

A worthy mother who can find?
  She must be gentle, loving, kind,
Wise, tactful, patient, firm and true,
  A diplomat, one who can do
The many things that children need;
  For their best good she must give
  heed.

Her husband's heart doth trust in her,
  He knows his children, in her care,
Are taught and trained as they should
  be;
  And he is glad to do his share.

For all her life she does them good;
  In childhood and in later years;
A mother and companion, too,
  She shares their joys and dries their
  tears.

With such a mother God is pleased,
  Her children know, in later days
How much their mother meant to them,
  Guiding them through their youthful
  ways.

Her husband praises her, and says,
  "Of all the mothers I have seen,
You are the best, though worthy ones
  Have done their part, where e'er
  they've been."

A mother, one who loves the Lord,
  When worth-while children she has
  raised,
And made her husband happy, too,
  The Bible says, "She shall be praised."

ADDA M. COLLAR
[Proverbs 31:10-31]

Being a Mother

Being a mother is sundry things. . .
It's baking cookies and pushing swings;
It's silver laughter, it's minor refrains,
It's coping with measles and growing
  pains.

It's making beds and sewing seams;
It's mending failures and broken dreams
With steady hands which wisely guide;
It's watching achievements with joy and
  pride.

Being a mother is learning the art
Of nurturing, in a growing heart,
Beauty and goodness; and, in body and
  mind,
Strength and wisdom to serve mankind.

SELMA JOHNSON BAKER

What Is A Mother

It takes a Mother's *Love*
  to make a house a home,

A place to be remembered,
no matter where we roam. . .
It takes a Mother's *Patience*
to bring a child
up right,
And her *Courage* and her *Cheerfulness*
to make a dark day bright . . .
It takes a Mother's *Thoughtfulness*
to mend the heart's deep "hurts,"
And her *Skill* and her *Endurance*
to mend little socks
and shirts . . .
It takes a Mother's *Kindness*
to forgive us when we err,
To sympathize in trouble
and bow her head in prayer . . .
It takes a Mother's *Wisdom*
to recognize our needs
And to give us reassurance
by her loving words
and deeds . . .
It takes a Mother's *Endless Faith*,
her *Confidence* and *Trust*
To guide us through the pitfalls
of selfishness
and lust . . .
And that is why in all this world
there could not be another
Who could fulfill God's purpose
as completely as
a *Mother!*

Analyzing Mothers

Mothers are good at drying tears,
Washing necks and scrubbing ears,
Forgiving each fault as it comes along
And seeing a right in every wrong.

Mothers are the appointed few
Who seem in league with the sandman's
crew,
And mothers know that feeding time
Is anywhere from nine to nine.

Mothers can scold but deep inside
Is a loving heart that has to hide
A hurt while reprimand is made
Or as the need, a hairbrush laid.

Mothers are made of the strangest
things,
And one is an angel minus wings . . .

Most of the time—but then, you see
Mothers are human like you and me.
                              ESTHER CUSHMAN RANDALL

A Mother

God sought to give the sweetest thing
In His almighty power
To earth; and deeply pondering
What it should be, one hour
In fondest joy and love of heart
Outweighing every other,
He moved the gates of heaven apart
And gave to earth—a mother.
                              G. NEWELL LOVEJOY

The Gift of Mother

When God looked down upon the earth
And chose to put new blessings there
He gave the sky the sunset's glow,
Gave laughter gay to children's play;
And then to every yearning soul
That gift of tenderest worth —
A mother.

The lily's sweetness is forgot
And sunsets' splendors fade to grey
But fresh and dear through changing
years,
Through quiet nights or eager days,
The love of her we love the best
Lives closely shrined within each heart—
Bless heaven for a mother.
                              AUTHOR UNKNOWN

Modern Mother

We read about the mothers
Of the days of long ago,
With their gentle wrinkled faces
And their hair as white as snow.

They were middle-aged at forty,
And at fifty donned lace caps;
And at sixty clung to shoulder shawls,
And loved their little naps.

But I love my modern mother,
Who can share in all my joys,
And who understands the problems
Of all growing girls and boys.

She may boast that she is fifty,
But her heart is twenty-three;
The laughing, fair-haired mother
Who is keeping young with me.
ERMA HILLABOUT in *Lookout*

Mothers

I walk into my garden fair,
And see the flowers blooming there;
I nestle in a shady nook
And listen to the babbling brook;
I seem to hear the lowing herds,
The honey bees, the song of birds.

In my dreams, I onward go
To watch the sunset's golden glow;
I look into the sky at night
And see the stars shining bright;
And in the distance covering all
I see the shadow moonbeams fall.

I stand beside the ocean blue
And think of all that's good and true;
Of all the lovely things God made
There's one above all others—
He took the best from all of these
And made them into "Mothers."
LAURA V. CLINE

Mothers

What a wonderful thing
Is a mother!
Other folks can love you,
But only your mother understands;
She works for you—
Looks after you—
Loves you, forgives you—
Anything you may do; ·
And then the only thing
Bad she ever does do—
Is to die and leave you.
BARONESS VON HUTTON

Mother

God took a ray from the shining sun,
A moonbeam, a starbeam, too;
Wove them together, the three in one,
And made the sweet smile of you.

God took the song of the nightingale,
At dusk, when the day is through;
The low throbbing notes of a violin,
And fashioned the voice of you.

God sought for virtues great and small,
All the bright heavens through,
Then chose the fairest of them all—
And made the pure soul of you!
THELKA HOLLINGSWORTH

What is a Mother?

A Mother can be almost any size or any age, but she won't admit to anything over thirty. A Mother has soft hands and smells good.

A Mother likes new dresses, music, a clean house, her children's kisses, an automatic washer and Daddy.

A Mother doesn't like muddy feet, having her children sick, temper tantrums, loud noises, or bad report cards.

A Mother can read a thermometer (much to the amazement of Daddy) and like magic, can kiss a hurt away.

A Mother can bake good cakes and pies but likes to see her children eat vegetables. A Mother can stuff a fat baby into a snow suit in seconds and can kiss little sad faces and make them smile.

A Mother is underpaid, has long hours and gets very little rest. She worries too much about her children, but she says she doesn't mind it at all.

And no matter how old her children are, she still likes to think of them as her little babies. She is the guardian angel of the family, the queen, the tender hand of love.

A Mother is the best friend anyone ever has. A Mother is love . . . God bless her.

When Is a Mother a Mother?

Many years ago a woman gave her child away for adoption. Years passed. The woman had a change of heart. She wanted to see the child and announce that she was the mother. The woman went to the adoption agency and asked for the current address of the foster parents of her child. The agency refused to give the woman that information.

Whereupon the woman brought a court action and it was fought in many courts until it reached the highest court in New York State—the Court of Appeals. Judge Benjamin Cardozo was then the chief justice of the N.Y. Court of Appeals. He later became a great justice of the U.S. Supreme Court.

Judge Cardoza wrote that giving birth to a child is an animal act and does not entitle one to the name of mother. It is the upbringing of a child with its attendant trials and tribulations that earns for one the sacred name of mother. The certainties and bonds, he continued to write, have grown up through the years between the foster parents and the adopted child. By virtue of what right should the woman who gave birth and abandoned the child now appear on the scene after years have elapsed and proclaim she is the mother and render asunder that cabletow that had been wrought through the years? By what right in law, morality, equity or ethics can this woman now say, "Presto, I am here. I am your real [sic] mother."

MARTIN RYWELL

The Watcher

She always leaned to watch for us,
  Anxious if we were late,
In winter by the window,
  In summer by the gate.

And though we mocked tenderly,
  Who had such foolish care,
The long way home would seem more safe
  Because she waited there.

Her thoughts were all so full of us,
  She never could forget!
And so I think that where she is
  She must be watching yet.

Waiting till we come home to her,
  Anxious if we were late—

Watching from heaven's window,
  Leaning o'er heaven's gate.

MARGARET WIDDEMER

What Is Mother?

I have three children. To each of them, the word "mother" means something different:

To Tommy aged 2, mother is a person who:
  Mops up spilled milk.
  Opens cans.
  Takes me to the potty when I don't want to be taken.
  Hands me cookies.
  Expects me to sit still in my high chair and eat oatmeal.
  Runs and loves me when I fall down.

To Mary Jane, aged 5, mother is a person who:
  Means to mend my cowboy suit but is always "too busy just now."
  Opens bureau drawers and says, "What a mess."
  Turns off the television in the middle of a cowboy picture.
  Hurries me all day long.
  Expects me to keep quiet and eat my oatmeal.
  Really is kind of pretty.

To Charles, aged 7, mother is a person who:
  Minds my business and meddles with my private things.
  Opens my bureau drawers and hollers, "Clean up this mess now."
  Turns out my lights when I've just started a new comic.
  Helps me with my homework but forgets to listen.
  Expects me to sit still, be quiet, and eat oatmeal.
  Really is pretty nice.

To daddy, middle-aged, mother is the person who:
  Mislays my Ladies Home Journal before I finish the serial.

Opens my mail and messes up the
paper.
Talks too much at breakfast.
Holds out her hand and says, "I need
a little money, dear."
Expects me to eat oatmeal and asks
me why I don't say something.
Really is my best girl.

I am "mother," the aged person who:
Mops, mends, and picks up messes all
day long.
Overworks and overeats.
Tries to keep the peace and to pick up
the pieces.
Hands out cookies all day long.
Eats up the family's cold leftover oat-
meal every morning.
Really believes that "Motherhood is
bliss."

NAN CARROLL

Mother

Our Lord hath showered us with gifts—
His love that He hath bid us share,
A faith that moves the heart of God,
A host of friends who love and care,
The greatest Gift of all—His Son.
To Him we would compare no other,
But next to Him who died for us,
The greatest gift He gave was MOTHER!

He used His finest workmanship
In fashioning a Mother's face.
Her heart He caused to overflow
With His pure love and truth and grace.
Her hands with tender care He made,
And gave to them a special power
To soothe small hurts, and by their
touch
Bring comfort sweet in sorrow's hour.

MOTHER!—how sweet that name to me.
'Twas at her knee I learned to pray,
And the example of her life
Caused me to seek the upward way.
The fairest one in all the world,
Exalted far above all other,
Is she whom I am proud to call
That dearest name on earth—MY
MOTHER!

AUTHOR UNKNOWN

Mother

I think God took the fragrance of a
flower,
A pure white flower, which blooms not
for world praise
But which makes sweet and beautiful
some bower;
The compassion of the dew, which gent-
ly lays
Reviving freshness on the fainting earth,
And gives to all the tired things new
birth;
The steadfastness and radiance of stars
Which lift the soul above confining bars;
The gladness of fair dawns; the sunset's
peace;
Contentment which from trivial rounds
asks no release;
The life which finds its greatest joy in
deeds of love for others . . .
I think God took these precious things
and made of them . . . mothers.

AUTHOR UNKNOWN

Mother

Your love was like moonlight
turning harsh things to beauty,
so that little wry souls
reflecting each other obliquely
as in cracked mirrors. . .
behold in your luminous spirit
their own reflection,
transfigured as in a shining stream,
and loved you for what they are not.

LOLA RIDGE

Only One Mother

Hundreds of stars in the pretty sky,
Hundreds of shells on the seashore to-
gether,
Hundreds of birds that go singing by,
Hundreds of lambs in the sunny
weather.
Hundreds of dewdrops to greet the
dawn,
Hundreds of bees in the purple clover,
Hundreds of butterflies on the lawn,
But only one mother the wide world
over.

GEORGE COOPER

Mother

The noblest thoughts my soul can claim,
The holiest words my tongue can frame,
Unworthy are to praise the name
  More sacred than all other.
An infant, when her love first came—
A man, I find it just the same;
Reverently I breathe her name,
  The blessed name of mother.

GEORGE GRIFFITH FETTER

Dedicated to All Mothers

There's an old fashioned house at the
    end of the lane,
  That has always seemed heaven to
  me,
For an old lady lives there, just simple
    and plain.
  An angel if ever there be.

Her eyes are pure springs of sweetness
    and love.
  The sun it just shines in her smile,
And I know the Lord sent her from up
    there above,
  To brighten this world for awhile.

Her sweet face is crowned with a halo
    white,
  Her robe is a calico dress,
And she goes about singing from morn-
    ing till night.
  Her voice like a soothing caress.

There isn't a queen in the world any-
    where
  Can look any finer than she
When mom's on her throne, just an old
    rocking chair,
  And smiles at her worshipper, me!

There are folks who think heaven is some
    far off place.
  They're hoping they'll find it some-
  where,
But I'm right here to say, if they'd
    glimpse Mother's face—
  They'd think she was already there.

Compassion Magazine

Mother—Daughter of a King

Dear little lady, this mother of mine,
The years may have left their sharp lines
    on her face
And bowed down her body, but she may
    be proud
That they have not marred her spirit's
    sweet grace.

Time, the great changer, puts his mark
    upon all;
There's never a person escapes this sad
    truth.
Fight hard as we will, the battle is lost,
For the ravage of years does away with
    our youth.

But "Grace is deceitful, and beauty is
    vain,"
She that loveth Jehovah shall know His
    dear praise.
The King's fairest daughter is glorious
    within,
And the King's image shines clear on her
    face.

MAY CLUTTER

Mother

I think when I look in your tender face,
  How most like God it was to give me
  you.
Music and laughter have their time and
    place,
  Beauty and sunlight, and a dream or
  two;
But oh my Mother, when my eyes look
    back
  Along the years, these other blessings
  fade—
I glimpse your face and nothing do I
    lack,
  Remembering the wonder *that* has
  made.
And how like God it was that other
    things
  He gave in measure: some have
  more, some less,
A limit to the smile, the songs, the
    wings.
  But all the love, the peace, the tender-
  ness

That make a mother, pure and undefiled,
God in His love gave once to every
child.

HELEN FRAZEE-BOWER

What's a Mother For?

What's a mother for? She cooks,
shops, washes dishes, takes care of
laundry, folds clothes, mends. Chauffeurs
the children, feeds the pets, helps the
children with homework, gets them to
brush their teeth and get ready for bed.
Countless times she bends down to tie
shoelaces, but she also points up to the
stars, directing inquiring minds to spiritual values that stand eternal. In these
unshakable standards of God's Word she
replenishes her own strength and faith
for she knows that she is unable to give
what she does not possess.

A mother's love makes home the one
place on earth where each member of
the family still feels he belongs. It is
where he finds shelter from the stress of
a competitive world that is often hard
and unfair, but in which he can live
courageously and in which he has a part.

BLAISE LEVAI

How slow we are to prove the height
and depth and deathlessness of perfect
mother love!

There is not in this hollow world a
fount of deep, strong, deathless love like
that which flows from a mother's heart.

The mother's heart is the child's schoolroom.

The sweetest sounds to mortals given
Are heard in Mothers, Home and
Heaven.

WILLIAM GOLDSMITH BROWN

To the man who has had a mother, all
women are sacred for her sake.

JEAN PAUL RICHTER

Don't cast aside the faith of your
mother for a faith your mother rejected.

Youth fades; love droops, the leaves of
friendship fall—
A mother's secret hope outlives them
all.

OLIVER WENDELL HOLMES

God's best gift to man is a good woman. I know this because of the mother I
once had and the wife I now have.

CHARLES W. GORDON

Mother's love is a cream of love.

CHARLES H. SPURGEON

Of all the men I have known, I cannot
recall one whose mother did her level
best for him when he was little, who did
not turn out well when he grew up.

FRANCES PARKINSON KEYES

A mother's love is indeed the golden
link which binds youth to age; and he is
still but a child, however time may have
furrowed his cheek, or silvered his brow,
who can yet recall with a softened heart,
the fond devotion or the gentle chidings
of the best friend that God has ever
given us.

BOVEE

The word Mother is indeed the golden
cord which binds the earth to God. She
is the keystone of the home. She is the
guiding star of the destiny of men. She is
the foundation of civilization. She has
enriched and ennobled the souls of men
and nations. Her love is the nearest ap-
proach to divine love that God grants to
men. For a mother's love there is no
substitute.

HARRY H. SCHLACT

A mother is the only person on earth
who can divide her love among ten children and each child still have all her
love.

Where there is a mother in the home,
matters speed well.

AMOS BRONSON ALCOTT

Mary kept her life pure inward, warm
and simple outward, and open upward.
This much we learn in Holy Writ of her
who was chosen by God to bring to the

birth, and to mother the growing human years of His Only Begotten.

S. D. GORDON

Most all the other beautiful things in life come by twos and threes, by dozens and hundreds! Plenty of roses, stars, sunsets and rainbows, brothers and sisters, aunts and cousins, but only one MOTHER in all the wide world.

KATE DOUGLAS WIGGINS

Like some mother forever going ahead into dark rooms with a lighted candle, she began taking all my troubles, leading me up to them gradually until suddenly they were luminous with beauty. That eternal feminine is her—maternally undaunted.

There is no friend to a man like his mother.

OSMANLI

Some children walk the high road
While others tread the low;
A mother can determine
Which way her child will go.

Mother's love grows by giving.

CHARLES LAMB

God pays a good mother. Mother, get your name on God's payroll.

BILLY SUNDAY

When God wants an important thing done in this world, or a wrong righted, He goes about it in a very singular way. He doesn't release His thunderbolts nor stir up his earthquakes. He simply has a tiny, helpless baby born, perhaps in a very obscure home, perhaps of a very humble mother. And He puts the idea or purpose into a mother's heart. And she puts it in the baby's mind, and then—God waits!

The great events of this world are not battles and earthquakes and hurricanes. The great events of this world are babies. They are earthquakes and hurricanes.

EDWARD T. SULLIVAN

I have not been able to find a single and useful institution which has not been founded by either an intensely religious man or by the son of a praying father or mother.

ROGER BABSON

What are Raphael's Madonnas but the shadow of a mother's love, fixed in permanent outline forever?

T.W. HIGGINSON

Mother: that was the bank where we deposited all our hurt and worries.

T. DEWITT TALMAGE

Maternal work is never done, mother concern never relaxed. A mother's anxiety goes on as long as she and her children live. Her apron strings are divinely elastic, and though stretched to the ends of the earth they will not break.

GEORGE N. LUCCOCK

All that is purest in man is but the echo of a mother's benediction.

FREDERICK W. MORTON

If you would reform the world from its errors and vices, begin with mothers.

C. SIMMONS

Show me the mothers of a people and I will show you the nation.

I don't think there are enough devils in hell to take a young person from the arms of a godly mother.

BILLY SUNDAY

Men and women frequently forget each other, but everyone remembers mother.

JEROME PAINE BATES

A beautiful mother, a more beautiful daughter.

HORACE, Carmina I.

A mother only knows a mother's fondness.

LADY MARY WORTLEY MONTAGU,
Letters to the Countess of Bute, 1754

But strive still to be a man before your mother.

WILLIAM COWPER

A mother is a mother still,
The holiest thing alive.

SAMUEL TAYLOR COLERIDGE
The Three Graves

Good mothers serve down here on this earth as angels without wings!

MOTHER'S DAY

How Mother's Day Started

In the early 1900's Anna M. Jarvis conceived the idea of setting aside one day of the year on which to pay homage to mothers.

The idea was enthusiastically received as Mrs. Jarvis talked about it. Her own mother had died on the second Sunday in May, 1905, so she suggested this particular Sunday for the observance.

Woodrow Wilson, then President, signed an Act of Congress in 1914 making the second Sunday in May a definite time when we might all think about mother, and express to her in the best way possible our love.

"Live this day as your mother would have you," Anna Jarvis urged, and she suggested that each person spend the day with his mother if she be alive, or at least write her a letter.

The carnation was chosen as the flower of the day—a red one to be worn for mothers still living, and a white one for mothers who have died. Mother's Day was first celebrated in a little church in Grafton, West Virginia, the town where Anna was born. Eventually the day came into universal observance because it found a warm response in the hearts of people everywhere.

On Mother's Day

As years ago we carried to your knees
The tales and treasures of eventful days,
Knowing no deed too humble for your praise,
Nor any gift too trivial to please,
So still we bring — with older smiles and tears —
What gifts we may, to claim the old, dear right,

Your faith, beyond the silence and the night,
Your love still close and watching through the years.

KATHLEEN NORRIS

This Is Her Day

This is her day — tho every day is hers,
Brimmed as they are with urgent tasks and deeds;
The glad young mother who must daily meet
Small children's constant needs.
This is her day: the mother who has seen
Her children grow like young corn in the sun;
Tall, straight, and clean; who takes a keen delight
And pride in every one.
This is her day — the mother now grown old,
Who folds her hands and slowly rocks her chair,
Who nods and smiles across the gathering dusk
At a child who is not there.
This is their day, the mothers of the world —
And the whole nation pauses as it should,
To honor them who know the poignant pain —
And the joy of motherhood.

Attributed to GRACE NOLL CROWELL

Mothers

Something of God is in a mother's love,
Something of His tenderness and care;
I never see a mother bent above
An ailing child, but I can see God there.

And I hear Him in the words she says
  To little children gathered at her
    knees:
God's own voice speaking through her
    lips the words
That will bring fruitage for eternity.

And I can feel Him in a mother's touch:
  Across the widening years her shielding
    hands
Will still reach out as if to keep from
    harm
  Her little child — how well God un-
    derstands.

A mother's heart, so like His own is it!
  True motherhood has touched His
    garment's hem
For strength and wisdom, and I am
    quite sure
  We honor Him the day we honor
    them.
                    GRACE NOLL CROWELL

A Mother's Request

What do I want for Mother's Day? you
    ask,
  My fair young daughter, and my stal-
    wart son.
Only that you should finish up the task
  That, in life's evening, seems but just
    begun—
The task that I can never now complete,
  Of setting forth the Way, the Life,
    the Truth,
Except you lend to me your eager feet,
  Your questing spirits and your gallant
    youth.

What do I want for Mother's Day? No
    gift
  That any purse could buy. But one
    request
I make of you: that, daily, you might
    lift
  The Cross of Christ and publish, east
    and west,
And north and south, the tidings of His
    grace.
  These feet grow slow, this fading eye-
    sight dim;
Only in you, my children, is my place

Of witness found—my going on with
    Him.

What do I want for Mother's Day? Just
    this:
  Your hands, your hearts, your voices
    for my Christ;
This is the ultimate of earthly bliss.
  There is no comfort I have sacrificed
For you that was too much. So do not
    bring
  The casual token . . . But, when ways
    grow rough,
Then light my twilight with remembering
  Your mother's God, for you, is still
    enough.
                    HELEN FRAZEE-BOWER

Mother's Day on Sunday?

Mother's Day on Sunday?
  Oh, no, that cannot be!
For mother's day is Monday
  Through Saturday, you see!
For mother's work is never done;
  Each day but finds new tasks begun.

Mother's Day on Sunday?
  The sentiment is good,
For other days she's busy
  With sewing or with food.
But who will do her work today
  While sentiment shall have its say?

Mother's Day on Sunday?
  The flowers you may bring,
Carnations for the button-hole
  A tender song may sing—
But don't forget on other days
  A word of "thank you" and of praise!
                    AUTHOR UNKNOWN

A Song for Mother

  Faith is a quiet thing.
  Faith is those mothering
  Women who pray and sing,
    Working away.

  Hope is an upward look.
  Hope, at an open Book,

Learning how Jesus took
  Strength for the day.

Love is a selfless thing.
Love is one comforting,
Tenderly shepherding
  Children who stray.

Mother, today is yours.
Mother, whom God assures
Beauty we know endures.
  Bless you this day.

                              PAULA SIEHL

Mother's Day

If I could follow in the path you trod
Oh precious mother mine,
And walk as you do, humbly with my
      God,
My life would grow divine!

I need not set one day apart
For Mother's day, you see;
As every day is "Mother's Day"
Throughout the year to me!
                            MARTHA MARTIN

A Mother's Wishes on Her Day

ON SECOND THOUGHT

A *pearl ring*   To hear my husband say
                  "I love you" more often

A *mink stole*   One bear hug from my
                  teenage son

An *orchid*   A compliment from my
  corsage   daughter

A *bottle of*   The aura of family serenity
  perfume   daily

A *box of*   Another chance to show
  candy   the measure of my love for
                  them
           RUTH PIERCE in Sunday Digest

Mother's Day is here again.
Let all the florists cry, Amen!

Now we shall all, as if on cue,
With Mom fill up our family pew;
We'll take her out and feed her well,
For she will not see us all together again
      in worship or meal time or any-
      where else for quite a spell!
                            BLAISE LEVAI

A foreigner commented, "You Amer-
icans are strange people. You devote one
day out of the year to your mothers and
an entire week to pickles.
                            Medford Star News

A Mother's Day essay by a small boy
said, "My mother keeps on speaking
terms with God and on spanking terms
with me."

On Mother's Day a minister gave this
perfect tribute: "My mother practices
what I preach."
                            Capper's Weekly

Mother's Day is a time observed by
all of us. With reference to it, it might
be a good deal of a surprise to some of
us to have us claim that civilization is
pretty much a feminine achievement.
              CLIFF COLE, Daily Pulpit

Judy: "Robby, where did you get that
cute little puppy? Please let me hold
him."
Robby: "He's our Mother's Day present.
If we give him to her then she'll have to
keep him!"

There are six children in our family,
and after years of remembering our parents on birthdays, anniversaries, Christmas, Mother's Day and Father's Day we
had just about run out of ideas for gifts
they would really appreciate. Then ten
years ago, toward spring, Mother and
Dad began talking of how they dreaded
spring housecleaning. This gave us an
inspiration. One morning shortly before
Mother's Day all 12 of us—six husbands
and six wives—paid our parents a surprise visit. We were armed with buckets,
ladders, cleaning equipment, a smile and
a potluck dinner, and before the day was
over the storm windows were down, the
screens were up, the yard was mowed, the

car was washed and the house was clean from top to bottom. Mother and Dad were delighted, and we had such fun that we haven't missed a year since.

MRS. RAYMOND HAHN in *Reader's Digest*

Thought for Mother's Day

We all remember Mother
  on her 'special day—
We send her gifts and flowers
  and lovely cards that say
How very much we thank her
  for the things that mothers do,
The sacrifices that they make;
  but when this day is through
We're prone to take for granted
  her precious love and care,
The fact that when we need her,
  Mother's always there.
She will never mention it,
  nor ask for any praise,
The joy of doing things for us
  is her reward always
But just the same it would be nice
  if we'd find the time to say
Just one small word of heartfelt thanks
  to Mother—every day!

NADINE BROTHERS LYBARGER

My Gifts to You—Mother

All the things you said
You wanted me to be—
Take them, Mom, instead
Of other gifts from me.

Here's an honest mind,
That tried to think things through;
Here's a heart that's kind,
And hands with work to do.

Here's a head held high,
Because I owe no man;
Here's a will to try,
To do the best I can.

Here's the place I live—
Each neighbor is my friend;
Here's the tenth I give,
The church we all attend.

Here's this lad of mine,
And here's his sister, Sue . . .
Yes, we think they're fine,
We hope you'll think so, too.

Nothing more to say,
I've written all but this,
"Happy Mother's Day" . . .
I'll seal it with a kiss.

GEORGE L. KRESS

Mother's Day

Mother! What a wealth
Of tender love and service
This simple word suggests.
Her days and nights are
Ever filled with thoughts of others,
Regardless of the cost to herself in
Sacrifice or toil or pain.

Dearest of all earthly friends
Acknowledged queen of the home.
Years can but enhance our love and
  memory of thee!

On This Mother's Day

Dear Mom, I love to send you gifts,
  Still on this special day.
I'd like to have the power to take
  So many things away.

I'd take away the worries
  That I've caused you through the
  years.
I'd take away the heartaches,
  And the cause for any tears,
I'd smooth away the wrinkles
  From the hands that once were soft—
The hands that touched so tender
  When they lifted me aloft.

And I'd remove the weary look
  From your eyes, so tired now;
I'd take away the burdens
  That have caused your wrinkled brow.
I'd leave my song of love within
  Your gentle heart to stay,
So every single day to you
  Would be like Mother's Day.

EVELYN BECKERT

Mother's Day

Let every day be Mother's Day.
Make roses grow along the way
And beauty everywhere.
Oh, never let her eyes be wet
With tears of sorrow and regret,
And never cease to care.
Come, grown-up children, and rejoice
That you can hear your mother's voice.

A day for her? For you she gave
Long years of love and service brave,
For you her youth was spent.
There was no weight or hurt or care
Too heavy for her strength to bear.
She followed where you went:
Her courage and her love sublime
You could depend on all the time.

EDGAR A. GUEST

To Mother on Her Special Day

I lacked the gold to buy a gem
Of azure like the skies,
But if I did, it could not match
The beauty of your eyes.

What coin could purchase anything
So very much worthwhile
As that which lights your happy face,
The treasure of your smile?

No gift I ever offered you
Could even pay, in part,
For that much greater gift you gave . . .
The kindness of your heart.

But Mother dear, today I hope
With some small gift to say
The words that best reflect my love
In an extra special way!

LOUISE WEIBERT SUTTON

Mother's Day

Mother's day is every day,
  And every moment in it;
She started when your life began,
  She does not stop a minute.
Her deep concern for you doth burn,
  Consuming heart and strength;

She follows you in all you do—
  She goes to any length.

Mother's day is every day
  With those who really love her;
They work and plan, as best they can,
  From weariness to save her.
Their love doth yearn to give return
  For all her lavish spending;
True children, like true mothers, strike
  A love chord that's unending.

ANNIE VIRGINIA YOUNG

Somebody's Mother on Mother's Day

Somebody's mother will be lonely today
For all of her family are far, far away;
Her companion has gone to the better
  land
And she longs for the touch of his loving
  hand;
Her children will greet her by cards and
  by 'phone—
They can't come to see her—she'll be so
  alone;
If you know such a mother, why not, I
  pray,
Pretend she's your mother—if just for
  today?
Pay her a visit and take her some flow-
  ers—
Her face will light up—and stay so for
  hours!
You will never regret the time it will
  take
To show her true kindness for Jesus' sake!

ROY J. WILKINS

Mother's Day Beatitudes

Blessed are the mothers of yesterday, for
  their memories shall be called beautiful and beneficent. They are like flowers growing by sunken garden and beside still water and in green fields, for
  they are like soft winds that blow with
  peace and love on wistful wings.
Blessed are the mothers of today, for
  they have the keeping of tomorrow in
  their hands and in their hearts; and
  the destiny of nations, hearts and
  homes.

Blessed are the mothers of tomorrow, for they have been summoned to a great and heroic hour. For they shall be called the mothers of men who shall make miracles of human life. The mothers of tomorrow shall breed a race of giants who handle lightning as a little thing, and make the clouds and thunder obey their wills, Blessed are the mothers of tomorrow.

Blessed are the mothers of scientists and statesmen; of laborers and poets; of preachers and prophets; of teachers and dreamers; for dreams and visions and prophecies and the glow and glory of creation is born in the hearts of mothers.

Blessed are the mothers, for they are conservers of the human race.

Blessed are the mothers, for they taught barbarian ancestors to grow grains and build shelters.

Blessed are the mothers of the world, for they have conserved the spiritual things of life for the sake of their children.

Blessed are the mothers of the earth, for they have combined the practical and the spiritual into one workable way of human life. They have darned little stockings, mended little dresses, washed little faces, and have pointed little eyes to the stars and little souls to eternal things.

Blessed are the mothers!

WILLIAM L. STIDGER

MY MOTHER

My Mother

Who fed me from her gentle breast
And hushed me in her arms to rest,
And on my cheek sweet kisses pressed?
    My Mother!

When sleep forsook my open eyes,
Who was it sang sweet hushaby
And rocked me that I should not cry?
    My Mother!

Who sat and watched my infant head
When sleeping in my cradle bed,
And tears of sweet affection shed?
    My Mother!

Who ran to help me when I fell,
And would some pretty story tell,
Or kiss the place to make it well?
    My Mother.

Who taught my infant lips to pray,
And love God's holy book and day,
And walk in wisdom's pleasant way?
    My Mother!

And can I ever cease to be
Affectionate and kind to thee,
Who wast so very kind to me,
    My Mother?

Ah! no, the thought I cannot bear,
And if God please my life to spare,
I hope I shall reward thy care,
    My Mother.

When thou art feeble, old, and grey,
My healthy arm shall be thy stay,
And I will soothe thy pains away,
    My Mother.

And when I see thee hang thy head,
'Twill be my turn to watch thy bed,
And tears of sweet affection shed,
    My Mother!

ANN TAYLOR

At My Mother's Knee

I have worshipped in churches and chapels;
    I've prayed in the busy street;
I have sought my God and have found Him
    Where the waves of His ocean beat;

I have knelt in the silent forest
　In the shade of some ancient tree;
But the dearest of all my altars
　Was raised at my mother's knee.

I have listened to God in His temple
　I've caught His voice in the crowd;
I have heard Him speak when the break-
　ers
Were booming long and loud;
Where the winds play soft in the treetops
　My Father has talked to me;
But I never have heard Him clearer
　Than I did at my mother's knee.

The things in my life that are worthy
　Were born in my mother's breast,
And breathed into mine by the magic
　Of the love her life expressed
The years that have brought me to man-
　hood
Have taken her far from me;
But memory keeps me from straying
　Too far from my mother's knee.

God, make me the man of her vision
　And purge me of selfishness!
God, keep me true to her standards
　And help me to live to bless!
God, hallow the holy impression
　Of the days that used to be,
And keep me a pilgrim forever,
　To the shrine at my mother's knee!

　　　　　　　　　JOHN H. STYLES, JR.

My Mother's Portrait

Artist—paint my Mother's portrait—
Let the lines and wrinkles show.
Let a silver halo crown her,
For she's growing old you know.
Let your brushes tell the story
Of her patient, tender care;
Mingle love with joy and sorrow,
Just as life has put them there.

Can you picture on the canvas
All the years of sacrifice—
Making life so right for others,
Never counting ought the price?
Blend your colors softly, artist,
Face her towards the setting sun,
Toward the calm and peaceful valley
For her task is almost done.

Can you paint the pathway brighter,
Toward the land of Endless Day—
Where blue forget-me-nots are bloom-
　ing,
All along a sunlit way?
Call the picture simply MOTHER—
All the world will understand;
Homes and hearts and heaven are
　brighter
Because she holds her Savior's hand!

　　　　　　　　　AUTHOR UNKNOWN

Softness

"What is the softest thing?" I asked.
I searched in vain.
I asked the sky; it brought me clouds,
I asked the sea; it washed my feet in
　foam.
I asked the woods; it placed cool moss
　upon my brow.
I asked the rose; it dropped a petal in my
　palm.
I asked the wind; it blew warm air to
　me.
I asked the doe; it pressed its nose into
　my hand.
I asked the snow; a snowflake fell upon
　my lips.
I asked the maid; her lover's eyes, said
　she.
I asked the soil; the rain, it said.
My mother wept; I kissed her cheek.
I search no more.

　　　　　　　　PATRICIA ANNE KAISER

My Mother's Name

No painter's brush or poet's pen,
In justice to her fame,
Has ever reached half high enough
To write my mother's name.

Make ink of tears and golden gems
And sunbeams mixed together,
With holy hand and golden pen,
Go write the name of Mother.

In every humble tenant house,
In every cottage home,
In marble courts and golden halls,
On every palace dome;

On mountains high, in valleys low,
In every land and clime
In every throbbing human head,
That blessed name enshrine.

Take childhood's light and manhood's
      age
Celestial canvas given,
In beauty trace her name and face
And go hang it up in heaven.

Thrice upward to the Heavenly Home
And midst music soft and sweet
Thank Jesus for your Mother's name,
And write it at His feet.
                          AUTHOR UNKNOWN

My Mother

I know someone with heart of gold
Full of patience, love untold
She taught me how to walk, to pray
And cared for me the livelong day—
      My mother.

And when my heart was full of grief
She gave me comfort and relief
When often ill and racked with pain
She nursed me until strength I'd gain—
      My mother.

And even though I knew defeat
Her love for me was still complete
In loss or sorrow, gain or fame
Her love for me was just the same—
      My mother.
                          AUTHOR UNKNOWN

My Mother's Hands

My mother's hands! So capable!
   I love them—every wrinkle there.
Though toil has made them rough and
      worn,
      These hands to me are wonderous
      fair.
                          AUTHOR UNKNOWN

God's Gift to Me

There's only one heart like my mother's
And that is the heart of God,

Forgiving, forgetting and loving
   The child who the wrong has done.

No eyes like the eyes of mother
   Can see in me all that is best,
Remembering all of my goodness,
   Forgetting all of the rest.

No feet like the feet of mother
   That hasten to be at my side
To comfort my hour of suffering,
   To share in the joys that betide.

No hand like the hand of mother
   So gentle to soothe and so kind,
When God gave to me a mother
   'Twas the choicest gift he could find.
                          AUTHOR UNKNOWN

May Her Way Be Fair

Her girlish charm has vanished now,
The lines are many on her brow;
No longer do her quiet ways
Bring atmosphere of spring-like days;
The years have tinged her hair with
      gray,
Her feet grow weary with the day;
But of the friends God gave to me
There's none so beautiful as she,
   My Mother!

How many stories she could tell
Of toilsome days, and nights as well,
Spent uncomplaining through the years
For those she loved! What cares and
      fears
Have burdened her! Perhaps her hope
Oft left her, till her heart could grope
By steps of prayer back to the light!
What faith was hers in God's great
      Right,
   My Mother's!

May every year now left to her
Be filled with joy. May few tears blur
Her hope-lit vision. May her way
But fairer grow with each good day
And dew-tipped roses make each dawn
A paradise to her. Upon
Her gracious form may God's love smile
And from her heart all cares beguile,
   My Mother!
                          THOMAS CURTIS CLARK

Mother

Yours were the hands that led my way
  Through the carefree paths of youth,
Yours were the faithful prayers each day
  That showed me the way of truth.

Yours were the precious golden hours,
  The cherished dreams, the rest
All sacrificed in mother love
  That I might have the best.

No gift I give can ever repay
  Such love or care so true. . .
But in my heart I'll always have
  The deepest love for you.

                 MARY R. DULING

To My Mother

The jealous fingers of Tomorrow pull me
  ever farther from Yesterday,
And I, on the endless belt of years between,
Turn and glance wistfully over my burdened shoulder
Coveting one fleeting glimpse of your
  face,
MY MOTHER.

For the memories come thronging,
  thronging—
Separating into pictures of the cookie jar
  in the pantry. . .
Of the long, snowy hill filled with
  sleds. . .
Of the matchless odor of home-cooked
  bread. . .
Of the family gathered around the fire
  sharing books. . .
Of breathless Christmas mornings. . .
The wonder of springtime. . .
The boisterous last day of school. . .
A small boy sprawled dreaming in the
  grass. . .
And all of this hallowed by you,
MY MOTHER.

Truly were you the creator,
The weaver, the artisan concerned
With filaments gossamer
For the fashioning of treasure-trove of
  visions and courage,

Shaping the soul of a lad to the wooing
  of his destiny,
MY MOTHER.

Never think, then, as you stand afar in
  my Yesterday
(Which was your Tomorrow),
That your day is done;
No, for whatever thing I do, whatever
  thing I am, or may become.
Whatever I may mean to men—
All have in them something of you:
Portions and particles of your very life
  flow,
Dauntless, unquenchable spirit,
Gift for sifting the lovely grain from
  homely chaff,
Some of your heart, in the long ago
  shared
With
  YOUR SON

                 GLENN H. ASQUITH

For My Mother

Dear little Mother, I thank you
For toil worn hands that show,
The many things you've done for me
That only God can know.

Dear little Mother, I thank you
For seeking help above,
For tired but willing little feet
And your great heart of love.

Dear little mother, it is good
That in your gentle way—
You taught me from God's Holy Word
And knelt with me to pray.

              ESTHER BELLE HEINS

My Mother

Thank God for you, Mother.
You helped lighten my heavy load;
Your smile so sweet, your word of cheer,
You helped me feel God was very near.
Thank God for you, dear Mother, thank
  God for you!

Thank God for you dear Mother of
  mine!
You shared all my joys, my sorrows too.
When I felt discouraged, weary and sad,

Your words of faith made my heart
glad.
Thank God for you, dear Mother, thank
God for you!

Thank God for a Mother's love, pure as
gold;

A beautiful seed planted by God above,
A helping hand in time of need to hold,
A rare and precious love God did
mould.
Thank God, dear Mother, thank God for
you!

DORIS PEACE

MOTHERHOOD

Motherhood

If I could write with diamond pen,
Use ink of flowering gold,
The love I have for my mother dear
Could then not half be told.

Her sympathy has been my sky,
Her love my guiding light.
Her gentle hand hath soothed my ills,
She's ever guided right.

A precious friend has mother been,
Stood by me all the way
The sacrifice has been too great;
Such love one can't repay.

So wonderful has mother been,
So gentle kind and good,
That I have learned to reverence
That sweet word, "Motherhood."

MRS. E.J. DANIELS

A Tribute to Motherhood

God made the streams that gurgle down
the purple mountainside
He made the gorgeous coloring with
which the sunset's dyed.
He made the hills and covered them with
glory; and He made
The sparkle on the dewdrop and the
flecks of light and shade,
Then knowing all earth needed was a
climax for her charms,
He made a little woman with a baby in
her arms.

He made the arching rainbow that is
thrown across the sky,

He made the blessed flowers that nod
and smile as we pass by;
He made the gladsome beauty as she
bows with queenly grace,
But sweetest of them all, He made the
love light in the face
That bends above a baby, warding off
the world's alarms—
That dainty little woman with a baby in
her arms.

A soft pink wrap embellished with a
vine in silken thread—
A filmy, snow-white cap upon a downy
little head—
A dress 'twould make the winter drift
look dusty by its side—
Two cheeks with pure rose-petal tint,
two blue eyes wonder wide,
And bending o'er—the mother face in-
bued with heaven's own charms,
God bless the little woman with a baby
in her arms.

AUTHOR UNKNOWN

The Builders

A builder built a temple;
  He wrought it with care and skill—
Pillars and doors and arches,
  All fashioned to work his will.
And men said, as they saw its beauty,
  "It shall never know decay.
Great is thy skill, O builder!
  Thy fame shall endure for aye."

A mother built a temple
  With infinite loving care,
Planning each arch with patience,
  Loving each stone with prayer.

None praised her unceasing effort,
　　None knew of her wond'rous plan,
For the temple the mother built,
　　Was unseen by the eye of man.

Gone is the builder's temple—
　　Crumbled into the dust;
Low lies each stately pillar,
　　Food for consuming rust.
But the temple the mother built
　　Will last while the ages roll,
For the beautiful unseen temple,
　　Was a child's immortal soul.

AUTHOR UNKNOWN

Motherhood the Glory of Womanhood

The glory of womanhood is motherhood. This is the highest dignity and honor to which she can aspire and hope to attain. "I have a son and am now a lineal descendant of Mary, the mother of God," wrote the Countess of Barclay to a friend.

No nation can rise higher than its mothers. The unit of national life is not the individual, but the home; and the home is what mothers make it. The American home is by far and away the most important of all its institutions. From the family came the school, the church, and the state. The future of America will depend very largely, if not entirely, upon the preservation and development of the ideals embodied in the American home, and the preservation of the American home will depend upon the preservation of high ideals concerning the glory, the influence and potency of motherhood.

Gibbon, the historian, declares with no hesitation that the decline and fall of the great Roman Empire began with the decline and fall of the Roman home.

Clarion

Motherhood

The world of tomorrow is being shaped by the Motherhood of today. The tomorrows of life will owe more to the Mothers of today than to any other force or institution. Motherhood is still the most potent force in the world.

The most beautiful word in the English language is Mother. That is true because of the universal conviction as to the primary position of the Mothers of our land. That opinion emphasizes the normal glory of a Mother's sphere and spirit, and the pathos and tragedy of a home and land where such an estimate cannot be given or understood.

Christian civilization honors itself when it honors Motherhood. Our better selves manifest no truer evidence of our chivalry and devotion than when we honor the memory and the inherent rights of our Mothers.

AUTHOR UNKNOWN

Motherhood is the launching of an immortal soul on the sea of life.

Maternal love: a miraculous substance which God multiplies as He divides it.

VICTOR HUGO

The girls who are to be the mothers of tomorrow will get their ideal of motherhood from the mothers of today.

How beautifully everything is arranged by Nature; as soon as a child enters the world, it finds a mother ready to take care of it.

JULES MICHELET

Maternity

Within the crib that stands beside my
　　bed
　　A little form in sweet abandon lies
　　And as I bend above with misty eyes
I know how Mary's heart was comforted.

O world of Mothers! blest are we who
　　know
　　The ecstasy—the deep God-given thrill
　　That Mary felt when all the earth was
　　still
In that Judean starlight long ago!

ANNE P.L. FIELD

The New Baby

"How funny and red!"
   That's what they said.
"Why, there's nothing but fuzz
   On top of his head."
And they lifted the covers
   To look at his feet.
"Oh, how tiny and wrinkled
   And red as a beet!"
And I heard them whispering
   Behind my back,
"Did you ever think
   He would look like that,
All wrinkled and red
   Like a baby bird?"
Of course they didn't
   Know that I heard.
But I had to smile
   When the baby was fed
To see how fast
   They lined up by his bed,
And in spite of the fact
   He was wrinkled and thin,
They all begged for a turn
   At holding him.

          OSIE HERTZLER ZIEGLER

The Mother's Hymn

Lord who ordainest for mankind
   Benignant toils and tender cares,
We thank Thee for the ties that bind
   The mother to the child she bears.

We thank Thee for the hopes that rise
   Within her heart, as, day by day,
The dawning soul, from those young
     eyes,
   Looks with a clearer, steadier ray.

And grateful for the blessing given
   With that dear infant on her knee,
She trains the eye to look to heaven,
   The voice to lisp a prayer to Thee.

Such thanks the blessed Mary gave
   When from her lap the Holy Child,
Sent from on high to seek and save
   The lost of earth, looked up and
     smiled.

All-Gracious! grant to those who bear

A mother's charge, the strength and
   light
To guide the feet that own their care
   In ways of Love and Truth and Right.

          WILLIAM CULLEN BRYANT

Ten Commandments
For a First-time Mother

1. Thou shalt not forsake thy womanhood for motherhood, for the two are compatible and a comely woman is a comely mother. In short, thou shalt not let thyself go.

2. Thou shalt impress upon thyself that thy housework must slide a bit, for it is a wise mother who recognizes her strength's limitations. Pamper thyself with frequent rests.

3. Thou shalt bestow upon thy tiny one a multitude of loving sounds and pats, that he may be assured of his position in thy heart.

4. Recalling that no two babies are alike, thou shalt listen to well-meaning advice and then adhere to thine own judgment of what is right for baby. When in doubt thou shalt cousult thy doctor.

5. Thou shalt accustom thyself to early morning hunger demands, recognizing that these feeding moments, when all about is soft stillness, give thee golden time to draw closer to thy child.

6. Thou shalt guard thy wee one against thoughtless visitors who come bearing sniffles. Thou shalt deal with these visitors with kind firmness, explaining that baby is susceptible to germ attacks.

7. Thou shalt not covet thy neighbor baby's five-month tooth, nor his agility in walking at 10 months, nor his first loving shout of *Mama*, for thy child will have his own abilities.

8. Thou shalt not suffer thy husband to bear a cutoff nose because baby receives more attention than he.

9. Thou shalt encourage thy husband to practice his fatherhood, for his arms, as thine, baby needs. Teach him to feed, to dress, even to bathe his child.

10. Thou shalt give thanks that where there were two, now there are three. And the glory of thy parenthood shall shine forth from thy face, for, truly, thou art blest.

DANA BROOKINS

Blessed Event

My motherhood is very new;
It touches everything I do. . .
Each humble task is edged with joy
Because of one small baby boy.

My thoughts for him at dawning start;
They climb the stairways of my heart
Like little prayers with wings of gold
To guard and bless the child I hold.

Words and music I have known
Come tiptoeing in softened tone. . .
Happy songs in sweet disguise
To masquerade as lullabies.

The dreams I cherished for a son
Are all unfolding, one by one;
Childhood's warm and eager charms
Have come to rest within my arms.

GERALDINE E. GOHN

A Creed for Mothers

I believe in little children as one of the most precious gifts of Heaven to earth.

I believe they have immortal souls created with a capacity for reflecting the image of God.

I believe that in every child there are infinite possibilities for good and evil, and that the kind of influences with which we surround their early childhood largely determine their future character.

I believe that the calling of Motherhood is one of the holiest and should be the happiest of all earth's tasks.

I believe that the Christ, who was once Himself a child, born of a human mother, is the one never-failing source of help for perplexed, discouraged, or wearied motherhood.

Since to this work, Father, Thou hast called me, help me to give to it all that Thou hast given me of insight and wisdom and strength and love and gentleness and patience and forgiveness!

Intelligencer Leader

Motherhood

From the earliest days women have called themselves blessed of God when life begins to palpitate within their bosom. Every one of a deep nature seems to herself more sacred and more especially under the Divine care while a new life, moulded by the Divine hand, is springing into being. For of all creative acts, none is so sovereign and divine. Who shall reveal the endless musing, the perpetual prophecies, of the mother's soul. . . . To others, in such hours, woman should seem more sacred than the most solemn temple; and to herself she must needs seem as if overshadowed by the Holy Ghost!

HENRY WARD BEECHER

Until I Was a Mother

I think I never truly knew
How very much I cared for you
Until I was a mother too;

Nor knew that any love could be
As deep as that you give to me.

A love that gives but does not ask;
That changes every little task

To joy; a love that stays the same,
A steady and enduring flame.

This love I give to her must be
The same love that you give to me;

And gave to me through all my years;
My joy, your joy, my tears, your tears.

Mother, I never truly knew

Until I was a mother too;
Your love for me and mine for you.
ABIGAIL CRESSON

Fourteen Points of Motherhood

1. Love suffereth long, and is kind.
2. Love envieth not.
3. Love vaunteth not itself.
4. Is not puffed up.
5. Does not behave itself unseemly.
6. Seeketh not her own.
7. Is not easily provoked.
8. Thinketh no evil.
9. Rejoiceth not in iniquity.
10. Rejoiceth in the truth.
11. Beareth all things.
12. Believeth all things.
13. Hopeth all things.
14. Endureth all things.
I Corinthians 13:4-7

The Christian faith has developed and encouraged the finest in human motherhood through the centuries.
SHERWOOD E. WIRT

A Partnership with God is Motherhood

Professor James in speaking on the subject of motherhood, told the story of a teacher who was giving her class a problem in fractions. Said she, "Suppose your mother baked a pie, and there were seven of you to eat it, five of you children and your parents; what part would you get?"

"A sixth, Miss," one boy answered.

"A sixth?" the teacher queried. "Johnny, I'm afraid you don't know much about fractions, if you say you would get a sixth when there were seven of you to share the pie your mother baked."

"I know a little about fractions," the boy said, "but I know a lot more about my mother. And I know she'd cut the pie in six pieces and go without herself in a case like that."

As the years of motherhood pass, the mother's influence is cumulative. Her steadfastness of faith becomes the standard of reference by which the child builds his concepts of reality. He ma-

tures but he does not forget. And the rock-bottom convictions that make up the difference between a good life and a bad life are still the same.

The joys of motherhood are many; but surely there is no greater joy than this, to see the fruit of one's womb stand before his or her Maker and acknowledge the Lordship of Jesus Christ. This is the real Mother's Day, the day for which she was born, the day for which she entered into marriage and bore her child. This too, is the hope of the future; for in all the marvels and risks and terrors of the space age, the place of motherhood is secure; and where there is Life, there is hope.
SHERWOOD E. WIRT

Expectant Mother's Prayer

Heavenly Father, I am about to go seeking a little soul, a thing that shall be mine as no other thing in the whole world has been mine.

Bring me through my hour strong and well for the sake of my baby. Prepare me for real motherhood. Preserve my mind from all doubts and worry, and take all fear-misgivings from me so that the little mind that is forming may become a brave, clean battler in this world of dangers.

And, God, when the child lies in my arms and draws its life from me, and when those eyes look up to mine to learn what this new world is like, I pledge Thee, the child shall find reverence in me, and no fear; truth and no shame; love, strong as life and death; no hates.

O God, make my baby love me. I ask no endowments of excellencies for my child, but only that place of motherhood, once given me, may never be taken from me.

As long as the soul lives that I shall bring forth, let there be in it one secret shrine that shall always be Mother's.

Give it a clean mind and a warm free soul. And I promise Thee that I shall study the little one to find what gifts and graces Thou hast implanted that I may develop them.

I shall respect its personality. And

now, Father, I fold my hands and place
them between Thy hands and pray, in
Jesus name, that it may be Thy Will to
give me a normal baby, and make me a
normal mother. Amen.

FRANK CRANE

Nobility of Motherhood

No orator, no singer, no artist-
worker, is to be compared with the
mother who is carving the image of God
in the soul of her little child. No mother
need long to go out of the household, as
if that were an obscure place. The Gate
of Heaven is inscribed over every humble family.

HENRY WARD BEECHER

Susannah Wesley, the mother of John
and Charles Wesley; Mary Edwards
Dwight, the mother of Timothy Dwight;
Nancy Hanks, the mother of Abraham
Lincoln. These and many others have
made motherhood a sacred vocation that
has blessed all humanity. It was for their
kind that Mary Thomson wrote:

Give of thy sons to bear the message
    glorious;
Give of thy wealth to speed them on
    their way;
pour out thy soul for them in prayer
    victorious,
and all thou spendest, Jesus will repay.

MOTHER'S BIBLE

We search the world for truth, we cull
The good, the true, the beautiful,
From graven stone and written scroll,
And all old flower-fields of the soul;
And, weary seekers of the best,
We come back laden from our quest,
To find that all the sages said
Is in the Book our mothers read.

JOHN GREENLEAF WHITTIER

My Mother's Bible

This book is all that's left me now!
    Tears well unbidden start—
With faltering lips and throbbing brow
    I press it to my heart.
For many generations past,
    Here is our family tree;
My mother's hand this Bible clasped;
    She, dying, gave it me.

Ah! well do I remember those
    Whose names these records bear;
Who round the hearth-stone used to
        close
    After the evening prayer,
And speak of what these pages said,
    In tones my heart would thrill!

Though they are with the silent dead
    Here are they living still!

My father read this holy book
    To brothers, sisters, dear;
How calm was my poor mother's look,
    Who loved God's word to hear.
Her angel face—I see it yet!
    What thronging memories come!
Again that little group is met
    Within the halls of home!

Thou truest friend man ever knew,
    Thy constancy I've tried;
Where all were false I found thee true,
    My counsellor and guide.
The mines of earth no treasure give
    That could this volume buy:
In teaching me the way to live,
    It taught me how to die.

GEORGE P. MORRIS

In The Bible Mother Read

There's a book I've always treasured,
    That I'll keep where'er I'm led;
It has brought me joy unmeasured,
    It's the Bible Mother read.

All the pages are so fingered,
    Many verses underlined;
Places worn where Mother lingered,
    Where she left a tear behind.

Yes, this precious book I'll cherish,
    I will read it ev'ry day,
For its truth will never perish
    Though the world should pass away.

                              JOHN W. PETERSON

Mother's Translation of The Bible

There is a story about four clergymen
who were discussing the merits of the
various translations of the Bible. One
liked the King James Version best because of its simple, beautiful English.

Another liked the American Revised
Version best because it is more literal
and comes nearer the original Hebrew
and Greek.

Still another liked Moffatt's translation
best because of its up-to-date vocabu-
lary.

The fourth minister was silent. When
asked to express his opinion, he replied,
"I like my mother's translation best."

The other three expressed surprise.
They did not know that his mother had
translated the Bible. "Yes, she did," he
replied. "She translated it into life, and it
was the most convincing translation I
ever saw."

                              The Pioneer

CHRISTIAN MOTHER

God's Ideal Mother

The mother who owns Christ as Lord
    And Saviour in her life;
The mother who has peace with God,
    Who has no inner strife;
The mother who knows how to trust
    The Father for all things;
The mother who is right and just,
    As punishment she brings.

The mother who knows how to pray
    For every daily need;
The mother who can point the way,
    Where God would have her lead;
The mother who knows how to guide
    A precious child to God;
The mother who walks by His side,
    Who walks the way He trod.

The mother who knows how to teach
    Her child the Holy Word;
The mother who knows how to reach
    A child who has not heard;
The mother who knows how to show
    A loving, tender face;
The mother who can help him grow
    In wisdom and in grace.

The mother who can make a home
    In any place on earth;
The mother, who, though children roam,
    Has love that knows no dearth;
The mother who is all of this,
    To whom her God is real;
The mother who is not remiss,
    She is her God's ideal.

                              CORA M. PINKHAM

Mothers

A woman with a heathen heart,
Stumbling down a dusty road,
Plays a sacrificial part,
Carrying a precious load.
Why this journey? Why this sad
Face and figure on the way?
Heathen gods must be made glad—
Mother throws her child away!

A woman with a worldly heart,
Dancing down life's short, short road,
Gaily plays a selfish part,
Touched by Satan's restless goad.
Will she pause and meditate
Ere eternity appear?
What about her children's fate
As she wastes each precious year?

A woman with a Christian heart,

Yielded to the Lord above,
Plays a missionary's part
Guiding little ones with love.
See the countenance aglow!
There is peace within her breast,
God has said, "I'll do the rest."

                    EDNA MOORE SCHULTZ

God's Will

God knows my heart is willing
    To serve Him to the end,
Across the seas, on mountain tops,
    To roads beyond the bend;
He only asks the simple things
    Of me with consecration.
A house to clean and clothes to mend;
    Plan meals with new creations;
Making sure the family
    Is neat from head to laces;
That hairs are combed and hands are
        scrubbed,
    And there're no dirty faces;
Little shoes to polish at night
    That hold the precious feet
Of children who will follow in
    Our steps where e'er they lead.
It's up to us to guide them
    Along the path of life,
And show them Christ's the answer
    Through all their stress and strife.
Sweet little ones to rock to sleep
    And lull with gospel songs;
Sweet little minds and hearts to mold
    For righteousness or wrong.
What privileges God gave me!
    What responsibility!
God knew my heart was willing, when
    He gave these tasks to me.
I'm happy in His service, through
    Novel paths I go.
I'd rather be a Christian Mother
    Than anything I know.

                    MAXINE T. CLARK

I Had a Christian Mother

I cannot join the cynics
    That some men will applaud,
I had a Christian mother
    Who kept her faith in God!

Though men may view the altar
    Of faith with hostile air,
I had a Christian mother
    Who proved the power of prayer.
Though all the earth be throbbing
    With selfishness and hate,
Though death wings make their thunder
    And envy shakes the state,
I do not doubt the goodness
    Of Him who rules above,
I had a Christian mother
    Who taught me God was love.

                    LON WOODRUM

My Mother

She carried me under her heart;
Loved me before I was born;
Took God's hand in hers and walked
    through the Valley of Shadows that
    I might live;
Bathed me when I was helpless;
Clothed me when I was naked;
Gave me warm milk from her own body
    when I was hungry;
Rocked me to sleep when I was weary;
Pillowed me on pillows softer than down,
    and sang to me in the voice of an
    Angel;
Held my hand when I learned to walk;
Suffered with my sorrow;
Laughed with my joy;
Glowed with my triumph; and while I
    knelt at her side, she taught my lips
    to pray.
Through all the days of my youth she
    gave strength for my weakness, cour-
    age for my despair, and hope to fill
    my hopeless heart;
Was loyal when others failed;
Was true when tried by fire;
Was my friend when other friends were
    gone;
Prayed for me through all the days,
    when flooded with sunshine or sad-
    dened by shadows;
Loved me when I was unlovely, and led
    me into man's estate to walk tri-
    umphant on the King's Highway
    and play a manly part.
Though we lay down our lives for her
    we can never pay the debt we owe
    to a Christian Mother.

                    AUTHOR UNKNOWN

My Christian Mother

God gave me a Christian Mother
  And so my path to Heaven
Was paved with prayer, with Scripture
    light,
  A lamp she held God-given.
No dreams of wealth or worldly fame,
  Or passion to excel
In things of little moment,
  Did she at all instill.
She taught me truth, no word was false
  That by chance I overheard,
No deep resentment by deceit
  In my youthful heart was stirred.
No words of shame fell from her lips
  That should I e'er repeat
Would bring a blush to her own cheek
  And sense of her defeat.
No thought of retribution
  Did she plant in my heart
When crushed by some injustice
  The burning tears would start.
No selfishness do I recall
  Which dwarfed her stature whole,
But memories of the gifts that hurt,
  Enrich my very soul.
No weakness did she show me
  When life was hard and bare,
But from her heart's deep anguish,
  She led the way to prayer.
I think of her human frailty
  Of eyes that at last grew dim,
But more I think of her faith in God,
  And of how she walked with Him.
For many years the golden streets,
  Her happy feet have trod,
But still her footprints lead me on—
  On, on the way to God.

ANNIE E. HITT

Mother of Sharon's Rose

She ponders and she prays,
She knows the power that stays . . .
Blest mother of God's Son,
Her child, her Little One.

Her soul seeks calm and rest.
The wee Babe at her breast,
The mother's lullabies
Are mingled with deep sighs.

Whatever God has planned,
Her Child is in His hand.
This thought brings her repose,
Mother of Sharon's Rose.

LYDIA REGEHR

Jochebed, A Bible Mother

Jochebed lived in Egypt four thousand
  years ago.
The Egyptians worshipped idols, but
  she our God did know.
Miriam was her daughter, Aaron her
  baby boy
When another baby brother came to fill
  the home with joy.

But Pharaoh, King of Egypt, made He-
  brew mothers mourn
By saying their boy babies should die
  when they were born.
"Where shall we hide our baby?" cried
  Miriam to her mother,
"We cannot let them kill him, our dar-
  ling little brother."

"We'll hide him in a closet while he is
  very small,
God can with ease protect him, for He is
  Lord of all."
But when the babe grew bigger, nothing
  could drown his cries;
He could no longer hide at home—God
  made his mother wise.

She made a strong rush basket, just like
  a little boat.
She put her baby in it and then she let it
  float.
It floated in the rushes along the river
  Nile.
The baby's sister Miriam kept watching
  all the while.

Along came Egypt's princess, the great
  King Pharaoh's daughter.
She saw the little basket still floating in
  the water.
She sent her maids to get it, and when
  she looked inside
She saw the Hebrew baby—When he
  saw her, he cried.

She said, "I'll keep this baby and save
  him from the grave."

She did not know this baby small would
    all the Hebrews save.
For this was Baby Moses, who later Is-
    rael led.
Let's not forget his mother. Her name
    was Jochebed.

VIVIAN GUNDERSON

A godly mother will point her children
to God by the force of her example as
much as by the power of her words.

Mothers are wonderful people. They
can get up in the morning before they
smell bacon frying.
    The Sparta (Ill.) *News-Plaindealer*

There are two things to do about the
Gospel—believe it and behave it.

SUSANNAH WESLEY

Mary

A little maid in years,
Shaken by vague dim fears,
Half hoping in her heart
This strangeness would depart.
Bewildered by the light
She'd glimpsed that wondrous night:
Her own familiar world
Through star-lit spaces hurled:
Praying, soul hushed and awed,
At the very knees of God.

The Babe in her arms at last,
The valley of shadow past,
And deep in her woman's eyes
An infinite knowledge lies—
The secret of pain and loss,
The crown of thorns, and the cross
(And her soft arms tighten their hold
'Round the Baby form they enfold.)
The vision that God had dreamed
Of a sinful world redeemed,
And afar on the shores of time
The light of love sublime.

She holds to a waiting earth
The Son she has brought to birth!

MARTHA SNELL NICHOLSON

A Mother's Prayer

As Thou didst walk the land of Galilee,
So, loving Saviour, walk with him for
    me,
For since the years have passed and he is
    grown,
I cannot follow—he must walk alone.
Be Thou my feet, that I have had to stay,
For Thou canst comrade him on every
    way.
Be Thou my voice when sinful things
    allure,
Pleading with him to choose those that
    endure.
Be Thou my hand that would keep his in
    mine,
All, all things else, that mother must
    resign.
When he was little I could walk and
    guide,
But now, I pray, that Thou be at his
    side.
And as Thy blessed mother folded Thee,
So, kind and loving Saviour, guard my
    son for me.

AUTHOR UNKNOWN

Young Mother

This wonder, welling in the heart,
    Another mother knew,
When Jesus lay upon her breast:
    For Mary loved Him, too.

Yet when they came to Calvary,
    Her love would not deter
His steps. She knew that He was God's,
    And only loaned to her.

Nor is this child completely mine.
    O Father, help me see
That mother fails who does not bring
    Her children up for Thee.

HELEN FRAZEE-BOWER

MOTHER'S COMFORT

Quick Change Artist

Little rough boy with grubby fists
And a teetering chip on your shoulder,
How your heart yearns and your hot
    spirit burns
To be bigger and tougher and older!

Yet when the shadows of dusk have
    grown long
And hunger and sleepiness find you,
You come to your mother—want HER
    and no other,
And leave all your battles behind you!

INEZ CREEKMORE

Haven

My lap is a refuge from a world
Of too-large dogs and darkened stairs,
And broken bubble-pipes, and bees,
And ill-discovered unripe pears.

And I thank God for this—but oh,
Small innocent so tightly curled,
You are the comfort that I grasp
Against my own sharp, bruising world.

BARBARA A. JONES in *Christian Living*

Mother

Shadows are dancing about on the wall,
Never a sound as they rise and then fall;
Softly the clock ticks the twilight away—
Children and Mother talk over the day.

Twilight with Mother! Their life she now
    shares;
Hears all their joys and their hopes and
    their prayers;
Faith that is perfect, no peace such as
    this—
Twilight with Mother, her guidance—
    and kiss!

NELLIE HURST

Incident in an Elevator

She got in the elevator
At the fifteenth floor
Of the Big hotel,
And the eight of us
Who were already in
Shuffled back a little
To make more room;
And she was pretty
And dressed in black
That seemed to add
To a touch of grief
That lay in her eyes;
And along with her
In a little blue coat
And a cute little face
Came a bit of a girl
Of perhaps four years;
And we shuffled again
And made more room,
Because little girls
Who are not very tall
And who can't reach up
Where there's lots of air
Must have more room
Than a grown up.
And so we stood
While the door clanged shut
And we started down,
And just as we did
There came an "Oh!"
In a frightened tone
From the little girl
As she hid her face
In her mother's skirt.
And mother reached down
And picked her up
And said to her,
"You mustn't be frightened—
Just open your eyes
And look up at the light."
And so she did;
And all the way down
She kept her eyes
On the bowl-like globe
With a clear white light.
And reaching the lobby
We all of us stood
With hats in hand
While mother and child

Went on thir way,
And I don't know
But I imagine
That most of us

Remembered the words
"You mustn't be frightened—
Just open your eyes and
Look up at the light."

KENNETH C. BEATON

MOTHER'S LOVE

Mother's Love

Blessed is the love of Mother,
    Gift divine, from God above;
On the earth there is no blessing
    Like her tender, guarding love.
Day by day she sacrifices,
    Gives to meet our every need;
Willingly she guides her children,
    If to her we will but heed.

Gentle are her words and actions,
    Hallowed is the smile she wears;
Falters not when duty calls her,
    As she journeys down the years.
Other earthly love excelling,
    Great her just reward shall be,
When the Father gives her welcome
    To His fair eternity.

JOHANN ZUNDEL

Measurement

Wide is the world
    And the sky above,
But no wider than
    A Mother's love.

Deep is the sea
    Too deep to sound,
But a Mother's love
    Is more profound.

High are the heavens,
    Bathed in blue,
But a Mother's love
    Is that high, too.

We thank Thee, God,
    So great and good,
For the depth and breadth
    Of Motherhood.

AUTHOR UNKNOWN

Mother's Doxology

Praise God for mother's gentle
    hand,
And love we cannot understand,
Praise Him who sent us from above,
The blessings of a mother's love.

AUTHOR UNKNOWN

Waiting Mothers

All over the world
Mothers wait for their children
To come home—
Their children who have gone away
Into the world.
If those children walk in sorrow,
Or if they walk in sin,
Even though they walk in forgetfulness
Of the loving heart,
They are to their mothers
Only as little children
Wandering in the dark.

Some mothers sit with folded hands
And wait—and wait—
Others knit with skillful fingers
Or work with busy preoccupation;
But in the evening,
When lamps are lighted,
Mothers all over the world
Go to their doors
And peer anxiously
Into the darkness.

All over the world there are mothers
    waiting—
Waiting for their children to come
    home.

ANNE ZUCKER

Mothers' Hands

What can be said of mother's hands
　　can also not be said,
For who can count the vast
　　drudgeries performed each day—
And who can surmise if drudgeries
　　are really joys, because:
　　it is their pride. . . .
And they also minister kindness.

LINDA CLARKE

A Mother's love, with its depth of sincerity and unselfishness, has done more to hold humanity to its highest ideals, and to provide an abiding anchor in the buffeting storms of life than any other emotion.

ELIZABETH DERIEUX

Mother Love

I bent my ears to a lily's cup,
　　And thought that it spoke to me
By the stainless white of its petals light,
　　Of a Mother's purity.

To the heart of a red, red rose I crushed
　　And it seemed that within my eyes
There was shadowed the gleam of the
　　crimson stream
　　Of a Mother's sacrifice.

I considered the sun and the moon and
　　the stars,
　　The winds, and the tides of the sea,
And found in the span of their beautiful
　　plan
　　All a Mother's constancy.

Then I lifted my eyes to a hilltop lone,
　　Where Love hung high on a tree.
And lo, it was there I could best com-
　　pare
　　My Mother's love for me!

JANIE ALFORD

There is an enduring tenderness in the love of a mother to her son that transcends all other affections of the heart. It is neither to be chilled by selfishness nor doubted by danger nor weakened by worthlessness nor stifled by ingratitude.

WASHINGTON IRVING

I had given my second-grade class a lesson on magnets. As a follow-up, I passed out mimeographed sheets with this question: "My name starts with M, and I pick up things. What am I?" Imagine my surprise when ten of the youngsters wrote, "Mother."

VELMA SMITH in Reader's Digest

A man may go over all the world; he may become a pirate, if you please; he may run through every stage of belief and unbelief; he may become absolutely apostate; he may rub out his conscience; he may destroy his fineness in every respect: but there will be one picture that he cannot efface; living or dying there will rise before him, like a morning star, the beauty of that remembered goodness which he called "Mother."

HENRY WARD BEECHER

I have seen a mother at a crib;
　　So I know what love is.

JOHN BOWEN

If the faith of all the mothers could blossom to its full fruition, there would be no unsuccessful men in the land.

In this wintry world, it is a tender mother's love and a pious mother's care that are the carpet on the floor and the blaze on the evening hearth of home.

Mothers are fonder of their children. For they have a more painful share in their production and they are more certain that they are their own.

ARISTOTLE, Nichomachean Ethics II

If I were asked to name the world's greatest need, I should unhesitatingly say wise mothers; and the second greatest, exemplary fathers.

DAVID O. MCKAY

Years to a mother bring distress,
But do not make her love the less.

WILLIAM WORDSWORTH,
The Affliction of Margaret

A class of third-grade children were asked to write a poem about mother. The teacher said that she would put a gold star on the blackboard beside the name of the pupil who wrote the best poem.

Roberto Jose Martinez seemed to have a difficult time with the assignment. When the teacher called on him to read his poem, this is what he read:

"I tried very hard. I just let the pencil put on paper the way I feel here," he said, pointing to his heart. "Mothers make you hurt inside when you haven't got one."

Needless to say, Roberto's poem earned him the gold star beside his name.

A sea captain not long ago captured a young seal, hoping to tame and raise it on board his ship. He placed it in a sack to secure it, but wide as the ocean was, and swiftly as the ship sped on, the mother was as swift, and followed in search of her young. When it was first caught the mother howled piteously, and the "baby" barked back its grief, but the man was relentless and coolly watched the agonized mother follow him till the ship reached the wharf in Santa Barbara. Here he thought his prize was safe, for surely no seal would venture there, and the ship was docked. Suddenly the mother gave a cry close to the ship and the little one, as if obeying instructions, struggled, still in the sack, to the edge of the deck, and rolled itself overboard. The mother was seen to seize the sack, rip it open with her sharp teeth, and joyfully claim her baby. She had swum after it for eighty miles.

The King's Business

Mother love is the best medicine, several British hospitals have discovered. Instead of confining mothers to infrequent visiting hours, hospital directors decided to let mother come in every night, tell baby a story, tuck him in bed, and kiss him good night.

The results were so successful in helping the children to get well faster that other hospitals are following suit. They've found that the best doctors and nurses in the world and the most sanitary conditions are not enough by themselves. There's no substitute for the love and devotion of a mother.

Chicago News, Foreign Service

The Fairest

They say . . . one time three angels
Were trying to agree
On earth's most lovely treasure.
They journeyed down to see.

The first one chose a baby's smile,
To take to heaven above.
The second chose a flower,
The third, a mother's love.

Alas! The smile soon faded,
The flower lived a day,
But Mother's love stayed fairest,
And never passed away.

ESTHER F. THOM

Mother Love

Of all the love that has been known
Since time and earth began,
Of all the faith that has been shown
Since God created man;
Of all the noble stirring deeds
That grace the written page,
A mother's love and faith and hope
Stand out through every age.

Her deeds have moved the sternest hearts
To wonder and to tears,
Her love has kindled faith and trust
Through all the changing years;
Her sacrifice, unselfishness,
Her trust through praise or blame
Have shrined her in the hearts of all
And glorified her name.

For though the world may frown or sneer,
Though failure may be ours,
Her love still folds, encircles us,
A garland of flowers;
A comforting, sustaining force,

A star that brightly gleams,
That softens every care and hurt
And shares our hopes and dreams.

KATHERINE EDELMAN

The baby has no skies
But mother's eyes;
Nor any God above
But mother's love;
His angel sees the Father's face,
But he the mother's, full of grace.

A Mother's Love

Life does not hold enough of years
    In which we can repay
A mother's love—so do your best
    Before she goes away.

No sweeter thought was given birth
    Amid the worldly throng;
No truer words were ever penned
    In verse or sacred song.

No purer theme could be discussed
    In mankind's vast domain;
And heaven's dream is far surpassed
    By this true, sweet refrain.

Life does not hold enough of years
    In which we can repay
A mother's love—then do your best
    Before she goes away.

AUTHOR UNKNOWN

Mother O' Mine

If I were hanged on the highest hill,
    Mother o' mine, O mother o' mine!
I know whose love would follow me
    still,
    Mother o' mine, O mother o' mine!
If I were drowned in the deepest sea,
    Mother o' mine, O mother o' mine!
I know whose tears would come down to
    me,
    Mother o' mine, O mother o' mine!
If I were damned o' body and soul,
I know whose prayers would make me
    whole,
    Mother o' mine, O mother o' mine!

RUDYARD KIPLING

A Mother's Love

A mother's love is something
    that no one can explain,
It is made of deep devotion
    and of sacrifice and pain,
It is endless and unselfish
    and enduring come what may
For nothing can destroy it
    or take that love away . . .
It is patient and forgiving
    when all others are forsaking,
And it never fails or falters
    even though the heart is break-
    ing . . .
It believes beyond believing
    when the world around condemns,
And it glows with all the beauty
    of the rarest, brightest gems . . .
It is far beyond defining,
    it defies all explanation,
And it still remains a secret
    like the mysteries of creation . . .
A many splendored miracle
    man cannot understand
And another wondrous evidence
    of God's tender guiding hand.

HELEN STEINER RICE

Mothers as well as fools, sometimes walk where angels fear to tread.

The Mother's Eye

When did a child ever look ugly to its mother! Larks doubtless think their featherless, discolored, yellow-mantled squabs more beautiful than full-grown humming-birds.

HENRY WARD BEECHER

Just Like a Mother

Bishop Quayle used to tell of a circuit rider who brought home four apples, a rare fruit on the almost orchardless frontier. When the preacher's wife had given one apple to each of her three boys, she placed the one meant for her on the mantle. After the boys had eaten their apples their mother saw them observing hers, whereupon she cut it into three pieces for them. The boys returned to the cabin porch and as they munched the fruit they discussed how strange it was that their mother did not care for apples. But when one of the sons was an old man he explained to the Bishop that he had come to understand that it was not because his mother did not like apples, but that she liked little boys better.

A Mother's Love

When Jim Brown left his Devonshire, England, home for a position in a New York bank, his mother gave him her own beloved and well-used Bible. With a parting kiss, she said, "Serve God, my son, and He will keep and bless you all the days."

Jim choked down a rising sob and said, "It is easy to promise, Mother; I will say nothing, but I will try to act and do my best."

When the *Umbrai* moved out of dock, the last sight seen on land by Jim was the frail figure of his mother. Her sad face, with unshed tears in her eyes, made the young man long to be on shore again, that he might comfort his mother by saying, "Mother, dear, smile again, and I will promise you anything."

Time passed on, and for seven years Jim had not seen his mother; promotion had come to him, and his mother rejoiced in his prosperity. No word in his letters ever referred to the parting advice of his mother. Jim had long since forgotten it, but his mother never doubted the answer to her constant prayer that her beloved son would someday honor God in his whole-hearted devotion to Him.

As Jim sat in his office one hot noon, a friend came in and proposed to take him out during the lunch hour.

"Where?" was Jim's question.

"Oh, to Fulton Street," replied his friend.

"That's a strange place to go this time of day," said Jim. "But perhaps you are bound for the fruit market?"

"Yes that's about it," said his friend. "Anyway, you will come?"

Jim consented, and they took a car, and before long Jim found himself entering, with dozens of city men known to him, the Fulton Street noon prayer meeting. He was annoyed, and resolved to leave as soon as possible. Presently his ears caught the words, "A mother desires prayer for her son, who, after seven years is farther from God, and given no sign of early Christian training." This was surely himself. His mother must have sent this appeal from Devonshire. Blair, his friend, knew it, and had brought him there to hear it.

He was furious, and wondered if every finger in the hall were pointing at him. But when the gentleman who read the request added, "The anxious mother is present with us in prayer," Jim looked around, expecting to see his own mother; he was disappointed to notice only city men. He listened to the short, fervent, pleading prayers of several men and felt sure they were on his behalf.

He left the meeting quietly, and for the rest of the day was silent, thoughtful, and unhappy. That evening, on entering his apartment, he saw the contents of a box of books he never used lying upon a table, and on top of all his mother's parting gift—her much-loved Bible.

What influence is this? he said to himself. He felt powerless in the face of such a combination of circumstances. Undoing the clasp of the Bible, a letter fluttered from between the pages—a letter in the handwriting of his mother. He flushed with shame.

For seven years this letter had lain between the pages of the Bible, perhaps needing an answer. How should he answer it? The letter commenced, "My son, remember thy Creator in the days of thy youth. Remember the tender hours of childhood which you gave to God at my knee. Remember, he loves you and seeks to save you. Remember, I shall live only to pray for you! God bless you! Christ guide you! The Holy Spirit teach you! prays your mother."

That was all; but it came just at the right moment to the heart of Jim Brown who said: "Here and now, O God, I give myself to Thee, to do with as Thou wilt, and keep forevermore. That is the answer to my mother's letter. Amen."

A gush of gladness filled his own soul, such as he had never known in all his successful business career, and he sat down at once to rejoice the heart of his darling mother whose picture he fondly kissed, and then wrote, "Mother, you have prevailed—you have won your son for God!"

Next day he was at the noon prayer meeting, and giving no name or circumstances, he passed up a slip of paper, stating: "A son desires to praise God for a mother's prayers."

He learned how the books came to be on his table.

"The box was moved by the workmen who were repairing the radiator," said the landlady; "the bottom fell out through dry rot, and so I put the books on your table."

That was all. Very simple are the divine methods. What a great and wonder-working God we have, who makes no mistakes! What seeming trifles He can use to bring about wise results!

"What do you mean to do?" asked his friend, Blair, on hearing the blessed news. "Nothing," was the reply. "It is done. I am a new man in Christ. He has turned me right around."

And so it proved, Jim (not his true name) is now one of our merchant princes. Though years have passed, he is still true as steel to his Saviour, a shining light in the dark places of the mercantile world; and an encouragement to every anxious mother, and a power for God, especially amongst young men.

AUTHOR UNKNOWN

Mother's Love

Her love is like an island
In life's ocean, vast and wide,
A peaceful, quiet shelter
From the wind, the rain, the tide,

'Tis bounded on the North by hope,
By patience on the West,
By tender Counsel on the South
And on the East by rest.

Above it like a beacon light
Shine faith, and truth, and prayer;

And through the changing scenes of life
I find a haven there.

A Mother's Version

(A paraphrase of the well known thirteenth chapter of First Corinthians, applied to the home maker.)

Though I speak with the language of the educators and the psychiatrists and have not love, I am become as blaring brass or a crashing cymbal.

And if I have the gift of planning my child's future and understanding all the mysteries of the child's mind and have ample knowledge of teen agers and though I have all faith in my children so I could remove their mountains of doubts and fears and have not love, I am nothing.

And though I bestow all my goods to feed and nourish them properly (vitamins and all), and though I give my body to backbreaking housework and have not love, it profiteth me nothing.

Love is patient with the naughty child and is kind to him. Love doesn't envy when he wants to move to Grandma's house because "she is nice."

Love is not anxious to impress a teenager with our superior knowledge.

Love has good manners in the home . . . does not act selfishly or with a martyr complex, is not easily provoked by normal childish actions.

Love does not remember the naughtiness of yesterday and love thinks no evil . . . it gives the child the benefit of the doubt.

Love does not make light of sin in the child's life (or in her own, either), but rejoices when he comes to a knowledge of the truth.

Love doesn't fail. Whether there be comfortable surroundings, they shall fail, whether there be total communication between parents and children, it will cease, whether there be a good education, it shall vanish away.

When we were children we spoke and acted and understood as children but now that we have become parents we must act maturely.

Now abides faith, hope, love . . . these

three are needed in the home. Faith in
Jesus Christ, eternal hope for the future
of the child, and God's love shed abroad
in our hearts, but the greatest of these is
love.

MRS. MERVIN SEASHORE
in *The Evangelical Beacon*

Your Mother

Nobody else may ever care because you
have a broken heart;
Nobody else, if you should err, may be
inclined to take your part.
But she will know and she will pray
That God may take your woes away.
When all fair weather friends forget,
when fortune turns and smiles no
more
Her faith in you will linger yet, she will
be faithful as before.

Nobody else may ever see your native
worth, your nobleness;
Nobody else may know, but she will
know, what talents you possess.
Though others enviously frown
Or slyly seek to drag you down,
She will in word and thoughts be true,
and with sweet triumph in her
breast
Achieve her rarest blessing through the
favors through which you are
blessed.

Nobody else may weep because your
dearest plans have come to naught;
Nobody else may deign to pause, if in
sin's meshes you are caught;
To ask if you had been to blame
Or seek to rid you of your shame,
But she would still, with all her heart
proclaim your innocence, your
worth.
Oh, strive, my child, to do your part to
gladden her brief days on earth.

S. E. KISER

Mother

There is just one,
And only one,
Whose love shall fail me never,

Just one who lives
From sun to sun,
With constant fond endeavor.

There is just one,
And only one,
On earth there is no other.
In Heaven a noble
Work was done
When God gave man a Mother.

AUTHOR UNKNOWN

Mothers and Others

Others weary of the noise,
Mothers play with girls and boys.
Others scold because we fell,
Mothers "kiss and make it well."
Others work with patient will,
Mothers labor later still.
Others' love is more or less,
Mothers love with steadiness.

Others pardon, hating yet,
Mothers pardon and forget.
Others keep the ancient score,
Mothers never shut the door.
Others grow incredulous,
Mothers still believe in us.
Others throw their faith away,
Mothers pray, and pray, and pray.

AMOS R. WELLS

Just for a Minute

I remember when I was only four,
Mother would bring me round to the
store.
And just outside the church she'd stand,
And "come in" she'd say, reaching down
For my hand—"just for a minute."

And then when I started going to
school,
She'd bring me down every day, as a
rule,
But first the steps to the church we'd
climb,
And she'd say, "We'll go in—you've always
Got time, 'Just for a minute.'"

Then I got real big, I mean seven
years old,

And I went by myself, but was always
told,
When you're passing the church, don't
forget to call
And tell our Lord about lessons and all,
"Just for a minute."

And now it's sort of a habit I've got,
In the evening, coming from Casey's lot,
Though it takes me out of my way a bit,
To slip into church with my bat and
mitt,
"Just for a minute."

But sometimes I feel like another fel-
low
Standing outside, and I just go yellow.
I pass by the door, but a voice from
within
Seems sadly to say: "So you wouldn't
Come in— 'Just for a minute.' "

There are things inside of me bad and
good,
That nobody knows and nobody could,
Excepting Our Lord, and I'd like Him to
know,
And He helps, when in for a visit I go,
"Just for a minute."

He finds it lonesome when nobody
comes
(There are hours upon hours when no-
body comes)
And he's pleased when any one passing
by
Stops in (though it's only a little guy)
"Just for a minute."

AUTHOR UNKNOWN

*If there be aught surpassing human deed
or word or thought it is a mother's love!*

MARCHIONESS DE SPADARA

The Unseen

What is the secret of a rainbow's charm?
  Its silent beauty after wind and storm?
Its multicolored rays above a farm?
  Its curve, its arch, and evanescent
  form?

How does a rainbow make my soul ex-
  pand?
  What does its tranquil brilliance fully
  mean?
The rainbow's hues have helped me understand
  Its deeper charm is in the part unseen.

What is the secret of a mother's love?
  A sense of duty to a helpless one?
A seed of kindness planted from above?
  An inner joy and peace for work well
  done?

How does a mother fill the needs she
  must?
  How can she scrub her universe so
  clean?
The angels know how she fulfills her
  trust—
  Her deeper charm is in her work unseen.

WILLIAM ARTHUR WARD

MOTHER'S INFLUENCE

Mother's Way

Oft within our little cottage,
As the shadows gently fall,
While the sunlight touches softly
One sweet face upon the wall,
Do we gather close together,
And in hushed and tender tone
Ask each other's full forgiveness
For the wrong that each has done.

Should you wonder why this custom
At the ending of the day,
Eye and voice would quickly answer,
"It was once our Mother's way."

If our home be bright and cheery,
If it hold a welcome true,
Opening wide its door of greeting
To the many—not the few;
If we share our Father's bounty

With the needy day by day,
'Tis because our hearts remember
This was ever Mother's way.

Sometimes when our hearts grow weary
Or our task seems very long,
When our burdens look too heavy
And we deem the right all wrong,
Then we gain a new, fresh courage
As we rise and brightly say,
"Let us do our duty bravely—
This was our dear Mother's way."

Thus we keep her memory precious
While we never cease to pray,
That at last when lengthening shadows
Mark the evening of life's day,
They may find us waiting calmly
To go home our Mother's way.

AUTHOR UNKNOWN

Mother Is Right

I can't see why mother doesn't like pretty
   snakes;
They don't hurt a thing, for goodness
   sakes!
I don't mean the big ones, just the kind
   in our yard,
They're those little green thin ones, but
   I'll try real hard
To please my mother with all my might
For Dad's always saying, "Your mother
   is right."

PHYLLIS MICHAEL

They say that man is mighty,
   He governs land and sea,
He wields a mighty scepter
   O'er lesser powers that be;
But a mightier power and stronger
   Man from his throne has hurled,
For the hand that rocks the cradle
   Is the hand that rules the world.

WILLIAM ROSS WALLACE,
The Hand That Rules The World

You may have tangible wealth untold;
Caskets of jewels and coffers of gold;
Richer than I you can never be—
I had a mother who read to me.

STRICKLAND GILLILAN,
The Reading Mother

And Dorcas in her daughters lives
   Industrious and kind;
For help her good example gives
   To willing hand and mind.

LYNCH

Just Like Glue

His mother had just returned from the
hospital. She had been away for such a
long time; at least it seemed long to her
little boy. But now she was at home
again, and he was beside himself with
excitement. As soon as he could put his
thoughts into words, he exclaimed,
"Mother, you're just like glue!" At first
she did not understand what he meant
by such an odd expression. But he continued, "I mean that you hold us together. When you are gone, we just fall
apart. Sister lives in one place, Buddy
somewhere else, and Daddy and I get
along by ourselves. You're just the stuff
that keeps us together."

The Upper Room

A Little Parable for Mothers

The young mother set her foot on the
path of life.
"Is the way long?" she asked.
And her Guide said: "Yes, and the
way is hard. And you will be old before
you reach the end of it. But the end will
be better than the beginning."
But the young Mother was happy, and
she would not believe that anything
could be better than these years. So she
played with her children, and gathered
flowers for them along the way, and
bathed with them in the clear streams;
and the sun shone on them, and life was
good, and the young Mother cried,
"Nothing will ever be lovelier than this."
Then night came, and storm, and the
path was dark, and the children shook
with fear and cold, and the Mother drew
them close and covered them with her
mantle, and the children said, "Oh
Mother, we are not afraid, for you are
near and no harm can come," and the

Mother said, "This is better than the brightness of day, for I have taught my children courage."

And the morning came, and there was a hill ahead, and the children climbed and grew weary, and the Mother was weary, but at all times she said to the children, "A little patience, and we are there." So the children climbed, and when they reached the top, they said, "We could not have done it without you, Mother." And the Mother, when she lay down that night, looked up at the stars, and said: "This is a better day than the last, for my children have learned fortitude in the face of hardness. Yesterday I gave them courage. Today I have given them strength."

And the next day came strange clouds which darkened the earth—clouds of war and hate and evil, and the children groped and stumbled, and the Mother said: "Look up. Lift your eyes to the Light."

And the children looked and saw above the clouds an Everlasting Glory, and it guided them and brought them beyond the darkness. And that night the Mother said, "This is the best day of all, for I have shown my children God."

And the days went on, and the weeks and the months and the years, and the Mother grew old, and she was little and bent. But her children were tall and strong, and walked with courage. And when the way was hard, they helped their Mother; and when the way was rough, they lifted her, for she was as light as a feather; and at last they came to a hill, and beyond the hill they could see a shining road and golden gates flung wide.

And the Mother said: "I have reached the end of my journey. And now I know that the end is better than the beginning, for my children can walk alone, and their children after them."

And the children said, "You will always walk with us, Mother, even when you have gone through the gates."

And they stood and watched her as she went on alone, and the gates closed after her. And they said: "We cannot see her, but she is with us still. A Mother like ours is more than a Memory. She is a Living Presence."

TEMPLE BAILEY

Today's Christian Leaders Had Mothers Who:

... fed their babies on a strict four-hour schedule.

... fed their babies on a hunger-demand schedule.

... avoided the habit of rocking their babies.

... enjoyed the habit of rocking their babies.

... did not force their children to eat.

... forced their children to eat the last bite.

... started bathroom training at four months.

... started bathroom training at two years.

... started cup feedings before six months.

... started cup feedings past two years.

... permitted thumb sucking.

... used thumb guards.

... refused to raise their voice to their children.

... rebuked their children vociferously.

... forbade frequent sweet treats.

... lavished their children with sweet treats.

... disciplined their children's toy purchases.

... allowed their children to accumulate toys.

... stressed child training over housework.

... stressed housework over child training.

... miraculously found the balance.

... related to each child in a similar manner.

... related to each child differently.

... followed an early-to-bed schedule.

... permitted a late-to-bed routine.

Though the methods were varied, these mothers bequeathed to their children one common gift: they were brought up in the nurture and admonition of the Lord; they are today's Christian leaders, rearing their own children by equally diverse methods.

JEANNE ALLEN
in *The Christian Mother*

Training to Love Others

David Hill was playing ball near his home in Scotland. His mother called him to help her take a basket of food to a poor family. "Can't the maid do it, Mother?" he asked.

"No," said the mother. "I want you to grow up to have a tender, loving heart for the poor." So she took him along. Not only that time did he go, but often. He became a missionary to China, popular because of his gentle kindness. His mother's training had made him unselfish.

MARTIN P. SIMON

Mother's Way

He criticised her pudding,
He didn't like her cake;
He wished she'd make the biscuits
His mother used to make.

She didn't wash the dishes,
And she didn't make a stew;
And she didn't darn his stockings
Like his mother used to do.

So when one day he went
The same old rigmarole through,
She turned and boxed his ears,
Just like his mother used to do.

Speaker's Library

I Must Make the Time Count
(A Mother's Last Letter to Her Son.)

Mother had died on Christmas Day and I was just back at home in Southern California following the funeral.

I leafed through the stack of mail which awaited me. There were cards of sympathy, thoughtful little notes from friends—but suddenly I found in the midst of them a card which was different. It was a birthday card. . . .

Holding it in my hand, it suddenly came back to me. It had been on my birthday that the call had come—the word that my mother had suffered a sudden stroke.

I opened the card, looked at the familiar handwriting . . . and at once realized what this was. This was a card from my mother—a card which apparently had been in the mails on its way to me at the very moment that I was rushing to her side.

You can imagine how eagerly I read the little personal note she had penned on the back . . . for I realized that this was the last thing she had ever said to me.

Yes, my mother had never regained consciousness during those days until she awoke in Heaven in the presence of the One whom she had loved so much and served so faithfully . . . and so these were her last words to me.

As I read them, the last phrase especially caught and gripped my attention. Writing on the first day of what proved to be her last week of conscious life, she commented on the busyness of the pre-Christmas season and then ended with these words: "I must make the time count, this week."

What a wonderful way, I thought, to begin one's last week of life: "I must make the time count."

Mother's fatal illness was sudden, unexpected. I really don't believe she had any particular apprehension of what was ahead as she wrote those words. I don't think she had any particular reason to write to me except for her usual cheerful busyness in "redeeming the time."

But I carry those words with me everywhere I go. I carry that little card in my Bible, and this reminder goes with me throughout the world.

And over and over again, as I think of these words, I thank God for one priceless gift He gives us.

Have you ever thought about it? Each day of our lives we receive a gift—a priceless gift—which comes from a royal source. It comes to us bright and sparkling, absolutely untouched, un-spoiled.

What is this gift? The priceless gift of time.

Yes, time. Each day we receive a fresh, new supply—24 hours . . . 1,440 minutes . . . 86,400 seconds. Twenty-four hours we have never lived before; twen-ty-four hours we shall never live again.

What a wonderful attitude for one to have in facing his last week—or his last day or month or year: "I must make the time count."

Ahead of us stretches a new year, as men measure time. This coming year, will be a year I have never lived before . . . a year I shall never live again.

So, adapting my mother's words, I make this my prayer: "This year I must make the time count . . . for Christ!"

LARRY WARD

You Invited Me There

When I arrive in that heavenly city
Where never comes sorrow or care,
I'll say to my dear precious mother,
"It was you who invited me here.

To Christ alone be the glory
He my sins in His Body did bare,
Yet to heaven I might not have come
Had you not invited me here."

AUTHOR UNKNOWN

She was the best of all mothers, to whom I owe endless gratitude.

THOMAS CARLYLE

In the man whose childhood has known caresses, there is always a fibre of memory that can be touched to gentle issues.

GEORGE ELIOT (MARY ANN EVANS)

Nothing is impossible to a valiant heart.

Motto of JEANNE D'ALBERT,
Mother of Henry IV

When the devil robs a man, the last thing he takes from him is what he learned at his mother's knee.

Every man got his high ideals from his mother or from some other good person or persons who got these ideals from the church.

O woman! lovely woman! Nature made thee
To temper man: we had been brutes without you;
Angels are painted fair, to look like you;
There's in you all that we believe of Heaven,
Amazing brightness, purity, and truth,
Eternal joy, and everlasting love.

THOMAS OTWAY, Venice Preserved

A mother takes twenty years to make a man of her boy, and another makes a fool of him in twenty minutes.

ROBERT FROST

All women become like their mothers; no man does.

Only God Himself fully appreciates the influence of a Christian mother in the molding of the character in her chil-dren. . . . If we had more Christian mothers we would have less delinquency, less immorality, less ungodliness and fewer broken homes. The influence of a mother in her home upon the lives of her children cannot be measured. They know and absorb her example and atti-tudes when it comes to questions of hon-esty, temperance, kindness and indus-try. . . .

BILLY GRAHAM

Samuel, was the child of his mother's prayers. "For weal or for woe a moth-er's influence is infinitely great. We are not surprised to learn that Byron's moth-er was proud, ill-tempered, and violent; or that Nero's mother was a murderess. On the other hand, we need not be as-tonished that Sir Walter Scott's was a lover of poetry; or those of Wesley, Au-gustine, Chrysostom, Basil, and others, remarkable for their intelligence and goodness. Like mother, like child. This is what led the good Lord Shaftesbury to exclaim, 'Give me a generation of Christian mothers, and I will undertake to change the face of society in twelve months.' "

E. MORGAN

The Legacy

She could not give her children gold
So she gave them faith to have and hold.
She could not give them royal birth . . .
A name renowned throughout the earth,
But she gave them seeds and a garden
   spot
And shade trees when the sun was hot.
She could not give a silver spoon
Or servants waiting night and noon.
She gave them love and a listening ear
And told them God was always near.

She could not give them ocean trips
Aboard majestic sailing ships,
But she gave them books and a quiet
   time,
Adventures found in prose and rhyme.

She could not give them worldly things
But what she gave was fit for kings,
For with her faith and books and sod
She made each child aware of God.

ALICE MASON

Thou must remember that this budding
   soul
Will see his God in thee,
And through thee—see God.

Selected

I do not ask for talents grand—
Just faith like my dear mother;
For then I'll have the art and grace
To understand my brother.

LES COX

When the will of Henry J. Heinz, wealthy distributor of the famous "57 Varieties" line, was read it was found to contain the following confession:

"Looking forward to the time when my earthly career will end, I desire to set forth at the very beginning of this will, as the most important item in it, a confession of my faith in Jesus Christ as my Saviour. I also desire to bear witness to the fact that throughout my life, in which there were unusual joys and sorrows, I have been wonderfully sustained by my faith in God through Jesus Christ. This legacy was left me by my consecrated MOTHER, a woman of strong faith, and to it I attribute any success I have attained."

A Mother's Influence

Had not Susannah Wesley been the mother of John Wesley, it is not likely that John Wesley would have been the founder of Methodism.

Susannah Wesley was the mother of John and Charles and seventeen other children. She was beautiful, energetic, devout. She knew Greek, Latin, French and theology.

In counsel to John she said, "Take this rule: Whatever weakens your reason, impairs the tenderness of your conscience, obscures your sense of God, or takes off the relish of spiritual things—in short, whatever increases the strength and authority of your body over your mind, that thing is sin to you, however innocent it may be in itself."

This Christian mother's counsel to her son John needs the attention of every mother and father and child today. If more parents would be Christian in character as Mrs. Wesley was, there would be less sabotaging of the children's lives with parental delinquency.

Gospel Banner

To be a mother is the greatest vocation in the world. No being has a position of such great power and influence. She holds in her hands the destiny of nations; for to her is necessarily committed the making of the nation's citizens.

HANNAH WHITALL SMITH

To Mother

You painted no Madonnas
  On chapel walls in Rome,
But with a touch diviner
  You lived one in your home.

You wrote no lofty poems
  That critics counted art,
But with a nobler vision
  You lived them in your heart.

You carved no shapeless marble
  To some high souled design,
But with a finer sculpture
  You shaped this soul of mine.

You built no great cathedrals
  That centuries applaud,
But with a finer sculpture
  Your life cathedraled God.

Had I the gift of Raphael,
  Of Michelangelo,
Oh, what a rare Madonna
  My mother's life would show!

THOMAS W. FESSENDEN

"In the Way He Should Go"

(Proverbs 22:6)

There is so much to do, how can one
    pair
  Of mother hands, one pair of tired
    feet
Give to the child today his proper care?
  There are so many fresh demands to
    meet—
The little bodies and the minds to dress
  In fitting garments, beautiful and
    right.
How shall she dare to undertake unless
  She keep the One who gave him in
    her sight?
Yet I have seen a mother turn away—
  "When he is older, he may make his
    choice":
Or "When I've time, perhaps, but not
    today."
  Oh, Mother, listen to the warning
    voice!
Tomorrow is so late; and time that stole

Your precious privilege may steal his
  soul.

RUBY WEYBURN TOBIAS
in *The Sunday School Times*

A Mother's Creed

I believe, with the gardener, that the youngest plants should have the tenderest care; that the habits of early youth should be so moulded as to develop fixed traits of good character in the adult.

I believe what one wills to be, one can be; "that education lays the foundation, but that self-education erects the building;" that the mind can only possess that which it does.

I believe that obstacles and reverses are but quality-testing stepping-stones to success; that the room for improvement is the largest room in the world.

I believe that within the breast of every child is an instinctive desire to be good; to grow; to learn; to work; to love; to achieve.

I believe in home encouragement; that a home without good useful books is like a home without windows; that where children are, there should be found the treasure thoughts of the greatest men and women of all ages which ever beckon on and on, inspiring to higher ideals and nobler ambitions.

I believe that the mind can only be rightly formed when it is rightly informed; that opportunity ever knocks at the door of those who are rightly equipped to fight life's battles; that the power to think grows by exercise.

I believe in the pleasure of self-sacrifice, the price paid by hundreds of mothers of world-renowned men.

I believe in the education that stimulates thought; develops self-reliance and leads to a delight in whatever is fair in nature, in whatever is true and beautiful in literature and art.

AUTHOR UNKNOWN

When Mother Reads Aloud

When Mother reads aloud, the past
Seems real as every day;

I hear the tramp of armies vast,
I see the spears and lances cast,
I join the thrilling fray;
Brave knights and ladies fair and proud
I meet when Mother reads aloud.

When Mother reads aloud, far lands
Seem very near and true;
I cross the desert's gleaming sands,
Or hunt the jungle's animal bands,
Or sail the ocean blue.
Far heights, whose peaks the cold mists
    shroud,
I scale, when Mother reads aloud.

When Mother reads aloud, I long
For noble deeds to do . . .
To help the right, redress the wrong;
It seems so easy to be strong,
So simple to be true.
Oh, thick and fast the visions crowd
My eyes, when Mother reads aloud.

AUTHOR UNKNOWN

Mother Goes Visiting

It makes me feel very odd
To write you this letter tonight,
When it seems, or it seems pretty nearly,
That you're somewhere around, out of
    sight.

I can hardly believe you're not sitting
Upstairs (though I know you are not),
Just doing your mending or knitting . . .
I miss you a lot!

I wish I had some news to tell you.
I'm not doing much that is sport.
I'm getting my lessons so well, you
Will smile when you see my report.

I've had a bad cold but I'm better;
I wasn't to tell, I forgot.
Please write me a very long letter.
I miss you a lot!

The kisses will count up to thirty
If you consider a kiss for each blot.
Heaps of love, from your little Bertie.
P. S. I miss you a lot!

AUTHOR UNKNOWN

Alma Mater

The oldest university
Was not on India's strand,
Nor in the valley of the Nile,
Nor on Arabia's sand;
From time's beginning it has taught,
And still it teaches, free,
Its learning, mild, to every child—
The School of Mother's Knee.

The oldest school to teach the law
And teach it deeply, too,
Dividing what should not be done
From what each one should do,
Was not in Rome or Ispahan,
Nor by the Euxine Sea;
It held its way ere history's day—
The School of Mother's Knee.

The oldest seminary where
Theology was taught
When love to God, and reverent prayer,
And the Eternal Ought
Were deep impressed on youthful hearts
In pure sincerity
Came to the earth with Abel's birth—
The School of Mother's Knee.

The oldest—and the newest, too—
It still maintains its place,
And from its classes, ever full,
It graduates the race.
Without its teaching, where would all
The best of living be?
'Twas planned by Heaven, this earth to
    leaven
The School of Mother's Knee.

PRISCILLA LEONARD

A young teen-age girl was being ex-
amined for church membership by the
officers of a certain congregation. "Do
you want to be like Christ?" was the
straightforward question of one of the
deacons. For a moment the girl hesitated
as if puzzled, but then she lifted her eyes
frankly to meet those of the speaker, "I
don't know," she replied slowly and
thoughtfully. "I never thought much
about that." Then with a look of tenderness in her face, she added, "But I know
I want to be like my mother."

GORDON MATTICE

If I am Thy child, O God, it is because Thou gavest me such a mother.

ST. AUGUSTINE

For when you looked into my mother's eyes you knew, as if He had told
you, why God had sent her into the
world . . . it was to open the minds of all
who looked to beautiful things.

JAMES M. BARRIE

The Parent's Life is the Child's Copy
Book.

O wondrous power! how little understood.
Intrusted to the mother's mind
alone.
To fashion genius—to form the
soul for good.

MRS. HALE

Mother—the essence of loveliness,
The beauty of a rose,
The sparkle of a dewdrop
And Sunset's sweet repose.

LYDIA M. JOHNSON

Man
The Bravest Battle

The bravest battle that ever was fought—
Shall I tell you where and when?
On the maps of the world you will find it
not:
It was fought by the Mothers of Men.

Not with cannon or battle shot,
With sword or nobler pen;
Not with eloquent word or thought
From the wonderful minds of men;

But deep in a walled-up woman's heart;
A woman that would not yield;
But bravely and patiently bore her part;
Lo! there is the battlefield.

No marshalling troops, no bivouac song,
No banner to gleam and wave;
But, Oh, these battles they last so long—
From babyhood to the grave!

But faithful still as a bridge of stars
She fights in her walled-up town;
Fights on, and on, in the endless wars;
Then silent, unseen goes down!

Ho! ye with banners and battle shot,
With soldiers to shout and praise,
I tell you the kingliest victories fought
Are fought in these silent ways.

JOAQUIN MILLER

I will desire for a friend the son who
never resisted the tears of his mother.

LACRITELLE

A little boy, who was told by his
mother that it was God who made people good, responded, "Yes, I know it is
God, but mothers help a lot."

CHRISTIAN GUARDIAN

If I prefer the truth it is due to my
mother's teaching.

CHRYSOSTOM

A woman's love is mighty, but a mother's heart is weak,
And by its weakness overcomes.

JAMES RUSSELL LOWELL,
Legend of Brittany

Mothers make men.

CHARLES H. SPURGEON

Mother's truth makes constant youth.

CHARLES H. SPURGEON

A child's first teacher is his mother.

Our nation has no better friend than
the mother who teaches her child how to
pray.

The mother's face and voice are the
first conscious objects as the infant soul
unfolds, and she soon comes to stand in
the very place of God to her child.

GRANVILLE STANLEY HALL

MOTHER'S PRAYERS AND PRAYERS FOR MOTHER

A Mother Prays

Father, teach my children how to grow
Through every loss or pain.
Let Your comfort give them strength
To make all sorrow gain.

Let them know Your joy and peace
Wherever life may lead;
And through them, bring Your healing
love
To meet our hurt world's need.

EMILY SARGENT COUNCILMAN

A Mother's Prayer

I do not ask riches for my children,
  Nor even recognition for their skill;
I only ask that Thou wilt give them
  A heart completely yielded to Thy
will.

I do not ask for wisdom for my children
  Beyond discernment of Thy grace;
I only ask that Thou wilt use them
  In Thine own appointed place.

I do not ask for favor for my children
  To seat them on Thy left hand or Thy
right;
But may they join the throng in heaven
  That sing before Thy throne so bright.

I do not seek perfection in my children,
  For then my own faults I would hide;
I only ask that we might walk together
  And serve our Saviour side by side.

PHYLLIS DIDRIKSEN

A Mother's Prayer

I pray I may unwind my spring,
Attune my heart so it can bring
Great peace and poise.

I pray to hear the pleasant word,
And act as if I hadn't heard
The din and noise.

MARGARET DOTY PIERATT
in *The Christian Mother*

A Mother's Dedication

Dear Lord, I bring to Thee my son
Whose tender years have scarce begun;
In this wee frame I know full well
A living soul has come to dwell
Who needs Thee now at childhood's gate
Ere he shall grow to man's estate.
I covenant through hours apart
To pray for him with fervent heart.
To teach Thy Word with winsome voice
By day and night until his choice
Be but Thy blood for sins' deep stain,
And my small son is born again;
Then onward shall I pray the more
And teach Thy precepts o'er and o'er
That he may grow, each boyhood hour
By Thine indwelling risen power.
Lord, some small boys with none to care
Will never hear a mother's prayer;
Prepare my son with love aflame
To reach them with Thy saving name;
And make him, Lord, a polished tool,
A learner in Thy highest school.
A mother's part seems, oh, so frail!
But Thy strong arm can never fail;
To teach, to pray, to stand are mine;
The miracles must all be Thine.
Expectantly, I yield to Thee
The little boy Thou gavest me.

LOUISE B. EAVEY

A Mother Dedicates Her Children

This is the promise that I claim for these
  Whom Thou hast given me, Lord, to
  guide.
Strong, straight and beautiful as living
  trees,
  Here in Thy house I'll set them side
  by side:
Down to the solid rock of Truth I'll go,
  Press close the soil of Faith with
  hands of love,
Out of its depths—magnificent—shall
  grow
  These that shall flourish in Thy courts
  above.
Daily I'll water them with Thy good
  Word,

And from their hearts I'll pull the
weeds of sin,
This is the best that I can do, O Lord;
But Thou wilt finish what Thou didst
begin,
And I can leave them with a quiet
peace:
Man sows the seed—God giveth the
increase.

HELEN FRAZEE-BOWER

Thank You for My Son

Dear God, today I brought my son
Into Your house on earth;
And had him baptized in Your name,
A "thank you" for his birth.
And as I held him close to me,
I breathed a silent prayer
And asked Your blessing on this child
You've placed within my care.

I did not ask for fame, dear God,
Nor gold beyond compare,
Or any of the earthly things
For which we've learned to care;
I only asked throughout his life
My son shall walk with Thee;
For then, O God, this child of mine
Richer than kings shall be.

MARY ROGERT PACKETT

A Happy Woman's Prayer

Dear God, there is so much pain and
sadness
Upon this earth, it almost seems that I
Must have more than my share of joy
and gladness—
The days are too full as they speed
by.

The little things—my baby's soft hand
lying
Like crumpled rose leaves tossed upon
my breast,
Yet other mother hearts like mine are
crying,
Sad hearts—unsatisfied, perhaps un-
guessed.

And other women sit alone in sorrow,

While there is ONE who walks with
me, Whose care
Paints in warm colors every new tomorrow,
Whose love is just as certain as the air!

The simple duties that I have, the sewing,
The dusting, and the cakes I bake
Leave me no time to feel that youth is
going—
I have so much to give, so much to
take.

I have no time to spend in vain regret-
ting,
My heart has never known a keen
despair;
I have no sadnesses that need forgetting,
And so dear Lord, I make to You this
prayer:

Take just a little of my boundless mea-
sure,
Take just a bit—for I am selfish,
Lord—
And place it, as You would a priceless
treasure,
In some poor woman's heart where
pain is stored.

And let her feel the love that is my
blessing,
And let her feel my comfort and my
peace,
And let her feel my baby's wee head
pressing
Down on her shoulder. Let her know
release.

For one fair moment from the doubts
that taunt her,
One moment drive her loneliness
away,
Let her forget the memories that haunt
her—
This is my prayer at the beginning of
another day.

The Sawdust Trail

My Opportunity

My opportunity! Dear Lord I do ask
That Thou should'st give me some high
work of Thine

Some noble calling or some wondrous
    task—
Give me a little hand to hold in mine.

I do not ask that I should ever stand
Among the wise, the worthy or the
    great;
I only ask that softly, hand in hand
A child and I may enter at the gate.

Give me a little child to point the way
Over the strange, sweet path that leads
    to Thee;
Give me a little voice to teach to pray
Give me two shining eyes Thy face to
    see.

The only crown I ask, dear Lord, to
    wear
Is this—that I may teach a little child
How beautiful, oh how divinely fair
Is Thy dear face, so loving, sweet and
    mild!

I do not need to ask for more than this;
My opportunity? 'Tis standing at my
    door.
What sorrow if this blessing I should
    miss!
A little child! Why should I ask for
    more?

MARION B. CRAIG

A Housewife's Confession

O, precious Lord,
You know how much
I'd like to sit and hear
The lessons that You once had taught,
Which fell on Mary's ear;
But Martha's tasks around me teem,
And duties press me sore.
O Lord, that I might have more time
To worship and adore.
There's the laundry,
And the cooking, Lord,
You know the hurts to heal.
There are dozens of immediate things
With which my hours must deal,
And so, like Martha, through the day
These simple tasks repeat,
But how my heart still yearns to spend
More time at Jesus' feet.

Lord, it is so,
I do not mind
The works of love I do,
But I, like Martha, fret a lot,
Even when I work for You.
As You knew Martha, know also me.
Please meet me in my need,
That I might show to others
The Christ, in word and deed.

DORIS REICHERT

A Mother's Prayer

Make each day a prayer, dear Lord
Let all the hours sing to Thee
As I go on about my work
Upheld by Thy sufficiency.

Give me the patience to endure
Fill my whole being with Thy grace
May all I do be unto Thee
As seeing only Thy dear face.

When the day draws to a close
And my sweet lambs are snuggled tight
My heart shall sing its praise to Thee
Here in the quietness of night.

MRS. WILLARD M. ALDRICH

A Mother's Prayer

Father, watch o'er my babe
    So little, and helpless and sweet!
You know how I love her, for You love
    her too.
Father, watch o'er her, and keep her
    with You!
    Guide Thou her dear little feet.

Shepherd, guard my little one!
    The world is so cruel and hard.
Help her to follow the path where You
    lead.
I know You will help her in each hour
    of need;
    Shepherd, be Thou her guard.

Lord, on Thy heavenly Throne
    Merciful, loving and kind,
Thou alone knowest what life will bring
This little babe that to me doth cling:
    Help her Thy peace to find!

Savior who lovest us all
    Listen to this my plea—
When my child's earthly journey is done,
Oh Blessed Savior, then take her home
    Ever to live with Thee.

                    MRS. A. O. OLIVER

On the Wing

Life, dear Lord, makes so many demands
    On a woman's heart, of a woman's
        hands!
Oh, I seldom have time for slipping
        away
    From my duties in some quiet corner
        to pray,
But like meadowlarks that soaring, sing,
    I must talk to you, Lord, as it were on
        the wing.
Do acknowledgements hold less of grati-
        tude
    If sent in the midst of preparing food?
Are petitions less fervent if one only asks
    As one works for strength for finishing
        tasks?

                    AUTHOR UNKNOWN

Morning Prayer

Dear God, be with me all the day,
In all I do and all I say:
Let my words be helpful, kind, and true,
My hands find useful things to do.
I would help another's load to bear,
I would another's sorrow share,
And when night comes, may others be
Happier because of me.

                    AUTHOR UNKNOWN

A Mother's Prayer

Lord, nothing I can say will be enough
    To keep him at my side;
But, when the way grows long and steep
        and rough,
    Be Thou his guide.

My love would hold him close, but dis-
        tance calls:
    The far horizon's rim

Beckons. Beyond the shelter of these
        walls,
    Remember him.

Thy mother knew the anguish, sudden,
        brief,
    That makes these eyes go blind
With woman's tears: But Thou didst
        know the grief
    Of all mankind.

Thou wast a young man once in Naza-
        reth . . .
    Henceforth I must forego
His secret thoughts, his dreams of life
        and death,
    But Thou wilt know.

This is the end: The work of heart and
        hands—
    The mother-task—all done;
But safely, with the One who under-
        stands
    I leave my son.

                    HELEN FRAZEE-BOWER

A Mother's Prayer

As I hold my own baby,
    So close to my breast,
With its tiny soft fingers
    Like pink rosebuds pressed.
Do I think of that Baby
    Of heavenly birth,
Who came bringing hope
    To the Mothers of earth?

As I clasp my own baby,
    So close with a prayer,
That the Savior will keep us
    With all-watchful care,
Do I think of the mothers
    Whose mute, nameless fears
Bow them low to blind gods
    With dumb lips and deaf ears?

In my home where my child
    Is a gift from the Lord,
Where the Mother is honored,
    The baby adored,
Do I think of far lands,
    Where at breaking of day,
The unwanted babies
    Are carried away?

Oh Father, Who gavest
  My baby to me
May the love of my child
  Bring me closer to Thee,
May the children of earth
  Who know not Thy Son
Be more precious to me
  Because of my own.

LAURA SHERER COPENHAVER

Prayer for Children

Father, our children keep!
  We know not what is coming on the
    earth;
Beneath the shadow of Thy heavenly
    wing
  O keep them, keep them, Thou who
    gav'st them birth.

Father, draw nearer us!
  Draw firmer round us Thy protecting
    arm;
Oh, clasp our children closer to Thy
  side,
  Uninjured in the day of earth's alarm.

Them in Thy chambers hide!
  Oh, hide them and preserve them
    calm and safe,
When sin abounds and error flows
  abroad,
  And Satan tempts, our human pas-
    sions chafe.

O, keep them undefiled!
  Unspotted from a tempting world of
    sin;
That, clothed in white, through the
  bright city gates,
  They may with us in triumph enter in.

HORATIUS BONAR

When Mother Prayed

When Mother prayed, ah then I knew
Within my soul that God was true.
I could no longer doubt His love
But yielded all—born from above.
And though the years may come and go,
This heart of mine can never know
A sweeter time than that blest hour
When Jesus came in saving power.

When Mother prayed she found sweet
  rest,
When Mother prayed her soul was blest,
Her heart and mind in Christ was stayed,
And God was there, when Mother
  prayed.

AUTHOR UNKNOWN

The Mother in "Snow-Bound"

The while, with care, our mother laid
The work aside, her steps she stayed
One moment, seeking to express
Her grateful sense of happiness
For food and shelter, warmth and
  health,
And love's contentment more than
  wealth,
With simple wishes (not the weak,
Vain prayers which no fulfillment seek,
But such as warm the generous heart,
O'er-prompt to do with Heaven its part)
That none might lack, that bitter night,
For bread and clothing, warmth and
  light.

JOHN GREENLEAF WHITTIER,
Snow-Bound

Mom prays informally and at any hour. At night, when members of the household are out and anxiety frays her nerves, she reminds God gently but firmly that they need watching over and she can't be there. At breakfast, eating early and alone, she looks from her window upon the loveliness of earth at dawn and murmurs, "Thank You, God, for You. And for their safe return." At table, Dad says grace, but Mom is not listening half the time. She is reasoning with God about a date for Daughter to the prom, or how she is to pay for the new wallpaper for the living room. She prays while washing dishes, ironing, hanging out clothes, making beds. "Help him get that big account today. Help her pass the examinations. Help me be serene and brave." Mom does not mind bothering God with small affairs. She believes God has lots of time to listen to her pleas, just as she always finds time to listen to her child's pleas.

News, Boonville, Mo.

Who Taught Me to Pray?

Who taught my childish lips to pray
On bended knee at close of day
For strength to spread along life's way
Sweet peace and joy? My Mother.

ALICE WHITSON NORTON

Prayer of a Mother

My little son was kneeling on the floor
Building with blocks. I stood by to
    adore.
He smiled,
And blue eyes, trusting, loving, raised
"You never touch things do you,
    Mother?"
Praised.

My little son will build his house of life
With press of other things, a house, a
    wife.
Please, Lord,
Help me to satisfy his eyes
And keep my hands from touching,
Mother-wise.

AUTHOR UNKNOWN

My Mother's Prayers

Among the treasured pictures
    That I'll hang on memory's wall,
There's one that's clearer than the rest
    And sweeter far than all.

'Tis a picture of my mother
    When I, a little chap,
Was folded in her loving arms,
    To slumber on her lap.

I felt her hands caress my head,
    I heard her softly say,
"Dear Jesus take this little life
    And use it every day."

There must have been a mighty weight
    Behind that simple prayer,
For through the seasons, year on year,
    The picture lingers there.

And whether I'm on hill or plain
    Or on the deep blue sea,

The memory of that sacred scene
Forever comforts me.

Among the treasured pictures
    That I've hung on memory's wall,
My mother's supplication
    Is the sweetest one of all.

AUTHOR UNKNOWN

A Busy Mother's Prayer

Dear Lord,
    Help me to patiently bear the sight
    Of unwashed clothes soaked over-
        night;
    Of sewing basket, running o'er with
        things to mend
    And seeming never to see the end
    Or bottom of that basket;
    Of never-ending dirty dishes
    And streaks on floors and half-voiced
        wishes;
    Of dampened ironing bundles rolled
        quite flat;
    Of market lists so long and purses so
        flat.

Help me not to think of all I have to
    do
'Til I forget to be patient, kind and
    true
May I have peaceful thoughts that
    when
I've done the day's routine (and 'twill
    be there to do again
Tomorrow), I may with quiet mind
Seek sweet repose
And know 'tis done for Thee and
    those
Whom Thou hast given me
And Lord, then thank Thee.

RUTH JAMES CORDING

The Housewife

Jesus, teach me how to be
Proud of my simplicity.

Sweep the floors, wash the clothes,
Gather for each vase a rose.

Iron and mend a tiny frock
Taking notice of the clock,

Always having time kept free
For childish questions asked of me.

Grant me wisdom, Mary had
When she taught her little lad.

CATHERINE CATE COBLENTZ

The Prayer of Martha

Lord, I am cumbered with so many cares,
  I needs must serve thro'out the live-
    long day,
Must keep the little clinging hands from
    harm,
  And guide the stumbling feet along
    the way,
Till weary head and heart may take their
    rest
  When prattling voices hush at set of
    sun.
O Jesus, Master! at Thy feet, for me,
  Keep Mary's place till Martha's work
    is done.

ANNIE JOHNSON FLINT

A Mother's Prayer

A mother needs Thee, Lord,
So often through the day
For tiny, mischief-making hands,
For little feet that play.

A mother needs Thee, Lord,
Especially at night,
To fill the darkened corners with
Thy steady, quenchless light.

As once in Galilee,
So by the sick one's bed,
Bless every anxious mother's heart
As well as each small head.

Who taught my heart to seek,
My stubborn knee to bow,
Trusted to me these little ones;
I need Thee greatly—now.

JEANETTE SAXTON COON

A Mother's Prayer

DEAR GOD,
  Help me to remember this time when
I can hold the whole of my baby's tiny
foot in the palm of my hand. Let me
remember all the other little things I
might take for granted today.
  The way she grasps my finger tightly
and gazes into my eyes.
  The sweet welcoming smile as I come
to her unexpectedly.
  The way she kicks her feet and spreads
her toes.
  Her little giggle when we play "peek-a-
boo."
  The happy hoots and shrieks with
which she welcomes the morning.
  The soft smoothness of the skin all
over her little body
  The way she kicks and splashes in the
bathtub.
  The way her eyes gleam when she sees
her bottle.
  The way she leans against me when she
is tired.
  The complete trust she has in me.
Help me never to unknowingly betray it.
  Help me to be a good mother to her, to
keep her healthy and happy, to teach her
wisely and well.
  Let me always be there when she
needs me, but give me the courage to
make her able to stand alone.
  Show me the right way to bring up
my baby to be a sweet little girl, a
charming young lady, and a fine woman.
And keep her happy. Amen.

RUTH HILDRETH ABILD

A Kitchen Prayer

God bless my little kitchen,
I love its every nook,
And God bless me as I do my work,
Wash pots and pans and cook.

And may the meals that I prepare
Be successful from above
With Thy blessing and Thy grace
But most of all Thy love.

As we partake of earthly good
The table before us spread
We'll not forget to thank Thee, Lord,
Who gives us daily bread.

So bless my little kitchen, Lord,
And those who enter in

May they find naught but joy and peace
And happiness therein.

M. PETERSEN

The Divine Office of the Kitchen

Lord of all pots and pipkins, since I have
    no time to be
A saint by doing lovely things and vigil-
    ling with Thee,
By watching in the twilight dawn, and
    storming Heaven's gates,
Make me a saint by getting meals and
    washing up the plates!

Although I must have Martha's hands I
    have a Mary mind,
And when I black the boots and shoes,
    Thy sandals, Lord, I find!
I think of how they trod the earth, what
    time I scrub the floor;
Accept this meditation, Lord! I haven't
    time for more.

Warm all the kitchen with thy love, and
    light it with Thy peace!
Forgive me all my worrying and make
    all grumbling cease!
Thou who didst love to give men food in
    a room or by the sea,
Accept this service that I do—I do it
    unto Thee!

CECILY R. HALLACK

This poem by a 19-year old servant girl
was read by Dr. G. Campbell Morgan at
one of his services at Westminster
Chapel in London, England.

Kitchen Prayer

Dear Lord, before I start this day
    Of tasks that it will bring,
May I refresh my soul right here
    Where pots and kettles sing.
This is my "realm" where I perform
    The work I best can do
And here I always seem to feel
    Especially near to You.

For You have planned in this small
    room
    Such homely tasks for me
That I can do them easily

And keep my mind on Thee
And writings of the Holy Book,
    The lessons they all teach.
I've but to live them day by day,
    Serenity to reach.

Again, when twilight time has come,
    Give me a short time too . . .
Here, through the deepening shadows,
    My tidied kitchen view,
And solace find in simple things
    Accomplished here by me,
A flaky pie, a loaf of bread,
    My family's joy to see
The things that in this little home
    I do with practiced skill.
Help me as well in other ways, O Lord,
    To do Thy will.

HARRIET ELMBLAD

A Mother Understands

Dear Lord, I hold my hand to take
    Thy body broken once for me,
Accept the sacrifice I make,
    My body, broken, Christ, for Thee.

His was my body, born of me,
    Born of my bitter travail pain,
And it lies broken on the field,
    Swept by the wind and the rain.

G. A. STUDDERT-KENNEDY

Hands

My hand is large and his is small,
And there is nothing on earth at all
More important than the task
That lies ahead of me. I ask
For wisdom, Lord, that I may lead
This child aright; his every need
Depends on me. Be Thou my guide
That I, in walking by his side,
May choose the right paths for his feet.
The days are swift, the years are fleet,
Make me alert in deed and word
As we go forward, blessed Lord:
His precious, clinging hand in mine,
With always, Lord, my hand in Thine.

GRACE NOLL CROWELL

A Mother's Prayer

I wash the dirt from little feet,
    And as I wash I pray,
"Lord, keep them pure and true
    To walk the narrow way."

I wash the dirt from little hands,
    And earnestly I ask,
"Lord, may they ever yielded be
    To do the humblest task."

I wash the dirt from little knees,
    And pray, "Lord, may they be
The place where victories are won,
    And orders sought from Thee."

I scrub the clothes that soil so soon,
    And pray, "Lord, may her dress
Throughout eternal ages be
    Thy robe of righteousness."

E'er many hours shall pass, I know
    I'll wash these hands again;
And there'll be dirt upon her dress
    Before the day shall end,

But as she journeys on through life
    And learns of want and pain,
Lord, keep her precious little heart
    Cleansed from all sin and stain;

For soap and water cannot reach
    Where Thou alone canst see
Her hands and feet, these I can wash—
    I trust her heart to Thee.

                BARBARA CORNET RYBERG

My Desire

Give me ears to hear the questions
Of a knowledge-seeking child;

Give me sympathetic insight
To his problems, great and mild;

Give me patience, never-ending,
For the things I teach and do;

Clear my vision—may I ever
Feel his needs and see his view.

Make me with the child to wander
Through his happy fairylands;

Let me skip with him and listen
To imaginary bands.

Soon his fairies will all vanish,
And the music fade away;

Fantasies will change to visions,
Work will rival happy play.

So if I may be companion,
Friend, and playmate of a child,

I shall never doubt his learning
While I teach the things worthwhile.

                AUTHOR UNKNOWN

A Mother's Prayer

I listen to my children pray
And oh, what simple things they say,
"Lord, thank You for the flowers and
    trees,
The butterflies and bumble bees.

"The pretty birds You made to sing
Oh God, thank You for everything
You put on earth to make it nice."
They might even thank Him for the
    mice.

And though sometimes a smile may play
Upon my lips when I hear them pray,
For blessings on the frog and toad,
From my heart lifts a mighty load

Of fear, that they might some day stray
To earth's own evil, wicked way . . .
Their faith is strong, their hearts are
    sure
That God made all things good and
    pure.

Oh Holy Spirit, so divine,
Completely fill this heart of mine;
Teach me the words that I should say
To guide my children day by day.

On up the path that leads above
To never doubt God's perfect love,
Give me that childlike faith I pray—
Oh, make me a child today.

                MARAMEL LEMARA

Dirty Dishes

Thank God for dirty dishes—
They have a story to tell;
For by the stack I have
It seems that we are living well.
While folks of some countries starve,
I haven't the heart to fuss,
For this stack of evidence shows to me
God's very good to us.

AUTHOR UNKNOWN

My Influence

My life shall touch a dozen lives
 Before this day is done;
Leave countless marks for good or ill
 Ere sets the evening sun.
So this the wish I always wish,
 The prayer I ever pray:
Lord, may my life help other lives
 It touches by the way.

AUTHOR UNKNOWN

A Mother's Thanksgiving

Now is the time for giving thanks,
 And I will give mine too:
Thanks be to God for simple tasks,
 And hands with which to do.

Thanks be to God for little feet,
 So happy in their play;
Lord, give me patience, love and faith
 To guide them on their way.

Thanks be to God for little lips,
 That can be taught to sing
The old, old songs, the tender tunes
 Of Jesus, Lord and King.

Thanks be to God, when feet shall fail
 And fading sight grow dim,
That Christ will do what I cannot.
 Thanks be to God—for Him.

HELEN FRAZEE-BOWER

Dear Lord,
A little child lies plastic to my touch;
I ask Thee for a love that understands
When it should reach and when
Withdraw its hands.

ELEANOR B. STOCK

Prayer Time

The while she darns her children's socks
 She prays for little stumbling feet.
Each folded pair within its box
 Fits faith's bright sandals, sure and
 fleet.

While washing out, with mother pains,
 Small dusty suits and socks and slips,
She prays that God may cleanse the
 stains
 From little hearts and hands and lips.

And when she breaks the fragrant bread
 Or pours each portion in its cup,
For grace to keep their spirits fed,
 Her mother-heart is lifted up!

Oh busy ones, whose souls grow faint,
 Whose tasks seem longer than the
 day,
It doesn't take a cloistered saint
 To find a little time to pray!

RUBY WEYBURN TOBIAS

Prayer for a Child

Dear Lord, she is so little! Take her
 hand—
 Go with her, when I cannot walk the
 long,
Dark road beside her, when she has to
 stand
 Upon her own small feet and face the
 throng.
She is so little and so very dear,
 So made for loving! When I cannot
 touch
Her any longer, she will feel You near,
 And need not miss me then, so very
 much.

I look with love into her upturned face.
 There were so many things I thought
 to ask
You once for her. But, somehow, as I
 trace
 The years ahead, I would not choose
 her task,
I would not seek for favors, great or
 small.
 Just take her hand, be with her—that
 is all.

HELEN FRAZEE-BOWER

As long as Mother lived I had a feeling that whatever I did, or failed to do, Mother would pray me through. Though she insisted that she was not her children's intercessor, that we must pray ourselves, yet I knew that her long hours of prayer were spent interceding for us.

MADAME CHIANG KAI-SHEK

Prayer for Mothers

Father of Life, fold in the everlasting arms of Thy love the torch-bearers of life—the mothers of the race. As they struggle up the steps of motherhood, through its travail of mind, body and soul, give them a clearer vision and a guiding wisdom. Grant them the compensation of a love returned and understood, and the ultimate satisfaction of knowing that they have lifted those entrusted to their care up into helpful harmony with Thy Kingdom. Bestow an especial tenderness on those who, having borne no children, nevertheless exert the sweet ministries of motherhood over their home circle. Comfort all lonely, unmothered hearts. Grant the ever-steadying power of Thy support through the daily discouragements, the clash and readjustments of ideals, and the anguish of bereavement that comes into all mothers' lives. Increase, we pray, their cheerful steadiness, their unselfish strength, and at the close of their days, may they enter into rest with faith undimmed, and unafraid. We ask through Christ, our Lord. Amen.

Prayer for Mother

Dear Father, keep my mother in
    The stillness of the night,
And let her sleep refreshingly
    Until the morning light.
God bless her as she goes about
    Her loving, working day,
Just doing things for all of us
    In her own precious way.
Please make her happy, as she makes
    Us time and time again,
And bless her daily, please, dear God,
    For Jesus' sake, Amen.
The Olive Leaf

MOTHER'S MEMORIES

Just We Two and Memories

The children all are flown, and fled the
    nest,
Again we are alone . . . unless a guest;
Just you and I, as all those years ago
When we began.

The quiet house seems queer, and now
    each day
As in our first wed year, my work is
    play,
There is so little left for me to do . . .
Or even plan.

The service large we've shelved . . . we
    need it not;
The pails and kettles, huge and cumbrous pot . . .
The rows of shining, tiny things we've
    purchased now anew,

They seem so wee, so small,
Like playthings cute; and yet I love them
    all,
They speak . . . though muted
The cunning little pots and pans and
    bowls
That serve, but two.

AUTHOR UNKNOWN

That Dear Old Kitchen

Our kitchen was the finest place
When we were girls and boys . . .
'Twas there we studied arithmetic
And mended broken toys.

The table had a red checked cloth . . .
The oil lamp gave good light . . .
The shiny cookstove threw out heat
That made the room so bright.

The parlor, it was fancy, and
Its furniture was fine . . .
But, we only had it heated when
The preacher came to dine.

But in the kitchen where we lived
And worked and played . . . and where
Mom's mending basket always sat
Close by her old cane chair,

What times we had popping corn
And pulling taffy brown!
And just before we went to bed
Dad would get the Bible down
And read some . . . then he'd pray a bit
While all our heads were bowed . . .
I wish that I was sitting in
That dear old kitchen now!

MAUD IRENE EVANS

My Mother's Gingham Apron

My mother's gingham apron
  Had uses by the score:
It fanned away the blow-flies
  that buzzed around the door;
It helped to carry dishes
  When they were piping hot,
And served her as a basket
  Down in the garden plot;
It was her muff in winter,
  Her towel every day;
And once, when I came running,
  It wiped my tears away!

GEORGE L. KRESS

My Mother Dear

There was a place in childhood
That I remember well,
And there a voice of sweetest tone
Bright fairy tales did tell.

SAMUEL LOVER

True wisdom lies in gathering the precious things out of each day as it
goes by.

E.S. BOUTON

Little Boy—Lost

Little boy—lost so long ago—
How did I bear it that you must go?
A seven-year old needs his mother so!

That terrible, empty, aching void
That was made by the absence of one
    small boy
Whose stay with me here was so briefly
    joyed!

The tenderest memories kept crowding
    in—
And I'd try not to think of your happy
    grin
The one with the space where two teeth
    had been!

But time has a way of healing pain,
And the constant grieving is quite in
    vain—
Soon life fills the gaps—and you live
    again,

In that place where you are you've
    reached man's estate,
But to me you're still seven—not twen-
    ty-eight—
Just a lad in blue jeans—racing home—
    quite late!

Now I'm happy remembering, and often
    smile
When I think of your ways that did
    heart beguile!
I'm so glad you were mine for a little
    while!

VIRGINIA LONG

I rose and gave my seat; I could not let
    her stand—
She made me think of my mother, with
    that strap held in her hand.

Do you remember when Mother's
meals were carefully thought-out instead
of carefully thawed-out?

Mothers of Men

"I hold no cause worth my son's life,"
    one said—

And the two women with her as she
    spoke
Joined glances in a hush that neither
    broke,
So present was the memory of their
    dead.
And through their meeting eyes their
    souls drew near,
Linked by their sons, men who had held
    life dear
But laid it down for something dearer
    still.
One had wrought out with patient iron
    will
The riddle of a pestilence, and won,
Fighting on stricken, till his work was
    done
For children of tomorrow. Far away
In shell-torn soil of France the other lay,
And in the letter that his mother read
Over and over, kneeling as to pray—
"I'm thanking God with all my heart
    today,
Whatever comes" (that was the day he
    died)
"I've done my bit to clear the road
    ahead."
In those two mothers, common pain of
    loss
Blossomed in starry flowers of holy
    pride,
What thoughts were hers who silent
    stood beside
Her son the dreamer's cross?

                                    AMELIA J. BURR

Are All the Children In?

I think ofttimes as the night draws nigh
Of an old house on the hill,
Of a yard all wide and blossom-starred
Where the children played at will.
And when the night at last came down,
Hushing the merry din,
Mother would look around and ask,
"Are all the children in?"

'Tis many and many a year since then,
And the old house on the hill
No longer echoes to childish feet,
And the yard is still, so still.
But I see it all as the shadows creep,
And though many the years have been,

Even now, I can hear my mother ask,
"Are all the children in?"

I wonder if, when the shadows fall
On the last short, earthly day,
When we say goodbye to the world out-
    side,
All tired with our childish play,
When we step out into that Other Land
Where mother so long has been,
Will we hear her ask, as we did of old,
"Are all the children in?"

And I wonder, too, what the Lord will
    say,
To us older children of His,
Have we cared for the lambs? Have we
    showed them the fold?
A privilege joyful it is.
And I wonder, too, what our answers
    will be,
When His loving questions begin:
"Have you heeded My voice? Have you
    told of My love?
Have you brought My children in?"

                                    AUTHOR UNKNOWN
                        (Last verse by MARION BISHOP
                                            BOWER)

Yesterday

Raiding the kitchen after school
    For cookies, jam and such,
They blithely tracked my new-scrubbed
        floors,
And left small smudges on the doors
    Where sticky hands would touch;
And then ran boisterous out to play.
(It seems like only yesterday!)

Bedraggled waifs with hopeful eyes
    They'd call me out to see.
"He's awf'lly hungry—cold to boot;
But see, he wags his tail so cute,
    And he—sorta—followed me!"
(Oh, what could any mother say?
I'm glad—I'm glad I let them stay!)

Today serenely I may go
    From room to quiet room,
And every book and chair and vase
Seems waiting in its ordered place
    Until the children come.

(But each has gone his chosen way;
I walk these rooms alone today!)

I longed for hours of quietness
  To read or paint or rest;
It seemed the day would never be
When I would know tranquillity.
  But now, within my breast
I know that always, come what may,
My heart will turn to yesterday!
                In Favor with God and Man

Dear Son of Mine—

  I am your mother ... the one who
gave you birth. I am the one who holds
you and whispers, "I'm so glad you're
mine!"

  While you grow from year to year, I'll
be near to comfort you when you cry,
and to cherish your every word. When
you are hungry, I'll be at your command
... and when you snuggle to me in
sleepy contentment, I'll stroke your hair
and kiss you goodnight.

  This will not be an easy world to
conquer, my son ... but you must learn
to make your way. You must learn
many things. At times you will find yourself rebellious, but as a boy you will
make your decisions.

  And as you grow older, I will know
that my role in your life has taken new
form. I will no longer be able to cuddle
you or kiss you when you join your
friends for school. There will be a time
when I must content myself with an
awkward pat and hear you say, "Mom,
you're a swell guy!"

  It will be hard for your mother to
realize she is not your only girl friend.
As surely as you start shaving with dad's
razor, I will spend many restless nights
wondering if you're having a good time
at the school party ... wondering if
you'll kiss your date good night.

  Time will go fast. One day it will be
time for college; I'll pack your clothes in
a shiny new bag ... I know a tear or
two will fall as I wave to you, but I'll
smile bravely and proudly when I say,
"Good luck to you, son."

  I'll worry, of course, as all mothers
do; but I'll know you are a man ... a
man ready to accept your place in the
business world.

  And then, some day you'll marry. I'll
love your wife and learn to share your
love.

  My son, the story goes on and on, just
as life itself, until a time will come when
I will try to remember life before you
came. The years will be squeezed together like an accordion. Joyous memories of
my baby ... my boy ... my son ... will
be the melodies played upon the keys.

                        Your Mother,
                        HUBIE ROSS

Come Into the Living Room

She never liked to call it parlor—
  The room where all of us would come
Together, evening after supper,
  Back in my happy childhood's home.
An oak-beamed room it was, and
    friendly,
For there were warmth and fragrance
    there,
And love—enough for everybody!
  And circling arms that banished care!
She'd stand, all smiling, in the doorway.
  "Let's go into the living room!"
Then, how the daily burdens lifted—
  We were together—we were home!
The living room! The family circle,
  With Father in his easy chair,
And Mother sewing in the lamplight—
  The room of laughter, song, and
    prayer!
                In Favor with God and Man

A Thousand Memories

Time, a clock, ticks off the years,
But leaves these memories through my
    tears.
Pitter-pats upon the floor,
Little jam-marks on the door.
Childish treble, gay and sweet,
Little wagons in the street.
Busy fingers and nimble toes,
Little worries to expose.
Crumpled pockets, overfilled,
Heartbreak of a sparrow killed.
Raids upon a cookie-jar,

Wishing . . . on a twinkly star.
Injured dollies, nursed with care,
And candle-light upon the stair.

And now, "I lay me down to sleep,"
A thousand memories . . . to keep.

PAMELA VAULL STARR

MOTHER'S THOUGHTS

Things That Honestly Thrilled Me

1. A corsage given "with love."

2. A tender remembrance of an event or date, or a gracious note of appreciation.

3. A colorful sunset with gold reflection on the water followed by a lovely full rising moon; a rainbow in a rain-washed sky.

4. A clean, trusting, smiling boy's face, or admiration in a man's.

5. Sharing a prayer of thankfulness.

6. A boys' choir, or a religious choir of special sacred music.

7. The first spring flower, or picking the first wild flowers with children, and hearing the little new sounds of life.

8. A high pure-white mountain peak, embracing the clear, blue sky.

9. Mellow peals of an old church bell, or tinkling ones in the distance.

10. Rays of the morning sun shining through dew-covered tall trees of the forest.

11. Unexpected gratitude shown, or an important moment shared with a loved one.

12. The spirit of love everywhere like that expressed at Christmas time by a tiny babe in the manger, or a little one's soft warm hand in yours.

MRS. N. J. CLINE
in Sunshine Magazine

A Woman's Happiness

A cake to bake and a floor to sweep,
A tired babe to sing to sleep;
What does a woman want but these—
A home, a child, and a man to please.

A Woman's Way

When a woman wants to celebrate
Or when she has the blues,
She raids the family budget
And buys a pair of shoes!
And when she's really angry
At something hubby's done—
She buys a very silly hat
And wears it—just for fun!

Sunshine Magazine

Have Baby, Will Travel

Have diapers (disposable), feeding chair
    (hoseable),
  Thermometer, bottle brush, milk;
Have plasticized sheeting, have gadget
    for heating
  And panties of waterproof silk.
Have vitamins, zwieback, a harness to
    tie back
  My son in inadequate crib;
Have aspirin, sleepers, applesauce,
    creepers,
  Can opener, orange juice, bib.
Have blanket, have teddy, have boiled
    water ready,
  Have tissue, have talcum, have Spock.
My thoughts I'll unravel; have baby, will
    travel,
  But never again past our own block!

ELIZABETH MACFARLAND

A Mother Speaks

It is not gratitude, my child, I ask,
  Nor do I seek to make my will your
    own;
The memory of your babyhood, though
    you are grown
  Enchants me still; nor ever was a task

Performed for you save lovingly; I do
    Indeed thank you that you have
      brought me days
Of bright felicity in all your ways,
    And hours of grieving and of tears, so
      few!

No, do not thank me now, but think
    upon
    Your childhood tenderly when I have
      gone,
And if in sudden sweet remembering,
    You, too, find deepening joy in each
      small thing
Done for your child, or in your ministry
To one beloved, you will be thanking
    me.
                AUTHOR UNKNOWN

Reflections

Life's not all light and sunshine,
    Nor is it all joy and cheer.
For each has his share of worries,
    His share of doubt and fear.

Seems that life's just a pattern
    Like the patches on a quilt,
And bits of shade and sunshine
    Are the squares from which it's built.

All the sunshine squares are pretty,
    While the shadow ones are plain;
But you know just how much brighter
    Is the sunshine after rain.

And you know that the pretty patches
    Simply never would be seen,
Were it not for all the plain ones,
    Sewn so neatly in between.
                AUTHOR UNKNOWN

Happiness is:
    a stack of clean, folded diapers.
    an empty ironing basket.
    a meal without spilled milk.
    Baby cradled in my arms.
    They were such little things to make
    me glad:
    A moonbeam dancing on a lily pad,
    A scarlet flower nodding in the breeze,
    And dappled sunlight thru the willow
    trees,

The brittle splendor of a winter's day,
The happy laughter of a child at play,
Crisp yellow curtains in a sunlit room,
And a bowl of tulips bursting into
    bloom,
A baby's hand around my finger
    curled—
Such little things to so enrich the
    world.
                AUTHOR UNKNOWN

I'd Rather Be a Mother

I'd rather be a mother
    With only a mother's name,
Than to gain all earthly glory,
    Or be known by world-wide fame.

I'd rather be a mother
    And press a little hand,
Than receive the highest favors
    As first lady of the land.

I'd rather be a mother
    And caress a little cheek,
Than possess the greatest riches
    That folks on earth may seek.

I'd rather be a mother
    And a baby's future hold,
Than live in costly palaces
    With kings, and queenly gold.

Because I am a mother,
    I hold God's greatest prize;
And He expects great things of me
    With a task of such a size.
                GRACE AITKENS

A Baby's Ministry

She came to me at Christmas time
And made me mother, and it seemed
There was a Christ indeed and He
Had given me the joy I'd dreamed.

She nestled to me and I kept
Her near and warm, surprised to find
The arms that held my babe so close
Were opened wider to her kind.

I hid her safe within my heart.
"My heart," I said, "is all for her."

But lo! she left the door ajar
And all the world came flocking there.

She needed me. I learned to know
The royal joy that service brings.
She was so helpless that I grew
To love all little helpless things.

She trusted me, that I who ne'er
Had trusted, save in self, grew cold
With panic lest this precious life
Not know His stronger, surer hold.

She lay and smiled, and in her eyes
I watched my narrow world grow broad;
Within her tiny, crumpled hand
I touched the mighty hand of God.

AUTHOR UNKNOWN

Little Hands

Oh, little hand, take care
  You have so much to learn!
For knives are sharp, and doors can
    pinch
  And stoves are hot and burn.

You must discover for yourself
  So much in life's hard school,
I only pray those little hands
  Will be the Master's tools—

Perhaps to play His songs of praise
  Perhaps to draw His art,
Perhaps through deeds of love to show
  His love within your heart!

AUTHOR UNKNOWN

Interlaced With Wonder

Blessed with two childhoods, mine and
    hers,
The space between them often blurs . . .
I can't be sure who caught and dressed
The bullfrog in a satin vest;
Who went to school in pinafores
And named her love by apple cores.
The dollhouse underneath the vine,
The acorn dishes . . . Mother's? Mine?
Impossible to tear asunder
These childhoods interlaced with won-
    der!

F. B. JACOBS

MOTHER'S TRAINING

By the Book

Mothers who raise
A child by the book,
Can, if sufficiently vexed,
Hasten results
By applying the book
As well as the text.

Evangelical Beacon

Doggie says Bow-wow,
Sheep says baa-baa,
Cow says Moo-moo,
Mommie says No-no.

A THREE-YEAR-OLD GIRL
quoted by MARTIN P. SIMON
in Points for Parents

A gracious, white-haired lady visited a
friend. When she left, a little girl said,
"Mother, if I could be an old lady like

she is—beautiful, calm, sweet, and lovable—I would not mind growing old!"
"Well, my dear," said the discerning
mother, "if you want to be that kind of
old lady, you had better begin making
her right now. She is not a picture that
was done in a hurry. It has taken a long
time to make her what she is. If you
want to paint that sort of picture of
yourself to leave to the world, begin
mixing the colors right now!"

Gospel Herald

Tucking-in Time

O tucking-in time is the best of all
The many good times of the day,
When the sun has hurried like a big red
    ball
Over the hills and away.

And Mother comes quietly up the
    stairs
To hug me ever so tight,
To hold my hands as I say my prayers
And tuck me in for the night.

Then carefully folding the counterpane,
She sits on the edge of my bed
And tells my favorite stories again . . .
Oh maybe we visit instead.

Then I'm kissed good-night, and I face
    the wall,
And Mother goes softly away . . .
O tucking-in time is the best of all
The many good times of the day!

AUTHOR UNKNOWN

Mother Mine

You loved me when I was a child,
    Rocked me when I was ill;
You always were so comforting
    When leading up life's hill.
And when at night, beside my bed,
I kneeled and there my prayer was
    said,
My hand and yours were close entwined;
God bless you, Mother, Mother mine.

You worked that I might stay in
    school,
    You soothed away my fears;
Oft when I came at eventime
    Your cheek was wet with tears.
And when the shadows lengthened,
    I came to you to hear
A word of gentle sympathy,
    To charm away my fears.

You told me of a Father
    Who knoweth and who cares;
God bless you, Mother darling!
    You're the heart of all my prayers.
And when, some day, I reach the home
    Of all the saints divine,
I'll say I'm here because God gave
    That precious Mother mine.

AUTHOR UNKNOWN

A Mother's Beatitude

Blessed is the mother who understands
her child, for she shall inherit a kingdom of memories.

Blessed is the mother who knows how
to comfort, for she shall possess a
child's devotion.

Blessed is the mother who guides by
the path of righteousness, for she shall
be proud of her offspring.

Blessed is the mother who is never
shocked, for she shall receive confidences.

Blessed is the mother who teaches respect, for she shall be respected.

Blessed is the mother who emphasizes
the good and minimizes the bad, for
in like manner the child shall make
evaluations.

Blessed is the mother who treats her
child as she would be treated, for her
home shall be filled with happiness.

Blessed is the mother who answers
simply the startling questions, for she
shall always be trusted.

Blessed is the mother who has character strong enough to withstand the
thoughtless remarks and resentments
of the growing child, for again, in due
time, she shall be honored.

LENORA ZEARFOSS
in Present Truth Messenger

Molding Life

I took a piece of plastic clay
And idly fashioned it one day;
And, as my fingers pressed it still,
It moved, and yielded to my will.

I came again when the days were past;
The bit of clay was hard at last;
The form I gave it still it bore,
But I could change that form no more.

I took a piece of living clay,
And gently formed it day by day,
And molded with my power and art
A young child's soft and yielding
    heart.

I came again when the years were
    gone,
It was a man I looked upon;
He still that early impress wore
And I could change him nevermore.

AUTHOR UNKNOWN

The Challenge

You have a son? Oh, teach his heart to
  be
  As gentle as the early morning light,
As sturdy as a pine beside the sea,
  As faithful as a star within the
    night.
Teach him to love the challenge of the
  long,
  Sun-lighted years when he will serve
    and share
The peace of silence and the joy of
  song,
  The fellowship of Christ through holy
    prayer.

You have no son? Then find a boy who
  needs
  The reassurance of your heart and
    hand.
Show him the upward-climbing path that
  leads
  To glory-lighted fortresses that stand
Impregnable, with flags of faith un-
  furled,
  Priceless beyond all treasures of the
    world.
               GRACE V. WATKINS

At a banquet the mother of George
Washington was sitting beside a distin-
guished French officer. Turning to
Washington's mother, the officer asked,
"How have you managed to rear such a
splendid son?"
  She replied, "I taught him to obey."

What Will He Become?

What will he become, this little one?
  So innocent is he today!
What will life unfold for him?
  Open, O Future and say!
The baby answers in tones so clear,
  "What will you have me be?
I belong to you, your bidding to do,
  You may do as you wish with me.
I am so little, I know not the way,
  My life is all yours to mold.
O, parents, prayerfully plan for me
  That my life may in beauty unfold.
This life can be a lovely thing
  Like a flower that is wondrously fair
Then train me carefully dear ones
  With faith, and hope and prayer."
               AUTHOR UNKNOWN

MOTHER'S WORK

Saturday Night

Placing the little hats all in a row,
Ready for church on the morrow, you
  know;
Washing wee faces and little black
  fists,
Getting them ready and fit to be
  kissed;
Putting them into clean garments and
  white—
That is what mothers are doing tonight.

Spying out rents in worn little hose;
Laying by shoes that are worn through
  the toes;
Looking o'er garments so faded and
  thin;

Who but a mother knows where to begin?
Changing a button to make it look
  right—
That is what mothers are doing
  tonight.

Calling the little ones all 'round her
  chair,
Hearing them lisp forth their soft evening prayer,
Telling them stories of Jesus of old,
Who loves to gather the lambs to His
  fold;
Watching them listen with childish delight—
That is what mothers are doing
  tonight.

Creeping so softly to take a last peep,
After the little ones all are asleep;
Anxious to know if the children are
   warm,
Tucking the blankets round each little
   form;
Kissing each little face, rosy and bright—
That is what mothers are doing
   tonight.

Kneeling down gently beside the white
   bed,
Lowly and meekly she bows down her
   head,
Praying as only a mother can pray,
"God guide and keep them from going
   astray."

AUTHOR UNKNOWN

Mother's Tasks—A to Z

Artist . . . as you arrange your home and
   become the daily example in the art of
   living.
Bookkeeper . . . as you balance the
   budget.
Censor . . . as you oversee the entertainment—television, books, friends—that
   flows into your home.
Clothes designer . . . as you create origi-
   nals and alter old clothing.
Counselor . . . as you listen to the problems and discuss solutions.
Dietician . . . as you plan menus to
   provide adequate nourishment.
Farmer . . . as you labor over a garden
   plot, trying to reap an abundant harvest.
Food conservationist . . . as you can and
   deep freeze the garden harvest.
Janitor . . . as you mop up messes and
   clean out closets.
Judge and jury . . . as you listen to cases
   and pass out sentences.
Laundry worker . . . as you strive for a
   whiter, wrinkle-free wash.
Musician . . . as you sing lullabies and
   play musical games with children.
News correspondent . . . as you write
   letters to loved ones about family epi-
   sodes.
Nobel Peace Prize possessor . . . as you
   try to keep the peace.

Nurse . . . as you spend sleepless nights
   beside a sick child.
Physician . . . as you apply bandaids and
   diagnose the ills.
Preacher . . . as you speak the Word of
   God to your children.
Psychologist . . . as you try to understand
   the psychological techniques used by
   your children.
Recreation director . . . as you plan
   family fun and fellowship.
Referee . . . as you call the fouls on the
   violators of the peace rules.
Shepherd . . . as you look after your
   flock, leading them into green pas-
   tures.
Teacher . . . as you instruct your children
   in everyday activities.
Waitress . . . as you serve graciously—
   your tips are appreciative words.
Zoo keeper . . . as you remind your children to feed and water cats, dogs,
   birds, turtles, fish, etc.

JEANNE ALLEN

Night Rules for Mothers

A mother must sleep as lightly as a
   cat,
To wake quickly at a baby's cry;
To step softly through a sleeping
   house,
And straighten sheets and blankets
   pulled away;
Add quilts against the cold, or draw
   away
Covers too heavy for a sultry night;
Close windows to the rain, and soothe
   the sleep
Of restless children caught in nightmare
   fright.
A mother must know, by dark as well as
   day,
The height of all the latches on the
   doors;
The buttons of the lights and which
   will shine
On tired eyes . . . which boards will
   creak in floors;
The places of the chairs, that soundlessly
Through soft and friendly darkness she
   may go
So quietly to solace pain or grief

That in the morning, children hardly
    know
Which one was real: the dream, the
    grief, or she.
And moving back to bed in darkness
    then,
Quickly and lightly, she must sleep
    again.

                            LOUISE OWEN

No Neurosis

Other girls have ropes of pearls,
    Other girls wear mink;
I have ropes of drying clothes,
    And dishes in the sink.

Other girls drive sporty cars,
    Other girls have maids;
I must steer a shopping cart,
    And eat meat's cheaper grades.

Other girls rely on cards
    To fill the empty hours;
I have noses to be wiped,
    No time for sulks and glowers.

Other girls use beauty parlors
    To keep them in the pink;
A laughing child and a husband's arms
    Are better aids, I think.

                    FLORENCE BELL WILLIAMS

Neatness

The beds are all made
    And the dishes are done.
The kids are all shiny
    And ready for fun;
The clothes are all ironed,
    No dirt on this floor.
No doubt you've guessed
    I'm calling next door.

                            M. M. FAY

Trail of Woe

There's a well-trodden path
    From nursery to sink
From eternal nocturnally
    Fetching his drink.

                        PAT CUNNINGHAM

Her Day

She cooked the breakfast first of all,
    Washed the cups and plates,
Dressed the children and made sure
    Stockings all were mates.
Combed their heads and made their
    beds,
    Sent them out to play.
Gathered up their motley toys,
    Put some books away,
Dusted chairs and mopped the stairs,
    Ironed an hour or two,
Baked a jar of cookies and
    A pie, then made a stew,
The telephone rang constantly,
    The doorbell did the same,
A youngster fell and stubbed his toe,
    And then the laundry came.
She picked up blocks and mended socks,
    Then she polished up the stove
(Gypsy folks were fortunate
    With carefree ways to rove!)
And when her husband came at six
    He said: "I envy you!
It must be nice to sit at home
    Without a thing to do!"

                        AUTHOR UNKNOWN

Tied Down

I am tied down . . .
By clothes lines
On which I hang
Small blue and yellow rompers.
By strings . . .
Just commonplace white threads
With which I sew on buttons,
Mend wee pockets,
Patch faded threadbare little suits.
Ropes tie me down
Red jumping ropes
And all those that pull
Small animals about.
Young, bleeding grimy thumbs there
    are
To kiss and bind with lengths
Of clean white gauze.
And baby arms about my neck . . .
O, yes . . . I am tied down . . . thank
    God!

                        AUTHOR UNKNOWN

A Mother Speaks

They call me just a mother
And I'm proud to bear the name,
I may not make the headlines,
I may not rise to fame.
To some, my work seems rather dull,
And hard at times I know,
With life a weary round of toil,
As seasons come and go.

They call me just a mother
But I do not ask for praise,
For in my humble household tasks,
I find a thousand ways
To make my home a shrine where trust
And faith and beauty dwell;
A place where I can proudly play
My part—and play it well.

They call me just a mother,
But they do not know the joys
That come with doing helpful things
For husband, girls and boys.
While many folks may seek success
As restlessly they roam,
I'm proud to do my very best
Each day—right here at home.

H. HOWARD BIGGAR

The Happy Tasks

Some work is drab work,
  Some work is gay—
Speaking of a woman's work,
  I like the way
Peas tinkle in their pods,
  I like the sound;
I like the heady scent
  That is always found
When I stem berries,
  Their delicious stain
Bring in-doors the whole out-doors
  Of sun and wind and rain.
When I dust my furniture,
  Lustrous, satin-fine,
I like the gleam of wood,
  I like the shine
Of bright dishes on a shelf;
  I like the glow
Of all vegetables washed clean and
  bright
  Oh, yes, I know

Some work is drab work,
  Some work is gay,
But many tasks about a house
  Are sparkling gay.

Attributed to GRACE NOLL CROWELL

Mommies

Do you know what mommies do
While they stay at home with you?

Mommies do just lots and lots,
Wash the dishes, scrub the pots.
Mommies cook and bake and fry,
And they are near to answer "Why?"

Tying shoes or combing hair,
Helping find a teddy bear.
Moms peel apples, Moms catch balls,
And scrub off crayon from the walls.

Busy as the busy bees,
Mommies shop for groceries.
Many mommies mend and sew,
And water flowers so they'll grow.

Mommies dress you while you squirm
Like a wriggly, little worm.
Moms bath dogs and save them bones,
And talk a lot on telephones.

Yes, they do so many things;
Hang the clothes and push the swings,
Iron and sweep and dust and mop,
And know where there's a lollypop.

Moms tell stories and cut your meat,
And sometimes say "Sit still and eat."

Mommies smile and hug and squeeze,
And run for hankies when you sneeze.
Many mommies read and knit,
Push and lift and make things fit.

Moms say "Play out in the air!"
Mommies tell you you must share.

Moms make beds and pick up toys,
And sometimes say, "Now stop that
  noise!"
Moms are there when you are sick;
They make you better pretty quick.

Mommies close and open latches,

Moms put Band-Aids on your scratches.
Moms sing songs so soft and sweet
But shout if you play near the street!

Moms pull sleds whenever it snows,
And bundle you up till none of you
 shows.
Moms make cake and lemonade;
And hold you tight when you're afraid.

They get the mail and call out, "Hi!"
To lots of people passing by.
Mommies do so much that—well,
It is just too much to tell.

They are busy all day through.
And here's a little secret . . .
Moms are busiest . . .
LOVING YOU!

      LONNIE CARTON

No Occupation

She rises up at break of day.
 And through her tasks she races;
She cooks the meal as best she may,
 And scrubs the children's faces,
While schoolbooks, lunches, ribbons,
 too
 All need consideration.
And yet the census man insists
 She has "no occupation."

When breakfast dishes all are done,
 She bakes a pudding, maybe;
She cleans the rooms up one by one,
 With one eye watching baby;
The mending pile she then attacks,
 By way of variation.
And yet the census man insists
 She has "no occupation."

She irons for a little while,
 Then presses pants for daddy;
She welcomes with a cheery smile
 Returning lass and laddie.
A hearty dinner next she cooks
 (No time for relaxation).
And yet the census man insists
 She has "no occupation."

For lessons that the children learn
 The evening scarce is ample,
To "mother dear" they always turn
 For help with each example.

In grammar and geography
 She finds her relaxation.
And yet the census man insists
 She has "no occupation."

      AUTHOR UNKNOWN

Mothers Are Found Everywhere

Mothers are found in various places:
Most often in the kitchen
Quite often in the laundry,
Very often walking here and there,
Sometimes in the sewing room
Once in a while in the bargain base-
 ment
And very seldom sitting in the living
 room.

A mother is a combination of things:
Information bureau, complaint depart-
 ment,
Chef, manager, baby-sitter, seam-
 stress,
Psychiatrist, accountant, interior decora-
 tor,
And everyone's best friend.
No one else is so early to rise or so late
 to bed.
No one else is too tired, yet so busy.

No one else is so much in demand:
Yet so often taken for granted.
No one else is so worried over the least
 little thing,
Yet so courageous in the time of real
 trouble.
No one else can cook, wash, iron,
 dust,
Straighten, scrub, tend to the children,
And still find time for church, club, or
 community project.

A mother is love with a dishcloth in her
 hand:
Beauty with flour on her chin
Patience in a gingham apron,
Efficiency with a child in her lap.
There isn't a more wonderful person in
 the whole world.

A Mother's Dilemma

Baby's in the cookie jar
Sister's in the glue

Kitty's in the birdie's cage
And I am in a stew!

Time for dad to come to lunch
Someone's spilled the roses
Breakfast dishes still undone
The twins have drippy noses.

Junior has the stove apart
Dinner guests at eight
Neighbors' kids swoop in like flies
How can I concentrate?

Telephone keeps ringing wildly
Someone's in the hall
Fido's chewed the rug to bits
The preacher's come to call!

Would mothers like to chuck their
    load?
They couldn't stand the rap
Easy, mild existences
Would cause their nerves to snap!

> HARRIET RUKENBROD DAY

Ruth Graham has a sign over the sink
in her kitchen, "Divine service conduct-
ed here three times daily."

Working Mother's Prayer

O God, it breaks my heart
    To leave this small but sheltered
    place,
To shut the door on motherhood
    And wear an eager, business face.

I want so much to stay at home.
    But since it cannot be
O Lord, along with daily bread,
    Give extra strength to me.

And let the other mothers know
    How fortunate are they
Who keep their happy brood in sight
    The long and wondrous day.

> JANNETTE CHAPMAN

And What Are Mothers For?

For tying tiny shoes
And kissing each new bruise?

For combing tangled curls
Of little wiggly girls?
For washing cups and plates
While many a pleasure waits?
For sweeping mud-tracked floors
And closing unlatched doors?
For mending jagged tears
Boys make in countless pairs
Of overalls and such?
And still not tiring much?

That's what mothers are for—
All this and yet for more.

They're for nightly climbing well-worn
    stairs
To hear their children's bed-time prayers;
For tucking all their sleepyheads
Safely in their little beds;
For giving every child true love
Like that which comes from God
    above;
For giving hope to every one,
Through each storm till the rain is
    done.

That's what mothers are for
All this and yet for more.

They're for planting seeds which are
    pure—
True faith that will always endure;
For teaching the right from the wrong
And making their children strong;
For giving them courage enough
To walk on when the pathway gets
    rough;
For smiling whatever may come—
Of all precious things they're the sum.
They're for building a world today
That's better in ev'ry way;
For paving the road ahead
So that long after they are dead
Others in faith may walk on
Toward a new and more glorious dawn.
Yes, *that's* what mothers are for—
That's what mothers are for.

> PHYLLIS C. MICHAEL

Of Things that Go Unsaid

Her fingers fashion day by day
    A piece of flimsy stuff.

A sleeve goes here, a collar there,
  And then a tiny cuff.
She sings and hums and nips her
  thread
  And whistles often, too.
Or accidentally pricks her thumb,
  As all good sewers do.
Her voice is not for minstrelsy,
  But meant for lullabies.
She couldn't weave a poem or song
  And never even tries.
But there's a poem in every sleeve,
  A song in every thread;
A prayer in every stitch she makes,
  Of things that go unsaid.
                    LAWRENCE J. SMITH

Mother's Work

Nobody knows of the work it makes,
  To keep the home together;
Nobody knows of the steps it takes,
  Nobody knows—but Mother.

Nobody listens to childish woes,
  Which kisses only smother;
Nobody's pained by the naughty
  blows,
Nobody—only Mother.

Nobody knows of the sleepless care
  Bestowed on baby brother;
Nobody knows of the tender prayer,
  Nobody knows—but Mother.

Nobody knows of the lessons taught
  Of loving one another;
Nobody knows of the patience sought,
  Nobody—only Mother.

Nobody knows of anxious fears
  Lest darling may not weather
The storm of life in after years,
  Nobody knows—but Mother.

Nobody knows of the tears that start,
  The grief she'd gladly smother,
Nobody knows of the breaking heart,
  Nobody can—but Mother.

Nobody clings to the wayward child,
  Though scorned by every other
Leads it so gently from pathways wild,
  Nobody can—but Mother.

Nobody knows of the hourly prayer,
  For him, our erring brother,
Pride of her heart, once so pure and fair,
  Nobody—only Mother.

Nobody kneels at the throne above
  To thank the Heavenly Father
For that sweetest gift—a mother's
  love,
  Nobody can—but Mother.
                    FLORA HAMILTON CASSEL

Working Mother

While I must work to earn your
  bread,
Provide a roof above your bed,
Diminish I not one small whit
Of our bless'd life or love of it.
When I'm away I learn the more
To cherish hours within our door.
                    FRANCES FIELDEN EPPLEY

Working as Unto Him

My household is away today,
  No one is coming in.
Ah! Then it doesn't matter when
  My housework I begin.

So then I'll leave the dishes,
  The beds are still unmade.
I do not care to dress—although
  The light bill should be paid!

It does not matter if I do
  Not do the ironing well.
I'll skip the dusting too, today
  The difference—who can tell?

I'm glad today is Monday
  For everyone is gone.
I'll do just as I want to,
  That now I am alone.

Hark! What is that? A whisper!
  "My child, take heed," He said
"The eyes of God are everywhere
  Beholding good and bad."

Then I must work as unto Him,
  My work I must do well.
For even if no other can
  The Lord Himself can tell.

I brace my shoulders, brush my hair,
  My work I do with care;
The eyes of God are looking on.
  To shirk—I will not dare.

BESSIE KINDLEY POOLE

Send Them to Bed With a Kiss

O mothers, so weary, discouraged,
  Worn out with the cares of the day,
You often grow cross and impatient,
  Complain of the noise and the play:
For the day brings so many vexations,
  So many things go amiss;
But, mothers, whatever may vex you,
  Send the children to bed with a kiss!

The dear little feet wander often,
  Perhaps, from the pathway of right,
The dear little hands find new mischief

To try you from morning till night;
But think of the desolate mothers
  Who'd give all the world for your bliss,
And, as thanks for your infinite bless-
    ings,
  Send the children to bed with a kiss!

For someday their noise will not vex
    you,
  The silence will hurt you far more;
You will long for their sweet childish
    voices,
  For a sweet childish face at the
    door;
And to press a child's face to your bos-
    om—
  You'd give all the world for just
    this!
For the comfort 'twill bring you in sor-
    row,
  Send the children to bed with a kiss!

AUTHOR UNKNOWN

TRIBUTES TO MOTHER

In Memoriam—My Mother

Her hands are folded now to rest,
  Hushed are those lips so pure;
Her spirit now among the blest,
  No pain or sorrow to endure.

Her chair is vacant now and lone,
  Her steps no longer heard;
Her voice is stilled forevermore,
  No longer gesture, look, or word.

She toiled for others day by day,
  With sacrifice her life was fraught;
Early began her day of toil,
  And late her tired fingers wrought.

May we who toil in life's hard way,
  A message from her share:
Live not for self nor selfish gain,
  Do all for Him and dare.

ALICE ANDIS OAKES

My Monument

I do not build a monument
Of carved white marble for your sake,

That only those who pass may read,
And only those memorial make.

My life must be the monument
I consecrate in your behalf;
My charity must carve your name,
My gentleness your epitaph.

And may some fragments of your
    strength
By God's great mystery fall on me,
That through this monument of mine
May shine your immortality.

CLAUDIA CRANSTON

My Mother's Hands

When I was younger I often wondered
why her hands were so large. They were
the largest woman's hands I have ever
seen—much larger than the ordinary
man's hands. They were hands whose
nails never knew the glamor of polish or
the efficient touch of a manicurist's file.
She always clipped the nails with scissors
for this was the quickest way, and they

were cut very close for she said long nails interfered with her work.

They were not always large hands, however, for when she was a young girl she said she had lovely hands and she wasn't ashamed of them then. How many times have I seen gloves on those hands! They were never seen in public without gloves for she was determined that no stranger was to see her rough, workworn hands.

To me those hands seemed the most beautiful ones in the world, and I wondered how she could have ever been ashamed of them—hands that had reared nine children; hands that could pick two hundred pounds of cotton a day, or hoe an acre of potatoes, as easily and willingly as they could prepare three tempting meals a day; hands whose very touch could ease a sick child's pain; hands always so eager to extend sympathy and help anyone in distress; hands that had the magic touch to lead so many to a richer, more abundant life.

Now I know why her hands were so large—she just couldn't have done so much with smaller hands!

HUGH W. PHILLIPS

Mother

I'm glad that God gave me no other
To guide me life's perilous way—
Than a dear, precious, old-fashioned
    Mother,
New-fashioned in Christ, I should say.

A Mother whose standards were taken
From a Holy, Infallible Book;
A Mother whose faith was unshaken,
Who led me toward Heaven to look.

She taught me to reverence the Bible,
God's Word to believe and obey;
She told me the way of Salvation;
From her, I learned early to pray.

Glad that my soul was entrusted
To one who knew Jesus divine,
Her joy in the Lord never rusted—
That good Christian Mother of mine.

There can never for me be another,
Sincerely and truly I say.
Thank God for that kind of a Mother,
God give us more like her today!

WILDA SCHROCK OATLEY

To Mother

A bit of heaven is in your eyes
Because God put it there.
The silver lining of the clouds
He placed amidst your hair.

A thoughtfulness and kindliness
He did to you impart.
A way of understanding things
He planted in your heart.

He gifted you with courage,
And with godliness so fine,
And then He placed His hand in
    yours,
And your hand into mine.

MARTINA M. THOMPSON

Fold her, O Father! in Thine arms,
    And let her henceforth be
A messenger of love between
    Our human hearts and Thee.

Still let her mild rebuking stand
    Between us and the wrong,
And her dear memory serve to make
    Our faith in goodness strong.

And grant that she, who, trembling
    here,
    Distrusted all her powers,
May welcome to her holier home
    The well-beloved of ours.

JOHN GREENLEAF WHITTIER

A Son's Tribute

James A. Garfield, as a boy working with a canal boat, fell to thinking of how he was throwing his life away. "I'll go back home get an education, and become a man."

Acting upon this resolution, he stood one night before the family log cabin in Cuyuhoga wilderness.

Through the window, by the firelight,

he saw his mother kneeling before an open Bible, reading with her eyes and praying with her lips.

He heard the words, "Oh, save the son of thy handmaid." He opened the door; she rose, he put his arms around her neck and his head on her bosom.

We do not know what he said to her, but we do know that he gave his life to God, graduated from Williams College, became the president of Hiram College.

When he was inaugurated president of the United States, he kissed the Bible; then kissing his mother, he said to her, "You brought me to this."

The Teacher

Mother

Mother, there is none more dear in all
    the world to me;
Your sweetness and your kindness and
    your generosity
Gave a meaning to my childhood that I'll
    treasure all my days;
Oh, the memories I harbor of your dear
    and loving ways!
I have never wished for riches, but this
    I've often said
If I had a crown of diamonds, I would
    place it on your head,
Hardship hasn't made you bitter—only
    seasoned and more true,
And when God was giving Mothers, I'm
    so glad He gave me you.

DOROTHY B. ELFSTROM

Devotion

How often we read or hear expressed
    Deep gratitude for a Mother's deeds
    done,
    Childhood hearts and love tender
    won,
That now inspires payment of a debt.
    Much deeper our devotion for you.

Yet others from depths of pity moved,
    And looking upon their mother grown
    older,
    Less agile, helpless, perhaps bitter,
    colder,

Try to make up, restore, their compassion prove. Much deeper our devotion for you.

There are even those who, for great expectations,
    Pander, trying by any means to
    please, even grovel,
    Killing within themselves a meagre
    soul,
Sycophants—meting out false adulations.

Some consider the Command, delivered
    in brevity,
    To progeny, who in the living God
    believe,
    Unequivocally honor parents, and thus
    receive
The resulting promise of longevity.

But to our Mother a tribute far to exceed
    Any obligation (though our debt to
    you be great)
    Or any feelings of duty we would satiate.
Your worth and worthiness is great indeed.

For you, having grown old with grace,
    Stability your character did not depart;
    Nor sense of humor, nor understanding heart;
Inner joy and gladness gladden your face.

What a delight to come within the existing sphere of you.
    To know you've not ceased to deeply
    live,
    And your awareness of still having
    much to give;
Nor expecting returns, though well they
    be due.

Our devotion is yours, care given with
    delight;
    No burden, for treasures we gather;—
    Not monetary, but spiritual rather.
For godly traits are your might.

What more expressive thought, Mother,
    could we proclaim,
    Than that to us an admirable prize,

As creeping shades of our old age we
  realize,
Our own attitudes and hearts, as yours
  be the same.

                              JACKIE MCGREGOR

A Memory of My Mother

As backward thru the passing years
  In Memory I roam
I find my mother once again
  Within our happy home.

Her pleasant smile would greet us all
  On our return each day
It seemed as though she never tired
  From morn to close of day.

A call from any one in need
  Was always gladly heard
She soothed the sick and cheered the
  sad
  With kindest deed or word.

She took great interest in the church
  And helped from day to day
She never failed where duty called
  Nor lingered on the way.

She found her place in God's wise plan
  As forward she would go
She did her best in everything
  For neither praise nor show.

She spent her life for others' sake
  This side the golden shore
Such influence will help the world
  And live forevermore.

                              WALTER VANCE

Mothers Make Nations

No biography of Abraham Lincoln of
sacred and immortal memory is complete which does not contain a copy of
the letter he wrote to Mrs. Bixby. No
tribute to the mother of men is complete
without a copy of the same letter, and a
place of honor reserved for the name of
Mrs. Bixby.

"I have been shown," wrote Lincoln,
on November 21, 1864, "in the files of
the War Department a statement of the
Adjutant General of Massachusetts that
you are the mother of five sons,[1] who
have died gloriously on the field of battle. I feel how weak and fruitless must
be any words of mine which should attempt to beguile you from the grief of a
loss so overwhelming. But I cannot re-
frain from tendering to you the consola-
tion that may be found in the thanks of
the Republic they died to save. I pray
that our heavenly Father may assuage
the anguish of your bereavement, and
leave you only the cherished memory of
the loved and lost, and the solemn pride
that must be yours to have laid so costly
a sacrifice upon the altar of freedom.
Yours very sincerely and respectfully,
Abraham Lincoln."

                                    Clarion

[1]Actually, only two of her sons had been
killed in action, but Lincoln did not know
this when he wrote this letter.

A Tribute to Mothers

When all is said, it is the mother, and
the mother only, who is a better citizen
than the soldier who fights for his country. The successful mother, the mother
who does her part in rearing and training aright the boys and girls who are to
be the men and women of the next generation, is of greater use to the community, and occupies, if she only would
realize it, a more honorable as well as a
more important position than any man
in it. The mother is the one supreme
asset of national life; she is more important by far than the successful statesman, or business man, or artist, or scientist.

                         THEODORE ROOSEVELT

In the same pious confidence, beside
her friend and sister, here sleep the remains of Dorothy Gray, widow, the
careful, tender mother of many children,
one of whom alone had the misfortune
to survive her.

        On the gravestone of the mother of
                              Thomas Gray

How little I appreciated her sacrifices
and how late comes the true appreciation of them. Alas, how inadequately

until the beloved mother who made them has gone beyond the reach of its manifestation.

THADDEUS STEVENS

Earth's noblest thing, a woman perfected.

IRENE LOWELL

But give her, Lord, in love profound
A crown with jewels all around,
These tribute words upon it found:
"She was a *Missionary Mother*."

CHARLES WILLOUGHBY

The Old-Fashioned Mother

There is home where an old-fashioned mother presides like a queen. Thank God, some of us have, and some have had, old-fashioned mothers. Dear, old-fashioned, sweet-faced mother! Eyes in which the lovelight shone, her brown hair threaded with silver, lying smoothly on the faded cheek; her dear hands, worn with toil, gently guiding our tottering steps in childhood and smoothing our pillow in sickness, ever reaching out to us in yearning tenderness. Precious memory of an old-fashioned mother! It floats to us now, like the powerful perfume of some fragrant blossom. The music of other voices may be lost, but the entrancing memory of her will echo in our souls forever!

J. WILBUR CHAPMAN

My Trust

A picture memory brings to me:
I look across the years and see
Myself beside my mother's knee.

I feel her gentle hand restrain
My selfish moods, and know again
A child's blind sense of wrong and pain.

But wiser now, a man gray grown,
My childhood's needs are better known,
My mother's chastening love I own.

JOHN GREENLEAF WHITTIER

The Portrait

Artist, be kind.
White hair clings to the furrowed brow,
And the sweet lips smile, but sadly now.

The eyes that were brave, and tender, and clear
Have been dimmed and faded by sorrow's tear.

The hands are tired, wrinkled and old . . .
Paint them slender, soft and gifted . . .
They were coarsened by burdens they have lifted;

The frail, bent form weathered storms of life,
But the soul is unscarred by the endless strife.

Artist,
Your model is dearer than any other . . .
Paint beauty, when painting
The portrait of Mother.

HELEN GRAY ROBERTSON

In Mother's Heart

When I was but a little girl,
I heard my Mother's name,
And then I heard them speak of God,
And thought they were the same.

I heard that God was very good,
And loved all children, truly;
My Mother loved me day and night,
And counselled when unruly.

They promised God would care for me;
My Mother was always there—
I took my childish wants to her,
My joys and hurts to share.

Now I have grown to womanhood,
And I found the two—apart—
But I feel I was not too wrong,
For God was in her heart.

MAMIE OZBURN ODUM

Such Beautiful Hands

Such beautiful, beautiful hands!
They are growing feeble now,
For time and pain have left their mark
On hand, and heart, and brow.
I've looked on hands whose form and hue
A sculptor's dream might be.
Yet are those aged, wrinkled hands
More beautiful to me.

AUTHOR UNKNOWN

In Gratitude

We're grateful, dear Mother, for so many
   precious things
That brighten countless hours along the
   way.
Your faith in us, your gentleness, your
   sweet unfailing love
Have meant far more than we could
   ever say.

We thank you for instilling an awareness
   in our hearts
Of nature's loveliness, of all that's fair,
By pointing to a sunset . . . to a flower
   . . . a butterfly;
And making each seem beautiful and rare.

For showing us a grand delightful world
   that's brimming full
Of wonder and enchantment, much to
   learn;
By pondering with us how many stars
   were in the sky,
What kind of bird, what made the windmill turn.

For taking disappointments with courage
   and hope;
For teaching honor, faith and loyalty . . .
No matter now what life may bring,
   these attitudes you taught
Are written in our hearts indelibly.

ROSE MARIE OVERMAN

Wonders to Share

She never said, "Run out and play
For Mother's busy now."
Housework will wait for one all day;
But little boys, somehow

Find wonders in the out-of-doors
About which mothers know;
Far better leave some daily chores
To help a young mind grow.

There's only one first butterfly
Afloat on airborne wings;
First bobolink that hurries by
In flight, the while he sings;
First dandelions like precious gold
Will tempt his eager hands
To gather all that they will hold . . .
Yes, mother understands,

Remembering that childhood joys
Will always, always be
The heritage for girls and boys . . .
They were for you and me.

ETHEL E. MANN

My Mother's Hymn

I sit alone at twilight
And watch the shadows dim,
And to me there comes stealing
The thought of mother's hymn;
Just as I heard it in childhood,
Her words float back to me;
I seem to hear her singing,
"Nearer, My God, to Thee."

I've strayed far in paths of sin,
Been reckless, weak and wild,
Forgotten the words she sang to me
When I was but a child;
Forgotten the God she loved so well,
Whose love she taught to me;
Forgotten my mother and her song,
"Nearer, My God, to Thee."

My soul is filled with deep remorse,
I'm tired of strife and sin,
I want to turn from worldly chaff
To the God of mother's hymn;
I thank Him for this quiet hour,
Which He has given to me,
In which I have again been drawn
"Nearer, My God, to Thee."

TALENA DIRKSON

Thy Mother

Lead thy mother tenderly,
   Down life's steep decline;

Once her arm was thy support,
Now she leans on thine.

See upon her loving face
Those deep lines of care?
Think—it was her toil for thee
Left that record there.

Ne'er forget her tireless watch
Kept by day and night,
Taking from her step the grace,
From her eyes the light;

Cherish well her faithful heart,
Which through weary years
Echoed with its sympathy,
All thy smiles and tears.

Thank God for thy mother's love,
Guard the priceless boon;
For the bitter parting hour
Cometh all too soon.

When thy grateful tenderness
Loses power to save,
Earth will hold no dearer spot
Than thy mother's grave.

AUTHOR UNKNOWN

Mother's Face

It was there, back there, in the dear,
sweet years,
When the world was gay, with no
clouds or tears,
I remember well how the sunlight
streamed,
In my laughing eyes—Ah, I never
dreamed
I should set my feet such a long, long
way
When I said "Good-by" at the gate
that day!
Ah, the yearning smile and the tender
glow
On my mother's face as I turned to go!

Oh, how could I know that the road was
long?
That my heart would ache for the
fireside song?
That the warmth and cheer of the hearth-
stone bright
Would bewitch my dreams in the
lonely night.

And how could I know that the coaxing
star
Would beckon me on to the lands
afar?
That through the sunshine fair and
through shadows grim
I would roam the earth to its farthest
rim?

But at last I'm home, and I stand and
wait,
With a haunting fear, by the little
gate.
There's a mystic change over mead and
wold
Which the years have wrought with
their cunning bold.
Will the dear scenes welcome me back
again?
Is it home, my home, just the same as
then?
But the wide door creaks, and a face I
see,
Ah, my mother's face—it is home to
me!

AUTHOR UNKNOWN

To Mother—At Set of Sun

As once you stroked my thin and silver
hair
So I stroke yours now at the set of sun.
I watch your tottering mind, its day's
work done,
As once you watched with forward-
looking care
My tottering feet. I love you as I
should.
Stay with me; lean on me; I'll make
no sign.
I was your child, and now time makes
you mine.
Stay with me yet a while at home, and
do me good.

AUTHOR UNKNOWN

Where's Mother?

I roam about the house like one be-
mused—
Here is her chair, her shawl, her tiny
shoes,

Her glasses, scissors, and some shiny
   thread,
A bookmark in the place where last she
   read,
A plant love-coddled near to blissful
   bloom,
A hallowed air about her vacant room.
Across some bridge I cannot even see
She went alone. She could not wait for
   me.

Then my anguished heart seems to hear
   her speak, impatiently:
"Begone about your daily tasks, child,
   look not here for me.
Waste not one minute bowed in grief.
   Wherever man has trod
Earth time is but his fertile path that
   leads at last to God.
Sow yours with faith, and love, and work
   . . ." How oft words she'd say;
Now her creed comes through, so alive,
   so true, she can't be far away.

                MARIE W. MUSSELWHITE

Dear Old Mothers

I love old mothers—mothers with white
   hair
   And kindly eyes, and lips grown soft
     and sweet
With murmured blessings over sleeping
   babes.
   There is something in their quiet
     grace
That speaks the calm of Sabbath after-
   noons;
   A knowledge in their deep, unfaltering
     eyes
That far outreaches all philosophy.

Time, with caressing touch about them
   weaves
   The silver-threaded fairy-shawl of age,
While all the echoes of forgotten songs
   Seem joined to lend sweetness to their
     speech.

Old mothers! as they pass with slow-
   timed step,
   Their trembling hands cling gently to
     youth's strength.

Sweet mothers!—as they pass, one sees
   again
   Old garden-walks, old roses, and old
     loves.

                CHARLES S. ROSS

Unspoken Thoughts

I wish I had told her
How the blue of her eyes
Was so soft and so clear,
Like the blue of the skies.
I wish I had said,
When she brushed back her hair,
That I thought she was pretty—
So slim and so fair.

And I might have whispered
A fond word of praise
When she toiled for my comfort
On long, busy days.
I wish I had said
Many times through the years,
"How patient you are with
My joys and my tears."

I wish I had told her
When steps grew more slow
And I knew that they had not
Much farther to go.
I wish I had said,
"You are precious to me.
Dear mother of mine,
And you always will be."

I thought these things over
Again and again,
But I did not express them,
With voice or with pen.
So long I was silent,
And now we're apart
I wish I had told her
The thoughts in my heart.

                AMY PERRIN

What Great Men Have Said About Their Mothers

JOHN QUINCY ADAMS: All that I am my
mother made me.

HENRY WARD BEECHER: The mother's
heart is the child's schoolroom.

Do you know why so often I speak what must seem to some rhapsody, of woman? It is because I had a mother. If I were to live a thousand years I could not express what seems to me to be the least that I owe to the fact that I had a mother.

NAPOLEON BONAPARTE: The future destiny of the child is always the work of mothers. Let France have good mothers and she will have good sons.

WINSTON CHURCHILL: When a London editor submitted a list of the people to this great statesman who had been his teachers, Mr. Churchill returned the list with one comment: "You have omitted to mention the greatest of my teachers—my mother!"

CHARLES DICKENS: I think it must be somewhere written that the virtues of mothers shall be visited on their children as well as the sins of the fathers.

THOMAS A. EDISON: My mother was the making of me.

JAMES A. GARFIELD: Upon his inauguration as president of the United States, he kissed the Bible; then kissing his mother, he said to her, "You brought me to this."

GEORGE HERBERT: One good mother is worth one hundred schoolmasters.

ABRAHAM LINCOLN: All that I am or hope to be, I owe to my angel mother. No man is poor who has had a godly mother.

HENRY W. LONGFELLOW: Concerning Jesus and His mother, this great American poet wrote the following: "Even He that died for us upon the cross, in the last hour was mindful of His mother as if to teach us that this holy love should be our last worldly thought—the last point of earth from which the soul should take its flight for heaven."

MARTIN LUTHER: There is nothing sweeter than the heart of a pious mother.

DWIGHT L. MOODY: All that is good in my life has come from my mother.

WENDELL PHILLIPS (great orator): Whatever I have done in my life has simply been due to the fact that when I was a child my mother daily read with me a part of the Bible, and made me learn a part of it by heart.

THEODORE ROOSEVELT: No state is greater than its mothers.

JOHN RUSKIN: My mother's influence in molding my character was conspicuous. She forced me to learn daily long chapters of the Bible by heart. To that discipline and patient, accurate resolve I owe not only much of my general power of taking pains, but the best part of my taste for literature.

ST. AUGUSTINE (who lived 1600 years ago): It is to my mother that I owe everything. If I prefer the truth to all other things, it is the point of my mother's teaching. If I did not long ago perish in sin and misery it is because of the faithful tears with which she pleaded for me.

CHARLES H. SPURGEON: My conversion took place—oh momentous hours— at my mother's knee.

BILLY SUNDAY: Mothers and teachers of children fill places so great that there isn't an angel in heaven that wouldn't be glad to give a bushel of diamonds to come down here and take their place.

WILLIAM MAKEPEACE THACKERAY: Mother is the name for God in the lips and hearts of children.

MARK TWAIN: It is at our mother's knee that we acquire our noblest and truest and highest ideals.

GEORGE WASHINGTON: I attribute all my success in life to the moral, intellectual, and physical education which I received from my mother.

DANIEL WEBSTER: If there is anything in my writings that is commendable, I owe it to my mother and the fact that in my youth she taught me to love and to read the sacred Scriptures.

JOHN WESLEY: My mother was the source from which I derived the guiding principles of my life.

BENJAMIN WEST (American Painter): A kiss from my mother made me a painter.

Mothers Who Made History

George Washington's mother taught her son the Biblical ideals of political and social morality which Washington kept before the nation throughout his life. Family prayers were held twice a day with regular readings from the Scripture.

Sir Isaac Newton's mother prayed with and for her son every day of her life. It was the grief of her deathbed that she left a son of seven years at the mercy of a rough world. But Newton said, "I was born in a home of godliness and dedicated to God in my infancy."

Queen Alexandria asked her son, King George VI, to read a chapter of the Bible every day. He kept the promise for 55 years.

William Penn's mother so impressed him with the importance of faith in Christ that he took as his life text. "This is the victory, even our faith which overcometh the world."

Ferdinand Foch's mother taught him to put his faith in God and to pray. As a result his men said of this great general of World War I, "General Foch is a man of prayer, a prophet whom God inspires." Throughout his life he continued the prayer habits learned in his mother's home.

James A. Garfield's mother was an earnest Christian who taught her children that "the fear of the Lord is the beginning of wisdom." A widow with four children, she not only managed her farm, but built with her own hands a log house which was also used as a church. There she taught her own children as well as others the Scriptures.

William E. Gladstone's mother led her son to faith in God when he was nine. He chose as his life's motto: "In practice, the great thing is that the life of God may be the supreme habit of my soul." This famous Englishman also wrote, "All I think, all I write, all I am is based on the divinity of Jesus Christ, the central hope of our poor wayward race."

Oliver Cromwell's mother taught him the simple truths of Scripture, and he chose as his favorite verse, "I can do all things through Christ which strengtheneth me."

Dwight L. Moody's mother struggled against poverty in a New England farm. A widow with many problems, she taught her son the importance of eternal values. At 17 Moody accepted Christ and a few years later dedicated his life for service.

from Log of the Good Ship Grace

John Ruskin's mother read the Bible to her son daily when he was a child and made him memorize a part of it. Of this Ruskin wrote years later, "All I have taught of art, everything I have written, whatever greatness there has been in any thought of mine, whatever I have done in my life, has simply been due to my mother."

Monica, the mother of *Augustine* went one day in tears to her bishop to ask for advice. Her son, the pride of her life, had left home to follow a disso-lute path. He had turned his back on God and had spurned his mother's love. What should she do? The bishop's answer to her was, "The faithful prayers of a loving mother are never lost." And they weren't! Augustine came back to the truths that he had been taught as a youth, and his writings have blessed the whole world.

CLIFFORD BARROWS, in *Decision*

PROVERBS ABOUT MOTHERS

The Mother's breath is ever sweet.

A bustling mother makes a slothful daughter.

LATIN

Whom will he help that does not help his mother.

TURKISH

A mother's love will draw up from the depths of the sea.

RUSSIAN

A mother's heart is always with her children.

A good mother will not hear the music of the dance when her children cry.

GERMAN

An indulgent mother makes a sluttish daughter.

DUTCH

An old mother in a house is a hedge.

GERMAN

The mother of a timid son never weeps.

TURKISH

No mother is so wicked but she desires to have good children.

ITALIAN

Mother's love is ever in its spring.

FRENCH

There is no mother like the mother that bore us.

He who takes the child by the hand takes the mother by the heart.

DANISH

Like mother, like daughter.

ENGLISH

Better the child cry than the mother sigh.

DANISH

His mother an onion, his father a garlic, himself comes out a conserve of roses.

TURKISH

Heaven is at the feet of mothers.

PERSIAN

A light-heeled mother makes a heavy-heeled daughter.

SCOTCH

Buy land that slopes toward the center and marry a girl whose mother is good.

JAPANESE

A supple mother makes an idle child.

IRISH

The daughter of a good mother will be the mother of a good daughter.

C.H. SPURGEON

A mother with a purse is better than a father with a plough team.

IRISH

Children who are obedient to their mothers will enter heaven.

PERSIAN

At cleaning time everyone should yield to the mother with the broom.

JAPANESE

The child says what he heard his mother say.

C.H. SPURGEON

An ounce of Mother is equal to a pound of clergy.

SPANISH

An elephant does not carry heavy on his tusks. Interpreted means: It is no burden for a mother to take care of her child.

WEST AFRICAN

He that coddles a child makes a rod for his own back.

C.H. SPURGEON

A mother's love is best of all.

WEST AFRICAN

The beetle is a beauty in the eye of its mother.

ARABIAN

The afflicted mother who has lost her children is not like the woman who weeps for hire.

ARABIAN

You may make bread and you may mix meal, but it is not rice. You may make an aunt and a father's sister, but she is not a mother.

INDIAN

God could not be everywhere, and so He made mothers.

JEWISH

SCRIPTURE CONCERNING MOTHERS AND FAMILIES

Adam called his wife's name Eve; because she was the mother of all living.

Genesis 3:20

Honour thy father and thy mother.

Exodus 20:12

These words, which I command thee . . . thou shalt teach them diligently unto thy children. . . .

Deuteronomy 6:6, 7

For this child I prayed; and the Lord hath given me my petition which I asked of Him: Therefore also I have lent

him to the Lord; as long as he liveth he shall be lent to the Lord.

I Samuel 1:27, 28

For he established a testimony . . .
which he commanded our fathers,
   that they should make them known to
      their children:
That the generation to come might know
   them,
   even the children which should be
      born;
who should arise and declare them to
   their children:
That they might set their hope in God,

and not forget the works of God,
but keep his commandments.

Psalm 78:5-7

Like as a father pitieth his children,
so the Lord pitieth them that fear him.

Psalm 103:13

Blessed is the man that feareth the Lord,
that delighteth greatly in his commandments.
His seed shall be mighty upon earth:
the generation of the upright shall be blessed.
Wealth and riches shall be in his house:
and his righteousness endureth for ever.

Psalm 112:1-3

He maketh the barren woman to keep house,
and to be a joyful mother of children.

Psalm 113:9

Except the Lord build the house,
they labour in vain that build it.

Psalm 127:1

Thy wife shall be as a fruitful vine
by the sides of thine house:
Thy children like olive plants
round about thy table.

Psalm 128:3

My son, hear the instruction of thy father,
and forsake not the law of thy mother.

Proverbs 1:8

I was my father's son,
tender and only beloved in the sight of my mother.
He taught me also, and said unto me,
Let thine heart retain my words:
keep my commandments and live.
Get wisdom, get understanding: forget it not;
neither decline from the words of my mouth.
Forsake her not, and she shall preserve thee:
love her and she shall keep thee.

Proverbs 4:3-6

A wise son maketh a glad father:

but a foolish son is the heaviness of his mother.

Proverbs 10:1

He that spareth his rod hateth his son:
but he that loveth him chasteneth him betimes.

Proverbs 13:24

A wise son maketh a glad father:
but a foolish man despiseth his mother.

Proverbs 15:20

Chasten thy son while there is hope.

Proverbs 19:18

A good name is rather to be chosen than great riches.

Proverbs 22:1

Train up a child in the way he should go:
and when he is old, he will not depart from it.

Proverbs 22:6

Withhold not correction from the child.

Proverbs 23:13

Hearken unto thy father that begat thee,
and despise not thy mother when she is old.
Buy the truth, and sell it not;
also wisdom, and instruction, and understanding.
The father of the righteous shall greatly rejoice:
and he that begetteth a wise child shall have joy of him.
Thy father and thy mother shall be glad,
and she that bare thee shall rejoice.

Proverbs 23:22-25

A child left to himself bringeth his mother to shame.

Proverbs 29:15

Correct thy son, and he shall give thee rest;
yea, he shall give delight unto thy soul.

Proverbs 29:17

Who can find a virtuous woman?
for her price is far above rubies. . . .

She is like the merchants' ships;
  she bringeth her food from afar.
She riseth also while it is yet night,
  and giveth meat to her household. . . .
She considereth a field, and buyeth it:
  with the fruit of her hands she plant-
  eth a vineyard. . . .
She stretcheth out her hand to the poor;
  yea, she reacheth forth her hands to
  the needy. . . .
Strength and honour are her clothing;
  and she shall rejoice in time to come.
She openeth her mouth with wisdom:
  and in her tongue is the law of kindness.
She looketh well to the ways of her
  household,
and eateth not the bread of idleness.
Her children arise up and call her blessed;
  her husband also, and he praiseth
  her. . . .
Favour is deceitful, and beauty is vain:
  but a woman that feareth the Lord,
  she shall be praised.

Proverbs 31:10-31

. . . and a little child shall lead them.

Isaiah 11:6b

Can a woman forget her sucking child,
that she should not have compassion on
the son of her womb? yea they may forget, yet will I not forget thee.

Isaiah 49:15

And all thy children shall be taught of
the Lord; and great shall be the peace of
thy children.

Isaiah 54:13

As one whom his mother comforteth,
so will I comfort you.

Isaiah 66:13

Behold, every one that useth proverbs
shall use this proverb against thee, saying, As is the mother, so is her daughter.

Ezekiel 16:44

And when they were come into the
house, they saw the young child with
Mary his mother, and fell down and worshipped him.

Matthew 2:11

And Jesus called a little child unto
him, and set him in the midst of them,
And said, Verily I say unto you, Except
ye be converted, and become as little
children, ye shall not enter the kingdom
of heaven. Whosoever therefore shall
humble himself as this little child, the
same is greatest in the kingdom of
heaven.

Matthew 18:2-4

Out of the mouth of babes and suck-
lings thou hast perfected praise.

Matthew 21:16

And he took a child, and set him in
the midst of them. . . .

Mark 9:36a

And they brought young children to
him, that he should touch them: and
his disciples rebuked those that brought
them. But when Jesus saw it, he was
much displeased and said . . . Suffer the
little children to come unto me, and
forbid them not: for of such is the
kingdom of heaven.

Mark 10:13, 14

. . . his [Jesus'] mother kept all these
sayings in her heart.

Luke 2:51

Children, obey your parents in the
Lord: for this is right. Honour thy father
and thy mother; which is the first commandment with promise; that it may be
well with thee, and thou mayest live
long on the earth. And, ye fathers [par-
ents], provoke not your children to
wrath: but bring them up in the nurture and admonition of the Lord.

Ephesians 6:1-4

Children, obey your parents in all
things: for this is well pleasing unto the
Lord. Fathers, provoke not your children
to anger, lest they be discouraged.

Colossians 3:20, 21

The . . . faith that is in thee . . . dwelt
first in thy grandmother Lois, and thy
mother Eunice.

II Timothy 1:5

MOTHERS-IN-LAW

To Mother-in-law

I wish Mother dear, I had known your
　　son
When he was just a boy;
I often wonder what he was like
What things would bring him joy.

I wish that I had seen the curls
That framed his baby face;
I wish I had seen you rock him to
　　sleep
There on the old home place.

I wish I had heard the little prayers
You prayed as you knelt by his bed;
I know they were meant to be heard by
　　God
But if I had heard what you said,

Perhaps I'd know why your little boy
Grew so perfect and strong and fine;
Then I could pray the same way to
　　day,
Make the same kind of man out of
　　mine.

PHYLLIS C. MICHAEL

To "His" Mother

"Mother-in-law" they say, and yet . . .
Somehow I simply can't forget
'Twas you who watched his baby
　　ways,
Who taught him his first hymn of
　　praise.
Who smiled on him with loving pride,
When he first toddled by your side.
And as I think of this today,
I think that I'd much rather say . . .
　　Just, Mother.

"Mother-in-law," but oh, 'twas you
Who taught him to be kind and true;
When he was tired, almost asleep,
'Twas in your arms he used to creep;
And when he hurt his tiny knee,
'Twas you who kissed it tenderly;
When he was sad you cheered him,
　　too,

And so I'd rather speak of you . . .
　　As Mother.

"Mother-in-law" they say, and yet . . .
Somehow I never shall forget,
How very much I owe
To you who taught him how to grow.
You trained your son to look above,
You made of him the man I love.
And so I think of that today.
And then, with thankful heart
　　　I say . . .
　　Dear Mother.

MINNIE PRICE

His Mother

I look at him and think of her;
　　So many years ago
She held him close, sang lullabies,
　　And rocked him to and fro.

Her loving prayers, her tenderness,
　　Hopes, care and sacrifice
Produced a man who seems to be
　　All virtue and no vice.

One plainly sees her honesty
　　In his clear eyes of blue.
Her sweetness is reflected in
　　His every action, too.

In him she realized her dreams,
　　Then gave him to another.
Yes, I'm the lucky girl, and oh!
　　So grateful to his mother!

LYLA MYERS

Mother, If You Wouldn't Mind

Why should I call you mother-in-law—
You who have been so kind?
I'd really rather just call you mother,
That is, if you wouldn't mind.

For I feel so like a daughter to you
And I need your love so much;
So why should I call you mother-in-
　　law
When it doesn't seem like you're such?

From the very first time I saw your
smile
I knew somehow inside
That your love was deep as the deepest
sea
And oh, just twice as wide.

I might have known it all along—
How could the man who's now mine
Be so perfect, so grand in ev'ry way
Without a mother so fine?

But I have something other than this
To call you mother for.
I'm sure that this would be reason
enough
But oh, there's so much more.

You took me into your heart, your
life,
You taught me many things
Like faith in God and in others, too,
Like love and its hidden springs.

Oh, why should I call you mother-in-
law
When you're everything nice com-
bined?
I'd rather just call you mother, please,
That is, if you wouldn't mind.

PHYLLIS C. MICHAEL

And What Does She Say?

And what does a fond mother say, I
wonder,
To a brand new daughter-in-law?
She must not bind her son too closely
Nor yet stand off in awe.

And what does a fond mother say, I ask
you,
When she longs to say what is right?
She must not seem too proud or posses-
sive
Nor yet too indiff'rent or light.

And what does a fond mother say,
please help me,
She who has treasured her son,
When she sees the two standing so near
her—
Two hearts that beat as one?

Then what does a fond mother say, I
wonder,
When she longs to hold both to her
breast,
Yet she knows she must let them go on
their way
Into their own little nest?

Oh, what does a fond mother say, I must
know,
When she aches with the pangs of
love?
"May the Lord of us all bless you both,
my dears,
As He watches us all from above."

PHYLLIS C. MICHAEL

Entreat Me Not to Leave Thee

Entreat me not to leave thee,
    or to return from following after
    thee:
For whither thou goest, I will go;
    and where thou lodgest, I will
    lodge:
Thy people shall be my people,
    and thy God my God:
Where thou diest, will I die,
    and there will I be buried:
The Lord do so to me, and more also,
    if aught but death part thee and me.

RUTH to Naomi (Ruth 1:16-17)

GRANDMOTHER

Grandmothers of America

It was back in 1934, when a group of Illinois Business and Professional women were meeting in convention, that Marie K. Brown, thrilled with the news that she had just become a grandmother, stood up and asked how many other women present were so blessed. The response was gratifying, and that common bond brought these grandmothers together for several years at convention time for a special breakfast. Ruth Cowan, of the Associated Press, released a story about this unique group. Her story created such interest throughout the United States, that the group, headed by Marie K. Brown, applied to the state of Illinois for a charter as the National Grandmother Club. This charter was issued April 11, 1938, and since that time the Federation has grown to include 725 clubs with a membership of some 18,000 grandmothers.

This National Federation of Grandmother Clubs of America is a nonsectarian, nonpartisan, and nonprofit organization. Its objects are these:

—To honor Grandmotherhood through the observance of the Second Sunday of October as National Grandmothers' Day, and to work to have it so established by legislation in the United States.

—To further the social and educational interests of its members.

—To promote better understanding of the privileges and obligations of American citizenship.

—To contribute to the research and study of children's diseases.

—To support charitable projects as adopted by the National Conventions.

—To promote interest in, to work for, and to contribute to the National Haven Building Fund.

The official colors of the Federation are gold and brown, the flower is the chrysanthemum, and the second Sunday in October is National Grandmothers' Day—all symbolic of Autumn, the time when women are blessed with grandmotherhood. The club emblem, a baby in swaddling clothes, engraved on a brown enamel background, was inspired by the famous Della Robbia plaque which decorates the Children's Hospital in Florence, Italy. From this emblem are suspended small bars, one for each grandchild. A star denotes great-grandmotherhood.

The official publication of the Federation is "Autumn Leaves." It contains reports of the social, educational, and charitable activities of the Grandmother Clubs, and is sent to all members.

A statement issued by the N.F.G.C.A. says in regard to its purpose:

"This organization came into existence at a time when there was dire need for concerted action among older women for self-reliance, companionship, and fellowship. In the Autumn of Life is when we need friends with similar interests, and in the National Federation of Grandmother Clubs we find such friends."

The National bylaws specify that one must be a grandmother through motherhood, marriage, or legal adoption to belong to a club, and must be sponsored by a member when seeking membership.

Headquarters of the National Federation of Grandmother Clubs of America is 4434 N. Monitor Ave. Chicago, Illinois.

Sunshine Magazine

The Lessons Learned . . .

My grandma used to sit and knit
  From morning till the night,
With her needles glancing, glancing,
  When the sun was shining bright.
She knitted stockings for us all,
  And all of us agreed
That she'd find a satisfaction
  Fitting out a centipede.

I used to watch her often then,
  And note her kindly smile,

And wonder if in heaven above
　　She'd knit 'most all the while
And say, "Now, ain't you weary?"
　　And she'd answer, "Dear, depend
If I just keep knitting, knitting,
　　I am sure to reach the end."

I've walked a toilsome way,
　　Have shaken hands with Care,
I have supped at times with Pleasure,
　　And have found her board was bare.
I have fainted in the struggle,
　　And my heart has made its plea:
"Dear God, a chance to rest a time
　　Were heaven enough for me."

I have toiled and striven vainly,
　　And the journey seems so long,
And I judge that I am vanquished
　　In the battle of the strong;
Yet I still take heart of courage,
　　For I hear while shadows bend:
"If you just keep knitting, knitting,
　　You are sure to reach the end."
　　　　　　　ALFRED J. WATERHOUSE

Taking Turns at Grandma's

We like to go to Granny's house
And spend a happy day
Where cooky jars are always full
It is such fun to stay.

Her garden now is bright with flowers
The honey bees are there
And from her trees the singing birds
Are flying everywhere.

Back in the barn our pony waits
With Rover at his side.
When brother leads the pony out,
He gives us each a ride.

Then Rover barks and runs ahead
Down to the shady lane
Oh, taking turns is fine—for soon,
Our turns come round again.
　　　　　　EMILIE BLACKMORE STAFF

Trifocals

Grandmother's glasses had two windows;

And I, a child at her aproned knee,
Would prod, "Grandmother, when you look
　　Through the bottoms, what do you see?"

And she would always smile and say
　　That she saw only me.
And "Grandmother, when you look
　　Through the tops, tell, what do you see?"

"The lane, the hill, the field of hay,
　　The collie dog, the maple tree. . . ."
When grandmother looked above her specs,
　　Then I would never prod,
For grandmother's eyes grew misty blue;
　　I knew that she saw God.
　　　　　　BEULAH FENDERSON SMITH

From a newspaper clipping: "Paul Williamson, M.C., of Jamaica, N.Y., said he found this in his notebook but has no idea how it got there:"

Grandmother, on a winter's day,
Milked the cows and fed them hay;
Slopped the hogs, harnessed the mule
And got the children off to school;
Did a washing, mopped the floors,
Washed the windows and did some chores;
Cooked a dish of home dried fruit,
And pressed her husband's Sunday suit;
Swept the parlor, made the bed,
Baked a dozen loaves of bread;
Split some firewood, lugged some in,
Enough to fill the kitchen bin;
Stewed some apples she thought might spoil,
Cleaned the lamps and put in oil;
Churned the butter, baked a cake,
Then exclaimed, "For goodness sake,
Those little calves are out again!"
Went and chased them into the pen;
Gathered the eggs and locked the stable,
Went back to the house and set the table,
Cooked a supper that was delicious,
And afterwards washed up all the dishes;
Fed the cat and sprinkled the clothes,

Mended a basket all full of hose;
Then opened the organ and began to
    play,
"When You Come to the End of a Per-
    fect Day."

I guess the answer is that Grandma
had no time for tranquilizers: plainly,
she was too busy to take them.

In Love Again

I looked at her, somewhat resigned
And guess the workings of her mind.
She's restless as a little wren,
And says that she's in love again.

Seems he has nice teeth, dark brown
    hair,
And wears his clothes with careless
    air.
Now I'm not jealous, Y'understand,
But when he's here, I'm contraband.

I grin, and that she can't condone.
She waits for him to telephone.
It rings—she leaps—to hear him say,
"Gramma, I gotta 'A' today."
                              PAUL P. WENTZ

Grandma

My grandma likes to play with God,
They have a kind of game.
She plants the garden full of seeds,
He sends the sun and rain.

She likes to sit and talk with God
And knows he is right there.
She prays about the whole wide world,
Then leaves us in his care.
                      ANN JOHNSON (age 8)

Grandma Says

When folks next to you act like those in
    the zoo,
    A grumblin', growlin', and spittin',
        It's a pretty good plan
        To be calm as you can,

And do somethin' useful—like knit-
    tin'.

When a gossipin' Susan, with poison-
    barbed tongue,
    Comes into the room where you're
        sittin'
        And starts to defame
        Some good neighbor's name
    Count stitches out loud—and keep
        knittin'.

When there's been a misunderstanding at
    church
    And others hint broadly of quittin',
        Why, the very best thing
        You can do is to sing,
    And stay at your post—and keep knit-
        tin'.

When Satan moves in with his cohorts of
    sin,
    Say, "You'll never find me a submit-
        tin' . . .
        You irk me, I find.
        So get thee behind.
    And please don't disturb me—I'm
        knittin'!"

In the middle of problems, the big ones
    and small,
    It's ALWAYS most proper and fittin'
        To trust and to pray
        Till the Lord shows the way—
    And go right ahead with your knit-
        tin'.
                           AUTHOR UNKNOWN

The Modern Grandma

The old rocking chair is empty today,
For Grandma is no longer in it.
She's off in her car to her office or
    shop,
And buzzes around every minute.

No one shoves Grandma someplace back
    on the shelf
For she's versatile, forceful, dynamic.
That's not a pie in the oven, my dear,
Her baking today is ceramic.

You won't see her trundling off early to
    bed,

From her place in a warm chimney
nook,
Her typewriter clickety-clacks thru the
night,
For Grandma is writing a book.

Grandma ne'er takes a look to the front
or the back
To suggest that her age is advancing.
She won't tend the babies for you any-
more,
For Grandma is taking up golfing.

She's not content with thinking old
thoughts,
With old-fashioned, second-hand knowledge;
Don't bring your mending for Grandma
to do,
For Grandma has gone back to college.

AUTHOR UNKNOWN

Patchwork Quilt

My grandmother's quilt
    was a royal affair,
Bright as her memory,
    soft as her hair.
Though patches were patterned
    like chords on a spinet,
There was more than color
    of calico in it.

The green-and-gold plaid
    was your Dad's kilted skirt;
He was wild as a colt,
    but handsome and pert.
The piece like a fire
    was a red flannel shirt.

The navy blue
    has a border of black—
I stitched it that way
    for your brave Uncle Jack—
He ran off to sea
    and never came back.

A shirtwaist of challis
    teen-agers won't wear—
But your grandfather liked it.
    He said at the fair
That my eyes were a match
    for the brown of his mare.

My grandmother's smile
    was honey on bread
As she hand-sewed gay patches
    and dreams with a thread.
She blinked back a tear;
    her head took a tilt.
"It's more like an album,"
    she said, "than a quilt."

LOUIS J. SANKER

The quickest way to be convinced that
spanking is unnecessary is to become a
grandparent.

Life

It's Spring—the tender, fragile blade
    Appears from out the frozen clay:
Reluctant, coy as if afraid
    To greet the cold and cheerless day.

It's Summer hour—the plant's in bloom
    Caressed and courted by the bee,
And gladdened by the sweet perfume
    The primrose sheds across the lea.

It's Autumn time—Hope's holy seed
    From drooping petals ripening fast,
Pride's trapping sheds upon the mead,
    Earth's grandeur gone—for now is
    past.

It's Winter bleak—the withered stem,
    Not mourning earthly hopes that
    flee,
But bears instead a diadem—
    The gems of immortality.

ELIZABETH GILES DONALDSON (age 83)

What a Grandmother Is

A grandmother is a lady who has no
children of her own, so she likes other
people's little girls. A grandfather is a
man grandmother. He goes for walks
with the boys and they talk about fishing
and tractors and like that.

Grandmas don't have to do anything
except be there. They're old, so they
shouldn't play hard or run. It is enough
if they drive us to the market where the
pretend horse is and have lots of dimes

ready. Or if they take us for walks, they should slow down past things like pretty leaves or caterpillars. They should never ever say "Hurry up."

Usually they are fat, but not too fat to tie kids' shoes. They wear glasses and funny underwear. They can take their teeth out and gums off.

It is better if they don't typewrite or play cards except with us. They don't have to be smart, only answer questions like why dogs hate cats and how come God isn't married. They don't talk baby talk like visitors do, because it is hard to understand. When they read to us they don't skip, or mind if it is the same story again.

Everybody should try to have one, especially if you don't have television, because grandmas are the only grown-ups who have got time.

By a nine-year old girl in the *Glendale News Press*

A *"Thank-You" Letter to Grandma*

Dear Grandma,
Mom said that I should be polite
And a well speld thank you letter
    write.
A "bread-and-butter note," but I
Would rather say "thanks" for the cho-
    clut pie!
And for your attatud when I played
    John Glen
And crashed my space ship in the den.
And I apprishiate that you diden't
    scold
When I broke that platter; I know I'm
    too old
To break things, but it happened so very
    quick'
(I wonder how waiters do that neat
    trick?)
Thank you for telling me about my
    Dad
And some of the axidents he had.
But I won't tell! I'll never say
"I know," when he asks why I act "that
    way."
Hope your head-ake is better—and let
    me know

When you're lonsum again—an I'll
    come,

> Love,
> Joe

RUTH BOWKER

Grandma, What's in There?

When I go to Grandma's house
    There's certain things to see,
The cuckoo clock, the push-button
    stove,
    Kitchen cupboards fascinate me.
Grandma has some special toys . . .
    She says they belonged to Dad . . .
A swing, a tractor, a pile of books . . .
    That he enjoyed as a lad.

LOIS BRUCE

Grandma

Grandma believes in the golden rule, but she also advocated a second maxim, her Iron Rule: "Don't do for others what they would not take the trouble to do for themselves."

The Christian Mother

Any grandmother can tell you what's new in people. And she has pictures to go with her wonderful story.

Herald, Azusa, California

One of the most influential handclasps is that of a grandchild around the finger of a grandparent.

High Bridge, N.J., *Gazette*

The old-time mother who used to wonder where her boy was now has a grandson who sometimes wonders where his mother is.

Grandmother's Apron

Grandma's garments made little impression on me as a child, except her apron. Its uses were unlimited. The apron made a basket when she gathered eggs, and if there were fluffy chicks to be carried to the back porch during a sudden cold spell, they made the trip peeping contentedly in Grandma's apron. When these same chicks grew to hens and hoed and pecked and scratched in Grandma's flowers, she merely flapped her apron at them and they ran squawking to the chicken yard. And I can see her yet tossing cracked corn to the hungry flock from her apron.

Lots of chips and kindling were needed to start fires in the big black range in Grandma's kitchen. Yes, she carried them in her apron. Lettuce, radishes, peas, string beans, carrots, apples and peaches all found their way to the kitchen in Grandma's "carry-all."

When she cooked, the apron made a handy holder for removing hot pans from the stove.

To men working in the field, the apron waved aloft was the signal "to come to dinner." At threshing time, Grandma hovered about a long table passing aromatic dishes and flipping the big apron at pesky flies.

When the children came to visit, the apron was ready to dry childish tears. If the little ones were shy, it made a good hiding place in case a stranger appeared unexpectedly.

The apron was used countless times to stroke a perspiring brow as Grandma bent over the hot wood stove or hoed the garden under a blistering sun. In chilly weather, Grandma wrapped the friendly apron around her arms when she hurried on an outside errand, or lingered at the door with a departing guest.

Hastily and a bit slyly the apron dusted tables and chairs when company was seen coming down the road. And in the evening when the day's work was done, Grandma shed her garment of many uses, and dropped it over the canary's cage!

AUTHOR UNKNOWN

FATHERS

Greetings to Dad

Best greetings to Dad
  On this, his day,
Who works for our good
  In every way.

He's gentle and kind,
  He's patient and true,
And he works with courage
  The whole day through.

There are battles each day
  That he must fight,
But he keeps his heart true
  And he stands for the right.

And then in the evening,
  His day's work aside,
He wends his way homeward
  The place of his pride.

And he knows there's a welcome
  All cozy within,
And that all in the family
  Are waiting for him.

Yes, we're proud of our dad,
  The others and me,
And we hope that all boys
  Will as fine someday be.

So, high honors to Dad
  On this his day,
Who helps, cheers and guides us
  Along the way.

ANN MORGAN

It's time to tell you, Father,
  I'm as proud as I can be
That when the dads were passed
  around,
  The best one came to me.

DOROTHY CONANT STROUD

On Father's Day

Send a card to Father
If he's far away;
Tell him you'll be thinking
Of him on Father's Day.

Tell him you remember
His patient, tireless teaching
And that his influence still guides,
Across the long miles reaching.

Tell him that you cherish
Fond memories of him
That neither time nor distance
Can ever change or dim.

Tell him that you understand
The battles fought for you,
Because you have the same to fight,
Since you're a parent, too.

Tell him you appreciate
The sacrifices made
And that your debt of gratitude
Can never be repaid.

Tell him that you realize
Since you have lived apart—
How large a place he always held
And still holds in your heart.

ELIZABETH LATHROP POWERS

Hats Off to Dad

Dear and good—dependable Dad,
　Always so steady and true;
A man of few words—he never says
　much
　Unless there is really need to.

Always the same—hard-working Dad,
　Plodding on day after day;
Thereby ready to meet all the bills
　That are ever around to pay.

He's really a patient, long-suffering
　Dad,
　Until he decides that the pranks
Have gone far enough, and then we
　know
　He is able to lay on the spanks.

You fill an important role, dear Dad,
　And we love you for all you do;
You seldom receive your due acclaim,
　So we're saying "hats off" to you!

Sunday School Banner

Just Like His Dad

"Well, what are you going to be, my
　boy,
　When you have reached manhood's
　years:
A doctor, a lawyer, or actor great,
　Moving throngs to laughter and
　tears?"
But he shook his head as he gave re-
　ply
　In a serious way he had:
"I don't think I care to be any of
　them;
　I want to be like my dad!"

He wants to be like his dad! You men,
　Did you ever think, as you pause,
That the boy who watches your every
　move
　Is building a set of laws?
He's molding a life you're a model for,
　And whether it's good or bad
Depends on the kind of example set
　To the boy who'd be like his dad.

Would you have him go everywhere you
　go?
　Have him do just the things you do?
And see everything that your eyes be-
　hold
　And woo all the gods you woo?
When you see the worship that shines in
　the eyes
　Of your lovable little lad,
Could you rest content if he gets his
　wish
　And grows to be like his dad?

It's a job that none but yourself can
　fill;
　It's a charge you must answer for;
It's a duty to show him the road to
　tread
　Ere he reaches his manhood's door;
It's a debt you owe for the greatest joy

In this old earth to be had;
This pleasure of having a boy to raise
Who wants to be like his dad!

AUTHOR UNKNOWN

My Daddy

My daddy is so strong and tall.
He lifts me to the ceiling.
He sets me on the garden wall,
Which makes a tickly feeling.

He works so very very hard,
To buy nice things for Mother.
And after dinner, in the yard
He plays with me and Brother.

When something breaks around our
    place,
He knows just how to fix it.
And if my toy lands in his face,
He never ever kicks it.

And when he spanks, he's never mean.
He loves his lass and laddy.
Of all the men I've ever seen,
I'm glad that this one's Daddy.

ALVEY E. FORD

Fun With Dad

Dad's going to take us fishing;
    He promised yesterday.
He knows the pools and shallows
    Where trout and catfish play;
He knows where plump blackberries
    Hang juicy-ripe today.
I'd rather go out fishing
    Than anything I know,
And tramp along the creek bank
    Where ferns and alders grow;
For even if the fish don't bite,
    It's dandy just to go!

MARJORIE HUNT PETTIT

The Ten Most Wanted Men

1. The man who puts God's business above any other business.
2. The man who brings his children to church rather than sends them.
3. The man who is willing to be a right example to every boy he meets.
4. The man who thinks more of his Sunday School class than he does of his Sunday sleep.
5. The man who measures his giving by what he has left rather than by the amount he gives.
6. The man who goes to church for his own sake rather than for the sake of the preacher.
7. The man who has a passion to help rather than to be helped.
8. The man who has a willing mind rather than a brilliant mind.
9. The man who can see his own faults before he sees the faults of others.
10. The man who is more concerned about winning souls for Christ than he is about winning worldly honor.

The American Holiness Journal

"Dad, I'm So Glad You Let the Field Wait"

A farmer had but one son. His conversion was the object of daily thought and prayer.

The time of camp meeting came before it was possible to finish the seeding. When the opening day came the farmer hitched up his wagon and invited the family to go to the camp meeting.

"But Dad," said the boy, "you aren't going to leave the field by the lane unseeded? It will never be in as good form again this season."

"The field will have to take its chances," said the father. "The meetings have first place."

During the meetings, the boy was converted. Less than a year later, he came down with a fatal illness. As the boy neared death's door, just before he slipped out into eternity, he put his arms around his father and drew him close. With a shining face the boy whispered, "Dad, I'm so glad you let the field wait."

GORDON R. UPTON

What Are Fathers Made Of?

A father is a thing that is forced to endure childbirth without an anesthetic.

A father is a thing that growls when it feels good ... and laughs very loud when it's scared half to death.

A father is sometimes accused of giving too much time to his business when the little ones are growing up.

That's partly fear, too.

Fathers are much more easily frightened than mothers.

A father never feels entirely worthy of the worship in a child's eyes.

He's never quite the hero his daughter thinks ... never quite the man his son believes him to be ... and this worries him, sometimes.

So he works too hard to try and smooth the rough places in the road for those of his own who will follow him.

A father is a thing that gets very angry when the first school grades aren't as good as he thinks they should be.

He scolds his son ... though he knows it's the teacher's fault.

A father is a thing that goes away to war, sometimes ...

And learns to swear and shoot and spit through his teeth and would run the other way except that this war is part of his only important job in life ... which is making the world better for his child than it has been for him.

Fathers grow old faster than people.

Because they, in other wars, have to stand at the train station and wave good-bye to the uniform that climbs aboard.

And while mothers can cry where it shows ...

Fathers have to stand there and beam outside ... and die inside.

Fathers have very stout hearts, so they have to be broken sometimes or no one would know what's inside.

Fathers are what give daughters away to other men who aren't nearly good enough ... so they can have grandchildren that are smarter than anybody's.

Fathers fight dragons ... almost daily.

They hurry away from the breakfast table.

Off to the arena which is sometimes called an office or a workshop ...

There, with calloused, practiced hands they tackle the dragon with three heads.

Weariness, Work, and Monotony.

And they never quite win the fight but they never give up.

Knights in shining armor ...

Fathers in shiny trousers ... there's little difference ...

As they march away to each workday.

Fathers make bets with insurance companies about who'll live the longest.

Though they know the odds they keep right on betting ...

Even as the odds get higher and higher ... they keep right on betting ... more and more.

And one day they lose.

But fathers enjoy an earthly immortality ... and the bet's paid off to the part of him he leaves behind.

I don't know ... where fathers go ... when they die.

But I've an idea that after a good rest ... wherever it is ... he won't be happy unless there's work to do.

He won't just sit on a cloud and wait for the girl he's loved and the children she bore ...

He'll be busy there, too ... repairing the stairs ... oiling the gates ... improving the streets ... smoothing the way.

PAUL HARVEY

Introspection

To get his goodnight kiss he stood
    Beside my chair one night
And raised an eager face to me,
    A face with love alight.

And as I gathered in my arms
    The son God gave to me,
I thanked the lad for being good,
    And hoped he'd always be.

His little arms crept 'round my neck,
    And then I heard him say
Four simple words I shan't forget—
    Four words that made me pray.

They turned a mirror on my soul,
    On secrets no one knew.

They startled me, I hear them yet;
He said, "I'll be like you."

HERBERT PARKER

By profession I am a soldier and take
pride in that fact, but I am prouder to
be a father. A soldier destroys in order
to build; the father never destroys. The
one has the potentialities of death; the
other embodies creation and life. And
while the hordes of death are mighty,
the battalions of life are mightier still. It
is my hope that my son, when I am
gone, will remember me not from the
battle, but in the home, repeating with
him our simple daily prayer, "Our Father Who art in Heaven . . ."

GENERAL DOUGLAS MACARTHUR

A Father Speaks

NOW

Of course he's sweet and precious
    And I'm proud to have a son
But I don't spend much time with him—
    You see, he's not yet one!

He's much too young to talk to,
    (Though experts don't agree),
And he's so small and fragile
    He almost frightens me.

I'll let his mother bring him up
    Until he's three or four:
I can't be bothered with him now,
    In fact, he's quite a bore!

IN FOUR YEARS

That son of mine is old enough
    To do things with his dad;
But he acts just like a stranger,
    What a disappointing lad!

I thought that when he'd grown a bit
    And walk and talk and learn,
I'd be the pal a father should
    And his devotion earn.

But now I see how wrong I've been
    He's grown away from me!
Oh fathers, listen! Watch your twig
    Before he becomes a tree!

AUTHOR UNKNOWN

A Father's Ten Commandments

BY MY EXAMPLE . . .

1. I shall teach my child respect for his fellow man.
2. I shall teach him good sportsmanship in work and play.
3. I shall instill in him an appreciation of religion and the family, the backbone of society.
4. I shall strive for companionship and mutual understanding.
5. I shall impart to him a desire to love and honor his country and obey its laws.
6. I shall encourage him to apply himself to difficult tasks.
7. I shall teach him the importance of participation in community affairs and local government.
8. I shall teach him self-reliance and help him develop an independent spirit.
9. I shall help him develop a sense of responsibility in planning for the future.
10. I shall, above all, prepare him for the duties and responsibilities of citizenship in a free society.

The Ten Commandments for Fathers

1. You shall so live as to transmit to your children physical bodies strong and clean.
2. You shall to the best of your abilities provide a satisfactory house, adequate clothing and necessary food for your family.
3. You shall be the head of the home and model it after God's law in love and justice.
4. You shall preserve the love between yourself and the mother of your children and promote love between them.
5. You shall not teach by precept alone but by personal example.
6. You shall seek to develop your child's potential to its greatest degree.
7. You shall provide and participate in recreational diversions and lead

the family in having fun and wholesome frolic.

8. You shall be the instigator and the leader in family worship daily, that your children may develop a relish for God's Word and a faith in the exercise of prayer.

9. You shall set the example by taking your wife and children to Sunday School and church regularly.

10. You shall make your primary objective the introduction of each child to Jesus, the Saviour, and thus fit him for life here and qualify him for life eternal and the reunion of the complete family circle in heaven.

RUSSELL V. DELONG

That Little Chap Who Follows Me

A careful man I ought to be;
A little fellow follows me.
I do not dare to go astray
For fear he'll go the selfsame way.

I cannot once escape his eyes;
Whate'er he sees me do he tries.
Like me he says he's going to be,
The little chap who follows me.

He thinks that I am good and fine,
Believes in every word of mine.
The base in me he must not see,
That little chap who follows me.

I must remember as I go
Through summer's sun and winter's snow,
I'm building for years to be—
That little chap who follows me.

AUTHOR UNKNOWN

Dad's Greatest Job

I may never be as clever as my neighbor down the street,
I may never be as wealthy as some other men I meet;
I may never have the glory that some other men have had,
But I've got to be successful as a little fellow's dad.

There are certain dreams I cherish that I'd like to see come true,
There are things I would accomplish ere my working time is through;
But the task my heart is set on is to guide a little lad
And to make myself successful as that little fellow's dad.

It is that one job I dream of; it's the task I think of most;
If I'd fail that growing youngster I'd have nothing else to boast;
For though wealth and fame I'd gather, all my future would be sad,
If I'd failed to be successful as that little fellow's dad.

I may never get earth's glory; I may never gather gold;
Men may count me as failure when my business life is told;
But if he who follows after is a Christian, I'll be glad—
For I'll know I've been successful as a little fellow's dad.

AUTHOR UNKNOWN

A Daddy's Prayer

Dear God, be good to him and take his hand
   Who never here was left one hour alone;
Being so young he will not understand
   A home so very different from his own;
And when the shadows fall let him kneel down
   Beside Your knee to say his evening prayers,
Then put on him his little woolen gown
   And lead him, as I used to, up the stairs.

And when he's tucked in bed kiss him goodnight;
   He knows an angel guards him night and day,
So he won't cry when You turn out the light
   And softly close his door and go away;

And then—oh, then, give courage to his
    dad!
You took him, God, and he was all I
    had.

                          T.E.B.

A Father Prays

Lord, who am I to teach the way
To this dear child from day to day
So prone myself to go astray?
I teach her power to will and do,
But in the teaching learn anew
My own great weakness through
    and through.

I teach her love for all mankind
And all God's creatures, but I find
My love comes lagging far behind.
Lord, if her guide I still must be,
Oh, may this child so dear to me
See I am leaning hard on Thee.

            LESLIE PINCKNEY HILL

When fathers are tongue-tied reli-
giously, need they wonder if their children's hearts remain sin-tied?

           CHARLES H. SPURGEON

When Father Prays

When father prays he doesn't use
    The words the preacher does;
There's different things for different
    days,
    But mostly it's for us.

When father prays the house is still,
    His voice is slow and deep.
We shut our eyes, the clock ticks loud,
    So quiet we must keep.

He prays that we may be good boys,
    And later on good men;
And then we squirm, and think we
    won't
    Have any quarrels again.

You'd never think, to look at Dad,
    He once had tempers, too.
I guess if father needs to pray,
    We youngsters surely do.

Sometimes the prayer gets very long
    And hard to understand,
And then I wiggle up quite close,
    And let him hold my hand.

I can't remember all of it,
    I'm little yet, you see;
But one thing I cannot forget,
    My father prays for me!

           AUTHOR UNKNOWN

A Father's Prayer

Dear God, my little boy of three
Has said his nightly prayer to Thee;
Before his eyes were closed in sleep
He asked that Thou his soul would
    keep;
And I, still kneeling at his bed,
My hand upon his tousled head,
Do ask, with deep humility,
That Thou, dear Lord, remember me.
Make me, kind Lord, a worthy dad,
That I may lead this little lad
In pathways ever fair and bright,
That I may keep his steps aright.
O God, his trust must never be
Destroyed or even marred by me.
So for the simple things he prayed
With childish voice so unafraid,
I, trembling, ask the same from Thee;
Dear Lord, kind Lord, remember me.

           Chicago Tribune

The Two Prayers

Last night my little boy confessed to
    me
Some childish wrong;
And kneeling at my knee,
He prayed with tears—
"Dear God, make me a man,
Like daddy—wise and strong;
I know You can."

Then while he slept,
I knelt beside his bed,
Confessed my sins,
And prayed with low-bowed head,
"Oh God, make me a child
Like my child here—
Pure, guileless,
Trusting thee with faith sincere.

           ANDREW GILLIES

A Father's Prayer

Build me a son, O Lord, who will be strong enough to know when he is weak —and brave enough to face himself in honest defeat, but humble and gentle in victory.

Build me a son whose wishes will not replace his actions—a son who will know Thee, and that to know himself is the foundation stone of knowledge.

Send him, I pray, not in the path of ease and comfort but in the stress and spur of difficulties and challenge. Here let him learn to stand up in the storm; here let him learn compassion for those who fail.

Build me a son whose heart will be clear, whose goal will be high—a son who will master himself before he seeks to master others; one who will learn to laugh, yet never forget how to weep; one who will reach into the future yet never forget the past.

And after all these things are his—this I pray—enough sense of humor that he may always be serious yet never take himself too seriously.

Give him humility so that he may always remember the simplicity of true greatness, the open mind of true wisdom, the meekness of true strength.

Then I, his father, will dare to whisper, "I have not lived in vain."

GENERAL DOUGLAS MACARTHUR

Letter to Dad

There are so many things I'd like
To tell you face to face;
I either lack the words or fail
To find the time or place.
But in this special letter, Dad,
You'll find, at least in part,
The feelings that the passing years
Have left within my heart.

The memories of childhood days
And all that you have done
To make our home a happy place
And growing up such fun.
I still recall the walks we took,
The games we often played;
Those confidential chats we had
While resting in the shade.

This letter comes to thank you, Dad,
For needed words of praise;
The counsel and the guidance, too,
That shaped my grown-up days.
No words of mine can tell you, Dad
The things I really feel;
But you must know my love for you
Is lasting, warm and real.

You made my world a better place
And through the coming years,
I'll keep these memories of you
As cherished souvenirs!

AUTHOR UNKNOWN

What Sort of a Father Are You?

What sort of a father are you to your
boy?
Do you know if your standing is
good?
Do you ever take stock of yourself and
check up
Your accounts with your boy as you
should:

Do you ever reflect on your conduct
with him?
Are you all that a father should be?
Do you send him away when you're anxi-
ous to read?
Or let him climb onto your knee?

Is a book more important to you than
his talk;
Do you find that his chatter an-
noys?
Would you rather be quiet than have
him about?
Do you send him away with his
toys?

Have you time to bestow on the boy
when he comes
With his question—to tell him the
truth?
Or do you neglect him and leave him
alone
To work out the problems of
youth?

Do you ever go walking with him in
hand?
Do you plan little outings for him?
Does he ever look forward to romping
with you,
Or are you eternally grim?

What memories pleasant of you will he
have
In the years that are certain to
come?
Will he look back on youth as a season
of joy,
Or an age that was woefully glum?

Come, father, reflect! Does he know you
today,
And do you know him as you
should?
Is gold so important to you that you
leave
It to chance that your boy will be
good?

Take stock of yourself and consider the
lad,
Your time and your thought are his
due;
How should you answer your God
should He ask;
"What sort of a father are you?"
AUTHOR UNKNOWN

A Father's Responsibility

This is the week set aside to salute
fathers. And it is good to have one day a
year to give special attention to the man
of the house.

The Bible has much to say to and
about fathers. It declares that his place
is one of headship in the family life. One
of the most influential areas in which he
exercises his divinely appointed leadership relates to rearing his children in the
"fear and admonition of the Lord."

Both parents are the representatives
of the Lord (Ephesians 6:1, Amplified
Version) and should be esteemed by the
children of the household. Honoring
one's parents is the Commandment that
promises prosperity and a long life,
taught both in the Old and New Testa-
ments.

One day after a meeting at which I
spoke, a mother and her tall teenage son
approached me. The mother said, "I am
so glad that you emphasized the biblical
teaching that children are to obey and
honor their parents." She had hardly
finished her sentence before the young
man said, "And I am glad you read the
Scripture, 'Fathers, do not irritate and
provoke your children to anger—do not
exasperate them to resentment—but rear
them [tenderly] in training and discipline and the counsel and admonition of
the Lord'" (Ephesians 6:4, Amplified
Version).

Discharging the privileged responsibility of parenthood is a tall order for any
man, and certainly calls for the full cooperation of you, the wife and mother.
Dealing with the complexities of childhood and teenage personality and the
problems of growing up in a world alien
to the Christian, is a task that can only
be accomplished with the help of an
omniscient God who gives insight and
the omnipotent God for whom nothing is
too hard. This God waits to be inquired
of and is ready to give unlimited help!

One of the sources for taking advantage of available help from God is to
gather the family together regularly for
worship. The name that we attach to this
spiritual exercise may be one of a number—family devotions, family quiet
time, family worship. It has been called
the family altar in some homes.

One night at a party the mother of the
home saw a boy looking around the living room in search of something. When
she inquired for what he was searching
he said, "Your son said you had a family
altar and I wanted to see what it looked
like."

It is not an easy task to bring all the
children together, especially the teenagers, in this day of diversified and individual activities. But have your family devotional period as often during the week
as possible, scheduling the time in advance, trying to accommodate everyone.
Hold to it, even though all cannot be
present occasionally.

The habit of family worship should be
started by the bride and groom before
the children arrive, and then continued

as a matter of course. If this was not done in your home in the beginning, begin now, no matter how long you have been married nor how old the children are.

The dividends accruing from such a spiritual exercise are inestimable. God indicates them to the Israelites in Deuteronomy 6:1-25 and means them for us in principle who are the Israelites by faith in Jesus Christ.

Perhaps for one of your family devotional periods you would be blessed by reading this portion of Scripture and discussing it. Make the matter of the content and conduct of your worship, the decision of the whole family if your children are old enough to participate. Involvement is more rewarding than spectatorship. Variety will be stimulating and add the element of expectation.

ANGELYN DANTUMA

Good Fathers

We need good fathers in our homes
  Whose hearts are full of grace,
Who by their love and earnest prayers
  Make home a pleasant place;

Who set examples that are clean
  For all their folks to see,
And long to be the noble men
  That God would have them be.

We need good fathers in the church
  To occupy the pews,
And help their fellow members seek
  The things they ought to choose;

Whose lives are such from day to day,
  Wherever they may go,
That others looking on may say,
  "The Lord they surely know."

We need good fathers o'er the land
  Who live and tell the truth
And have at heart along life's way
  The welfare of our youth;

Who want to keep our country free
  On ocean and on sod,
And help their fellows on their way
  To heaven and to God.

Such fathers then deserve our prayers,
  Our honor and respect,
And never should they suffer from
  Our spirit of neglect;

And by the living grace of God
  We ought to boost them on,
Until their battles all are fought
  And the glory's day shall dawn.

WALTER E. ISENHOUR

A Legacy

I, CHARLES LOUNSBURY, being of sound and disposing mind and memory (he lingered on the word memory), do now make and publish this my last will and testament, in order, as justly as I may, to distribute my interests in the world among succeeding men.

And first, that part of my interests which is known among men and recognized in the sheep-bound volumes of the law as my property, being inconsiderable and of none account, I make no account of in this my will.

My right to live, it being but a life estate, is not at my disposal, but these things excepted, all else in the world I now proceed to devise and bequeath.

ITEM: And first, I give to good fathers and mothers, but in trust for their children, nevertheless, all good little words of praise and all quaint pet names, and I charge said parents to use them justly, but generously, as the needs of their children shall require.

ITEM: I leave to children exclusively, but only for the life of their childhood, all and every the dandelions of the fields and the daisies thereof, with the right to play among them freely, according to the custom of children, warning them at the same time against the thistles. And I devise to children the yellow shores of creeks and the golden sands beneath the waters thereof, with the dragonflies that skim the surface of said waters, and the odors of the willows that dip into said waters, and the white clouds that float high over the giant trees.

And I leave to children the long, long days to be merry in, in a thousand ways, and the night and the moon and the train of the Milky Way to wonder at, but subject, nevertheless, to the right hereinafter given to lovers; and I give to each child the right to choose a star that shall be his, and I direct that the child's father shall tell him the name of it, in order that the child shall always remember the name of that star after he has learned and forgotten astronomy.

ITEM: I devise to boys jointly all the useful idle fields and commons where ball may be played, and all snow-clad hills where one may coast, and all streams and ponds where one may skate, to have and to hold the same for the period of their boyhood. And all meadows, with the clover blooms and butterflies thereof; and all woods, with their appurtenances of squirrels and whirring birds and echoes and strange noises; and all distant places which may be visited, together with the adventures there found, I do give said boys to be theirs. And I give to said boys each his own place at the fireside at night, with all pictures that may be seen in the burning wood or coal, to enjoy without let or hindrance and without any incumbrance of cares.

ITEM: To lovers I devise their imaginary world, with whatever they may need, as the stars of the sky, the red, red roses by the wall, the snow of the hawthorn, the sweet strains of music, or aught else they may desire to figure to each other the lastingness and beauty of their love.

ITEM: To young men jointly, being joined in a brave, mad crowd, I devise and bequeath all boisterous, inspiring sports of rivalry. I give to them the disdain of weakness and undaunted confidence in their own strength. Though they are rude and rough, I leave to them alone the power of making lasting friendships and of possessing companions, and to them exclusively I give all merry songs and brave choruses to sing, with smooth voices to troll them forth.

ITEM: And to those who are no longer children, or youths, or lovers, I leave memory, and I leave to them the volumes of the poems of Burns and Shakespeare, and of other poets, if there are others, to the end that they may live the old days over again freely and fully, without tithe or diminution; and to those who are no longer children, or youths, or lovers, I leave, too, the knowledge of what a rare, rare world it is.

WILLISTON FISH

My Dad

He couldn't speak before a crowd;
    He couldn't teach a class;
But when he came to Sunday School
    He brought the folks en masse.

He couldn't sing to save his life,
    In public couldn't pray;
But always his jalopy was just
    Crammed on each Lord's day.

And although he couldn't sing,
    Nor teach, nor lead in prayer,
He listened well, he had a smile,
    And he was always there

With all the others whom he brought
    Who lived both far and near—
And God's work prospered, for
    I had a consecrated dad.

AUTHOR UNKNOWN

PARENTS

Advice to Parents

1. Be loving to children.
2. Don't expect impossibilities of children.
3. Never deceive children.
4. Keep promises.
5. Correct shortcomings early.
6. Never exaggerate values of material things.
7. Do nothing or say nothing you would not want children to repeat.

8. Show no favoritism.
9. Make the house a home.
10. Establish a religious faith.

JULIUS MARK

Ten Commandments
For Modern Parents

I. Thou shalt look upon thy child, not as a possession belonging to thee, but as a sacred trust in God.
II. Thou shalt be honest in all dealings with thy child; then honesty and obedience can be expected of him.
III. Thou shalt regard thy child's respect and love, not as a duty to be demanded, but as an achievement to be earned.
IV. Remember when thou art out of patience with thy child's faults to take time to count then—of thine own.
V. Remember that the surest way to make it hard for thy child is to make it too easy for him. He should learn early the meaning of discipline and responsibility.
VI. Thou shalt have daily prayers and Bible reading with thy family, and thou shalt always thank God for food before partaking of it.
VII. Thou shalt early teach thy child to love and trust in God, and thou shalt wisely help him to choose Jesus Christ as his Lord and Saviour.
VIII. Remember that the example of thy life is more effective than thy fault-finding and moralizing.
IX. Thou shalt practice the teachings of Christ in thy home by being kind, unselfish and loving.
X. Remember the Sabbath Day by worshiping God in thy church as a family, for this is necessary if thy home is to be truly Christian.

GORDON H. SCHROEDER

If He Were Mine

I met a man and his heart was broken because his only son had come to noth-ing. He searched his soul, for he truly felt that the fault was all his own. In retrospect he sought to discover when, where, how he had failed his son. He never did learn the answer.

When his loving wife, the boy's mother, had passed into the shadows beyond, he had vowed to do everything possible for the son. He managed to send him off to the "proper" schools and to provide competent and intelligent tutors to guide him through his formative years. There is no doubt he gave his son everything any young boy's heart desired.

He worked hard, traveled widely and amassed a tidy fortune. This man had wealth, titles, prestige, respect; people humbled themselves before him. But son and father never did get to understand each other.

Is there any wonder the father never knew his own son? He never managed to take time off from his many duties to reach his boy spiritually. He never set aside a moment to reflect—what did the boy truly need? What were his hopes, his desires, his fears.

A boy needs perspective and parents' guidance, the opportunity to think for himself, to form his own opinions, to have someone listen to his views and correct him if necessary, to learn his own capabilities and accept responsibilities, to have respect for himself and to respect others, to be appreciated, to learn faith and discover God, to know what courage means and have the strength to carry on through periods of adversity. And what is more, before, beyond and above everything else, he needs the warmth and the comfort of parental love.

Ye parents hear what Jesus taught
When little ones to Him were brought;
  Forbid them not, but heed My plea
  And suffer them to come to Me.

Obey your Lord and let His truth
Be taught your children in their youth
  That they in church and school may dwell
  And learn their Savior's praise to tell.

For if you love Him as you ought,
To Christ your children will be
   brought.
  If thus you place them in His care,
  You and your household well shall
  fare.

LUDWIG HELMBOLD

What Every Parent Learns

He cleaned his room all by himself—
  There's that much to be said.
(The things that should be on the
  shelf
  Are underneath the bed.)

ELEANOR GRAHAM VANCE in Home Life

R For Parents

Take heart, even while you consider
  these days
  Perpetual clashes of wills;
Your child will outgrow his recalcitrant
  ways.
  Take heart—and vitamin pills!

MAY RICHSTONE

Prayer for All Parents

Great Parent of mankind,
Help me in my divine task of parenthood.

Help me to see my children's problems
  through their eyes.

Keep ever before me my own childhood
so that I will not expect too much.

Give me the patience of the silent
  stars.

Give me a sense of humor.

Help me to win them through love
instead of compelling them through
  fear.

Help me to teach them to see straight
and to play the game according to the
  rules.

Help me to teach them that every home
  is an altar
and that every wish is a prayer.

Help me to live my own life above
  doubt and skepticism.

Help me to radiate faith in the basic
  goodness of life.

Help me to keep the ideals of youth
  aglow in my own life.

Give me the strong hand for guidance
When youth falters and would turn
  back.

Help me to teach them to live bravely
and to meet defeat courageously.

Help me to teach them that a man's real
  character is
what he is when he is alone with himself in the dark.

Help me to teach them that the value of
  their lives
will be measured by the service they
  give.

Help me to teach them that true happiness is found,
not in things, but in the unfolding of
  their minds
and their souls.

Help me to make my life go on in theirs,
bigger, finer, nobler, than I ever dared to
  be.

AUTHOR UNKNOWN

Parents

Parents gather all your children,
To the altar in your home.
Daily follow His commandment
Teach them, that they may not roam.

Let not earthly cares and pleasures
Occupy your time and thought
Stay your mind upon Jehovah,
With a price you have been bought.

Therefore in your soul and body,
Glorify the Lord and show

In your home among your loved ones,
Whose you are and whom you know.

Oh, be earnest with your children.
Teach them daily God's sure word.
Pray with them, that they may know
    Him
As their Saviour and their Lord.
           Christian Home League

Sparents

Sparents are those
    That "spare the rod"
When offspring need
    Attention.
They find their troubles
    Multiplied
In ways too sad
    To mention!
        ALICE MARIE GRAVES

Prayer for Parents

Dear Heavenly Father,
Help us both to be good parents;
Let us love with a love that sees beyond
All selfish aim;
Help us learn to look to Thee each mo-
    ment of our lives
For guidance
In this great task which You have given
    us.
Lord, may we always feel it is not only a
    great task
But a wonderful privilege to be
A parent.

Help us to unite our hearts and our
    minds
In one common goal . . .
The good of our family and the good we
    may do
For others.
In so doing, help us remember that good
    does not
Always consist in
Giving all and requiring nothing.
Little oaks grow strong by standing
    alone
Against the wind.
So, dear Lord, help us think twice before
    making things

Too easy
For those You have entrusted to our
    care.

Help us laugh the genuine laugh of
Companionship
As we work and play with our chil-
    dren.
Let us be a part of their lives, yet
Not such a dominant part that we hin-
    der
Their growth.
Let us always take time to listen
To their hopes, their joys, and their trou-
    bles,
Knowing that sometimes all a child
    needs
Is just someone to listen
To him.

Help us not to talk
Too much
But to mean every word that we say.
    Let us keep
Each promise
For faith is so easily broken.
Above all, dear Father, help us keep our
    children
Close to You, and this
Not by our words, but by our daily liv-
    ing.
Keep our faith always strong
That theirs may be strong, also.

Give us wisdom, O Lord,
That we may teach them the joy
Of fair play
And of living both honestly and
    bravely
Even when the field
Is rough.
Help us teach them to love,
To be understanding, to be patient
    and
To be trustworthy.
Their lives will be judged by others, but
    let them be
Untroubled by what others may say.
Let them know that
When evening comes
If they can kneel and truly say,
"Lord, I bring this day to You, I've done
    my best,"
Then this is all
Anyone can ask.

Now, Lord, we must go and see that the
    children
Are all "tucked in" and sleeping peace-
    fully.
I don't know what else we should ask
    for,
But just let us do our best to be
The kind of parents
You
Want us to be,
Won't You, Lord?
Amen."

PHYLLIS MICHAEL

The Parents' Task

Give to your children a home wherein
Love's fires are lit and never grow dim.
A place where the children may always
    know
That they with their pleasures and trou-
    bles may go.
The place may be small with scanty
    board,
Or rich with the wealth of Croesus
    stored.
It matters not where the house may
    sit,
For the home is just what we make of it.

Help your child build a memory chest
Where all that is noble, all that is best,
Can be stored away for the time when he
Needs help and guidance away from
    thee . . .
Some time when he needs must stand
    alone,
When no longer little, not yet hardly
    grown . . .
When back to his memory chest he'll
    go,
And find there the things that he needs
    to know.

Teach him these truths lest he should
    fall:
That a loving Father is over all;
There's a time and a place for everything,
And virtue its own reward will bring;
That if he the flames of kindness would
    fan
He must live in peace with his fellow
    man;

That life must be lived both clean and
    pure,
And God will take care of the rest, I am
    sure.

AUTHOR UNKNOWN

A Parent's Thoughts

What can I give him.
These childhood days
To aid him in growing,
To remember always?

I can teach him compassion
For each helpless thing.
I can show him that kindness
Will make his heart sing.

I can give him the wisdom
To know right from wrong,
Instill in him pleasure
In laughter and song.

I can give him a love
That is deep as the sea,
But still leave him finally
Unfettered to me.

And when it is ended . . .
His childhood's span,
May my heart know with sureness
I've helped make a man.

VIRGINIA BLANCK MOORE

Whatever you write on the heart of a
    child
  No water can wash it away.
The sands may be shifted when billows
    are wild
  And the efforts of time may decay.
Some stories may perish, some songs be
    forgot,
  But this engraved record, time chang-
    eth it not.

Whatever you write in the heart of a
    child,
  A story of gladness or care
That heaven has blessed or that earth
    has defiled,
  Will linger unchangeable there.

Who writes it has sealed it forever and
 aye.
 He must answer to God on that great
 Judgment Day.

CLARENCE E. FLYNN

A Parent's Prayer

Heavenly Father, make me the parent
 Thou dost want me to be.
Give me poise, I pray, and self-
 control.
Make me sympathetic with my child and
 wise enough to understand him.
Allow me not, O Lord, to laugh at the
 mistakes my baby makes.
Help me listen patiently to all that he
 tries to say and always to answer his
 questions kindly.
Teach me to let my child create and
 play.
Lead me with him into the land of
 make-believe.
Help me to overlook the things that are
 unimportant.
Turn my eyes upon the good things that
 my baby does; not to condone the
 wrong but to direct him aright.
Teach me the power to praise, and show
 me how to celebrate my child's successes wisely.
Help me to teach him early self-
 control.
Give me the courage to say "No" as rarely as possible, but to be honest when I
 say it.
May my baby learn from me to be con-
 siderate of others and to grow up to be
 lovable and useful.
Help me to be humble in Thy sight, O
 Lord.
Give to us as parents and partners in
 marriage a constant mutual love and
 understanding.
Before our baby, make us both as one.
With all Thy gifts, O great Jehovah,
 make us worthy to be loved and imi-
 tated by our child.
In the Saviour's name I pray. Amen.

The Christian Parent

A Mother's and Father's Litany

To respect my children and in return
To be worthy of their respect—
 May Love and Understanding help me.
To praise much and blame little,
To emphasize their successes
And minimize their failures—
 *May Love and Understanding teach
 me.*
To make no promise to my children
That I cannot keep—
 May Love and Understanding help me.
To have unbounded faith in my chil-
 dren,
To be loyal to them both at home and
 abroad—
 May Love and Understanding lead me.
To allow them the dignity of their own
 personalities,
Not trying to make them over to my
 own desire—
 May Love and Understanding help me.
To care well for my children's bodies
But not at the expense of their minds
 and spirit—
 May Love and Understanding help me.
To be cheerful and ready to laugh
Because children love laughter as they
 love sunshine—
 May Love and Understanding help me.
To have infinite patience with my chil-
 dren,
And to make allowances for them,
Because they have so much to learn
And I myself am not so very wise—
 May Love and Understanding help me.
To protect my children from my own
 nerves,
Ill temper, personal prejudice, pessimism,
 and fears—
 May Love and Understanding lead me.
To help them to choose
The life work they are best fitted for,
Instead of gratifying through them
My personal ambition—
 May Love and Understanding lead me.
To reserve time and fresh energy for my
 children,
So that I can be their close and interested
 friend—
 May Love and Understanding help me.
To fit my children to meet life and peo-
 ple
Bravely, honestly and independently—

May Love and Understanding help me.
To give my children freedom, but
To teach them how to use that free-
     dom,
So they will not confuse liberty with
     license—
  *May Love and Understanding guide
     me.*
To show my warm love for my chil-
     dren
As well as conscientiously care for them—
  May Love and Understanding lead me.
To manage them with intelligence and
     affection,
And not by punishment, condemna-
     tion,
Fear, faultfinding, and nagging—
  May Love and Understanding help me.
To guide my children instead of driving
     them,
To direct their energy instead of repress-
     ing it—
To try to understand my children
Instead of sitting in judgment of them—
And through all misdemeanors both
     trivial and serious
To love them steadfastly—
  May Love and Understanding help me.

                GLADYS HUNTINGTON BEVANS

A Sacred Trust

Reach down your hand!
The little one who trudges by your
     side
Is striving hard to match your grown-up
     stride;
But oh! his feet are very tiny yet,
His arms so short—I pray you don't
     forget—
Reach down your hand!

Keep soft your voice!
For it was such a little while ago
This small one left the place where tones
     are low,
His ear still holds the cadence of that
     land
Where no one ever gave a stern com-
     mand.
Keep soft your voice.

Lift up your heart.

The little child you struggle so to
     teach
Has resource far above the human
     reach;
Lift up your heart.

                AUTHOR UNKNOWN

Lord Jesus Christ, our Lord most dear,
As thou wast once an infant here,
So give this child of thine, we pray,
Thy grace and blessing day by day.
Thy saving grace on him bestow
That he in thee may live and grow.

                LAUFENBERG

If being a Christian parent is a challenge to you—good! For no role or relationship planned of God for mankind is
of greater significance.

Find help to meet the challenge of
parenthood. Act upon this Scripture
promise:

If any one of you lacks wisdom, let
him ask God, who gives to everyone
without reserve and without faultfinding,
and it will be granted him. But ... ask
in faith. (James 1:5, 6, Berkeley Version).

In writing an essay a student in the
fourth grade wrote, "The trouble with
parents is that when we get them they
are so old that they are very hard to
change."

A young student of child psychology
gave a lecture titled: "Ten commandments for Parents." Then he married
and a year later became a father. He
altered the title of his lecture to "Ten
Hints for Parents." After his second child
arrived, he gave a lecture on "Some Suggestions for Parents." After the third
child arrived, he stopped lecturing!

An Appeal to Parents

Parents, I urge you to make the Bible
the sweetest, the dearest book to your
children. Not by compelling them to
read so many chapters each day, which
will have the effect of making them dis-

like the Bible, but by relaxing its pages with them, and by your tender parental love, so showing them the beauty of its wondrous incidents, from the story of Adam and Eve to the story of Bethlehem and Calvary, that no book, in the home will be so dear to your children as the Bible: and thus you will be strengthening their minds with the sublimest truths, storing their hearts with the purest love, and sinking deep in their souls solid principles of righteousness, whose divine stones no waves of temptation can ever move.

A.E. KITTRIDGE

Some Parents Say—

"We will not influence our children in making choices and decisions in matters of religion!"
WHY NOT?
The ads will!
The press will!
The radio will!
The TV will!
The movies will!
Their neighbors will!
Their business will!
Their politicians will!
We can use our influence over flowers, vegetables, cattle.
Shall we ignore our children?

AUTHOR UNKNOWN

Christian Parent

C heerful, courageous, a church-goer, converts others.
H opeful, honest, helpful, hospitable, humble.
R everent, responsible, righteous, reliable.
I ndustrious, informed, inspiring.
S incere, slow to anger, shares with others, serene.
T olerant, temperate, thankful, trustworthy.
I nstrument for good, increasing in grace.
A lert, appreciative.
N eighborly, never coveting or gossiping.

P atient, practical, participates in children's activities.
A ppreciative, affectionate, approachable.
R eligious, reasonable, relaxed.
E nthusiastic, even-tempered.
N eighborly, never breaks a promise.
T olerant, tactful, temperate in all things.

AUTHOR UNKNOWN

Recipe for Raising Children

Love—Oceans of it.
Self Respect—Give generous portions.
Cultural Advantages—Plenty of the best available.
Music ⎫
Laughter ⎬ Use generously for seasoning.
Play ⎭
Money—Scant and sparingly.
Religion—Use judiciously to thicken; makes the best foundation.

Parents

To babies they're handy
   For warming bottles,
They're dandy props for
   The tot that toddles.
For all birthday parties
   They're elementary,
At grammar grade programs,
   Most complimentary.
But when the years come
   That we call adolescent,
Most parents are found
   To be quite obsolescent.

LAURENCE C. SMITH

If (for Parents)

If you can stay the spanking hand
And truly say you understand;
If you can keep your savoir-faire
When your offspring's in your hair;
If you can quietly listen to
The cute things others' children do;
And when the neighbor's kids are naughty
And their parents cold and haughty
Blame your little "innocence,"

If you do not take offence;
And if you find you're in position
To keep a sunny disposition
When Junior's friends daub him with
    paint
—You're no parent—you're a saint!

ALICE DUCH

Resolutions for Parents

I will show my children daily that I love
    them—by what I say and what I
    do.
I will go regularly with my children to
    church, recognizing that religion
    will give us both strength and
    guidance in a family relationship.
At least once each day I will praise some-
    thing about my children and be
    wary of excessive criticism.
I will give my children freedom and pri-
    vacy and teach them the proper use
    of both.
I will listen to my children and make
    opportunities for them to talk with
    me—never being too busy.
I will keep our home usable for the
    children's activities, a place for hob-
    bies, storage for personal treasures,
    a ready welcome for their
    friends.
I will do those things with my children
    as well as for them: read, walk,
    picnic, sight-see, visit.
When I am tired and nervous, I will be
    extra careful before I speak.
I will recognize and respect my chil-
    dren's individual personalities and
    not expect them to be of the same
    pattern.
I will keep the promises I make to my
    children, and teach them to be de-
    pendable.

From The Christian Mother

My Baby

With dimpled cheeks and twinkle toes,
    With laughing eyes and turned up
    nose,
He's just as precious as can be.
    This tiny tot God gave to me.

Of all his charms I am aware,
    Yet they musn't blind me to take care,
As I assume a parent's role,
    To guide the future of his soul!

AUTHOR UNKNOWN

No parent should spend all his time in
the garden of a child's life digging up
weeds; there is always the danger of
scratching out flowers not yet above the
ground.

Recipe for having beautiful children:
be a beautiful parent!

ELBERT HUBBARD

The imprint of the parent remains
forever on the life of the child.

There is no friendship, no love, like
that of the parent for the child.

HENRY WARD BEECHER

A four-year-old daughter demanded
that her father read the story "The
Three Little Pigs" night after night. Finally the father tape-recorded the story.
When she asked for the story he switched
on the recorder.

This was fine for several nights. Then
one evening the little girl pushed the
story book at her father.

"Now honey," he said, "you know
how to turn on the recorder."

"Yes," she replied, "But I can't sit on
its lap."

Every child, regardless of age, longs
for relationships, not things. Yes, relationships with both parents—Daddy and
Mother.

Let every father and mother realize
that when their child is three years of
age, they have done more than half they
will ever do for its character.

HORACE BUSHNELL

Parents have a job that requires lots
of experience to perform and none at all
to get.

Parents are just baby-sitters for God.

Children live to bless the memory of a true parent.

Said a proud father, "Our baby was taking his first steps—faltering and uncertain. How proud and happy he was as he tottered across the room! His mother followed closely with outstretched arms, ready to catch him if he fell."

"I am not carrying him, nor am I hiding from him. My arms are so close to him that I can immediately catch him if he falls," said his mother.

Our heavenly Father is always near His faltering children. He is "within the shadows, keeping watch above His own." The eternal God is our refuge, and "underneath are the everlasting arms" (Deuteronomy 33:27).

WALTER B. KNIGHT

Young Ruth had wearied her father with questions. She asked the meaning of "transatlantic" and was told, "Across the Atlantic."

"Does 'trans' always mean across?"

"Yes!" was the retort.

"Then is 'transparent' a cross parent?" she asked meekly.

The Instructor

To understand your parents' love, you must raise children yourself.

Among those things which are so simple that even a child can operate them are parents.

I Take Thee, Young One,

to be my dearly beloved child—

I take thee to have:
  As my God-given trust and responsibility,
  This mortal parenthood my proud calling.

I take thee to hold:
  Close while you are small and helpless,
  Close as you grow—when my arms, eyes, ears,
  My hands, tongue and heart can give comfort,
    But with pliable heart strings, not apron strings.

I take thee for better:
  My life better for your being, the world lovelier,
  For pride in your growth, first steps, first words,
  Your unfolding talents and ideas;
    For joy, for fun, for friend and companion.

I take thee for worse:
  Whenever need be, not knowing now its shape.
  If it touch you as sore affliction
    I shall seek God's help to lighten it.
  If it engulf us in the dark of dispute
    I shall relight our path with affection.
  If it strike as calamity or disgrace
    I shall never forsake you.

I take thee for richer:
  Richer now, I endow thee with all my worldly goods—
  With food, clothing and shelter.
    More: my time, my inner self, a growing parent.
  With family as your rightful inheritance,
    Intact insofar as I can preserve it;
    Inviolable ties with loved ones,
    Pride in forbears, humble or mighty.
  With home, wherein to enjoy family and friends
    While retaining rights to solitude.
  With country to honor and serve,
    Yours its rich heritage and potential future.
  With a world of growing horizons and multitudes
    Awaiting your personal offering.
  With my respect for your individuality—
    Encouragement to do for yourself what you can do,
    Free will to choose one day your own life's work,

Your own life's partner, whom I
  shall welcome.
With loyalty, myself your steady advo-
  cate.
With reverence for our Creator,
  source of strength.

I take thee for poorer:
And count myself no martyr if I must
  sacrifice.
I dedicate my work to your outer
  needs,
My shared leisure to your inner yearn-
  ings—
  So you may learn the dignity of
  giving.

I take thee in sickness:
To nurse tenderly, guarding your
  physical safety
By my vigilance, foresight and instruc-
  tion,
Sparing you neglect always,
  Sparing you injury or harsh punish-
  ment.

I take thee in health:
Knowing health combines sound body,
  mind and soul.
I regard your body as your spirit's
  vessel,
  Teach you cleanliness and zest for
  healthful food.
I dissuade self-indulgence, encourage self-mastery
  Through balanced work, recreation
  and repose.
I respect learning, provide its atmosphere
  That you may seek an educated
  mind.

I further your skills, accept your
  limitations,
and put no kindred child before
  thee . . . or after.
I discipline you sensibly,
Guide you to moral and social values.
I arm you against the lure of false
  banners
  But welcome those who inspire you
  rightfully.
I explain life's processes as sacred
And foster the highest attributes of
  your sex,
I strive to model health's daily
  therapy:
  Praise for success, sympathy for
  failure,
  A cheerful voice and laughter within a happy home.
I observe all things about you
And keep them in my heart . . . as
  compass.

I take thee child:
Resolving to renew these vows de-
  voutly,
Reviewing my own values, lest they
  dim,
Expressing sorrow when I misjudge
  you,
Starting anew each time I fail.

In lieu of a ring:
I pledge you my fidelity with a ring of
  love
To encircle us both, woven of word
  and deed
And the shining thread of spirit.

                DOROTHY ROSE

FAMILY

Twelve Beatitudes for the Family

Blessed is the home where love abides
and friendship is a guest, for there
shall peace dwell all unafraid.

Blessed is the home where mutual trust
and confidence abide, for there shall
strength of character be fashioned.

Blessed is the home where sympathetic
understanding characterizes every attitude, for there shall healing of mind,
heart, and spirit occur.

Blessed is the home where each member
acknowledges and reverences the integrity of character inherent within the
personality of others, for there shall

full and abundant life be experienced.

Blessed is the home where each counts the other members of the family better than himself, for there shall jealousy and selfishness be erased.

Blessed is the home where each seeks to possess and employ the mind of Christ, for there shall great dreams be born and noble visions be encompassed by heroic effort.

Blessed is the home where each entertains charity of thought and intent toward all others, for therefrom shall the fragrance of good will issue for the blessing of all.

Blessed is the home which seeks daily to communicate with Him who is the Father of all men, for there shall great spiritual power reside for the encouragement and upbuilding of all others.

Blessed is the home which so saturates itself with Biblical truth that it constantly affirms, "Thy word is a lamp to my feet and a light to my path," for therefrom shall emanate light sufficient to direct others to moral and spiritual virility and victory.

Blessed is the home which seeks above all else to be the incubator not only of growing physique but also the generator of high dreams, noble visions, worthy aspirations, goodly ambitions, for therefrom shall come folk who can boast, "We are more than conquerors through Him who loved us."

Blessed is the home which seeks first the kingdom of God and His righteousness, for therefrom shall come lives dedicated to the high task of building God's realm of love and peace in the day that is now.

Blessed is the home that makes the teachings of the Church the guideposts for its daily pattern of life, for therefrom shall walk people full of Christ-

like compassion and rich in all the attributes of heaven.

WESLEY E. MCKELVEY
in *Together* magazine

Family

The family is a little book,
  The children are the leaves,
The parents are the cover that
  Protective beauty gives.

At first, the pages of the book
  Are blank, and smooth, and fair;
But time soon writeth memories,
  And painteth pictures there.

Love is the little golden clasp
  That bindeth up the trust;
O break it not, lest all the leaves
  Shall scatter and be lost.

AUTHOR UNKNOWN

Wanted

FATHERS like Abraham. "He will command his children and his household after him, and they shall keep the way of the Lord" (Genesis 18:19).

MOTHERS like Hannah. "As long as he [her son] liveth he shall be lent to the Lord" (I Samuel 1:28).

BOYS like Jesus. He returned with His parents to Nazareth, "and was subject unto them" (Luke 2:51).

GIRLS like the little maid who told her mistress that God could heal Naaman's leprosy (II Kings 5:1-3).

BROTHERS like Nehemiah and Hanani who served God together (Nehemiah 7:2).

SISTERS like Mary and Martha who received Jesus into their home and into their lives (Luke 10:38).

Ten Reasons for a Family Altar

1. It will sweeten home life and enrich home relationship as nothing else can.

2. It will dissolve all misunderstanding

and relieve all friction that may enter the home.

3. It will hold our boys and girls to the Christian ideal and determine their lasting welfare.

4. It will send us forth to our work for the day, in school, home, office, store, and factory, true to do our best and determined in what we do to glorify God.

5. It will give strength to meet bravely any disappointments and adversities as they come.

6. It will make us conscious through the day of the attending presence of a divine Friend and Helper.

7. It will hallow our friendship with our guests in the home.

8. It will reinforce the influence and work of the Church, the Sunday school, and agencies helping to establish the Christian ideal throughout the world.

9. It will encourage other homes to make a place for Christ and the Church.

10. It will honor our Father above and express our gratitude for His mercy and blessing.

Christian Digest

A Family's Prayer

O God, we pray that Thou wilt bless
This kitchen clean and light;
Fill it with loving thoughts and deeds
And sun to keep it bright;
We also pray that Thou, O God,
Wilt bless the lady fair
Whose gifted hands prepare our food
And worship thee in prayer.

CURT A. MUNDSTOCK

Family Prayer

In all the world there is no holier sight
Than families at prayer; mothers beside
Their children bowing down, and fathers, too,
The little ones who echo heaven here,
Whose joy is prayer; the tempted older ones,

Who hear clear calls to honor God in all
Their ways.
What joy is His to hear their pleas
For guidance from home's quiet altar place!
All families are dear to Him who once
Knew home's true love and kindly care, and joined,
A child and son himself, in family prayer.
"Thy kingdom come! Thy will be done!"
Were these
Prayers made in all earth's homes, each desert place
Would blossom as the rose; all hate would cease,
And his true peace untie men's hearts and hands.
But peace he gives to every home on earth
Where families in humble reverence pray,
"Thy kingdom come, Thy will be done each day."

NORMAN C. SCHLICHTER

The Message of Love

"My mommy understands me when I'm good, but not when I'm naughty."

"Mother, don't wash me so fast."

"Daddy, love me with your hands."

"Don't just say it with your mouth, Daddy. Say it with your eyes."

The above quotes are out of the mouths of babes. And little children may tell us more about ourselves and our homes than we realize.

Our love for our children is often hurried and too shallow for their needs. Have we sought to spare ourselves by turning our children over to modern conveniences and gadgets? Can we expect a TV set to give our child the personality God desires? Gadgets are wonderful things—but only things. Attitudes of consideration, warm compassion, sacrificial love and mercy, are not transmitted by gadgets. We may, by providing outwardly for every necessity, say we love our children, but our eyes betray us. Eyes that are worried, eyes that are narrow in impatient selfishness, eyes clouded over in thoughtlessness—these are the windows to our souls through which the child sees clearly what we really are!

WILSON B. FAGERBERG

Here are seven simple suggestions that have helped our family live together as a team:
1. Develop mutual respect for each member of the family.
2. Thoughtfully listen to each other.
3. Hold informal discussions where each member can express himself unafraid.
4. Get aside alone as husband and wife so that problems may be shared and appraised intimately.
5. Maintain a sense of humor to help lift morale in conflicting situations.
6. Keep in focus a sense of identity and purpose.
7. Attempt in some way at some time during the day to have family devotions together.

BLAISE LEVAI

Family Worship

Rear you an altar that will last forever:
Longer than any shaft or marble dome;
Erect it there beside your own hearthfire,
The chaste, white family altar in the home.
Chisel the Word of God upon the waiting
Hearts and minds of the dear ones gathered there—
The blowing sands of time will not erase it;
No friction dim the imprint of your prayer.

For memory will hold those chiseled letters,
And prayer shall be embedded in the heart.

O Father, Mother, rear that lasting altar,
And the children whom you love will not depart
From the way of life . . . The Word will last forever,
Though earth and heaven itself should pass away—
If you have not as yet begun the building
Of that eternal altar—start today!

Attributed to GRACE NOLL CROWELL

Family Ties

Family ties are precious things
  Woven through the years
Of memories of togetherness . . .
  Of laughter, love and tears.

Family ties are cherished things
  Forged in childhood days
By love of parents, deep and true,
  And sweet familiar ways.

Family ties are treasured things,
  And far though we may roam,
The tender bonds with those we love
  Still pull our hearts toward home.

VIRGINIA BLANCK MOORE

The Family

God bless the close-knit family
  Whose ties of love extend
Throughout the home in little ways
  And to each precious friend.

God bless the father who works hard
  To keep his family fed . . .
Who strives to give them spiritual
  As well as earthly bread.

God bless the mother who each day
  Labors from morn till night
To keep the home a welcome place,
  A clean and humble sight.

God bless the close-knit family
  Whose bonds of love extend
To each one in the home and
    then
  To each and every friend.
                    GEORGIA B. ADAMS

Stick-Together Families

The stick-together families
  Are happier by far
Than the brothers and sisters
  Who take separate highways
    are;
The gladdest people living
  Are the wholesome folks who
    make
A circle at the fireside
  That no power but death can
    break,
And the finest of conventions
  Ever held beneath the sun,
Are the little family gatherings
  When busy days are done.

There are some who seem to
    fancy
  That for gladness they must
    roam,
That for smiles that are the
    brightest,
  They must wander far from
    home.
That a strange friend is a true
    friend,
  And they travel far astray,
And they waste their lives in striv-
    ing
  For a joy that's far away.
But the gladdest sort of people
  When the busy day is done,
Are the brothers and the sisters
  Who together share their fun.

It's the stick-together family
  That wins the joy of earth,
That hears the sweetest music
  And that finds the finest mirth.
It's the old home roof that shelters
  All the charm that life can give,
And oh, weary wandering brother,
  If contentment you would win,
Come you back into the fireside,
  And be comrade with your kin.
                    AUTHOR UNKNOWN

Prayer for the Household

Lord, behold our family here assembled. We thank Thee for this place in which we dwell; for the love that unites us; for the peace accorded us this day; for the hope which we expect the morrow; for the health, the work, the food, and the bright skies, that make our lives delightful; for our friends in all parts of the earth, and our friendly helpers in this foreign isle.

Let peace abound in our small company. Purge out of every heart the lurking grudge. Give us grace and strength to forbear and to persevere. Offenders, give us the grace to accept and to forgive offenders. Forgetful ourselves, help us to bear cheerfully the forgetfulness of others.

Give us courage and gaiety and the quiet mind. Spare to us our friends, soften to us our enemies. Bless us, if it may be, in all our innocent endeavors. If it may not be, give us the strength to encounter that which is to come, that we be brave in peril, constant in tribulation, temperate in wrath and in all changes of fortune, and down to the gates of death, loyal and loving one to another.

As the clay to the potter, as the windmill to the wind, as children to their sire, we beseech of Thee this help and mercy for Christ's sake.

                    ROBERT LOUIS STEVENSON

All happy families resemble one another; every unhappy family is unhappy in its own fashion.

        LEO TOLSTOY, *Anna Karenina*

What Is a Family?

Take one husband, one wife, four walls, one small dog or stray cat; mix well; add a generous portion of time; and you are almost certain to have a family. The dog or cat isn't absolutely necessary for the recipe, but somehow or other it seems to give Mother Nature the right idea.

"Why just look at that!" she will say. "I can do better than *that* for them!"

The family always seems to start at exactly the wrong time. When the snow is the deepest or the hour the latest, the traffic the heaviest or the tires the flattest, the wife will whisper, "Honey, I think you'd better get the car ready." So the husband and wife become a family in an awesome, frightening, expensive, terrible hour of crisis, but Mother Nature, who is really in charge of the whole affair, just smiles and hums a tune. Families are her business and she knows it well—no fretting, no rush, the springtime of life for the ten billionth time . . . *There!*

"It's over!" sighs the husband.

"It's here!" thinks the wife.

"It's just begun," says Mother Nature.

The family, from Dad's point of view, could be the best collection of people in the whole world—a pretty and efficient wife, a highly intelligent son, an angel of a daughter, a well-behaved dog, and, of course, himself—very nearly handsome and with a real head for business. And how he works and slaves for them, never thinking of himself. Yet what does he usually see—a wife in pin curls, who didn't *mean* to forget to enter the check in the stubs; a freckled-faced mischief-maker who didn't *mean* to kick the football through Mr. McGonigal's greenhouse; a jeans-clad daughter, who didn't *mean* to burn the dinner (But, Daddy dear, I was talking on the telephone!); a miserable mongrel, who looks so sad and sorry, sitting in the middle of what used to be Dad's straw hat, a pooch with eyes that say, "But I didn't *mean* to—I was just playing catch-the-rabbit." If only the rest of the family could have a little of Dad's intelligence.

Mother comes to view her family with fatalistic resignation. No matter how she slaves at cleaning, cooking, washing, polishing, sewing, mending, or ironing, Dad will never notice it. To him, home is a place of loafing. Then there's Sonny. She spends her life starting him on the right path, and what does he do? Spends his Sunday school money for jelly beans. Sister, the one she has always felt so close to, has drifted away and started using lipstick and getting phone calls from strange boys. And that four-legged monster! He's tracked up her kitchen again. If only the family would appreciate all that Mother does for them.

Sonny thinks he has a keen family. He loves everybody in it, too. Of course, it would be nice if Dad were a little smarter. You know, able to make a kite that would fly instead of diving into the telephone wires. And tight! Getting a quarter out of Dad is harder than getting out of practicing the piano. Mom is an angel—but a strict angel. Do this, run here, stop that, pick it up, put it away—gosh! Sister? Well, she's better than most girls. A pretty good sport about those old gags with worms and frogs. Well, all right, she's pretty. Not so pretty as Hortense, of course. But what a dope about movie heroes and disc jockeys. She can't help it; all girls are dopey, even Hortense. Old Spot has the right idea—the heck with everything, run like crazy, and have a good time.

Sister is tenderly tolerant of her old-fashioned family. Dad is a lovable old man (he must be thirty-five at least)—a nice, fattish Daddy, who is so easy to persuade with a smile and a kiss. Mother is just a dear, but so far behind the times and so impossible every once in a while. Remake that old rag of a party dress indeed! It just can't be! I simply won't go to the party dressed like old Mother Hubbard. Sonny? Ugh! A person who would eavesdrop on a private telephone conversation has positively no sense of proprietariness. He and his dog. If Spot could walk on two legs, I'd rather have *him* take me to a dance.

What does Spot think of the family? We'll never know because he keeps it all to himself behind those big brown eyes. Most likely he has a better and truer view of the family than any of them.

When God made the family, He must have meditated a long time. The family must have food, shelter, and clothing, so there must be a father. He will also repair doorknobs, mow lawns, and stand on stepladders.

The family must have care, affection, and guidance, so there must be a mother. She will be in charge of shopping, spanking, praising, and worrying.

The family must not be dull or tiresome, so there must be a boy to shout, jump, run, get in the way, and hang by his knees from trees.

The next family must not be forgotten, so there must be a little girl, an angel who will love them, bewilder them, and make them so very, very proud.

So all are accounted for except poor old Spot. How did he get in the family? Most of us might say that Spot just happened along, liked the free meals, and decided to stay. But perhaps he was *intended* to become a member of the family. His job? Well, maybe it is to be a constant example of love and devotion for all the others.

The family is a storehouse in which the world's finest treasures are kept. Yet the only gold you'll find is golden laughter. The only silver is in the graying hair of Dad and Mom. The family's only real diamond is on Mother's left hand; yet can it sparkle like the eyes of the children at Christmas or shine half as bright as the candles on a birthday cake? The mines of the earth yield no sapphires or rubies so precious as a baby's smile when it sleeps or a child's prayer at bedtime: "God bless Mommy and Daddy and Brother and me."

The small pleasures, the great sorrows, the hopes, the loves, the dreams of the world are contained within these four walls called Home. Though you may search the far corners of the world for your heart's desire, you'll find that if it's worth having at all, it has been right at home all the time—right at home with the family.

ALAN BECK

The church is not a convention to which a family should send a delegate.

The most thrilling sight a minister sees from the pulpit is a whole family sitting together in a pew.

EDWIN C. HOUK

The family is ultimately responsible for personal faith.

The Success Family

The Father of Sucess is—Work. The Mother of Success is Ambition. The eldest son is Common Sense. Some of the older boys are Perseverance, Honesty, Thoroughness, Foresight, Enthusiasm, Cooperation. The eldest daughter is Character. Some of the sisters are, Cheerfulness, Loyalty, Courtesy, Care, Economy, Sincerity. The baby is, Opportunity.

Get acquainted with the Father and you will be able to get along pretty well with the rest of the family.

The family circle is the supreme conductor of Christianity.

HENRY DRUMMOND

The family that prays together stays together.

The family is the nucleus of civilization.

WILL DURANT

True family worship is a vase of perfume that sheds fragrance over all. It softens harshness; it quells anger; it quiets impatience; it settles differences; it subdues evil passions. Hearts that are drawn together at God's feet every day cannot wander far apart. The altar in the midst wonderfully hallows and sweetens the home fellowship. It smooths out the wrinkles of care. It keeps the fire burning on every heart's altar.

The Sunday school with a solid foundation, one that will grow steadily, must be built with families. Let's aim for them!

A family jar is no good for preserving the peace!

A family will hold together across the years if each member refrains from pointing the accusing finger.

JOHN MILLER

Count me as a firm believer in the family altar. I am thoroughly convinced that a wide-spread return to the practice of regular worship in the home would work miracles in meeting the many critical problems of modern life. Let the family altar become the center around which life revolves and we will regain the spiritual resources so badly needed.

LUTHER W. YOUNGDAHL

The average person can get a big laugh out of the family album, and then look into a mirror without a smile.

HOME

What Is a Good Home?

I have come to have a deep and abiding appreciation for those fathers and mothers who strive valiantly to create a good home for their children.

And what is a "good" home?

I am sure that everyone who has had the priceless experience of being reared in such a home has his own personalized image of it. For him, the past conjures up beloved memories. The mirror of his mind reflects simple things—perhaps a fireplace, the odor of cinnamon rolls and fresh baked bread, tall shelves with books. And the strand of each loved memory of childhood traced back further still, becomes indissolubly entwined with the memory of the man and woman who made that house a home.

The longer I live the more certain I become that material things—the architecture and the furnishings—mean little in the creation of a true home. The essential items are intangible—love, sympathy, understanding, encouragement, and faith.

An English clergyman of another century said:

"Six things are requisite to create a 'happy home.' Integrity must be the architect, and tidiness the upholsterer. It must be warmed by affection, lighted up with cheerfulness; and industry must be the ventilator, renewing the atmosphere and bringing in fresh salubrity day by day; while over all, as a protecting canopy and glory, nothing will suffice except the blessing of God."

I believe that a good home, as a place for living, should be comfortable. I think it should be adequate in size and in appearance. But these are externals and a truly good home can exist in the absence of these desirable items.

The good home does not have its source in material things. Its roots are to be found in fixed principle and in morality, both of which stem solely from the spiritual. The good home is a place of learning in which example is the teacher and the values taught are sound. The good home is a place of discipline leavened with affection. It is a place of good faith and understanding. It is a place in which the priceless attributes of living are taken for granted because they are solely given.

What is the test of a good home?

I know of none except that to be found in after years in memories marked with love and gratitude.

J. EDGAR HOOVER

Home

I try to make my home
  A place that's beautiful to see,
To fill each room with lovely things
  And perfect harmony,
To polish up the copper pots,
  The silver and the brass,
And rub the walnut table
  Till it gleams like crystal glass.

But home is not mere furniture . . .
  The objects we see here
Are visible expressions
  Of a wonderful idea,
A power that draws with ties of love
  Wherever we may roam
The center of the universe,
  And of the heart . . . the home.
                    PATIENCE STRONG

Hymn for a Household

Lord Christ, beneath Thy starry dome
We light this flickering torch of home,
And where bewildering shadows throng
Uplift our prayer and evensong.

Dost Thou, with heaven in Thy ken,
Seek still a dwelling-place with men,
Wandering the world in ceaseless
    quest,
O Man of Nazareth, be our guest!

Lord Christ, the bird his nest has
    found,
The fox is sheltered in the ground,
But dost Thou still this dark earth
    tread
And have no place to lay Thy head?

Shepherd of mortals, here behold
A little flock, a wayside fold
That wait Thy presence to be blest—
O Man of Nazareth, be our guest!
                    DANIEL HENDERSON

Home and Mother

How precious are life's memories
  I treasure and recall;
But "home" and "mother" are the two
  That blessed me most of all.

Though home was just a humble shack
  I thanked God much in prayer;
For it was like a palace, grand;
  With darling mother there!

Our Bible was like one of us,
  And never would we eat
Until we thanked the Lord in prayer
  For blessings dear and sweet.

Mom helped me polish all my dreams,
  And when they'd fade with wear
She'd help me build them once again—
  My "castles in the air."

She'd kiss away each tear and hurt,
  And love me like a pup;
Then worry when I wasn't home,
  And always would wait up.

Then later on when years had passed
  I found that time stood still
'Cause mother's children all stay kids,
  Just like they always will.

Yes, "home" and "mother" are sweet
    notes
  That form a sacred tune;
And when God calls I'll smile 'cause
    I'll
  Be home with mother soon!
                    LES COX

What a Home Is

A world of strife shut out, a world of
    love shut in.
The place where the small are great and
    the great are small.
The father's kingdom, the mother's
    world, and the child's paradise.
The place where we grumble the most
    and are treated the best.
The center of our affection around
    which our heart's best wishes
    twine.
The place where our stomachs get three
    square meals daily, and our hearts a
    thousand.
The only place on earth where the faults
    and failings of humanity are hidden
    under the sweet mantle of char-
    ity.
                    AUTHOR UNKNOWN

That Is a Christian Home

Where family prayer is daily said,
God's word is regularly read,
And faith in Christ is never dead,
    That is a Christian home.

Where father, mother, sister, brother,
All have true love for one another
And no one ever hates the other,
    That is a Christian home.

Where family quarrels are pushed
    aside
To let the love of God abide
Ere darkness falls on eventide,
    That is a Christian home.

Where joy and happiness prevail
In every heart without a fail
And thoughts to God on high set sail,
    That is a Christian home.

Where Jesus Christ is Host and Guest,
Through whom we have eternal rest
And in Him are forever blest,
    That is a Christian home.

            The Bible Institute of Los Angeles

The Christian Home

How God must love a friendly home
Which has a warming smile
To welcome everyone who comes
To bide a little while!

How God must love a happy home
Where song and laughter show
Hearts full of joyous certainty
That life means ways to grow!

How God must love a loyal home
Serenely sound and sure!
When troubles come to those within,
They still can feel secure.

How God must love a Christian home
Where faith and love attest
That every moment, every hour,
He is the honored Guest!

            GAIL BROOKS BURKET

A Prayer for a Little Home

God send us a little home,
To come back to when we roam—
Low walls and fluted tiles;
Wide windows, a view for miles;
Red firelight and deep chairs;
Small white beds upstairs;
Great talk in little nooks,
Dim colors, rows of books;
One picture on each wall;
Not many things at all.
God send us a little ground—
Tall trees standing round,
Homely flowers in brown sod,
Overhead Thy stars, O God!
God bless, when winds blow,
Our home and all we know.
            FLORENCE BONE

So Long As We Have Homes

So long as we have homes to which men
    turn
    At the close of day,
So long as we have homes where chil-
    dren are
    And women stay,
If love and loyalty and faith be found
    Across these sills,
A stricken nation can recover from
    Its gravest ill,
So long as we have homes where fires
    burn
    And there is bread,
So long as we have homes where lamps
    are lit
    And prayers are said,
Altho a people falter thru the dark
    And nations grope,
With GOD, Himself, back of these little
    homes,
    We still have hope.
            GRACE NOLL CROWELL

Every Home a Kingdom

The Christian home is a sphere where
love rules but where proper discipline is
maintained.

It takes more than beautiful walls and
comfortable furniture to make a home.
To grow up in a home where Christ is

known, loved, honored and recognized daily in consistent living means more than wealth or fame.

The Christian home is an abode where the family dwells together in love and harmony, each delighting in the company of the others and seeking the good of all. Such a place cannot be maintained without the Bible, prayer, praise, playing, and planning together.

There is more to having a Christian home than having all members Christian. It's "togetherness" at the Christian level that makes a home Christian.

No home can be Christian until Christ has been invited, received, and made central in the thinking and actions of the family.

Every Christian does not have a Christian home, but if he remembers to be a Christian even when his home is not, his testimony before other members of the family is the greatest sermon they will ever hear. His life becomes a wedge for Christ and eternity or a block between the family and Christ.

It takes effort to have a Christian home. True happiness doesn't just happen. It takes planning and leadership to make the right things happen. The results of selfishness and laziness are costly, both here and hereafter.

God intends every man to be a king, his wife a queen, every child a prince or princess with their home as their kingdom.

May God grant that every king and queen, and every prince and princess, will thoughtfully determine and assume his rightful share of the responsibility to make his kingdom a real Christian home.

CLATE A. RISLEY

Keeping House

"Keeping House" some lightly call it.
"Keeping Home" I'd rather hear,
Since against what may befall it
Love must guard it, year by year.
It must keep it gay with laughter,
And with comradeship and song,
And with faith for what comes after,
Since no joy can last for long.

"Keeping Home" needs patient labor,
And a woman's lovely skill;
Needs the art of being a neighbor
When someone nearby is ill.
"Keeping House" is done by others
With the strength that money hires.
"Keeping Home" needs dads and mothers
Whose devotion never tires.

Lest its growing youth forsake it,
Love must keep it warm and bright,
And a safe, sure haven make it,
Where all things are set aright.
"Keeping House" means sweeping, dusting.
It is listed as a trade,
But by stout hearts and by trusting—
The enduring Home is made.

EDGAR A. GUEST

Home

Two birds within one nest;
Two hearts within one breast;
Two spirits in one fair,
Firm league of love and prayer,
Together   bound   for   aye,   together blest.

An ear that waits to catch
A hand upon the latch;
A step that hastens its sweet rest to win;
A world of care without,
A world of strife shut out;
A world of love shut in.

DORA GREENWELL

For the only happy toilers under earth's majestic dome
Are the ones who find their glories in the little spot called "home."

VALLI ROSE

Our Home

May our home be a haven
Of peace
And contentment,
Knowing laughter
And love

Without strife;
May our home be a harbor
Where we find
New courage
To sail
The sea
Of life.

PHYLLIS C. MICHAEL

Home Lights

I love the autumn twilight
When the dusk grows ever deep:
The first sweet breath of evening
Lulls the birds and flowers to sleep.

The home-lights in the valley,
On the hilltop, on the plain,
Shine out in friendly welcome
Leading footsteps home again.

Each cheery light that flickers
Through the darkness and the gloam
Conveys a tender meaning,
For someone calls it home—

A place where joys and sorrows blend,
A home like yours and mine,
With youthful voices ringing
And a mother's smile divine.

In the quiet of the evening
I watch each light that gleams,
And think of all the human hearts
That surge with hopes and dreams.

Each has his own ambitions,
His loves, his work and play;
And every light is made to shine
Each in a different way.

INEZ CULVER CORBIN

Bless This House

Bless this house, O Lord, we pray,
    Make it safe by night and day;
Bless these walls, so firm and stout,
    Keeping want and trouble out;
Bless the roof and chimneys tall,
    Let thy peace lie over all;
Bless this door, that it may prove
    Ever open to joy and love.

HELEN TAYLOR

Winter Nights at Home

A stretch of hill and valley, swathed
    thick in robes of white,
    The buildings blots of blackness, the
    windows gems of light;
The moon, now clear, now hidden, as in
    its headlong race
    The north wind drags the cloud-wrack
    in tatters o'er its face;
Mailed twigs that click and clatter upon
    the tossing tree,
    And, like a giant's chanting, the deep
    voice of the sea;
As mid the stranded ice-cakes the burst-
    ing breakers foam,
    Comes the familiar picture—a winter
    night at home.

The old familiar picture—the firelight
    rich and red,
    The lamplight soft and mellow, the
    shadowed beams o'erhead;
And Father with his paper, and Mother,
    calm and sweet,
    Mending the red yarn stockings
    stubbed through by careless feet.
The little attic bedroom, the window
    'neath the eaves,
    Decked by the Frost King's brushes
    with silvered sprays and leaves;
The rattling sash which gossips with idle
    gusts that roam
    About the ice-fringed gables—on win-
    ter nights at home.

JOSEPH C. LINCOLN

At Home

Adventure and travel haunt my
    dreams
And foreign names have magic glow—
Zanzibar and Mandalay
And where the trade winds blow.

So I set off when gypsy blood
Wells up and urges me to start,
I wander on and on until
Homesickness strikes my heart.

World travel has its golden days
And it is nice at times to roam,
But far the best part of adventure:
Return to Home Sweet Home.

DAWN FLANERY PARKER

Home

Beneath the roof of your own home
May love and happiness abound.
Let laughter ring within its walls,
And all feel comradeship's close tie.
Let little ones express their joys
In merry songs and romping play.
May hospitality be shared
To cheer the hearts of many friends.
Teach love of God and country too,
And in the quiet evening hours
Repose beside your warm hearth fire
To read or chat or just to dream . . .
Forgetting all the worldly cares,
Enjoy the peace and love of home.

GENEVIEVE BRUNSON

Happiness

Happiness has many houses
And dwells in many places;
It lives in many moments
And shines in many faces.

It laughs with little children
Whose hearts are free from pride,
It seeks a sunny meadow
Or a quiet fireside.

It haunts the house of service
And knows the place of prayer;
Where broken hearts are mended,
Happiness is there.

Happiness has many houses,
But mostly it will come
Where faith and love are living,
Where God can make His home.

AUTHOR UNKNOWN

The Sweetest Home

The sweetest home is a little home,
    With a dear little mother in it;
And if in your heart there's a little
        song
    For the mother you love, begin it;
For this is her hour and this her day,
    Though she's living afar or near
        you;
In a mansion fair or a shack out
        there,
    The mother you love will hear you!

The sweetest home is a quiet home,
    With a peace that a mother wills it;
And you're still her child, though you're
        far away,
    For she holds to your heart and fills
        it
With the memories of a time gone by
    When you whispered the prayers she
        taught you;
And she can't forget, though her eyes be
        wet,
    How great was the price that bought
        you.

The sweetest home is a God-blest
        home
    That rests near a humble by-way,
And always the fairest one within
    Is a mother who shuns the highway
Where evil struts in a robe of red,
    Where devilish imps will call you.
Go back to her knee, to her warm arms
        flee,
    And never shall ill befall you!

AUTHOR UNKNOWN

A Home Song

I read within a poet's book
    A word that starred the page:
"Stone walls do not a prison make,
    Nor iron bars a cage!"

Yes, that is true; and something more
    You'll find, where'er you roam,
That marble floors and gilded walls
    Can never make a home.

But every house where Love abides,
    And Friendship is a guest,
Is surely home, and home-sweet-home,
    For there the heart can rest.

HENRY VAN DYKE

If they (the children) have the background of a godly, happy home and this unshakable faith that the Bible is indeed the Word of God, they will have a foundation that the forces of hell cannot shake.

MRS. BILLY GRAHAM

The father is the head of the house,
The mother is the heart of the house.

It takes a heap o' livin' in a house t'
    make it home,
A heap o' sun an' shadder, an' ye some-
    time have t' roam
Afore ye really 'preciate the things ye
    lef' behind,
An' hunger fer 'em somehow with 'em
    allus on yer mind.

        EDGAR A. GUEST, Home

Let me live in my house by the side of
    the road
    Where the race of men go by;
They are good, they are bad, they are
    weak, they are strong,
    Wise, foolish—so am I.
Then why should I sit in the scorner's
    seat,
    Or hurl the cynic's ban?
Let me live in my house by the side of
    the road
    And be a friend to man.

            SAM WALTER FOSS,
    The House by the Side of the Road

Home Influence

The power of a home shown.
It never lets go its hold.
A mother has often reeled in a boy by
    the line of love,
And a father's memory has brought
    many back.

        HENRY WARD BEECHER

The lights of home . . . they bring us
    A sense of warmth and peace.
They promise untold loveliness,
    Rest, laughter and release.

They are like hands that beckon us,
    Like arms that draw us near . . .
The lights of home! They whisper
    words
    Of comfort and good cheer.

        AUTHOR UNKNOWN

Home Blessings Radiated

Oftentimes it is the case that a person
can do work as a candle does, which
gives light to all that are in the room,
but, not stopping there, throws light
through the window and along the road
as well. What mothers and fathers do in
their homes may be reflected far beyond
the human sphere to which they are
confined, and bless many others besides
their own families.

        HENRY WARD BEECHER

Children need a spiritual example set
in the home. All too often parents take
their children to Sunday school but never set the example by going themselves.
One of the greatest insurances against
juvenile delinquency is faithful church
attendance.

        BILLY GRAHAM

What Makes a Home?

"What makes a home?"
I asked my little boy.
And this is what he said,
"You, Mother,
And when Father comes,
Our table set all shiny,
And my bed,
And, Mother, I think it's home,
Because we love each other."
You who are old and wise,
What would you say
If you were asked the question?
Tell me, pray.
Thus simply as a little child, we learn
A home is made from love,
Warm as the golden hearthfire on the
    floor,
A table and a lamp for light,
And smooth white beds at night—
Only the old sweet fundamental things.
And long ago I learned—
Home may be near, home may be far,
But it is anywhere that love
And a few plain household treasures are.

        AUTHOR UNKNOWN

Home

God's mercy spread the sheltering roof;
Let faith make firm the floor.
May friend and stranger, all who come,

Find love within the door.
May peace enfold each sleeping place,
And health surround the board.

From all the lamps that light the halls
Be radiant joy outpoured.
Let kindness keep the hearth aglow,
And through the windows shine;
Be Christ-like living, on the walls
The pattern and design.

T. L. PAINE

A Prayer for Our Homes

God give us homes!
Homes where the Bible is honored and
taught:
Homes with the Spirit of Christ in their
thought:
Homes that a likeness to heaven have
caught.
God give us homes!

God give us homes!
Homes with the father in priest-like em-
ploy;
Homes that are bright with a far-
reaching joy;
Homes where no world-stain shall come
to annoy.
God give us homes!

God give us homes!
Homes where the mother is queen-like in
love;
Ruled in the fear of the Saviour
above;
Homes that to youth most inspiring
shall prove.
God give us homes!

God give us homes!
Homes with the children to brighten the
hours;
Budding and blooming like beautiful
flowers
Places of sunshine—sweet, sanctified
bowers.
God give us homes!

The Prophetic Witness

Bless This Home

Bless this home, O Lord, we pray,
Guard it safely night and day.
Bless the family living here;
Bind them close with love and cheer.

Bless the food which is prepared,
And each guest with whom it's shared.
Bless the children through the years,
Guide them in their joys and tears.

Bless the mother—tender, kind—
And the father by her side;
Bless their pure and faithful love
Making home like heaven above.

Bless this home, O Lord, we pray,
Where we live and work and play.
Bless us all that ever we
May live, O Lord, with Thee.

AUTHOR UNKNOWN

Motto for Every Home

Who'er thou art that entereth here,
Forget the struggling world
And every trembling fear.

Take from thy heart each evil thought,
And all that selfishness
Within thy life has wrought.

For once inside this place thou'lt find
No barter, servant's fear,
Nor master's voice unkind.

Here all are kin of God above—
Thou, too, dear heart: and here
The rule of life is love.

AUTHOR UNKNOWN

A Home Without a Bible

What is a home without a Bible?
'Tis a place where day is night,
Starless night; for o'er life's pathway
Heaven can shed no kindly light.

What is home without a Bible?
'Tis a place where daily bread
For the body is provided,
But the soul is never fed.

What is home without a Bible?
  'Tis a vessel out at sea,
Compass lost and rudder broken,
  Drifting, drifting, aimlessly.

What is home without a Bible?
  Listen, ponder, while I speak:
'Tis a home with Bibles in it,
  But not opened once a week!

Monday comes and goes, and Tuesday
  Comes and goes, and Wednesday, too;
Thursday, Friday, Saturday, Sunday,
  Book unopened all week through!
                League Echoes

In the quiet home-life, showing love's
    bright ray,
More and more like Jesus living every
    day,
We may guide a dear one to the heaven-
    ward way
By the things we practice, by the words
    we say!
                AUTHOR UNKNOWN

Joys of Home

Curling smoke from a chimney low,
And only a few more steps to go.
Faces pressed at a window pane
Watching for someone to come again.
And I am the someone they want to
    see—
These are the joys life gives to me.
So let me come home at night and
    rest
With those who know I've done my
    best;
Let the wife rejoice and children
    smile,
Showing by their love that I'm worth-
    while.
For this is conquest and world success—
A home where abideth happiness.
                EDGAR A. GUEST

The New House

"I don't like our old house,
  It's not nice any more,"
I told Mother one day

When we went to the store.
"Wish we had a new house
Like the Jones family has;
It is made of red brick,
And the door is all glass."
Mother said, "Ruthie dear,
Their house is nice and new,
But God gave us some things
That the Jones never knew.
They have no boys or girls
And are often so sad.
Let's be happy for them
If their house makes them glad."
                AUTHOR UNKNOWN

Blessings 'Round My Door

Dear Lord,
I thank Thee for my friendly home,
Simple though it be;
I thank Thee for the cool, green grass,
And for the spreading tree;
For many days with sunny skies,
And gentle cooling showers
That wash afresh the windowpanes
And quench the thirsty flowers.

Dear Lord,
I thank Thee for the lilac bush
That blooms beneath the eaves,
And for the trusting little birds
That nest among its leaves;
I thank Thee for the daisy field
And for the flowers of May,
And for the joyous little brook
That hurries on its way.

Dear Lord,
For many blessings round my door
I lift my heart to Thee,
As do the happy little birds
That sing within my tree.
I thank Thee for my daily strength
And for Thy constant care,
For work to do and friends to love.
Dear Lord, accept my prayer.
             JOSEPHINE COURTRIGHT

Old Familiar Place

We may rove the wide world o'er
  But we ne'er shall find a trace
Of the home we loved of yore,

Of the old familiar place.
Other scenes may be as bright,
But we miss, 'neath alien skies,
Both the welcome and the light
Of the old, kind, loving eyes.

Home is home; of this bereft,
  Memory loves again to trace
All the forms of those we left
  In the old familiar place.

We may sail over every sea,
  But we still shall fail to find
Any spot so dear to be
  As the one we left behind;
Words of comfort we may hear,
  But they cannot touch the heart
Like the tones of memory dear,
  Of the friends from whom we part.

Home is home; the wanderer longs
  All the scenes of youth to trace,
And to hear the old home songs
  In the old familiar place.

C. W. GLOVER

What a Real Home Is . . .

A real home is a gymnasium. The ideal of a healthy body is the first one to give a child.

A real home is a lighthouse. A lighthouse reveals the breakers ahead and shows a clear way past them.

A real home is a playground. Beware of the house where you "dassen't frolic" —there mischief is brewing for someone.

A real home is a workshop. Pity the boy without a kit of tools or the girl without a sewing basket. They haven't learned the fun of doing things—and there is no fun like that.

A real home is a forum. Honest, open discussion of life's great problems belongs originally in the family circle.

A real home is a secret society. Loyalty to one's family should mean keeping silent on family matters—just this and nothing more.

A real home is a health resort. Mothers are the natural physicians.

A real home is a cooperative league. Households flourish where the interest of each is made the interest of all.

A real home is a business concern. Order is a housewife's hobby. But order without system is a harness without the horse.

A real home is a haven of refuge. The world does this for us all: it makes us hunger for a loving sympathy and a calming, soothing touch.

A real home is a temple of worship.

EDWARD PURINTON
in Covenanter Witness

Five Cornerstones of a Good Home

1. Must have a great desire to have a home of beauty filled with love and harmony.
2. Must have faith—a wife needs to have faith in herself, her husband, in others and especially in God.
3. Prayer—to stay together every couple must pray together.
4. Knowledge—to know the Bible and what it says about a good home.
5. Enthusiasm—about themselves and the things they can do together.

And finally—an extra—Humor, the saving grace of many family situations.

MRS. DAN POLING in Christian Herald

Love
(A Paraphrase of I Corinthians 13)

Though in the glamour of the public eye I sway the emotions of man by my oratory, or by my silver singing, or by my skillful playing, and then go home and gripe because supper is late, or because my clothes weren't made to suit me, I am become as sounding brass or a tinkling cymbal.

And though I am able to impress others with my vast knowledge of the deep things of the Word of God, and though I am able to accomplish mighty things through faith so that I become famous among men as a remover of mountains, and have not the love that reads the deep longings of the hearts around the family circle and removes the barriers that grow up in shy and tender hearts, I am nothing.

And though in the glamour of public praise I bestow all my goods to feed the poor, and though I win the name and fame of a martyr by giving my body to be burned, and yet close up like a clam at home, or behave like a snapping turtle, knowing nothing of the glory of giving myself in unstinted, self-denying service to those nearest and dearest, it profiteth me nothing.

Love is never impatient, but kind; love knows no jealousy; love makes no parade; gives itself no airs.

Love is never rude, seeks not her own, nor fights for her own rights, is never resentful, never imagines that others are plotting evil against her.

Never broods over wrongs; never exults over the mistakes of others; but is truly gladdened by goodness.

Love suffers silently, is always trustful, always cheerful, always patient.

Home is the acid test of the truly yielded life, for in all other phases of Christian service there is a certain amount of glamour; but in the home one is confronted with the bare facts of life, stripped of all glamour. The home is given to help every Christian "not to think more highly of himself than he ought to think." And it is in the home that we have the privilege of demonstrating that the Christian life is "faith which worketh by love."

AUTHOR UNKNOWN

H - onesty, that, first of all,
A - nd lots of loving too;
P - raise whenever possible,
P - erhaps a gift or two;
I - nsight into soul of mate,
N - agging? Oh, no, never!
E - njoy each other's company—
S - weethearts be, forever;
S - pend cash wisely, saving some,
   All adds up to "Happy Home!"

In 1923, when Herbert Hoover was president of Better Homes in America (before it became a department of Purdue University), that organization offered a prize for the best definition of a better home written by a school child.

The award was won by a Tennessee mountain lad, who wrote: "A better home is a place my dad is proud to support, my mother loves to take care of, and we like to be in. It is a place to grow old in!"

R and R Magazine

The true civic center of our municipalities will be found not in some towering edifice with stately approaches, nor in broad avenues flanked with magnificent mansions, but around the family altar of the American home, the source of that strength which has marked our national character, where above all else is cherished a faith in the things not seen.

CALVIN COOLIDGE

A good home is one where the attitudes and habits of the parents can be safely and happily copied by the children.

WILFRED GRENFELL

Motto for a Home

Lord, enter Thou my home with me,
Until I enter Thine with Thee.
AUTHOR UNKNOWN

Home is the place where character is built, where sacrifices to contribute to the happiness of others are made, and where love has taken up its abode.

ELIJAH KELLOGG

The spirit of the household reaches farther than from the front door to the back. It shines forth from a child's eyes and shows in the way a man hurries back to his home.

AUTHOR UNKNOWN

Peace and rest at length have come,
   All the day's long toil is past,
And each heart is whispering, "Home,
   Home, at last."
THOMAS HOOD, Home at Last

Without hearts there is no home.

LORD BYRON

Men make a camp;
A swarm of bees a comb;
Birds make a nest;
A woman makes a home.

ARTHUR GUITERMAN

No Place Like It!

It may be a mansion, it may be a
    dump;
It may be a farm with an old broken
    pump;
It may be a palace, it may be a flat;
It may be a room where you just hang
    your hat.

It may be a house with a hole in the
    floor;
Or a marble hotel with a man at the
    door.
It may be exclusive, or simple, or
    swell.
It may have grand fixin's, like curtains,
    and—well,
Just kindly remember, wherever you
    roam,
That old song is right, folks, there's no
    place like home!

AUTHOR UNKNOWN

There's nothing half so pleasant as coming home again.

MARGARET SANGSTER

A glance of heaven to see,
    To none on earth is given;
And yet a happy family
    Is but an earlier heaven.

SIR JOHN BOWRING

The kind of homes we have deter-
mines the kind of nation or church we
have.

What a Home Should Have

A home should have a mother
    Waiting every day

When children hurry home from school
    In their eager way;
For children come on flying feet
    When Mother's waiting there,
To greet them with a loving kiss
    And all their secrets share.

A home should have a father
    Coming home at six
To join a lusty game of ball
    Or a bike to fix;
For children need a father
    To enter in the fun
And help with all their problems
    Before the day is done.

A home should hold the secret
    Happy families share
Of joyful times together—
    Loving, helping there;
And homes should have the blessing
    That comes to those who pray
And worship God together,
    And serve Him every day.

ELIZABETH B. JONES
in *Together with God*

Home

A house is built of logs and stone,
    Of tiles and posts and piers;
A home is built of loving deeds
    That stand a thousand years.

VICTOR HUGO

Home

A little house—a cozy house,
    Paint-scarred, low-eaved, and humble;
Bright morning glories round the door—
    Their hues a gorgeous jumble;
A small red wagon—one wheel gone;
    A tree with blossoms swinging;
A kettle humming on the fire;
    A cheerful mother singing;
A place where loved ones gather
    round
    When evening prayers are given—
The dearest spot we'll ever know
    Till we go home to heaven!

KATHRYN BLACKBURN PECK
in *In Favor with God and Man*

What Have They Seen in Thy House?
(*II Kings* 20:15)

Perhaps there is not one who reads this but who has had callers or visitors at some time in his home, room or dwelling place. What did they see in your house? Things that advertise Christ and His cause or Satan and his cause? Have you pictures and texts on the walls that preach for Christ? Does your library testify that you are a child of God? Or is your house just cluttered with questionable things of this world? My Christian friend, do you realize your position in Christ? You are born from above, hence your citizenship is in heaven. While here on this earth you are an ambassador for Christ and heaven. This makes your abode, no matter how humble or palatial, heaven's embassy. In traveling in foreign lands we have occasion to visit the American embassies and they are easily recognized because they have their flag flying, and signs out informing us in no uncertain words that it is an American embassy. So our flag should be flying and signs out that all may know we are ambassadors of heaven and our homes are heaven's embassies. We are known by what is seen in our houses.

It is said of G. Campbell Morgan that he invited his father into his new home, showing him every room. He then asked his father his opinion of it. His father replied with words something like, "Yes, it is very nice, but nobody will know, walking through here, whether you belong to God or the devil." Mr. Morgan, thinking his father right, set about to place some picture or wall text in every room that would speak of his Saviour.

C. ROBERT HUNTRESS in *Living Faith*

What Is a Home?

A HOME

is the Laugh of a BABY,
the Song of a MOTHER,
the Warmth of LOVING HEARTS,
the Light from HAPPY EYES,

KINDNESS, LOYALTY
and COMRADESHIP.

HOME

is the First School
and the First Church
for Young Ones,
where they learn what is RIGHT,
what is GOOD,
and what is KIND.
Where one goes for COMFORT
when hurt
or ill.

HOME

is where JOY is shared
and SORROW is eased.

HOME

is where Fathers
and Mothers
are respected and loved,
where Children are wanted,
where the simplest good
is good enough for Kings,
because it is earned.

HOME

is where Money is not so important
as Loving-Kindness,
where even the Tea-kettle
sings for happiness.
That is HOME—
God bless it!

MADAME SCHUMANN-HEINK

Recipe for a Happy Home

To 3 cups of love and 2 cups of understanding add 4 teaspoons of courtesy and 2 teaspoons each of thoughtfulness and helpfulness. Sift together thoroughly, then stir in an equal amount of work and play. Add 3 teaspoons of responsibility. Season to taste with study and culture, then fold in a generous amount of worship. Place in a pan well greased with security and lined with respect for personality. Sprinkle lightly with a sense of humor. Allow to set in an atmosphere of democratic planning and of mutual sharing. Bake in a moderate oven. When well done, remove and top with a thick coating of Christian teachings. Serve on a platter of friendliness garnished with smiles.

PAULINE and LEONARD MILLER

What Makes a Good Home?

It is a good home for a child if:

1. He is loved and wanted—and knows it.
2. He is helped to grow up by not having too much or too little done for him.
3. He has some time and some space of his own.
4. He is part of the family, has fun with the family and belongs.
5. His early mistakes and "badness" are understood as a normal part of growing up; he is corrected without being hurt, shamed, or confused.
6. His growing skills—walking, talking, reading, making things—are enjoyed and respected.
7. He plans with the family and is given real ways to help and feel needed throughout childhood.
8. He has freedom that fits his age and his needs; he has responsibilities that fit his age, abilities and freedoms.
9. He can say what he feels and talk things out without being afraid or ashamed; he can learn through mistakes as well as successes. And his parents appreciate his successes rather than dwell upon his failures.
10. As he grows older, he knows his parents are doing the best they can; they know the same about him.
11. He feels his parents care as much about him as they do his brothers and sisters.
12. The family sticks together and the members help one another.
13. He is moderately and consistently disciplined from infancy, has limits set for his behavior and is helped to take increasing responsibility for his own actions.
14. He has a personal knowledge of

Christ as Savior and is learning the joy that comes from serving Jesus . . . at home and at school!

Recipe for a Home

Half a cup of friendship
  And a cup of thoughtfulness,
Creamed together with a pinch
  Of powdered tenderness.

Very lightly beaten
  In a bowl of loyalty,
With a cup of faith, and one of hope,
  And one of charity.

Be sure to add a spoonful each
  Of gaiety-that-sings
And also the ability
  To-laugh-at-little-things.

Moisten with the sudden tears
  Of heartfelt sympathy;
Bake in a good-natured pan
  And serve repeatedly.

AUTHOR UNKNOWN

If Every Home Were An Altar

If every home were an altar
  Where holiest vows were paid,
And life's best gifts in sacrament
  Of purest love were laid;

If every home were an altar
  Where harsh or angry thought
Was cast aside for kindly one,
  And true forgiveness sought;

If every home were an altar
  Where hearts weighed down with care
Could find sustaining strength and grace
  In sweet uplift of prayer:

Then solved would be earth's problems.
  Banished sin's curse and blight;
For God's own love would radiate
  From every altar light.

AUTHOR UNKNOWN

Home

Home's not merely four square walls,
　　Though with pictures hung and
　　gilded;
Home is where affection calls,
　　Filled with shrines the heart hath
　　builded!
Home! go watch the faithful dove,
　　Sailing 'neath the heaven above us;
Home is where there's one to love!
　　Home is where there's one to love us!

Home's not merely roof and room,
　　It needs something to endear it;
Home is where the heart can bloom,
　　Where there's some kind lip to cheer
　　it!
What is home with none to meet,
　　None to welcome, none to greet us?
Home is sweet—and only sweet—
　　When there's one we love to meet us!
　　　　　　　　　　　　CHARLES SWAIN

To be happy at home is the ultimate
aim of all ambition; the end to which
enterprise and labor tends, and of which
every desire prompts the prosecution.
　　　　　　　　　　　SAMUEL JOHNSON

The first essential in a happy Christian
home is that love must be practiced.
　　　　　　　　　　　　BILLY GRAHAM

The Christian psychiatrist, the late
Dr. Smiley Blanton, commended the
calming effect Bible reading can have in
family life. "It's the greatest textbook on
human behavior ever put together."

Where we love is home,
Home that our feet may leave, but not
our hearts.
　　　　　　　OLIVER WENDELL HOLMES,
　　　　　　　　　　　Homesick in Heaven

There can be no freedom or beauty
about a home life that depends on bor-
rowing and debt.
　　　　　　　　　　　　HENRIK IBSEN

He is happiest, be he king or peasant,
who finds peace in his own home.
　　　　　　　JOHANN WOLFGANG GOETHE

Sweet is the smile of home;
The mutual look, when hearts are of
　　each other sure.
　　　　　　　　　　　　JOHN KEBLE

The Crown of the house is Godliness.
The Beauty of the house is Order.
The Glory of the house is Hospitality.
The Blessing of the house is Content-
　　ment.
　　　　　　　　　　AUTHOR UNKNOWN

Many homes are on the rocks today
because God has been left out of the
domestic picture.
　　　　　　　　　　　　BILLY GRAHAM

A house is built by human hands, but a
home is built by human hearts.

The next way home's the farthest way
about.
　　　　　　　　　　　FRANCIS QUARLES

The many make the household,
but only one the home.
　　　　　　　JAMES RUSSELL LOWELL

Home is the chief school of human
virtues.

Home is never perfectly furnished for
enjoyment unless there is a little child
rising up in it.

The greatest heritage anyone can re-
ceive is the influence of a Christian
Home.
　　　　　　　　　　　RAYMOND L. COX

A real home is a picture of heaven on
earth.

Education begins at home. And if you
are a Christian parent, your job outranks
all others. For yours is the task of rais-
ing children in the nurture and admonition of the Lord.
　　　　　　　　　　　ROBERT STEWART

It takes a hundred men to make an
encampment, but one woman can make
a home.

Home is the pattern table on which the pieces of life are cut for size.

LOUIS PAUL LEHMAN

Wherever a true woman comes, home is always around her. The stars may be over her head, the glow-worms in the night-cold grass may be the fire at her foot; but home is where she is. For a noble woman it stretches far around her, better than houses ceiled with cedar, or painted with vermillion, shedding its quiet light far for those who else are homeless.

JOHN RUSKIN

A little girl who was asked where her home was, replied: "It is where my mother is."

CHILDREN

A Child's Garden

I know a little garden, dear,
    Where weeds and flowers grow;
The weeds must all be rooted out:
    They choke the flowers so.

This garden is your little heart,
    Where faults and virtues grow;
And you, the little gardener,
    Must tend it well, you know.

You must pull out the growing weeds,
    And cultivate the flowers;
And you must toil with patient care
    Through long and weary hours.

For weeds are of a ranker growth,
    And grow despite your care;
But you must weed them, one by one,
    And help the flowers grow there.

And toiling, you must pray for help;
    God's sunshine and His rain;
For, without these, my little one,
    All toiling is in vain.

But with His help, dear, as you toil
    Through life's long, passing hours,
You'll have, instead of ugly weeds,
    A garden full of flowers!

MYRTLE CONGER

Days of Youth

They pass so soon, the days of youth;
    The children change so fast:
Quickly they harden in the mold,
    And the plastic years are past.

Then shape their lives while they are young;
    This be our prayer, our aim—
That every child we meet shall bear
    The imprint of His name!

MARTHA SNELL NICHOLSON

Baby Shoes

Two worn little shoes
    with a hole in the toe!
And why have I saved them:
    Well—all mothers know,
There's nothing so sweet
    as a baby's worn shoe,
And patter of little steps
    following you.
The feet they once held
    have grown slender and strong;
Tonight they'll be tired
    after dancing so long—
I guided her feet
    when she wore such as these.

Dear God—may I ask—
    won't You guide them now, please?

ISLA P. RICHARDON

When Your Child Grows Up

Oh, never hold a loved one clenched so tight
And carefully within protective hands

That like a frightened bird he takes his
  flight
  Into a gentler and more sunny land.

Have faith that as you freely let him
  dare
  His wings to seek the outposts of the
    sky
That he will send his love across the air,
  More "yours" than some tame bird
    that cannot fly.

For what you hold you lose, and learn to
  weep;
But what your heart sets free you always
  keep.

JEAN HOGAN DUDLEY
in Home Life

Prayer at Bedtime

"Lo, children are an heritage of the Lord."
  —Psalm 127:3
Here in the dusk I watch them kneel to
  pray,
  And all the gratitude I cannot speak
And all the loving words I long to say
  Are written in the tears upon my
    cheek.

How can I thank thee, Lord, for such as
  these,
  This blessed heritage vouchsafed to
    me—
My children, confident, upon their
  knees,
  This simple faith, their hushed expec-
    tancy?

Oh, I will open wide the sacred Book
  And speak to them of all thy match-
    less grace;
So shall they come, in fancy, to look
  Beyond all other faces to thy face.
Yes, I will share the treasures of thy
  Word
With these, I cannot thank thee better,
  Lord.

HELEN FRAZEE-BOWER

Guide Our Children

O God, great Father, Lord and King!
Our children unto Thee we bring;

And strong in faith and hope and love,
We dare Thy stedfast Word to prove.

Thy covenant kindness did of old
Our fathers and their seed enfold;
That ancient promise standeth sure,
And shall while heaven and earth en-
  dure.

Look down upon us while we pray
And visit us in grace today;
These little ones Thou didst receive,
Thy precious promise we believe.

Guide Thou their feet in holy ways,
Shine on them through the darkest days;
Uphold them till their life be passed
And bring them all to heaven at last.

E. EMBREE HOSS

A little child, a limber elf,
Singing, dancing to itself,
A fairy thing with red round cheeks
That always finds and never seeks,
Makes such a vision to the sight,
As fills a father's eyes with light.

SAMUEL TAYLOR COLERIDGE, Cristabel

We need love's tender lessons taught
  As only weakness can;
God hath His small interpreters;
  The child must teach the man.

JOHN GREENLEAF WHITTIER, Child-songs

But hope will make thee young, for
  Hope and Youth
Are children of one mother,
  Even Love.

PERCY BYSSHE SHELLEY

The Heart of a Child

The heart of a child is a tremulous
  thing;
Lovely and frail as a butterfly's wing.

Kissed by the beam of a summer sun,
Or crushed by the word of a careless
  one.

A look or a smile will cause it to sing,
For the heart of a child is a tremulous
thing.
MILLICENT M. SLABY

Some mothers love their children self-
ishly—
Their children exist for them.
Other mothers love their children slav-
ishly—
They exist for their children.
But some mothers love their children
sacrificially—
Their children and they exist for God.
JAMES SPRUNT

In Sight

Of children's mischief, I for one
Find this the most disturbing view:
It's not so much what they have done
As it is what they're apt to do!
S.H. DEWHURST in Home Life

Recipe for Raising Children

"Self-will is the root of all sin and
misery," wrote Susanna Wesley, who
from their babyhood put her children
into a regular routine. To insure a calm,
quiet household, she taught them to cry
softly. Children ate what they were given
at meals, were allowed nothing between,
and went to bed at eight except in case
of sickness, when they were expected to
take medicine without complaint. Here
are some of Susanna's other rules for
child training. Though two hundred
years old, many of them could serve as a
guide for modern Christian Mothers!

1. To prevent lying, do not punish a
   child who confesses his fault and
   promises to amend.
2. No sinful act should ever pass un-
   punished.
3. No child should be punished twice
   for the same fault, and he should
   not be upbraided with it afterwards.
4. Obedience should be commended
   and rewarded.
5. Any effort to please, even if badly
   performed, should be commended.
6. Allow no one to take property
   from the owner, though it were the
   value of a pin, without his consent.
7. Strictly observe promises, and leave
   a gift once given, to the disposal of
   him to whom it was given, unless it
   were conditional and the condition
   not observed.
8. Require no girl to work until she
   can read very well.
9. Teach the Lord's Prayer as soon as
   the child can speak.
10. Require all to be still at family
    prayers.
11. Give them nothing they cry for,
    and only that which they ask for
    politely.
12. Subdue self-will in a child so as to
    work with God in renewing and sav-
    ing his soul.
SUSANNAH WESLEY

Five things needed for a child to feel
that he is wanted and loved:
1. Love from the father.
2. Love from the mother.
3. Discipline governed and set up by
   the father who should establish the
   principles of control.
4. Supervision by the mother working within the framework of discipline established by the father.
5. A family that sticks together at
   all times.
WAYNE SWENSON in the Wheaton Daily

How Do You Rate Your Children?

How foolish those fathers and mothers
Who think that their children are
saintly.
Now ours show the same faults as oth-
ers—
Although (to be honest) more faintly!
ELLA MAY MILLER

Twelve Rules for Raising Delinquent Children

1. Begin with infancy to give the child
   everything he wants. In this way

he will grow up to believe the world owes him a living.

2. When he picks up bad words, laugh at him. This will make him think he's cute. It will also encourage him to pick up "cuter" phrases that will blow off the top of your head later.

3. Never give him any spiritual training. Wait until he is 21 and then let him "decide for himself."

4. Avoid use of the word "wrong." It may develop a guilt complex. This will condition him to believe later, when he is arrested for stealing a car, that society is against him and he is being persecuted.

5. Pick up everything he leaves lying around—books, shoes, and clothes. Do everything for him so that he will be experienced in throwing all responsibility on others.

6. Let him read any printed matter he can get his hands on. Be careful that the silver-ware and drinking glasses are sterilized, but let his mind feast on garbage.

7. Quarrel frequently in the presence of your children. In this way they will not be too shocked when the home is broken up later.

8. Give a child all the spending money he wants. Never let him earn his own. Why should he have things as tough as you had them?

9. Satisfy his every craving for food, drink, and comfort. See that every sensual desire is gratified. Denial may lead to harmful frustration.

10. Take his part against neighbors, teachers, policemen. They are all prejudiced against your child.

11. When he gets into real trouble, apologize for yourself by saying, "I never could do anything for him."

12. Prepare for a life of grief. You will be likely to have it.

Economic Intelligence

Twelve Rules for Raising Responsible Children

1. Begin with infancy to teach the child he cannot have everything he wants.

2. When he picks up bad words, correct him.

3. Give him spiritual training early in life.

4. Make frequent use of the word "wrong" in correcting bad acts.

5. Make him pick up his own things and do as many other things for himself as he can.

6. Be careful what you let him read.

7. Keep the home atmosphere pleasant and warm.

8. Make him earn his spending money.

9. See that sensual desires and cravings for food, drink and comfort are satisfied only in moderation.

10. Back him only when he's right and let him know you won't back him when he's wrong.

11. Accept your responsibility for his actions until he's of age to accept them himself.

12. Prepare for a life of satisfaction with your child. You are likely to have it.

ROBERT D. NORTON

From Children . . . Advice to Parents

"If you could write a book for parents," some 8-12 year-olds were asked, "what advice would you give them?"

In spite of their misspelling and split infinitives they came up with some interesting tidbits on such subjects as togetherness, drinking, punishment, chores and devotions. Not all of the co-authors came from Christian homes, but all attended church. Here are a dozen excerpts:

"I would advise them to be more careful when driving and to not drink."

"Try to put yourself in the shoes of the child before you punish," suggested an 11-year-old. She added, for her peers, "Remember when your folks spank you, it's for your own good." Her one other comment to parents: "Raise them in the Lord."

"Go to church and make children go to

church and help with homework"—a ten-year-old boy.

"Do things together as a family," wrote a girl.

"If parents give their children love and care they need, and let them have certain privileges, then the least I can do is my share of work around the house, respect my parents and try to do things when asked"—an 11-year-old girl.

"I would tell parents not to get onto them [the kids] too much"—a boy.

"Don't tell them what your parents used to say and what you had to do as a kid."

"Give some allowance."

"Give some time to play"—a 10-year-old girl who has to "wash dishes, clean my room, take out the garbage, dust and run errands." Asked if she thought she had to do too much work, however, this girl said, "No, because my mother and father probably did the same things."

"I would advise parents to have devotions every day"—a 10-year-old.

"I would advise them to teach their children about the Bible"—a 10-year-old.

"To give more attention or expression when it comes to spiritual needs and thoughts." To her Sunday school classmates she added, "Don't take everybody's advice on religion before you hear from Christians; and those who are Christians better get to the kids before they decide unwisely." This came from a barely-niner!

from *Today*

Our Buds for the Master

Two little soft toddling feet,
　To be led in the upward way;
Two knees, that are dimpled and sweet,
　To be taught how to kneel and pray.

Two weak little fluttering hands,
　To be shown how to help someone;
Two ears, just waiting commands,
　So they'll know what to shun and
　　choose.

Two eyes that should learn to behold,
　Only things that are true and right;
A tongue to be trained not to scold,
　Or to say bitter words that smite.

A body, still perfect and pure,
　To protect from all lust and pride;
A temple that long may endure,
　Where the Master can now abide.
　　　　　　　　JESSIE F. MOSER

He Takes My Hand

She's just a little kiddie
　Who walks by her mother's side,
And she'd rather go out walking
　Than to take a little ride.
She likes to skip and hop along,
　To run ahead and wait
For mother to catch up to her
　Down by the garden gate.
But sometimes when they go walking
　It gets hard for her to stand,
And when the road gets rocky,
　She says, "Mother, take my hand."
It's all right when paths are easy
　For her to skip along,
But when it's getting hard to walk
　She wants a hand so strong,
To reach down and take hold of hers
　To help her find the way,
"Mother, mother, hold my hand,"
　Is what you'll hear her say.
I guess that we're all children,
　Sometimes the way is bright,
Then we like to run along;
　But when the day grows night,
When the shadows lengthen,
　When the sky is overcast—
Or when we walk the valley
　When the day is done at last:
I think that we shall reach right up,
　I know He'll understand,
And we'll cry like weary children,
　"Lord Jesus, take my hand,"
I know that he will reach right down
　To help us in our need,
For when we cannot help ourselves

He'll always intercede.
Then when the journey's over
And we stand on yonder strand,
Methinks that we shall ask again,
"Lord Jesus, take my hand."
                    LOUIS PAUL LEHMAN, JR.

The Child's Appeal

I am the Child.
All the world waits for my coming.
All the earth watches with interest to see
    what I shall become.
Civilization hangs in the balance,
For what I am, the world of tomorrow
    will be.

I am the Child.
I have come into your world, about
    which I know nothing.
Why I came I know not;
How I came I know not
I am curious; I am interested.

I am the Child
You hold in your hand my destiny.
You determine, largely, whether I shall
    succeed or fail.
Give me, I pray you, those things that
    make for happiness.
Train me, I beg you, that I may be a
    blessing to the world.
                    MAMIE GENE COLE

Dressing Up

When she was only three or four
She played at being grown,
And oft her mother's garments wore
As though they were her own.

She strutted in a trailing dress
And wore a bonnet gay,
For that was Janet's happiness
On many a rainy day.

She loved the game of dressing up
And having friends for tea.
The way she held her little cup
Was proper as could be.

For capes and robes and pretty things
She robbed both hook and shelf,

Took brooches, bracelets, pins and rings
And hung them on herself.

I've chuckled many a rainy day
To see her thus attired
And have her curtsey low and say:
"Your company is desired."

"A few friends I have asked for tea.
I've known them all my life;
And very happy I should be
If you should bring your wife."

Now to those grand and lofty airs
Has Janet fully grown,
And still her mother's trinkets wears,
As though they were her own.

But what is more than silk and lace
And Jeweled neck and arms,
She also wears with youthful grace
Her mother's many charms.
                    EDGAR A. GUEST

If they learn nothing else, I want my
boys to learn to be thoughtful of their
mother—not just to love her, that's easy
—but to think about sparing her. Too
many boys grow up to think of a mother
as somebody to wait on them, an attitude that probably carries over when
they eventually marry.
                REX GOGERTY in *Farm Journal*

Other people's harvests are always the
best harvests, but one's children are always the best children.

Though a mother gives birth to nine
sons, all nine will be different.
                        Chinese Proverb

The future destiny of the child is always the work of the mother.
                    NAPOLEON BONAPARTE

Children: Today's investment, tomorrow's dividend.

The thing most apt to drive a parent
    wild,
Is a child behaving like a child.

Children are God's apostles sent forth day by day to preach of love and hope and peace.

JAMES RUSSELL LOWELL

Rearing children is like drafting a blueprint; you have to know where to draw the line.

The Hand You Hold

When a boy or girl thrusts his small hand in yours, it may be smeared with chocolate ice cream, or grimy from petting a dog, and there may be a wart under the right thumb and a bandage around the little finger.

But the most important thing about his hands is that they are the hands of the future. These are hands that some-day may hold a Bible or a Colt revolver; play the church piano, or spin a gambling wheel; gently dress a leper's wound, or tremble wretchedly uncontrolled by an alcoholic mind.

Right now, that hand is yours. It asks for help and guidance. It represents a full-fledged personality in miniature to be respected as a separate individual whose day-to-day growth into Christian adulthood is your responsibility.

"Mamma, what are men?" asked the little girl.

"Why, men are what we women marry," Mother explained.

"We don't have much choice, do we?" mused the little girl.

MARTIN P. SIMON in *Points for Parents*

Two little girls were playing wedding with mother's trunkful of old clothes. One was the bride, the other was the bridesmaid.

"Who is the groom?" Mother asked.

"Oh, we don't have any," one girl explained, and the other added, "This is a small wedding."

MARTIN P. SIMON in *Points for Parents*

A Child Shall Lead

You, little child, with your shining eyes and dimpled cheeks . . . you can lead us along the pathway to the more abundant life.

We blundering grown-ups need in our lives the virtues that you have in yours:

The joy and enthusiasm of looking forward to each new day with glorious expectations of wonderful things to come . . .

The vision that sees the world as a splendid place with good fairies, brave knights and glistening castles reaching toward the sky . . .

The radiant curiosity that finds adventure in simple things: the mystery of billowy clouds, the miracle of snowflakes, the magic of growing flowers . . .

The tolerance that forgets differences as quickly as your childish quarrels are spent—that holds no grudges, that hates never, that loves people for what they are . . .

The genuineness of being oneself; to be finished with sham, pretense, and empty show; to be simple, natural, and sincere . . .

The courage that rises from defeat and tries again, as you with laughing face rebuild the house of blocks that top-ples to the floor . . .

The believing heart that trusts others, knows no fear and has faith in a divine Father who watches over His children from the sky . . .

The contented, trusting mind that, at the close of day, woos the blessing of childlike slumber.

Little child, we would become like you that we may find again the kingdom of heaven within our hearts.

AUTHOR UNKNOWN

Parents' Creed

If a child lives with criticism,
    He learns to condemn.
If a child lives with hostility,
    He learns to fight.
If a child lives with ridicule,

He learns to be shy.
If a child lives with jealousy,
   He learns to feel guilty.
If a child lives with tolerance,
   He learns to be patient.
If a child lives with encouragement,
   He learns confidence.
If a child lives with praise,
   He learns to appreciate.
If a child lives with fairness,
   He learns justice.
If a child lives with security,
   He learns to have faith.
If a child lives with approval,
   He learns to like himself.
If a child lives with acceptance and
     friendship,
   He learns to find love in the world.

                      DOROTHY LAW NOLTE

A babe in the house is a wellspring of pleasure, a messenger of peace and love, a testing place for innocence on earth, a link between angels and men.

            MARTIN FARQUHAR TUPPER,
                      Of Education

Give a little love to a child, and you get a great deal back.

  JOHN RUSKIN, *The Crown of Wild Olive*

After the mad rush of getting the older children ready for a party and putting the young ones to bed for a nap, a harried mother rested her aching head on the cool kitchen table. At this point, she felt her four-year-old's hand on her shoulder. "What's the matter, Mommy?" he asked sympathetically. "Don't you have anything to do?"

A Little Girl's Essay

People are made up of girls and boys, also men and women. Boys are no good at all until they grow up and get married. Men who don't get married are no good either. Boys are an awful bother. They want everything they see except soap. My ma is a woman and my pa is a man. A woman is a grown-up girl with children. My pa is such a nice man that I think he must have been a girl when he was a boy.

Your Children

Take time to laugh and sing and play,
And cuddle them a bit.
Tell them a story now and then.
And steal a little time to sit
And listen to their childish talk,
Or take them for a little walk.

You do not know it now—but soon
They will be gone—the years are swift—
For life just marches on and on,
And heaven holds no sweeter gift
Than a small boy with tousled hair,
Who leaves his toys just anywhere.

Take time to hear their prayers at night
To really cherish and enjoy
A little girl with flaxen curls,
And the small wonder of a boy.
They ask so little when they're small,
Just love and tenderness—that's all.

                AUTHOR UNKNOWN

New Shoes

Strap shoes, buckle shoes,
   Shoes of every size;
Shiny patent-leather shoes
   Shoes with bows and ties.

Moccasins and saddle shoes,
   Shoes for work and play,
Shoes to keep for Sunday best,
   Shoes for everyday.

Black shoes, brown shoes,
   Warm shoes and cool—
Everyone's buying new shoes
   Because it's time for school.

                MARIAN KENNEDY

Mother's Helper

Oh, it's cookie-making morning
And our kitchen looks a sight.
There is flour spread on the table,
There is flour to left and right;
There is ginger mixed with sugar,
And each spice-can on the rack
Bears the fingerprints of someone
Who was going to put it back.

There are raisins and molasses
All in all pools around
Where some happy little fingers
Think such morsels should be found;
There is butter on the mixer
And on someone's mouth and hair,
But my darling little daughter
Thinks she ought to help me there.

Oh, it's cookie-making morning
And our kitchen looks a sight . . .
But what mother here among us
Would deny her child this right?
                    PHYLLIS C. MICHAEL

The world has no such flower in any
    land,
And no such pearl in any gulf the sea,
As any babe on any mother's knee.
ALGERNON CHARLES SWINBURNE, *Pelagius*

The child, the seed, the grain of corn,
The acorn on the hill,
Each for some separate end is born
In season fit, and still
Each must in strength arise to work
The Almighty will.
                    ROBERT LOUIS STEVENSON

Children Everywhere

Children at the window,
Children at the door;
Tiny in the baby cab,
Toddler on the floor.

Helpful in the kitchen,
Happy up the stair—
An overflowing, small house,
And not a child to spare.
                    ETHEL ROMIG FULLER

Sweetest thing on earth,
Loveliest out of heaven—
Baby, little angel, to my
Longing spirit given:

In thy tiny hand
Lies God's dearest gift,
In thine eyes the fairest light
Heaven on earth can lift.
                    AUTHOR UNKNOWN

Weariness

O little feet! that such long years
Must wander on through hopes and
    fears,
    Must ache and bleed beneath your
    load;
I, nearer to the wayside inn
Where toil shall cease and rest begin,
    Am weary, thinking of your road!

O little hands! that, weak or strong,
Have still to serve or rule so long,
    Have still so long to give or ask;
I, who so much with book or pen
Have toiled among my fellow men,
    Am weary, thinking of your task!

O little hearts! that throb and beat
With such impatient, feverish heat,
    Such limitless and strong desires;
Mine, that so long has glowed and
    burned,
With passions into ashes turned,
    Now covers and conceals its fires.

O little souls! as pure and white
And crystalline as rays of light
    Direct from heaven, their source di-
    vine;
Refracted through the mist of years,
How red my setting sun appears,
    How lurid looks this soul of mine!
                    HENRY WADSWORTH LONGFELLOW

A Child's Thought of God

They say that God lives very high!
But if you look above the pines
You cannot see our God. And why?

And if you dig down in the mines
You never see Him in the gold,
Though from Him all that's glory shines.

God is so good, He wears a fold
Of heaven and earth across His face—
Like secrets kept, for love, untold.

But still I feel that His embrace
Slides down by thrills, through all things
    made,
Through sight and sound of every place:

As if my tender mother laid
On my shut lids, her kisses' pressure,
Half waking me at night; and said,
"Who kissed you through the dark, dear
    guesser?"
        ELIZABETH BARRETT BROWNING

I have no answer for myself or thee,
Save that I learned beside my mother's
    knee;
"All is of God that is, and is to be;
And God is good." Let this suffice us
    still,
Resting in childlike trust upon his will
Who moves to his great ends unthwarted
    by the ill.
        WILLIAM COWPER

But, children, you should never let
    Such angry passions rise;
Your little hands were never made
    To tear each other's eyes.
        ISAAC WATTS, *Divine Songs*

The Little Prayer

It was a very little prayer
    The small child prayed, alone.
How could it climb up Heaven's stair
    To reach the Father's throne?

The stumbling speech, the faltered word,
    Must vanish on the air.
And yet, distinctly, God had heard
    The very little prayer.

It was not lost to Him at all,
    He met it at the Gate—
For though the prayer was very small,
    The faith was very great.
        HELEN FRAZEE-BOWER

From The Children's Hour

Between the dark and the daylight,
    When night is beginning to lower,
Comes a pause in the day's occupations,
    That is known as the Children's Hour.

I hear in the chamber above me
    The patter of little feet,

The sound of a door that is opened,
    The voices soft and sweet. . . .

A sudden rush from the stairway,
    A sudden raid from the hall—
By three doors left unguarded,
    They enter my castle wall . . .

Do you think, O blue-eyed banditti,
    Because you have scaled the wall,
Such an old mustache as I am
    Is not a match for you all?.

I have you fast in my fortress,
    And will not let you depart,
But put you into the dungeon
    In the round-tower of my heart.
        HENRY WADSWORTH LONGFELLOW

Keep holy the being of the little child. Protect it from every touch of the vulgar; a touch, a look, a sound is often sufficient to inflict savage wounds. A child's soul is often more tender and vulnerable than the finest or tenderest plant.
        FROEBEL

Bewildered five-year-old Johnny, who, feeling that he was lost, ran down the aisles of the supermarket shouting at the top of his lungs, "Martha! Martha! Where are you, Martha?"

Soon his mother, Martha, heard him and dried his tears.

"But you shouldn't have called me Martha," she chided. "You should have shouted, 'Mama, Mama.'"

"Yeh," he sighed, "but the store is full of Mama's. I didn't think there'd be many Martha's."

A Sunday school teacher reported that the excuse of a little girl for not having her memory work was "because the only copy of the Bible we have at home is the reversed version."

Proud father to mother as they watch their small son, lying on the floor studying by the light from the TV screen: "Reminds you of Abe Lincoln, doesn't it?"

Happy are the families where the government of parents is the reign of affection, and obedience of the children the submission of love.

FRANCIS BACON

Adult education is what goes on in a household containing teen-age children.

Very seldom do parents have trouble with children when the Bible is read regularly in the home, grace is said at the table and family prayers take place daily.

BILLY GRAHAM

The world has only one problem before it: How should we best transmit to children the fruits of our effort? How best, in education, put them in possession of the knowledge we have gained? in the church, how hand on to them the gains of our spiritual life? in art and literature, how pass on to them our visions? in business, how give them the products of our work? And so in government, in law, and in all phases of life.

FRANK CRANE

Parents do wrong by failing to exercise wise and loving authority over their children. Children are born with an innate instability and with a desire to be directed and guided. If they discover that their parents are weak instead of strong, and incapable of leading them properly, their personalities are affected. They will then seek and find unwholesome and improper leadership in hoodlum gangs, terror clubs and sadistic rings.

BILLY GRAHAM

The great man is the man who does not lose his own child's heart.

KEITH L. BROOKS

He who helps a child helps humanity with a distinctness, with an immediateness, which no other help given to human creatures in any other stage of their human life can possibly give again.

PHILLIPS BROOKS

Children are banners inscribed plainly with the inside story of the family life at home.

The parent who does not teach his child to obey is being cruel to him. The habit of implicit obedience to parental authority is the foundation of good citizenship. More than that, it is the foundation of subjection to God's authority.

BILLY GRAHAM

Sweet childish days, that were as long
As twenty days are now.
WILLIAM WORDSWORTH, *To a Butterfly*

The scenes of childhood are the memories of future years.

J. O. CHOULES

Who Wants the Boys and Girls?

God wants the boys, the merry, merry boys,
The noisy boys, the funny boys,
    The thoughtless boys;
God wants the boys with all their joys
That He as gold may make them pure,
And teach them trials to endure,
    His heroes brave
        He'd have them be.
    Fighting for truth
        And purity,
    God wants the boys!

God wants the happy-hearted girls,
The loving girls, the best of girls,
    The worst of girls;
God wants to make the girls His pearls,
And so reflect His holy face,
And bring to mind His wondrous grace,
    That beautiful
        The world may be,
    And filled with Love
        And purity.
    God wants the girls!

AUTHOR UNKNOWN

A Tribute to Childhood

When God made the child he began early in the morning. He watched the golden hues of the rising day chasing away the darkness, and He chose the azure of the opening heavens for the color of childhood's eyes, the crimson of the clouds to paint its cheeks, and the gold of the morning for its flowing tresses. He listened to the song of the birds as they sang and warbled and whispered, and strung childhood's harp with notes now soft and low—now sweet and strong.

He saw little lambs among the flock romp and play and skip, and He put play into childhood's heart. He saw the silvery brook and listened to its music and he made the laughter of the child like the ripple of the brook. He saw angels of light as upon the wings of love they hastened to holy duty, and He formed the child's heart in purity and love.

And having made the child, He sent it out to bring joy into the home, laughter on the green and gladness everywhere. He sent it into the home and said to the parents, "Nourish and bring up this child for Me." He sent it to the state and said, "Deal tenderly with it and it will bless and not curse you." He sent it to the nation and said, "Be good to the child. It is thy greatest asset and thy hope."

GEORGE W. RIDEOUT

A Child Is Compensation

You are the trip I did not take,
You are the pearls I cannot buy,
You are my blue Italian lake,
You are my piece of foreign sky.

You are my Honolulu moon,
You are the books I did not write,
You are my heart's unuttered tune,
You are a candle in my night.

You are a flower beneath the snow,
In my dark skies a bit of blue,
Answering disappointments' blow,
With, "I am happy," I love you.

ANNE CAMPBELL

The Faith of a Little Child

God, give me the faith of a little child!
  Who trusts so implicitly,
Who simply and gladly believes Thy
    Word,
  And never would question Thee.

God, give me the faith of a little child!
  A faith that will clasp Thy hand,
And willingly go where Thou see'st best,
  Though he may not understand.

God, give me the faith of a little child!
  A faith that will look to Thee,
That never will falter and never fail,
  But follow Thee trustingly.

AUTHOR UNKNOWN

Thoughts for the Children
(Selections from the Bible)

Praise ye the Lord:
    for it is good to sing praises unto our
      God:
He telleth the number of the stars;
    he calleth them all by their names.
Sing unto the Lord with thanksgiving;
    who covereth the heaven with clouds,
    who prepareth rain for the earth,
    who maketh grass to grow upon the
      mountains.
He giveth to the beast his food,
    and to the young ravens which cry.
He giveth snow like wool:
    he scattereth the hoarfrost like ashes.
Praise ye the Lord.

From *Psalm 147*

A Devotional Reading

Oh, I think the summer is the nicest time
    of all.
I like to wake up early and hurry out-of-
    doors.
The birds are singing in the treetops.
The leaves on the trees whisper a little
    song
As the wind goes by.
The flowers are wet with dew and spar-
    kling
In the morning sunlight.
I can see the fields of golden wheat

And the dark green corn that is now
    higher
Than my head.
I can smell the sweet hay drying in the
    meadow.
The summer apples are ripening in the
    orchard.
The garden is filled with fresh vegetables
    ready
To gather for the table.
What fun we have the whole day long:
    Playing beneath the orchard trees, or
    Walking through the tall corn, or
    Wading in the little stream!
When evening comes, and a big yellow
    moon
Shines through the treetops, I whisper a
Little prayer to God for all His wonderful
    gifts:
    The sunlight, the flowers, the birds,
    the fields and meadows, the happy
    hours to run and play.
                    From *Together with God*

I'm Glad Today

Dear God, I'm very glad today
For sturdy legs to run and play;

For eyes to see each lovely thing;
For ears to hear the birds that sing.

I'm glad for things I have to eat:
For rich, brown bread and cookies sweet.

I'm thankful too for teachers kind,
And books that help to train my mind;

And for a chance to work and share
Your love with children everywhere.
                    From *Together with God*

The Soul of a Child

The soul of a child is the loveliest flower
    That grows in the garden of God.
Its climb is from weakness to knowledge
    and power,
    To the sky from the clay and the clod.
To beauty and sweetness it grows under
    care,
    Neglected, 'tis ragged and wild.

'Tis a plant that is tender, but wondrous-
    ly rare,
    The sweet, wistful soul of a child.

Be tender, O gardener, and give it its
    share
    Of moisture, of warmth, and of light,
And let it not lack for the painstaking
    care,
    To protect it from frost and from
    blight.
A glad day will come when its bloom
    shall unfold,
    It will seem that an angel has smiled,
Reflecting a beauty and sweetness un-
    told
    In the sensitive soul of a child.
                    AUTHOR UNKNOWN

Childlike Trust

"Now I lay me"—say it, darling;
    "Lay me," lisped the tiny lips
Of my daughter, kneeling, bending,
    O'er her folded finger tips.

"Down to sleep"—"to sleep," she mur-
    mured,
    And the curly head drooped low;
"I pray the Lord," I gently added,
    "You can say it all, I know."

"Pray the Lord"—the words came
    faintly,
    Fainter still—"My soul to keep,"
Then the tired head fairly nodded,
    And the child was fast asleep.

But the dewy eyes half opened
    When I clasped her to my breast,
And the dear voice softly whispered,
    "Mamma, God knows all the rest."

Oh, the trusting, sweet confiding
    Of the child-heart! Would that I
Thus might trust my Heavenly Father,
    He who hears my feeblest cry.
                    THOMAS H. AYERS

Little Cradles

All over the earth they are swaying,
The nests where the little ones lie,

And the faces, black, brown, white or
    yellow,
Are watched by the Father's kind eye.
AUTHOR UNKNOWN

The Mother's Sacrifice

The cold winds swept the mountain's
    height,
  And pathless was the dreary wild,
And mid the cheerless hours of night
  A mother wandered with her child:
As through the drifting snow she pressed,
The babe was sleeping on her breast.

And colder still the winds did blow,
  And darker hours of night came on,
And deeper grew the drifting snow:
  Her limbs were chilled, her strength
    was gone.
"O God!" she cried in accents wild,
"If I must perish, save my child!"

She stripped her mantle from her breast,
  And bared her bosom to the storm,
And round the child she wrapped the
    vest,
  And smiled to think her babe was
    warm.
With one cold kiss, one tear she shed,
And sunk upon her snowy bed.

At dawn a traveller passed by,
  And saw her 'neath a snowy veil;
The frost of death was in her eye,
  Her cheek was cold and hard and
    pale.
He moved the robe from off the child,—
The babe looked up and sweetly smiled!
SEBA SMITH

If you have lost your faith in yourself
just go out and get acquainted with a
small child. Win his love and your faith
will come stealing back to you before you
know it.

NICK KENNY

A first grader told her teacher that she
was one of seven children. "My but it
must be expensive to have so many
children," the teacher said.

"Oh," said the child, "we don't buy
them; we just raise them."

The mother who can manage her children with dispatch can get them ready
and sent to play with the youngsters next
door before the youngsters there can
come over here.
Press, St. Charles, Minn.

Children are what we make them.
FRENCH PROVERB

We are apt to forget that children
watch examples better than they listen
to preaching.
ROY L. SMITH

Be careful of your life lest a child
stumble over you.

Children are contagious to character
and conduct.

Rule your children, or you'll ruin
them.

Little children are still the symbol of
the eternal marriage between love and
duty.
GEORGE ELIOT

It is important that the significant person in a child's life has faith in the
potentialities of that child.
ERICH FROMM

What does it profit a youngster to have
plenty of pocket money and his own
radio, TV set, and car if he lacks his parents' understanding and encouragement?
WILLIAM COGREVE in *PTA Magazine*

How many troubles are with children
  born!
Yet he that wants them counts himself
  forlorn.
DRUMMOND of Hawthornden

A baby is God's opinion that the world should go on. . . .

CARL SANDBURG

When a little boy's mother asked him who he loved the most he replied, "Well, I like you best, and then comes daddy and teacher last—but in between come a lot of dogs."

QUIN RYAN

Mother: "Aunt Becky won't kiss you with that dirty face."
Small boy: "That's what I figured."

The Secret World of Kids

A little girl was reading with her mother in the New Testament. When they came to John 3:16, her mother stopped a moment in the reading and asked, "Isn't that wonderful?"

"No," the girl answered, looking surprised.

Her mother repeated the question.

"Why, no," the girl said again. "It would be wonderful if it were anyone else, Mother, but it is really just like God."

Today

A child cried one night
Outside,
And I said, That is my child.
But I found him to be another lad,
So I went back to my room and said,
There is nothing for me to do;
Now I can sleep.

The child cried again
And I went out and looked into his face
And said, Why, This is my child!
And I brought him in
And gave him something to eat
And put him in a warm bed;
And I slept.

A child laughed
And I followed the sweet laughter
Out to a place called the Kingdom of
    God,

Where many children were.
The Lord of the Place asked me,
Which child did you help?
And I could not tell!

HERBERT R. WHITING

Comfort

"I'll lend you for a little time
    A child of mine," He said,
"For you to love the while she lives,
    And mourn for when she's dead.
It may be six or seven years
    Or twenty-two or three,
But will you, till I call her back,
    Take care of her for Me?
She'll bring her charms to gladden you,
    And should her stay be brief,
You'll have her lovely memories
    As solace for your grief."

"I cannot promise she will stay,
    Since all from earth return,
But there are lessons taught down there
    I want this child to learn.
I've looked this wide world over
    In my search for teachers true,
And from the throngs that crowd life's
        lanes
    I have selected you.
Now will you give her all your love,
    Nor think the labor vain,
Nor hate me when I come to call
    To take her back again?"

I fancy that I heard them say,
    "Dear Lord, Thy will be done;
For all the joy Thy child shall bring,
    The risk of grief we'll run.
We'll shelter her with tenderness,
    We'll love her while we may,
And for the happiness we've known,
    Forever grateful stay.
But should the angels call for her
    Much sooner than we've planned,
We'll brave the bitter grief that comes
    And try to understand."

AUTHOR UNKNOWN

The bearing and training of a child is woman's wisdom.

ALFRED, LORD TENNYSON

There are only two bequests we can leave children—roots and wings.

We live again in our children. The whole attitude of life is determined by the atmosphere of the home. And mothers are largely responsible for creating this.

I don't see why bringing up children should be such a problem—all you've got to do is:
dress 'em up,
feed 'em up,
and beat 'em up!

When a neighbor once asked Mrs. Mary Scannell of Boston, mother of 12, if she had a lot of trouble with so many children, she replied: "Never trouble. Bother at times, maybe. Bother is in the hands. Trouble is in the heart."

Our children are the only earthly possessions we can take with us to glory.

Children are poor men's riches.

When a mother was disciplining her small boy, he begged, "Don't say 'must,' Mother. It makes me feel 'won't' all over."

The children of men that are wandering by,
Each with his packet of dreams and sandals of pain . . .
Little and lonely under the evening star.

Children have neither past nor future; they enjoy the present which very few of us do.

JAMES A. GARFIELD

I do not love him because he is good, but because he is my little child.

RABINDRANATH TAGORE,
The Crescent Moon

BABIES do not want to hear about babies; they like to be told of giants and castles, and of something which can stretch and stimulate their little minds.

SAMUEL JOHNSON

Blessed be the hand that prepares a pleasure for a child for there is no saying when and where it may bloom forth.

DOUGLAS JERROLD

The kind of a world we live in tomorrow depends, not partially, but entirely, upon the type and quality of the education of our children today.

MARTIN VANBEE

Gathering Roses

Two little girls wanted to help mother. So mother sent them into the garden to gather some roses for the table. One soon came running back crying and said, "I just can't cut roses; they are full of thorns and they hurt me." Later the other girl came in with a lovely bouquet of long-stemmed roses. "Why, how could you get them?" said mother. "Didn't the thorns hurt you too?" "Yes, a little, but I kept thinking how happy you would be when you saw these lovely flowers and I looked more at the blossoms than at the thorns."

Children may tear up a house but they never break up a home.

DAUGHTERS

Prayer for a Daughter

Lord, for my daughter I beseech
A scope of love, that she may reach
And hold with very gentle hands,
Each heart that comes for life's demands.

Oh, may she have a faith as deep
And endless as the ocean's sweep.
May wisdom be her guide each day,
With strength to stand, and time to pray.

Let goodness shine upon her face,

Unselfishness, and peace, and grace.
A sense of humor, too, she needs,
With patience for the little deeds.

Oh, may her life be full and free,
And may she always trust in thee!

IRIS O'NEAL BOWEN in Home Life

Mother's Prayer

Eternal God and Father,
   I humbly bow in prayer,
And thank Thee for this jewel
   Entrusted to my care.

May she never turn to folly,
   Never seek the path of sin,
But as a noble Christian worker
   Strive a wandering soul to win.

In the name of Jesus, asking
   Thou wilt hear this humble prayer,
Bless, guide, and protect
   By Thy love, this jewel rare.

ANNIE STEPHENSON CHAPMAN

I had a little daughter,
   And she was given to me
To lead me gently backward
   To the Heavenly Father's knee,
That I, by the force of nature,
   Might in some dim wise divine
The depth of His infinite patience
   To this wayward soul of mine.

JAMES RUSSELL LOWELL, The Changeling

Just Women Talk

I'm glad I have you, daughter dear—
   Who else could understand?
We talk just "women talk," we two,
   And oh, it seems so grand.

No other one can have this joy,
   The kind a mother knows—
When Daughter tells her this and that,
   Her heart within her glows.

It's not so much the bigger things,
   Which anyone could hear;
It's just the common "women talk"
   That makes us feel so near.

I'm glad I have you, daughter dear,
   The little things you say,
The little things that we two share
   Make this a perfect day.

PHYLLIS C. MICHAEL

Just Like Mama

Little girls like stylish hats
With ribbons on . . . and telephone chats,
And bubbly baths and brick-a-bracks,
Just the same as mama.

They don't like a frock, visibly patched;
They wince when expensive furniture's
   scratched;
They delight in china, properly matched,
Just the same as mama.

They love shined shoes, with nary a
   scuff,
Long white gloves and starched white
   cuff,
And a pat from a scented powder
   puff . . .
Just the same as mama.

Someday the little girls will grow
With the grace and poise of a darting
   doe,
Then, all of her womanly choices will
   show
Just the same as mama.

Will she crave world's pleasures and
   neon lights,
Where temptations lure and sin incites,
And yearn to explore wild appetites,
Just the same as mama?

Or will she be found in the house of
   prayer,
Ministering souls that gather there,
A jewel in the crown of the Lord, so fair
Just the same as mama?

Little girls are a loan from Him
On the sea of life, they will sink or
   swim,
Become an imp or a cherubim,
Just the same as mama.

So mom, step carefully, life's long hike,
And wisely select the choices to like.

After you walks a lovely tyke,
Just the same as mama.

Careful choices can shelter from harms,
And cause that bundle of nylon charms
To flee one day to the Saviour's arms
Just the same as mama!
                                    ROMAYNE ALLEN

Oh, my son is my son till he gets him
a wife,
But my daughter's my daughter all of
her life.
            DINAH MARIA MULOCK CRAIK

Mother, to small daughter who
wanted the light left on: "But you sleep
in the dark at home, dear. Why not here
at Grandma's?"
Daughter: "Yes, but it's my own dark
at home, Mommy."

My small daughter had spent some
time with her grandmother and broke
something for which she had been repri-
manded.
    A few days later, she was listening to
a discussion a friend and I were having
about weapons, and afterward my
daughter asked me what the word
meant. I answered that it usually referred
to an object that did damage.
    She thought about this for a moment,
then asked in a little voice, "Mother, am
I a weapon?"
            MRS. W.H. DE MOURE in *Coronet*

Daughter am I in my mother's house;
But mistress in my own.
                                RUDYARD KIPLING

A fluent tongue is the only thing a
mother don't like her daughters to resemble her in.
            RICHARD BRINSLEY SHERIDAN,
                            St. Patrick's Day

As long as a woman can look ten
years younger than her own daughter,
she is perfectly satisfied.
                                    OSCAR WILDE

Raise your daughter to know the Lord
and she will have a built-in Chaperone.

I will dare to say "No" to a daughter
as well as "Yes" and for the same reason. Yes, you may confide in me that
that certain boy causes strange stirrings
in you. You will find me not shocked but
openly ready to confide in you that I
also had such feelings. No, you may
not stay out with that boy alone in a car
for several hours—because those strange
and wonderful stirrings in you will someday make you partners with God in the
creation of a new companion for Him.
This can be done to His glory only in the
context of a mature marriage. I will help
you to avoid betraying the trust He
placed in you when He made you female. I will help you to hold the reins on
your feelings until you are able, with His
help, to hold them in check yourself.
                        MIRIAM PHILIPS PLATIG

A Girl Is a Girl

A girl is a girl so frilly and sweet
You'd just like to hug her the moment
    you meet.

She's little pink ruffles and nylon and
    lace;
She's an innocent look on a little pink
    face;

She's dozens of dollies of ev'ry known
    size—
This cute little angel with stars in her
    eyes;

She's little toy dishes and parties and
    teas—
A princess at heart, you can say what
    you please;

She's all kinds of ribbons and buttons
    and bows,
A pleasure to have as any one knows.

She's little play houses and red rocking
    chairs,
Soft pink eyed bunnies and brown teddy
    bears;

She's the pictures she colored and wants
    you to see,
This wee little pixie who climbs on your
    knee;

She's roses and sunshine, yes, she's all
    that—
Wearing pink gloves and a little pink
    hat;

In Mother's lace curtain this miniature
    bride
Is really quite charming it can't be de-
    nied.

She's an artist, a teacher, a nurse all in
    white,
Yet the mother of four from morning till
    night;

She's perfume and powder and all pretty
    things
Like bracelets and beads and play dia-
    mond rings;

She's ice cream and candy and pink
    birthday cake
She's also the cookies she helped Mother
    bake;

She's the one perfect nuisance to each
    little boy
But she's Daddy's own sweetheart, his
    pride and his joy;

She can pout, she can stomp, she can
    tease, she can cry,
But still she's his pet, the very apple of
    his eye.

She's kittens and everything cuddly and
    nice—
Ah, sure 'n' she's a bit of God's own
    paradise.

                          PHYLLIS C. MICHAEL

A Tribute to Daughters

Of all the joys of motherhood,
    That give your heart a whirl;
There's really nothing to compare,
    With just a little girl.

A little girl with pretty curls,
    And shining, laughing eyes;
Can bring a mother happiness,
    That money never buys.

Now daughters do not stay the same,
    In age, or stage, or size;
And each day for a mother,
    Brings a new and fresh surprise.

One day a daughter cares for things,
    Like frills, and dolls, and toys;
The next she thinks of different things;
    Like cars, and sports—AND BOYS!

To lead her daughter in God's truth;
    Is mother's special task,
And so wise mothers seek the help,
    Of God, who bids us ask.

So now to daughters we extend,
    Our tribute and this prayer:
"That God may bless you every one,
    And keep you in His care."

                          ROGER F. CAMPBELL

What Is a Girl?

Little girls are the nicest things that
happen to people. They are born with a
little bit of angel-shine about them and
though it wears thin sometimes, there is
always enough left to lasso your heart—
even when they are sitting in the mud, or
crying temperamental tears, or parading
up the street in mother's best clothes.

A little girl can be sweeter (and bad-
der) oftener than anyone else in the
world. She can jitter around, and stomp,
and make funny noises that frazzle your
nerves, yet just when you open your
mouth, she stands there demure with
that special look in her eyes. A girl is
Innocence playing in the mud, Beauty
standing on its head, and Motherhood
dragging a doll by the foot.

Girls are available in five colors—
black, white, red, yellow or brown, yet
Mother Nature always manages to select
your favorite color when you place your
order. They disprove the law of supply
and demand—there are millions of little
girls, but each is as precious as rubies.

God borrows from many creatures to make a little girl. He uses the song of a bird, the squeal of a pig, the stubbornness of a mule, the antics of a monkey, the spryness of a grasshopper, the curiosity of a cat, the speed of a gazelle, the slyness of a fox, the softness of a kitten, and to top it all off He adds the mysterious mind of a woman.

A little girl likes new shoes, party dresses, small animals, first grade, noise makers, the girl next door, dolls, make-believe, dancing lessons, ice cream, kitchens, coloring books, make-up, cans of water, going visiting, tea parties, and one boy. She doesn't care so much for visitors, boys in general, large dogs, hand-me-downs, straight chairs, vegetables, snow-suits, or staying in the front yard. She is loudest when you are thinking, the prettiest when she has provoked you, the busiest at bedtime, the quietest when you want to show her off, and the most flirtatious when she absolutely must not get the best of you again.

Who else can cause you more grief, joy, irritation, satisfaction, embarrassment, and genuine delight than this combination of Eve, Salome, and Florence Nightingale? She can muss up your home, your hair, and your dignity—spend your money, your time, and your temper—then just when your patience is ready to crack, her sunshine peeks through and you've lost again.

Yes, she is a nerve-racking nuisance, just a noisy bundle of mischief. But when your dreams tumble down and the world is a mess—when it seems you are pretty much of a fool after all—she can make you a king when she climbs on your knee and whispers, "I love you best of all!"

ALAN BECK

The Sweetest Story
(from the inside cover of a daughter's Bible)

Between these pages, dear, you'll find
The keys to perfect peace of mind;
You'll see the truth, you'll hear, you'll
feel,—
Within your heart, you'll know God's
real.

You'll find new strength for ev'ry need
In ev'ry chapter that you read;
You'll find true faith though dark the
night;
You'll know true joy, true hope, true
light.

Between these pages, dear, you'll find
The secret ties of love that bind
This life to that beyond the blue,
Eternal life, God's gift to you.
Accept God's mercy, truth and grace,
They go beyond all time and space.
Read well these pages, heed each word—
It's the sweetest story ever heard.
—PHYLLIS C. MICHAEL

The Girls That Are Wanted

The girls that are wanted are good girls,
  Good from the heart to the lips,
Pure as the lily is white and pure
  From its heart to its sweet lip tips.

The girls that are wanted are home girls,
  Girls that are Mother's right hand,
That fathers and brothers can trust in,
  And the little one understand.

Girls that are fair on the hearthstones,
  And pleasant when nobody sees;
Kind and sweet to their own folks,
  Ready and anxious to please.

The girls that are wanted are wise girls
  That know what to do and say.
They drive with a smile and a loving
    word
  The gloom of the household away.
          Youth's Counsellor

To My Daughter

I call you mine a million times,
And do believe you are—
'My Own'—'My Sweet'—'My Darling
  Girl'—
'My Precious one'—'My Shining Star!'

Yet in my heart I know that you
Do not belong to me,
For no one ever owned a star
Or really, truly, owned a tree!

No cloud was ever bought on sale,
No sunset ever given.
No one in all this great wide world
Can own a part of heaven.

For gifts like these belong to Him
Who gave the world His love—
In every precious growing thing
On earth—in every cloud above.

No—you do not belong to me,
I must admit it's true.
You still are His whene'er He wills—
I only borrowed you!

JUNE BURCHAM

To A Young Mother

We have watched through the years
     your growing,
From babyhood, girlhood and now . . .
We look to behold a woman
With greater love to endow.

A wife and a mother maturing,
Ideals of your youth still held dear;
A bud that has blossomed in beauty,
Seeing beyond life's veneer.

We are happy and proud of you, dear,
And will watch ever eager to see
Each step newly taken and mastered
Toward the one you aspire to be.

Your choice is the wisdom of ages,
Without qualm, you stand in your place,
Following the best and the highest,
The wondrous path of His Grace.

PAMELA VAULL STARR

Just One Little Girl

She's little and shy
With a smile in her eye
And a bright golden bow in her hair,
A hug and a kiss,
What a dear little miss
With never a worry or care.

She's up with the dawn
When the nighttime is gone
Though sweeter than morning could be,
Just one precious word

And she knows she's adored
And brings heaven closer to me.

I watch her at play
Through the cloudiest day,
She's always the same it would seem,
There's a song in her heart
And a smile from the start
With her mind all aglow in a dream.

She's my sunshine in spring,
Every song that I sing,
My summer that's shining in June,
My autumn and all . . .
Every snowflake to fall,
She keeps my world ever in tune.

She is all that I love
And my stars up above,
Like a fairy she flits on her way.
When she's close by my side
I am beaming with pride . . .
She's the laughter that's all of my day.

Just one little girl
With a ribbon and curl
But the reason for all that I do,
Though small she may seem,
She's the end of my dream,
She's lovely and I love her too.

GARNETT ANN SCHULTZ

To You My Daughter

The world is yours my child
     A gift from God,
But not for you alone to keep
     Yet you may share in its great wealth
And all its beauties now enjoy.

Each child of God is privileged
     With this gift,
But she must learn to understand
     Full well
That harvest time comes only after
     spring.

And after night the dawn
     Is sure to come;
Your world holds treasures rich
     And happiness
If you but work
     And ever true remain;
Keep clean of mind

Be kind and reverent too.
This my daughter
Is your mother's heritage to you.

GRACE MATHEWS WALKER

A writer who was having a hard time making a living was asked by his young daughter this question: "Daddy, what does penury mean?"

"Penury, my child, means the wages of the pen."

From birth to age 18, a girl needs good parents.
From 18 to 35, she needs good looks
From 35 to 55, a woman needs personality,
And from 55 on, she needs cash!

A teenage girl does her homework in the same length of time it takes her mother to do the dishes.

Dreams Do Come True

Daughter of mine, little daughter of
  mine,
  You've grown up so quickly it seems;
Ah, sure and 'twas only yesterday
  You were just a part of my dreams,

I dreamed of a daughter with soft brown
  curls
  And eyes of delphinium blue;
I dreamed of the hours we'd spend in
  play
  Of the many things we'd do.

I dreamed of the moments of joy we'd
  share,
  The secrets—just you and I—
Mother and daughter, daughter and
  mother,
  Together as the days passed by.

But daughter of mine, little daughter of
  mine,
  You've grown up so quickly it seems;
Ah, sure and 'twas only yesterday
  You were just a part of my dreams.

PHYLLIS C. MICHAEL

To My Daughters: A Spiritual Will and Testament

They say, these days, that we should all make a will, a statement in black and white which would be carried out in case of death. Few are our possessions, my daughters; little have we to pass on. But "all that glitters is not gold," and thank God life's most valuable possessions are subject neither to inflation nor taxation. I would pass on to you, my daughters, treasures without price, a few gems gathered from costly inheritance and through rich experience.

Rich I am, rich in the wealth of sons and of daughters. What tax assessor could place a value upon a warm hug, a dimpled smile, a look of mischief from behind a half-closed door? Rich I am, in a true husband's love. Nor do I pay a property tax upon the priceless memories of quiet talks along a wooded path, tea just for two, the many daily joys incomplete until shared with your dad. And how utterly untaxable are the riches of Christ, sustenance for the soul "without money and without price."

And so, my daughters, since I cannot tell how long my torch will burn, and since God has bestowed upon me unlimited wealth, I want to pass on, in writing, a sort of spiritual will and testament. I hope that you, in turn, will pass on these valuable possessions to your children, who will then give them to the third and fourth generations.

(1) Take love. Love is the substance, without which we are but noisy gongs and clanging cymbals (I Corinthians 13:1, RSV). I did nothing to deserve the love of your grandmother, then young and golden-haired and, yes, inexperienced, who poured upon her first-born child a mother's devotion. Nor did I anything to earn the adoration of your grandfather, slight of build and full of humor, who plopped me down in a field of daisies to take my picture for the family album. Nor did I need to beg of them their sympathy and understanding during the days of my childhood, but they are mine. And by God's help this treasure will be yours, yours to grow by and yours to grow in, yours, my daugh-

ters, to pass on in full measure to friends, a love-hungry world, and later to good husbands and welcome children.

(2) *Take faith.* And while I say this, well do I know that faith is caught, not taught. Daughters mine, I would pass on to you a mother's faith, tested, tried, proved. Passing on such a virtue is not like willing you the piano or the record player. For these possessions would be yours at once, while faith is a miniature living thing which comes to fruition only with time. It is walking through an obstacle course, blindfolded, with your hand securely in God's. I would live by faith, my daughters, that it will also become a part of you. And when you reach those thoughtful teens, I would help you see that the doubts Satan throws in your pathway can be stepping-stones to a stronger faith. Faith in what? Faith in a personal, loving, understanding Saviour, Companion, and Friend. Faith in your spiritual leaders. Faith in your friends. Faith in us, your parents. Faith in God's working in your own lives.

(3) *Take courage.* What a world we have brought you into, our daughters! Surely we can pass on to you no flowery optimism about the future, worldly-wise. There is no security to be found in present peace negotiations. Nor is there in the United Nations. The world boasts of military security, as its watchdogs glare ferociously at one another. All we can give you is His word, "When these things . . . come to pass . . . look up . . . for your redemption draweth nigh" (Luke 21:28). And that is enough, my daughters.

(4) *Take health.* My mother tells of the day when it was stylish for an attractive girl to lie back on her pillow, appearing delicate and expecting to be waited on hand and foot. What a misfit such a frail creature would be in our modern world! You, my daughters, have been endowed by God with strong bodies, minds, and spirits. Keep them that way. You know the rules of health and recreation. Discipline your lives to observe them, for what you *do* is not so important as what you *are*. Enjoy a wide variety of hobbies and skills. Pause

for the aesthetic pleasures that enrich life—inspiring books, fine music, flaming sunsets. Remember that your bodies are God's house, and carefully guard His gift to you, the very foundation of your future happiness, your Christian purity. Think on those things which are "true . . . honorable . . . just . . . pure . . . lovely . . . gracious . . . (excellent) . . . (and) worthy of praise." (Philippians 4:8, RSV).

(5) *Take home.* I am glad, my daughters, that the word "housewife" has given way to the more expressive "homemaker" or "home builder." And I thank God for the privilege of creating a home for you, your brothers, and your dad. Take home, my daughters. Live in it, love it, wear out the carpet with the hurry of your play. Learn to do by doing; learn to love by being loved. I hope you will grasp life's difficult lessons right here in our home, so you will not need to sweat them out with tears after you have gone. Learn from your parents to forgive and be forgiven. Learn from us to live above criticism, unsympathetic judgment. Yet we acknowledge that we are all to human and subject to error. We pray that we may, by example, help you to master those two magic expressions: "Thank you," and "I'm sorry; I was wrong."

(6) *Take joy.* There is a boisterous humor, my daughters, which is not for you as Christian girls. It struts itself upon the screen, making ridiculous faces, and tiresome, superficial gestures. It is weighed in the balances and found wanting. For it leaves in its wake a weary emptiness. Take fun, my daughters, real Christian fun. Take a sense of humor, the ability to laugh even at yourself (you'll need it). Take the merry heart the Bible speaks about. Fill up with joy and let it bubble over. But never at the expense of anyone else. Nor at the expense of principle. Nor at the expense of your relationship with Jesus Christ.

(7) *Take a correct sense of values.* A college professor, addressing a group of young mothers, once said, "I'm glad your families are so fortunate: in your homes people will be more important

than things." I never could forget that. When you are small, you may be tempted to think that children who own the most toys are happiest. When you are older, you may be enticed by extravagant wardrobes. And when you are older still, you will be introduced to a fairyland of picture windows, sterling silver, and fine linens.

Be not deceived: a woman's happiness consists not in the abundance of *things* which she possesses. Some of the happiest people I have met were destitute refugees; some of the world's most desperate characters live on Easy Street.

The things which mean the most to you, my children, are time, love, companionship, and understanding. They cost nothing in dollars and cents. Pass on to others these inexpensive pleasures. And let the Joneses keep up with themselves.

(8) *Take Character.* I realize, my daughters, that when you are old enough to read this, your characters will long have been basically formed. I hope that you will never need to say that you were but a side line in your mother's life. For my highest calling is bringing you and your brothers to a mature Christian adulthood.

I hope that you will always be eager to learn, that you will be enthusiastic and dependable, and that you will rejoice in each day the Lord has made as an adventure with God. I hope that you will begin making decisions for yourself long before you are eighteen or twenty-one, and that you will learn self-discipline, so vital to a happy life. I want you to grow spiritually tall, as you grow physically mature, abounding in such graces as honesty, understanding, kindness, and respect for others. I want you to know that I have faith in you, just as my mother's trust lighted a torch for me, even when I was thousands of miles from her hearth.

Does all of this sound as though I expect perfection of you, my daughters? Of course not, for I fall short in all these things. Yet, as your grandmother so diligently taught me, "If we aim for the sky, we may at least hit the treetops."

(9) *Take womanhood.* Pearl Buck wrote that, when she rebelled at learning the arts of homemaking, her mother said, "Pearl, you cannot escape being a woman." I beg of you my daughters, accept gladly the fact that you are girls. For God has planned for you a satisfying fulfillment of the best that is in you in womanhood, motherhood, and companionship with some earnest disciple of His.

Although my mother allowed me many opportunities for personal enrichment, she also taught me to do the ordinary tasks around the house. How I chafed when the mother of a friend remarked, "Helen is so domestic!" At the time her daughter's glamour seemed more exciting than my dishwashing. But I would not change places with her daughter today.

I want you to learn early, my daughters, that God didn't mean work to be distasteful. I want you to see homemaking as a creative vocation, with such tangible rewards as shining dishes, attractive meals (well-balanced and home-prepared), and a harmonious family life. Be glad you are girls, my daughters. Women were not meant to compete with men, but to complete them. If you struggle only for self-realization, you will end in frustration; if you lose your life for others, you will find it.

(10) *Take Christ.* And as I write these things, I am keenly aware that you could become gracious, lovely, young ladies in the eyes of your friends, yet be motivated by Self instead of Christ. Many are the cultured, refined persons who have appropriated some of the by-products of Christianity, but who have missed the Person of the Lord Jesus Christ.

More than anything in all this world, my daughters, I pray that you will become intimate with Christ, that His Spirit will bear His gentle fruits in your lives. Then will your faces radiate an inner joy that needs no artificial improvements. Then will you be endowed with an inner peace and poise unobtainable at a charm school. Then will your life have meaning, purpose, and enthusiasm which cannot be induced by natural means.

Then will you find your place—His plan
—in the world. Then will your mother's
prayers for your lives be answered.

HELEN GOOD BRENNEMAN

A Tribute to All Daughters

Every home should have a daughter,
　　for there's nothing like a girl
To keep the world around her
　　in one continuous whirl! . . .
From the moment she arrives on earth,
　　and on through womanhood,
A daughter is a Female
　　who is seldom understood . . .
One minute she is laughing,
　　the next she starts to cry,
Man just can't understand her
　　and there's just no use to try . . .
She is soft and sweet and cuddly,
　　but she's also wise and smart,
She's a wondrous combination
　　of a mind and brain and heart . . .
And even in her baby days
　　she's just a born coquette,

And anything she really wants
　　she manages to get . . .
For even at a tender age
　　she uses all her wiles
And she can melt the hardest heart
　　with the sunshine of her smiles . . .
She starts out as a rosebud
　　with her beauty unrevealed,
Then through a happy childhood
　　her petals are unsealed . . .
She's soon a sweet girl graduate,
　　and then a blushing bride,
And then a lovely woman
　　as the rosebud opens wide . . .
And some day in the future,
　　if it be God's gracious will,
She, too, will be a Mother
　　and knows that reverent thrill
That comes to every Mother
　　whose heart is filled with love
When she beholds the "angel"
　　that God sent her from above . . .
And there would be no life at all
　　in this world or the other
Without a Darling Daughter
　　who, in turn, becomes a Mother!

HELEN STEINER RICE

BOYS

When all the world is young, lad,
　　And all the trees are green;
And every goose a swan, lad,
　　And every lass a queen;
Then hey for boot and horse, lad,
　　And round the world away:
Young blood must have its course, lad,
　　And every dog his day.

CHARLES KINGSLEY, Water Babies

What Is a Boy?

Between the innocence of babyhood
and the dignity of manhood we find a
delightful creature called a boy. Boys
come in assorted sizes, weights, and
colors, but all boys have the same creed:
To enjoy every second of every minute of
every hour of every day and to protest
with noise (their only weapon) when

their last minute is finished and the adult
males pack them off to bed at night.

Boys are found everywhere—on top
of, underneath, inside of, climbing on,
swinging from, running around, or jumping to. Mothers love them, little girls
hate them, older sisters and brothers
tolerate them, adults ignore them, and
Heaven protects them. A boy is Truth
with dirt on its face, Beauty with a cut
on its finger, Wisdom with bubble gum
in its hair, and the Hope of the future
with a frog in its pocket.

When you are busy, a boy is an incon-
siderate, bothersome, intruding jangle of
noise. When you want him to make a
good impression, his brain turns to jelly
or else he becomes a savage, sadistic,
jungle creature bent on destroying the
world and himself with it.

A boy is a composite—he has the appetite of a horse, the digestion of a sword swallower, the energy of a pocket-size atomic bomb, the curiosity of a cat, the lungs of a dictator, the imagination of a Paul Bunyan, the shyness of a violet, the audacity of a steel trap, the enthusiasm of a fire cracker, and when he makes something he has five thumbs on each hand.

He likes ice cream, knives, saws, Christmas, comic books, the boy across the street, woods, water (in its natural habitat), large animals, Dad, trains, Saturday mornings, and fire engines. He is not much for Sunday School, company, schools, books without pictures, music lessons, neckties, barbers, girls, overcoats, adults, or bedtime.

Nobody else is so early to rise, or so late to supper. Nobody else gets so much fun out of trees, dogs, and breezes. Nobody else can cram into one pocket a rusty knife, a half-eaten apple, 3 feet of string, an empty Bull Durham sack, 2 gum drops, 6 cents, a sling shot, a chunk of unknown substance, and a genuine super-sonic code ring with a secret compartment.

A boy is a magical creature—you can lock him out of your work shop, but you can't lock him out of your heart. You can get him out of your study, but you can't get him out of your mind. Might as well give up—he is your captor, your jailer, your boss, and your master—a freckled-face, pint-sized, cat-chasing, bundle of noise. But when you come home at night with only the shattered pieces of your hopes and dreams, he can mend them like new with the two magic words —"Hi Dad!"

ALAN BECK

Boys

A boy is a piece of existence quite separate from all things else, and deserves separate chapters in the natural history of man. The real lives of boys are yet to be written, the lives of pious and good boys, which enrich the catalogues of great publishing societies, resemble a real boy's life about as much as a chicken picked and larded, upon a spit, and ready for delicious eating, resembles a free fowl in the fields. With some few honorable exceptions, they are impossible boys, with incredible goodness. Their piety is monstrous. A Man's experience stuffed into a little boy is simply monstrous. And we are soundly sceptical of this whole school of juvenile *pate de foie gras* piety. Apples that ripen long before their time are either diseased or wormbitten.

Your Boy

There are little eyes upon you, and
    they're watching night and day;
There are little ears that quickly take in
    every word you say;
There are little hands all eager to do
    everything you do,
And a little boy who's dreaming of the
    day he'll be like you.

You're the little fellow's idol; you're the
    wisest of the wise;
In his little mind about you no suspicions
    ever rise;
He believes in you devoutly, holds all
    that you say and do,
He will say and do in your way when
    he's grown up just like you.

There's a wide-eyed little fellow who be-
    lieves you're always right,
And his ears are always open, and he
    watches day and night.
You are setting an example every day in
    all you do
For the little boy who's waiting to grow
    up to be like you.

AUTHOR UNKNOWN

The Love of a Boy

Thank you, God, for the love of a boy,
For the warm, tight squeeze of his hand,
For the eyes that sparkle and feet that
    dash,
And his feeling that life is grand!

Thank you, God, for the love of a boy,
For his rough-and-tumble fun,

For his towsled hair and his cap awry,
And his shouting when school is done.

Thank you, God, for the love of a boy,
For the silent depths of his soul,
For his questioning mind and his halting
    speech
As he struggles to find life's goal.

Yes, thank you, God for the love of a
    boy—
Whole-hearted, impetuous, free—
Thank you for all that he is today,
And for all he is going to be!

ERIC S. HORN

A boy is a bank where you can deposit
your most precious treasures—the hard-
won wisdom, the dreams of a better
world. A boy can guard and protect
these, and perhaps invest them wisely
and with a profit—a profit larger than
you ever dreamed. A boy will inherit
your world. All the work will be judged
by him. Tomorrow he will take your
seat in Congress, own your company,
run your town. The future is his and
through him the future is yours. Perhaps
he deserves a little more attention now.

AUTHOR UNKNOWN

For Any Mother of a Small Boy

Was it for this I rendered sterile
Bottles, blankets, and apparel,
Scrubbed and boiled and disinfected,
Let no one touch unless inspected,
That now, quite innocent of soap,
My erstwhile pride, my one-time hope,
In spite of all the books assert,
Should thrive on good old-fashioned dirt?

ELIZABETH-ELLEN LONG

The Boy of Today

A boy is a person who is going to carry
    on what
    You have started.
He is going to sit where you are sitting
    and
    When you are gone, attend to those
things which you think are impor-
    tant.
You can adopt all the policies you
    please, but how long they will be
    carried out depends on him.
All your work is for him and will be
    judged,
    Praised, or condemned by him.
Your reputation and your future are in
    his hands.
He will take over your schools and your
    universities, your churches and your
    prisons, your charities and your
    corporations.
He will assume control of your cities,
    states and nations.
Even if you make leagues and treaties,
    he is the one who will enforce
    them.
The fate of nations and humanity is in
    his hands.
So it might be well to pay some atten-
    tion to
    him—the boy of today.

The King's Highway

To make a man, begin with a boy.

Mother of small boy to psychiatrist,
"Well, I don't know whether he feels
insecure, but everybody else in the neighborhood certainly does."

A Boy

Nobody knows what a boy is worth,
    A boy is his work or play,
A boy who whistles around the place,
    Or laughs in an artless way.

Nobody knows what a boy is worth,
    And the world must wait and see,
For every man in a honored place,
    Is a boy that used to be.

Nobody knows what a boy is worth,
    A boy with his face aglow,
For hid in his heart there are secrets deep
    Not even the wisest know.

Nobody knows what a boy is worth,
    A boy with his bare, white feet;

So have a smile and a kindly word,
For every boy you meet.
AUTHOR UNKNOWN

Sons are the anchors of a Mother's
life.
SOPHOCLES, *Phaedra*

The Boy We Want

A Boy that is truthful and honest
And faithful and willing to work;
But we have not a place that we care to
disgrace
With a boy that is ready to shirk.

Wanted—a boy you can tie to,
A boy that is trusty and true,
A boy that is good to old people,
And kind to the little ones too.

A boy that is nice to the home folks,
And pleasant to sister and brother,
A boy who will try when things go awry
To be helpful to father and mother.

These are the boys we depend on—
Our hope for the future, and then
Grave problems of state and the world's
work await
Such boys when they grow to be men.
AUTHOR UNKNOWN

A Man Twelve Years Old

There's a man that I know, and he lives
near you,
In a town called Everywhere;
You might not think he's a man from his
hat
Or the clothes he may chance to
wear;
But under the jacket with many a patch
Is a heart more precious than gold—
The heart of a man 'neath the coat of a
boy,
A man who is twelve years old.

We never may know what the future
will make
Of the boys that we carelessly meet,
For many a statesman is now at school,
And presidents play in the street.
The hand that is busy with playthings
now
The reins of power will hold;
So I take off my hat and gladly salute
This man who is twelve years old.
MAURICE SMILEY

READINGS

If Jesus Came to Your House

If Jesus came to your house to spend a
day or two—
If He came unexpectedly, I wonder what
you'd do.

Oh, I know you'd give your nicest room
to such an honored Guest,
And all the food you'd serve Him would
be the very best,
And you would keep assuring Him
you're glad to have Him there—
That serving him in your own home is
joy beyond compare.

But—when you saw Him coming, would
you meet Him at the door
With arms outstretched in welcome to
your heav'nly Visitor?
Or would you have to change your
clothes before you let Him in
Or hide some magazines and put
the Bible where they'd been?

Would you turn off the radio and hope
He hadn't heard
And wish you hadn't uttered that last
loud, hasty word?
Would you hide your worldly music
and put some hymn books out?
Could you let Jesus walk right in, or
would you rush about?

And I wonder—if the Saviour spent a
day or two with you,

Would you go right on doing all the
things you always do?
Would you keep right on saying all
the things you always say?
Would life for you continue as it does
from day to day?

Would your family conversation keep up
its usual pace,
And would you find it hard each meal to
say a table grace?
Would you sing the songs you always
sing and read the books you read
And let Him know the things on
which your mind and spirit feed?

Would you take Jesus with you everywhere you'd planned to go,
Or would you maybe change your plans
for just a day or so?
Would you be glad to have Him meet
your very closest friends,
Or would you hope they'd stay away
until His visit ends?

Would you be glad to have Him stay
forever on and on?
Or would you sigh with great relief when
He at last was gone?
It might be interesting to know the
things that you would do
If Jesus Christ in person came to
spend some time with you.

LOIS KENDALL BLANCHARD

Mother

In the history of human speech, in the
language of all nations, and in the dictionary of men and angels, there is no
word so full of meaning, or that fills our
soul so full of sentiment, as "Mother"!

The word "Mother" is the sweetest
and the most forceful of all words wherever the footsteps of civilization have
left their imprints. Any movement that
deepens home ties, that inspires better
national life, that makes better sons and
daughters, has the sentiment of Mother
as its source.

Songs have been sung, poems have
been written, and pictures have been
painted by master hands, yet none has

been or will be able to express that love
which glows in a Mother's heart, the
finest inspiration life offers.

Someone[1] has wisely declared that
most beautiful things in life come by
twos and threes, by dozens and hundreds
—plenty of roses, stars, sunsets, rainbows, brothers and sisters, aunts and
cousins—but there is only one Mother in
all the wide world!

[1] Kate Douglas Wiggen. See p. 34.

ANNE MCCOLLUM BOYLES

The Apron String

Once there was a mother and her
small son running by her side. And as
the son was very little, the mother tied
him to the string of her apron.

"Now," she said, "when you stumble,
you can pull yourself up by the apron-
string, and so you will not fall."

The little boy held on tight, and all
went well. And the mother sang at her
work.

By and by the boy grew up until his
head came above the window sill; and he
looked through the window, and saw far
away green trees waving in the wind,
and a flowing river that flashed in the
sun; and rising above all, blue peaks of
the mountains that looked like spires in
the sky.

"O, Mother!" he cried, "untie the
apron-string and let me go!"

But the mother said, "Not yet, my
child. Only yesterday you stumbled, and
would have fallen but for the apron-
string. Wait yet a little, until you are
stronger."

So the boy waited, and all went well
as before, and the mother sang at her
work.

But one day the son found the door of
young manhood standing open, and it
was in the Springtime, and he stood on
the threshhold and looked across the valley, and saw the green trees waving, and
the swift-flowing river with the sun flashing on it, and the blue mountains rising
beyond. And this time he heard the
voice of the river, and it said, "Come!"

Then the young man started forward
and he took a blade and severed the

apron-string, and he ran out into the world with one end of the apron-string hanging by his side.

The mother gathered up the other end of the string and put it into her bosom, and went about her work. But she sang no more.

The young man ran on and on in the fresh air and the morning sun, rejoicing in his freedom from the apron-string. He crossed the valley and began to climb the foothills, among which the river flowed swiftly, angrily beating the rocks and cliffs. At times it was easy climbing, and again it was steep and craggy, but always he looked upward at the blue peaks beyond, and always the voice of the river was in his ears, saying, "Come!"

Suddenly one day the young man came to the brink of a precipice, over which the river dashed in a cataract of fury, foaming and flashing, and sending up clouds of silvery spray. The mist filled his eyes and he could not see his footing clearly. He grew dazed, stumbled and fell.

But as he fell, something about him caught on a point of rock at the very edge of the precipice, and held him so that his feet were dangling over the abyss. When he put his hand up to see what held him, he found that it was the apron-string which was still fastened to his side.

And then the young man remembered what his mother told him many years ago: "When you stumble, you can pull yourself up by the apron-string." Then he drew himself up, and said, "Oh, how strong my mother's apron string is!" And he stood firm on his feet, and went on climbing toward the blue peaks of the mountains.

From *Golden Windows*

Mothers Are Like That

No! I'm busy just now. Ask Daddy to tie your shoes.

No dear, I didn't see your Bible.

I know it counts ten points, but where did you leave it? Perhaps you didn't bring it home last Sunday. I haven't seen it all week.

You found it?

Good!

Yes, your blue dress. No, not that one—the new one.

No, I'm sure I don't know who you can get for a substitute teacher. We have no extras in our department.

Yes, try her. She might do it.

Too bad your teachers don't call you earlier.

Oh, she just took sick.

Stop son! Don't tease your sister. No! No! Be a good boy. Are you clean? Let's see.

Your face is dirty. Go and wash it again. And use *hot* water and *soap!*

Just a minute. I'll be right up as soon as I set the oven for dinner.

What is it now?

Your part; what part?

Your class has charge of the worship programme.

Look under your desk blotter. Sometimes I put loose papers under there when I find them around.

You found it? Good!

You have to learn it yet? Why *do* you leave things till the last minute?

Yes, I know you have been busy.

Isn't this a lovely corsage Daddy gave me for Mother's Day?

Get your coats on now, it's nearly time to leave.

Hurry! Daddy has gone out to get the car.

Carry your little sister. She may fall and get her clothes dirty.

All out now?

Your trumpet? Of course. Better get it. We'll wait.

Now can I lock the door? Everybody have a Bible?

You haven't.

Run and get it then.

Now. All set?

Here, you can't take that pea shooter to Sunday School.

Hand it over.

Yes, dear, I know you want to say

your verse to me. I'll hear it at church. Daddy is waiting now.

No, you can't all sit by the window. Let your little sister there.

You come in the front with Mom and Dad, son.

No, you can't take your pea shooter. Not even if you leave it in the car. That's enough!

There.

Not yet, I'll hear your verse at church.

Help your little sister out of the car. Better carry her again. There's a bit of a puddle by the curb. No, you take her to class. I have to hear memory work. And Daddy will take little brother with him.

Good morning, Pastor. Yes, it's a fine day.

Don't slide on the railing. No, you'll get your hands dirty. Come into the church.

I know it's early but you can wait inside.

Don't cry, dear, go with big brother and see your teacher. No, Mommy will come for you after Sunday School.

Now, your memory verse.

Matthew 25: 21.

All right.

You want the first word?

"Well done."

Yes.

Now what?

You can't remember the rest.

Listen carefully. I'll say it for you.

"Well done thou good and faithful servant . . . enter thou into the joy of our Lord."

Now try it again.

Good girl. You know it now.

Tears in my eyes? Well that's hard for Mommy to explain to her little girl.

No, dear, I'm not sad.

Just thinking.

What about?

Oh, about your memory verse.

Here's your offering.

Now, off to your class!

Yes, yes, I'm all right. I'm fine.

She's a sweet child. And what a verse she has given me for Mother's Day!

ELLEN MCKAY TRIMMER
in *The Fellowship Baptist*

They Call Her Mother

(A modern adaptation of Proverbs 31:10-31)

Who can find a virtuous woman? for the value of her life is beyond monetary calculations. Her husband has absolute trust in her so that he has no need of satisfaction from other women. She will do him good and not evil all the days of her life.

She keeps his clothing up-to-date, clean and tidy. She willingly works around the house. She provides variety at mealtime by wise selection of nutritious and delicious foods. She gets up early each morning to make his breakfast and sees that her children also eat properly.

She knows a bargain when she sees one and is always concerned about the future stability and supply of her home. The strength of her character is shown in her attitude toward her household tasks. She takes pride in a job well done even if she must work late hours to accomplish it.

She knows how to use a sewing machine and needle. She has a compassionate heart and hand toward those who have great needs. Those in her home especially benefit from her domestic talents. Her own clothing shows good taste and modesty. Even her husband is known by her concern for his wearing apparel. She often uses her household talents to provide extra income for her family.

She is known as a woman of honorable character. The humble expression of this character gives her an inner joy.

She is wise in her speech and especially knows how to say kind words. She is concerned about the interests and problems of all in her house. She is not a gossip or kaffeklatcher. Her children are happy to talk about her to their friends. Her husband also praises her to others.

Other women have done great deeds, but this type of mother and wife ranks highest.

Popularity is deceitful and glamor is shallow, but a woman who has personal contact with the holy God, she shall be praised. She shall receive great satisfaction from her labors and others shall talk about her good deeds wherever they go.

WILLIAM J. KRUTZA in *Moody Monthly*

What Mothers Are

Mothers can begin being mothers when they are around sixteen, and they sometimes keep it up until they are past eighty, which must make it about the longest career on record.

They come in all sizes, shapes, and colors, but don't be fooled; the tiny ones can pack a powerful punch, and the big ones can faint at the sight of a spider.

When vandals besieged Rome, it was a stately mother, who, when the despoilers demanded her jewels, placed an arm around her children and proclaimed: *Hic sunt ornamentis!* ("These are my jewels!")

A mother will scold quite hard when you pout for a party dress that costs fifty dollars. Then, just when you have resigned yourself to wearing the old blue tulle, she will dig down under the newspaper lining the top bureau drawer, and come up with five old ten-dollar bills, which she presses into your hand.

A mother will scream like a banshee at dirty dishes left in the sink, and then stay up until one A.M. baking the three cherry pies which you promised for the bake sale.

In a recent newspaper account, a pretty young mother offered one of her eyes for an operation for her son, who was losing his sight. Said the hard-bitten old surgeon: "In the face of love like this, I stand speechless."

A mother will remain dry-eyed when Junior falls out of the apple tree and breaks an arm. She is not particularly moved at funerals or sad movies, but her eyes fill up when you come down the aisle in the beautiful white gown.

Mothers will ask fathers if they think mothers are getting fat, and when fathers say yes, then mothers get mad.

One mother whose little runaway boy was brought home by the police, got on her knees and hugged him tightly, and then got up and gave him the worst licking he ever had!

Mothers can remember the birthdays and anniversaries of all the aunts and cousins, but they forget who called you from the malt shop right after school.

Your mother will take a folded newspaper and give the dog a spanking for getting up on your bedspread. Then, when he gets a piece of glass in his paw, she drives him to the vet, ten miles away and holds him on her lap while the vet fixes him.

You take one day a year to think especially about your mother; she takes the other three hundred and sixty-five to think about you.

But that's the way she wants it!

IRENE STEIGERWALD

MOTHER'S DAY DEVOTIONAL TALKS AND MESSAGES

What Can a Mother Do?

What can a mother do? The question is as old as motherhood itself and it may be that we can find a few answers if we will look back over the centuries.

Mother Noah, perplexed by the problems of an age whose moral standards so closely parallel our own, must have asked herself, "What can a mother do?"

Undoubtedly she had to listen to scoffing. To the antediluvian equivalent of, "What's the matter with you folk. Are you crazy or something? Old Noah trying to 'save' everybody. Him and his ark and his gloomy predictions of judgment!"

And when her sons would come home, their feelings hurt, and appeal "Mom, can't you do something? Everybody in town's making fun of our whole family," did this mother resort to rationalization? Did she take the attitude that "We have to think of what all of this talk is doing to the boys' personalities. You know, Noah, a boy shouldn't have to go around explaining and apologizing for what his dad is doing — even in the name of religion."

. She didn't. Apparently this mother found a solution, and when the flood came, her sons were safe in the shelter ordained by God for those who believed His message.

The New Testament has its sampling of mothers who likewise must have questioned at times how best to fill their role. The mother of James and John, for instance. Possibly she had lived for the day when the sign over the business would read, "Zebedee and Sons, Inc." Instead, as her sons grew up to be responsible young citizens they took themselves off to be disciples of an almost unknown — though coming — Prophet. This spelled the death of the family expectations and certainly jeopardized the financial future of the two young men.

How would the average mother have reacted?

"Son," we can almost hear, "I hope you're really thinking this thing through. I can see that there's a certain glamor in all this miracle business, but what will it get you in the end? Think of the business your dad has built up . . ."

There is not one indication of any such conversation ever having taken place. We are given a glimpse of this mother in Matthew 20:20:

"Then came to him the mother of Zebedee's children with her sons, worshipping him, and desiring a certain thing of him."

Some have criticized this mother for the request she made, but the fact is that she asked nothing but the best for her two sons, and what mother would not join her in such a request? We should note that, first, she came with her sons (she didn't send them) and, secondly, she had the right order: she worshipped — acknowledging Christ as the One to be worshipped — then she asked, "Could

You arrange for my two boys to have a place close to You — for all eternity?"

What more can a mother ask?

Another from whom we can get an answer to "What can a mother do?" is the mother of young Timothy. Both his mother and his grandmother would say to each mother today, "Give the scriptures an important place in your home." And for Timothy this must have been more than rote learning or mere parroting verses, for when the Apostle Paul encountered Timothy he found a young man with whom the Spirit of God could deal because Timothy had a working knowledge of the soul-saving Scriptures (II Timothy 3:15).

We can well believe that this mother and grandmother had to sandwich their Bible teaching in between many conflicting schedules, for Timothy's dad was a Greek. His boy would be required to learn the lore and literature of the Greeks and quite possibly give much time to his athletic activities in that Olympian culture.

Nevertheless Mother Eunice and Grandmother Lois did their work for God in the heart of a boy whose name lives on.

Conflict there will be, we can be sure. Situation ethics would require that we accommodate to the times in which we live. But the Christian who sincerely asks God, "What can a mother do?" will receive the timeless answers from God's Word.

JEANETTE W. LOCKERBIE

A Beautiful Picture

There is nothing more beautiful in the world than seeing an entire family engaged in religious devotions. The home may be small, poor and scantily furnished, but God is there with His love and comfort, and His presence gives strength to resist temptation. Family devotions keep us in touch with God and give us strength in the day of trial and testing.

Dale Carnegie tells the experience of a woman who was a student in one of his classes. She told him how, in the great financial depression of the early thirties, her husband's salary was only $18.00 a week, and often it was less than that because of his illness. In the course of time they lost the little home they had built with their own hands. They owed money at the grocery store and had five children to feed. Conditions grew worse until the woman became so worried over successive misfortunes that one day she took her five-year-old daughter into the bedroom, plugged up the window, turned on the gas and lay in the bed with her child at her side and listened to the gas escaping from the heater.

Suddenly she heard music. She had forgotten to turn off the radio in the kitchen and now someone was singing, "What a Friend we have in Jesus, All our sins and griefs to bear." As she heard these words she realized she had tried to fight all her battles alone. She sprang from the bed, turned off the gas, opened the door and raised the window.

Then she fell on her knees and prayed to God. She prayed and wept all the rest of the day. She did not pray for help. She poured out her soul in thanksgiving to God for the blessings He had given her—five splendid children—all of them healthy and strong in body and mind.

Then, in time, conditions improved as the depression lightened. Her children grew up and married, and as she looked back to that terrible day when she turned on the gas, she thanked God over and over that she woke up in time. What joys she would have missed had she died that day.

Listen, mothers! No matter what your circumstances in life may be, whether you live in a home of poverty or of plenty, if God has blessed you with children, give them the training as taught in the Word of God, and by precept and example, lead them in the way of righteousness. If at present you have sons and daughters who are not Christians, let them feel your anxiety about their soul's salvation. Let them know they have been cradled in prayer since babyhood, and how your heart has yearned for God to plan their lives. Tell them the story of your conversion and of the mysterious workings of the Spirit of God in your life. Let there be times when they hear your voice lifted in prayer for them, praying that they might know the blessed joy of Christian faith.

If some mother who reads this message be not sure of her own salvation, I kindly urge her to attend to it as soon as possible. How can you lead your children right unless you be right yourself? How can you lead them heavenward unless you are on the way to heaven? Open your Bible to John 3:16 and put your trust in Jesus Christ, the Son of God. He will save you now. Begin to serve Him who died to save you. Oh, what a joy it will be then to teach and guide your children in the way of life everlasting.

Having received Christ as your Saviour, you will find it easy to influence your children to attend Sunday school and church. There you, with them, will find real joy in Christian living. Then you will strive continually to throw a mantle of Christianity around them.

In closing this message, I would add a few words to fathers. Fathers, according to the Bible, you are supposed to be the head of the house. You should take the lead and set the example in Christian living. You should join hands with the mother of your children and bring them to Christ. Go with them to Sunday school and church. It is not a difficult matter to bring the children to church if the parents lead the way.

It is said that some years ago a Canadian farmer and his wife were going home on a cold winter night. With them was their little son. To save several miles they took a short cut through an immense, frozen wheat field. After awhile as they walked along the father said, "Wife, you have hold of the boy, haven't you?"

"No," she replied, "I thought you had him. Don't you have hold of him?"

"No," he replied, "we must have lost him!"

They turned back to look for their child, and all night the distracted parents sought for their boy in that wide field, but they failed to find him. The next day the entire town turned out to find the lad. They finally joined hands and combed the whole field. One of them stumbled over the boy. He was still and cold in death! When they brought the frozen body to the father, he moaned, "Our child is dead. Why didn't we join hands before? Why didn't we keep hold of him?"

Fathers and mothers, let us join hands to bring the children to the blessed Saviour and He will save and hold them for eternity.

CHARLES F. WEIGLE in *Listen, Mothers*

A Mother's Calling to Make and to Mend

What child has not watched with wonder as mother wielded a needle and thread? How comforting it is for children to see mother making new clothes for them or mending their old garments, particularly their favorites.

But mothers not only make and mend clothes. They make and mend character! To do this sometimes requires "needling."

The greatest heritage anyone can receive is the influence of a Christian home. But children do not always respond favorably to mother's efforts. Sin often snares the sons and daughters of the saintliest parents. But a godly mother never gives up. She ever encourages righteousness and redemption.

"Stop needling me, mother!" If Robert Moffatt did not say it, at least he was thinking it when his mother volunteered some advice as her son prepared to leave home. Earnestly she sought to solicit his promise that he would read his Bible and pray twice daily.

Robert tried to ignore her entreaties. But at the moment of parting his mother once again implored, "Son, please promise me to read the Bible."

The youth recognized that he dare not refuse. "Yes, Mother," he replied. "I promise." Later he explained to acquaintances who inquired about his practice, "My promise once made, must be kept." So you see, if mother had not "needled," South Africa might have missed its pioneer missionary!

Some mothers raise their children to serve God from infancy. Others grieve as they see their offspring detour from the straight and narrow. Instead of making, they must then strive to mend. Such a mother was Monica. Her son Augustine broke her heart by departing from the faith and living a life of wild abandon. But Monica would not give up. She talked to Augustine and she talked to God. At the last she apparently was successful in dissuading him from sailing to Italy where she feared the influence would wreck him beyond recovery. He said he would not go, but his cronies persuaded him to sail anyway. Monica, distraught, feared God had failed her. But she continued praying for her wayward Augustine. And in Italy he met Ambrose who led him to Christ. God saved St. Augustine in the very place his mother feared to have him venture lest he be lost beyond recovery!

Christian mother, never give up in your efforts to make or to mend your offspring according to God's revealed pattern. Scripture encourages us to "Train up a child in the way he should go and when he is old, he will not depart from it" (Proverbs 22:6).

What more wonderful assurance could you ask this Mother's Day and every day of the year than a promise from God's Word that your efforts will be rewarded?

RAYMOND L. COX

Mother's Day

SUGGESTED MUSIC:
Sweeter as the Years Go By (C. H. Morris)
I Know God's Promise Is True (C. H. Morris)
SCRIPTURE:
Proverbs 31:11-15, 30, 31
TEXT:
"House and riches are the inheritance of fathers: and a prudent wife is from the Lord" (Proverbs 19:14).
MEDITATION:
A man who has neither a good wife nor a good mother is at an extreme disadvantage; for back of every man who has made an impact upon the world

is a good woman, either a wife or mother or maybe both.

It is always interesting to read about the mothers of great men. But of all the famous mothers of history, my favorite is Susanna Wesley, mother of John and Charles Wesley. Susanna was the twenty-fifth child of Rev. Dr. Annesley. Even in those days a family of twenty-five aroused considerable interest. Just after the parish pastor had baptized Susanna, a friend asked, "How many children has Dr. Annesley now?"

The pastor answered, "I am not sure whether it is two dozen or a quarter of a hundred."

Mrs. Wesley, who was known for her beauty, ran her home by the sheer force of her personality. She had nineteen children of her own. Ten died in infancy and of the nine left, two became world famous.

In her own words, Mrs. Wesley tells how she trained the children. "When turned a year old and some before, they were taught to fear the rod and cry softly, by which means they escaped abundance of correction which they might otherwise have had; and that odious noise of the sound of crying children was rarely heard in the house: but the family usually lived in as much quietness as if there had not been a child among them.

"None of the children were taught to read until they were five years old. One day was allowed the child wherein to learn its letters and each of them in that time did know all its letters. After learning their letters, the children were taught to spell out the first chapter of Genesis with the happy result that long before they were six years of age, they were able to read."

Susanna had one room of the parsonage turned into a school where the children sat from 9:00 to 12:00 and from 2:00 to 5:00.

"And it is almost incredible," says Mrs. Wesley, "what a child may be taught in a quarter of a year by vigorous application. . . ."

In addition to all this, Mrs. Wesley had a set time each week when she had special conversations with each child,

Thursday with John, Saturday with Charles, etc.

According to modern progressive methods in education, Mrs. Wesley would have hampered the personality of her children, warped their out-look on life and in short made them general misfits in life; an abundance of knowledge but no ability in application. All this severe discipline would cause the youngsters to grow afraid of their parents, hate the Bible and dislike church. However, it did not seem to work that way in her family. John, her fifteenth child, took the world as his parish. He traveled over a quarter of a million miles on horseback and preached forty thousand times, literally saving England from a revolution. Charles traveled on both sides of the Atlantic, served as a companion to his brother, John, and wrote six thousand hymns, many of which we sing today.

Concerning that special time of conversation which Susanna gave each child, John later wrote to her, "If you can spare me only that part of Thursday evening which you formerly bestowed on me in another manner, I doubt not it would be as useful now for correcting my heart as it was in forming my judgments."

There was never a time until her death that John Wesley ever got away from the guidance and counsel of his great mother, Susanna.

PRAYER:

All of us pause, our Heavenly Father, to thank Thee for our mothers. We pray that Thy love and Thy tender care shall abide with us each and every one and make us good parents to our own children. In Thy Name we pray. Amen.

LORA LEE PARROTT

I'm the Only Mother My Children Will Ever Have—I'd Better Be a Good One!

I had only one mother—and she was a good one! The memories I retain of life at home are warm and good.

She gave herself to the task of motherhood. She penned in her diary: "Training my children is the most important task I have while they are under my care and nothing shall interfere with that training. The housework, church demands, social obligations—all must be subservient to my children's welfare."

This she practiced!

Despite the demands as a busy wife, she always found time to spend with us. Under a large tree, she would tell us the stories from the Bible, illustrating them in the sand with rocks and stones for houses and mountains and representing the patriarchs of old with twigs. She captured our imaginations, and our heroes became David instead of Fabian, and Mary instead of Liz Taylor.

We were taught the Scriptures and to pray before we could say much else. Before we started school, we could recite the books of the Bible in order, the twelve disciples, and quote more Scripture than many ministers. We grew up with the Word of God as an integral part of our lives.

The only mother I ever had, penned in her diary: "The sculptor spends hours in shaping the features of the face; the painter labors to give color to the hair or expression to the face. Their work is to stand for ages to come. But I, as a mother, am shaping substances more imperishable than canvas or marble. I can afford to be patient and wait long for results. I have all eternity in which to watch developments."

My mother worked patiently and consistently. When we grew older, she would pick out chapters and portions of Scriptures, give us scissors, glue, a bundle of magazines, and a scrapbook. Then she would challenge us to illustrate these chapters with pictures from the magazines. We accepted the challenge, loved every minute of it—and, not incidentally, memorized those chapters word for word.

She played Bible games with us! If we ran out of new ones, she created some. She could always be counted on for fun, companionship, and—although we were often unaware of it—religious training.

She told us the Bible stories and then challenged us to live like the heroes we came to adore. We could listen to the story of the sweet spirit of Joseph, the trust of David, and dream that "some day" we would live like that! She gave to our dreams of service an outlet so they could find fulfillment.

She soothed me when I was sick. She played ping-pong with me in the basement, dolls in the house, and baseball in the street. She listened to my opinions and made me feel important. She made me believe she enjoyed my numerous parties. She joked about it when she had guests and discovered too late that I had used all of the sugar the night before in a fudge party. She liked my friends.

My only mother was proud when I won honors, and built me back up when I lost. Her eyes flashed tears of joy when I was happy. Her arms held me tightly when I was sad. My mother filled my world with happiness, love, and God. She kept her spiritual life so lovely and radiant that I lived in the splendor of it all of my life.

I had only one mother—and she was a good one! She shaped my life for good. If she had not been a good mother, my life would be different. How I thank God for my mother and all the mothers who have given of themselves for their children.

I occasionally slip into the nursery in my house and look at the sleeping forms of my children. I am now fashioning their memories of home. I am now molding their adult lives and influencing their relationships with God.

Unless accident comes, I am the only mother my children will ever have. I'd better be a good one!

RUTH VAUGHN

A Contrast in Mothers

Ahaziah, King of Judah, reigned a year in Jerusalem. He "walked in the ways of the house of Ahab: for his mother was his counsellor to do wickedly. Wherefore he did evil in the sight of the Lord like the house of Ahab: for they were his counsellors after the death of his father to his destruction" I Chronicles 22:2-4).

Athaliah was the mother's name. She was the daughter of Ahab. She and the members of the house of Ahab counseled Ahaziah to disobey the Word of the Lord. Hence, it is not to be wondered at that Athaliah is called, "that wicked woman" in I Chronicles 24:7. "There is no wisdom or understanding or counsel [that can prevail] against the Lord" (Proverbs 21:30, Amplified Version).

There is no record of her children rising up and calling her "blessed" (Proverbs 31:28).

By way of contrast, Mary, the mother of Jesus, said: "All generations shall call me blessed" (Luke 1:48). She counseled people to obey the word of the Lord. While at a wedding feast in Cana of Galilee, she said to the servants: "Whatsoever he saith unto you, do it" (John 2:5). They acted upon His word, and immediately that which was lacking was abundantly supplied.

Mary's good counsel should be heeded by people everywhere. Every father, mother, son, and daughter of us should do as He says.

Who has a better right to tell us what to do? He is our Creator, and also the One who died for our sins and rose again.

All who heed His command to "repent" (Luke 13:3,5) and respond to His invitation "Come unto me" (Matthew 11:28) shall find rest of soul.

What a blessed day for mothers that will be when the Lord Jesus shall reveal to them the full results of their godly example and counsel to their children and others!

NOW

Your Privilege

Recently a young mother asked me, "How can I find time to work for my church? I have two young children in school and a new baby at home."

Another young mother asked, "I have four little children—I'm busy every moment. I want to do my share in church, but what can I do?"

May I reply?

Dear Young Mother,

The calendar reminds us that soon we will observe Mother's Day. In the week preceding that day the candy stores and florist shops will do a flourishing business. Sentimental cards portraying love of mother will be dropped into many a mailbox. While listening to the radio, we will hear stories of outstanding mothers—and in church some sermon will be based on mother love. Through advertising or custom no one will be allowed to forget Mother's Day.

It is a beautiful thought—a day set aside to honor motherhood. But how often, as all eyes are upon us, do we feel unworthy. We know of all the times we have failed to be the kind of mother we wanted to be.

Perhaps at this time of the year all Christian mothers should evaluate themselves. Quietly and conscientiously we should look back over this past year.

How would you answer God if He asked you these questions: "Have you been faithful in the stewardship of motherhood? Have these children drawn you closer to Me or have you used them as an excuse when called upon to serve Me? I gave you these children you love so dearly, but surely you know that with this gift there also were given many responsibilities."

Mother's Day . . . a day to evaluate ourselves! A day for all Christian mothers to read again the vows they made when an infant son or daughter was brought into the Lord's house. Do you remember how proudly you stood before the members of the congregation and made a promise to be a faithful mother?

The minister asked of you, "Do you promise to instruct this child in truth of God's Word and in the way of salvation through Jesus Christ; to pray for him and teach him to pray; and to train him as God may give you grace?" And you answered, "I do."

Now if you are faithful to your promise, you should bring your children before the throne of grace each day. Not only should you be concerned for their safety, but for their salvation, beseeching God to come into their lives—to be a reality, a living Presence so that your child will serve Him completely and joy-ously. You must ask God to remove the sins that a true mother sees in her child—selfishness, temper, rebellious spirit, etc.

To train a child is a full-time job—no one can take a mother's place. Your child's love cannot be forced, but God, through His wisdom, has instilled with-in the hearts of all children a desire to love their parents. There should be a bond of love between mother and child that is so sweet no mother would want to lose it through neglect.

Often a mother exclaims, "How help-less a little child is!" But have you ever thought of this, young mother, that though your child is helpless, he is also hopeless unless someone teaches him the way of salvation? *And you did promise!* You are his first teacher. Day by day, through Bible stories, simple prayers, quiet talks and Christian family life you must teach him to love God.

> Ere a child has reached to seven,
> Teach him of the way to heaven,
> Better yet the work will thrive
> If he learns before he's five.

An old proverb says, "An ounce of mother is worth a pound of clergy." Surely this is true if the mother is a Christian mother. You who are young mothers could learn much by reading about some mothers of the Bible—Elizabeth, for instance, of whom we read that she "walked in the command-ments and ordinances of the Lord blame-less."

You must not talk about loving oth-ers; you must show love to all people. "*Children have no natural prejudices,* but early in life they *learn* to be preju-diced." How automatically we push our child toward the empty place beside the *white* person in the bus; how often we allow our children to see television shows where the Indian or man of red skin is always the villain; how many times our children hear the words "nigger," "Jap," or "wop" used in a belittling manner. Dare you teach your little child this song unless you *show* him the truth of it?

> Jesus loves the little children.
> All the children of the world,
> Yellow, black and red and white

They are precious in His sight.
Jesus loves the little children of the world.

Early in life children must learn to understand the spirit of brotherhood within God's world-wide family. Yes, why sing this song unless your Christian attitude towards others is such that it will teach your child that real worth is not based on physical appearance?

You must not only talk missions; you must instill within your own children the willingness to answer God if He should call them to serve Him as full-time servants. As you read I Samuel 1:27, 28 (Berkeley Version), you see the attitude of a true Christian mother. Han-nah's words should be your words, "For this lad I prayed, and the Lord has granted me what I prayed Him for; I have therefore handed him back to the Lord; as long as he lives he is returned to the Lord." Education and dedication go hand in hand.

Religion in the home must be a seven-day-a-week matter. During his very early years, your child will understand your loving care better than he understands your words. If you cultivate a sense of God's presence in all of your home ex-perience, he too will speak naturally about God, Jesus, and the Bible.

Such a long letter! You think I have digressed, gone far afield in answering your question?

You asked me how you can work for the church? I think now you already know the answer. You are working for the church every day. You are creating the church of the future—you are train-ing the leaders for the church of Jesus Christ.

In Christ's commission, He said we must preach and teach—beginning in Jerusalem. To you, young mother, Jeru-salem is your home. Begin there and be faithful!

ANN HOEK

Every Day Is Mother's Day

Now that May is here, we will be honoring our mothers on Mother's Day. All over the country on her special day, Mother will have her breakfast served in bed; Mother will be taken out for dinner; Mother will receive a corsage, a plant, or some other gift—all tokens of our love for, and our appreciation of, Mother. On that one day, everything will be done for her enjoyment.

But when the sun rises the next morning, will Mother still be the center of attention? Will our concern for her only last one day?

I know that among teen-agers the tendency is to take Mother for granted. For example, when a boy needs a clean white shirt, he relies on Mother to wash and press one for him. He also rests assured that a tasty supper will be prepared for him each night.

Let's remember to thank Mother for the everyday tasks she performs for us. We should be thankful not only for mothers who provide for our material needs but those who care enough about our spiritual lives to teach us the things of God. We read in II Timothy 1:5 that "unfeigned faith . . . dwelt, first in . . . [Timothy's] mother Eunice." Timothy's mother had the love of God in her heart and faithfully taught her son the Scriptures and trained him in the way befitting one who loved God.

Because of the great responsibility our mothers have of leading us spiritually, we should accept what they teach us and practice it daily in our lives. We should "forsake not the law of [our] mother" (Proverbs 1:8).

Teen-agers, let's definitely remember our mothers on Mother's Day, but also show that we appreciate them every other day of the year.

BETH O'KEEFE

Mothers Must Be Taught

Napoleon Bonaparte once asked a woman what was needed to right the wrongs of the education system in his empire. "Mother," was her immediate reply. "Yes," said Napoleon. "Here is a system of education in one word. Be it, then, your care to train up mothers for the empire."

In order to teach, a mother must be taught. Beyond all human agencies, to whom better can she go for learning than to God. The Bible says, "Behold, God exalteth by his power: who teacheth like him" (Job 36:22). Every Christian mother's heart reaches up to God with the petition of the Psalmist: "Teach me good judgment and knowledge: for I have believed thy commandments" (Psalm 119:66).

Children can safely trust in the mother who diligently searches the Bible for wisdom to guide them, and love to secure them. Sooner or later, this mother's children "will rise up and call her blessed."

But mothers must be taught from the Book of all Books, the Bible, by the Teacher who excels all others, the Holy Spirit.

Let's consider the devotional use of the Bible. This exercise will help furnish the Christian woman in her own life to be the kind of mother she longs to be.

Meditation is basic to a satisfying and rewarding devotional life. It means reflection, continued thought, contemplation. It differs from study which is attention to learning. Meditation is *attention with intention.*

The Christian meditates upon the truth of God until it catches hold of her thinking, warms her heart, fires her will and results in action that causes her to live to please God. Following are some suggestions that may be helpful to you:

1. *Be definite* about having a devotional time. Suit it to your time and temperament. If you can manage undisturbed time alone with God early in the morning, excellent. Perhaps the best time for you is just before retiring. Or maybe it will be during the day, when everyone is out of the house or the baby is napping. Adapt the time to fit into your schedule and, if possible, make it habitual. By temperament I mean the state of mind and disposition when you are most alert to this spiritual exercise, when you "get going" best. Some are alert early in the morning, others late at night.

2. *Have a plan* for a steady, continuing devotional experience. Jumping from one passage to another, willy nilly, may frustrate concentration. Neither is it stim-

ulating to spiritual growth to turn repeatedly to familiar passages. You may want to use devotional helps. Never let them displace the Bible.

3. *Exercise sanctified imagination.* For instance, if you are using the women of the Bible for your devotions, let your mind transport you to where they are geographically, into the conversations, as it were, visualizing the situations. (Sit with the Samaritan woman at the well as the Lord Jesus talked with her.) Let the incidents come alive. You will find yourself being affected and stimulated to turn to God, asking Him to work in your life, too.

4. Open every devotional time with *prayer for the Holy Spirit's illumination.* Pray as you meditate, asking God to help you to apply each truth unfolded to your practical living.

5. *Test yourself* on the basis of the portion of Scripture you use each day:
What precept does it teach *me?*
What counsel does it give *me?*
What warning does it sound to *me?*
What promise does it extend to *me?*
What command am *I* to obey?

6. *Try using a notebook* to briefly write down items that have especially impressed you. As you look back over a mother's devotions you will be gratified by the treasury of truth you have gleaned.

7. *Thank God* that He personalizes the teachings of the Bible to you. Don't fall short of gratitude and worship.

8. *Yield to His Holy Spirit* and trust Him to translate the truth into your life today.

ANGELYN DANTUMA

The Lasting Gift

Today was Mother's Day—a special day. It was not special because I received an automatic washer, a new outfit of spring clothing, a new chair for the living room, or any one of the many items the merchants had advertised as the perfect gift for Mother on her day. Actually, the gifts I received were inexpensive items in keeping with the children's limited finances.

It was not the material things that made the day special. It was the things which money cannot buy that I treasure most. My teen-age daughter arose before anyone else. She arranged the table tastefully upon a bright tablecloth, and had everything ready for breakfast when we came downstairs. The other two children helped with the dishes afterward. When church was over and we were home again, the children took over in the kitchen, preparing the dinner and doing up the work afterward.

This vacation from the kitchen was appreciated very much because it was given from hearts of love.

There are the year-round blessings which I would not, if I could, exchange for money or any expensive gift—the blessings of a family circle complete, with each member knowing the Lord as his personal Saviour, the unexpected words of appreciation from husband and children, and the good times we enjoy together playing games or picnicking. Yes, even shopping trips could be included, for the children have made these delightful times of fun and enjoyment. There have been the little surprises planned so carefully. Maybe some little chore was done around the house so I would not have to do it, or perhaps something was baked for Sunday when I was away on Saturday.

All these combine to make Mother's Day a special day for me as I consider each one now. What richer gifts could a Mother ask?

ALMA YOUNG

Mother's Day

This day has been set aside as a national observance to honor Mother. A true mother is worthy of praise and honor (cf. Proverbs 31:10-31), and we welcome this day.

Although motherhood carries with it a great responsibility, it is one of God's greatest gifts to womanhood. The thrill and ecstasy of joy when the precious baby says "Mamma" can only be realized by Mother herself. With no foreknowledge of that baby's future, true motherhood loves on through the days and years.

True Mother's love can only be exceeded by God Himself. Isaiah 49:15 says that a mother "may forget" her child, but God says, "yet will I not forget thee."

All through time, mothers have been highly honored for the success won by their sons and their daughters. It has been well said: "The hand that rocks the cradle rules the world." It is the mother that is continually with the child in its formative years.

The Bible gives us some examples of true motherhood.

Hannah was childless. To be childless among the children of Israel, brought reproach upon the woman. Thus, we find Hannah praying that God would bless her with a son. Realizing that this would be a gift from God, she made a vow to the Lord and said, "O Lord of hosts, if thou wilt indeed look on the affliction of thine handmaid, and remember me, and not forget thine handmaid, but wilt give unto thine handmaid a man child, then I will give him unto the Lord all the days of his life" (I Samuel 1:11). God answered her earnest prayer and gave her Samuel. She then did just as she had vowed (vss. 20-28). Samuel became one of the greatest judges of Israel.

Eunice, the mother of Timothy, taught Timothy the Scriptures from his youth. When Paul needed a faithful helper, Timothy was the man of his choice. Paul reminded Timothy of his godly heritage. "I call to remembrance the unfeigned faith that is in thee, which dwelt first in thy grandmother Lois, and thy mother Eunice; and I am persuaded that in thee also" II Timothy 1:5). What a blessing Christian heritage is!

Let us honor Mother on this, her day. Many of us do not have our own mothers to honor. She has gone on before. But some mothers do not have their children to give honor. They likewise have gone on before. So let us choose a mother on whom we will bestow love and honor. By doing so, both the giver and the mother will enjoy Mother's Day.

ANNA L. MEISINGER

Beautiful Hands

Recently my little mother and I sat at the breakfast table. After she had folded her hands in prayer, my eyes thoughtfully, tenderly, lingered on her. How infinitely kind God has been that He should so graciously spare Mother's life past man's "alloted time." How wonderful that at eighty-five she still is the meticulous little lady I have always remembered—the tidy housekeeper, the tender guardian of the roses and other flowers!

If I were permitted but one word to describe Mother, I think I would reach for gentle. Yes, Mother is a gentle lady in every sense of the word. So often I say, "But Mother, surely you remember —I told you several times."

"Why yes, I believe you did mention it before—you see—" and a rather perplexed look fleetingly crosses her face as she continues gently, "I'm getting so forgetful! I'm sorry, dear."

Gratefully I recall, as I study Mother's aged, toilworn hands, the many kind deeds they performed for me when I was a little girl. The times she sat up late to finish sewing a dress for me—a dress I just had to wear the next day! The times she comforted me through the long night hours of illness!

I shall always remember the great amount of "canning" she did for our family and others. My brother and I smile when we remember the ginger cookies! Many were the flower gardens she planted at each parsonage, even though she knew that in true "preacher tradition" we would soon be moving.

Little hands—old hands now—but they are beautiful hands. They finger the leaves of her Bible morning, night and often through the day. They place it under her pillow before she sleeps. They are hands scarred with service to God.

"O heavenly Father," I pray, "help me to always look at Mother's hands when I grow impatient. Help all sons and daughters—the world over—likewise to be reminded by their mothers' hands. Grant our hands, too, shall toil for others. Oh, that they might reach out to give; might draw in to love; touch gently to caress; be strong in trouble; reach down to lift up, and reach up to bring down Thy help!

"Blessed Saviour, above all else, help us to remember your hands and why they bear the scars of nails. Amen."

ESTHER BELLE HEINS

The Great Woman

... Shunem where was a great
woman ... (II Kings 4:8)

It takes only one person to make a city remembered forever. There were many homes in Bethany but Mary, Martha and Lazarus make Bethany an unforgettable place. Many people lived in Shunem, but one woman gave it an indestructible spot in sacred history.

What makes a woman a great woman?

Some people are so anxious to be even, they have no time to be great. The time wasted proving the equality of the sexes would be better spent in achieving the greatness of the individual.

The woman of Shunem was great in hospitality. "She constrained him (the prophet Elisha) to eat bread . . . as oft as he passed by" (II Kings 4:8). The house with an open door is always subject to blessing, "for thereby some have entertained angels unawares." (Hebrews 13:2). Every church with a going, growing ministry needs households which are open to missionaries, gospel workers and journeying believers. Pity the church which is a household of closed doors. Each generation has seen a portion of Christian homes which have become traffic centers of Christian workers. During the war more Christianity was dispensed at some dinner tables than from some pulpits, and as many men in uniform were won for Christ in front rooms, patios and recreation rooms as at altars and prayer rooms. Many a great woman has made her household and its spirit of welcome a living Bible with covers made of patch quilts and printed in the glowing letters of Christian love.

The woman of Shunem was great in spiritual perception. "She said unto her husband, Behold now, I perceive that this is an holy man of God ... Let us make a little chamber ... set for him there a bed, and a table, and a stool, and a candlestick ... he shall turn in thither" (II Kings 4:9, 10). This passage gave birth to the designation, "a prophet's chamber." Many of the old-fashioned Christian homes had such chambers in all literal style of this Scripture, but the real secret is not just the room that was prepared, but the woman's understanding of the man of God and his needs. It is sometimes thought that a heavenly ministry does not need any earthly support, but this woman was wise to a necessity.

Women have rolled millions of bandages to bind up the wounds of people they have never seen, they have quilted and sewed blankets and clothes, they have packed boxes and slicked labels and knotted ropes to provide missionaries with necessary items for a ministry to the "have-nots" of the world: have not the Gospel, have not the Light, have not the Lord and have not human help. True, some people may put such tasks to disproportionate strain, as though they were a means of getting to heaven, and some have given useless gifts in such adventures of faith as the missionary barrel; yet those who in fullness of the love of Jesus and with a sacrificial heart have given their best in such service have blessed thousands of workers and poor people in darkness, and God has been pleased to accept their gift of love. They have perceived the need and met it.

The woman of Shunem was great in reward. The prophet inquired of this woman as to her desire, and found that she was content with her lot. That was a mark of spiritual maturity. Her lack of desires for material and social gains was no substitute, however, for the emptiness of her home without children. God promised to give her a son, and fulfilled the promise twice: once in the birth of the child, and again in the resurrection of that child from death. Her reward was a living child—twice alive.

A mother of spiritual perception knows the hazard of having a child. It is a tragedy to have a dead child. It is triumph to have a living child. The loss of a child in physical death leaves a deep scar of sorrow not healed by time. The old wound can always bleed again, and the empty room can weep any lonely night. For a Christian parent, however, the worst tragedy is a child spiritually dead. You wanted that little life born into your home, but the loss of that life to sin and sin's entanglements leaves upon the spirit a deep gash that pains with prayer and bleeds like fire. But the God of Elisha is still the God of new life. Godly parents have a right to ask Him to restore their children to Himself and to them, to breathe upon them the miracle breath of the Holy Spirit. What a triumph to have a living child. It is triumph over natural birth, which was the best you could do for him. It is a triumph over the aims of Satan, triumph over the encircling temptations, triumph over the present world, triumph over the bent of the flesh, triumph over the doubts of your own heart, triumph over the inconsistencies of your own life and the fears of your own failure. That is a triumph wrought only by the Cross of Jesus.

Nothing keeps a family together in time like faith in the Lord Jesus, and nothing can keep a family together in eternity but faith in the Lord Jesus.

Many fathers and mothers would spend a fortune to have their children introduced at court to the Queen of England or to the royal circle of a continental empire or to the political artistocracy or social top-drawer of a democratic system, but what will you give to introduce your boys and girls to Jesus?

LOUIS PAUL LEHMAN

This is a mother's first Mother's Day letter to her three-month-old daughter. Four years later it was the last letter she read to her little girl on Mother's Day, shortly before leaving her to be with Jesus Christ, her Saviour and Lord.

Dear Cynthia:

Every woman experiences magic moments whether she is a mother or not. She reaches out to hold on to them— only to find that they have vanished. It probably is this very elusiveness that gives them their magical quality. Perhaps pen and ink will help me capture some of my magic moments, many of which have been inspired by you and your brothers.

Sitting in a rocking chair holding a wee daughter is a new experience for me. It is a time for loving and thinking and praying. My thoughts are not very profound, but I believe God has gotten through to me during some of these rocking sessions.

"What can I give you?" I ask myself as I look down in your little face. There are so many *things* for children these days. A loving impulse makes me want every*thing* for you. But I am beginning to realize that what you will need most is more of me and my time. Not *things*— but someone to play with—to pray with; not *things* as much as a listening ear to hear your problems, joys, plans— every*thing* that concerns you.

Of all the *things* I would like to give you, a living faith in God is first on the list. Unfortunately this is some*thing* that cannot be handed down from mother to daughter. Your daddy and I will try to teach and show you the Christian way of life, but one day you must accept Jesus as your own Saviour and Lord and believe that He died for your sins.

The miracle of your birth is still fresh in my mind—the sound of your lusty soprano cry that indicated you were a lively little girl. As wonderful a moment as this was, it cannot compare with the wonder of your second birth, when you become a member of God's family. No magic here, but miraculous!

Sometimes mothers get tired because extra people make extra work—especially extra little people. But believe it or not, there is even magic in work— when you are working for those you love. I discovered this one day at the ironing board of all places! Blue jeans to be pressed—! Then this thought welled up inside: if I had no sons, there would be no blue jeans to press. Suddenly the blue jeans took on a different quality. They belonged to someone I loved and this made all the difference. Instead of feeling sorry for myself because of the ironing still to be done, I began to thank

God for my family and the strength to work for them. A prayer began to accompany each piece—for the one who would rest on this sheet; or wear this shirt to school or the office, and so on down through the pile. Not a thing got scorched either as a result of my preoccupation. Little girl's dresses still seem a bit strange in my laundry. Do I dare confess to you though that I'm glad so many dresses are "wash and wear" now?

Yes, there is magic in your crooked little smile, in hearing your boisterous brother say in a tender moment, "She's the nicest thing that's happened to our family" and in watching the joy your coming has already brought into many lives, even outside of your family.

You may not remember, Cynthia, but I whispered three words into your tiny ear the moment I first held you in my arms, and have repeated them to you often since that time. These three words, however, I hope you will remember always—"Jesus loves you."

I love you, too,
Your mother,
JEANNE TEPLY

Mothers, Makers of Men
by
Mrs. Arthur Tylee

(The following Mother's Day message was written and first published in 1939 in the *Chattanooga News-Free Press*. At that time the late Mrs. Arthur Tylee was the director of extension work for the Chattanooga Bible Institute. Prior to this Mrs. Tylee and her husband had been missionaries in Brazil, working with various Indian tribes. One day a nomadic tribe came to the mission station, scalped Mr. Tylee, a two-year-old child and the nurse. They thought they had also killed Mrs. Tylee for she carried a scar at the top of her forehead until she died. After Mrs. Tylee was rescued she was sent back to the United States and a few months later her baby daughter, Mildred Francis, was born.)

The greatest instrument in the hands of God for making men is a God-fearing mother. The world's crying need today is for men of vision, faith, self-control, purity and power. The need exists because God cannot find mothers. Cigarette smoking, bridge-playing flappers do not make mothers of men. The qualities a mother wishes to be found in her son must first be found in the heart of the mother.

There is no greater example of this fact than the slave mother of long ago: Jochebed. Her name is little known but that of her illustrious son, Moses— general, statesman, lawgiver—shines as brightly today as it did over 3,500 years ago.

Her freeborn, proud race was at the time of the child's birth a slave people, suffering cruelly under Egyptian taskmasters' lash; but there was nothing slavish about Jochebed's mind. She was not bound by any slavish fear of the inhuman monster who sat on the throne and when God spoke to her heart, as He must have done, telling her something of the work He had planned for the little life entrusted to her, she was willing to brave all the fury of an Oriental despot to carry out God's plans and purposes for his life.

A woman of faith, vision and courage by the grace of God was able to inculcate in her son these same qualities.

Her first act of faith was to entrust the child to God's keeping as she put him in the small basket and put the basket among the rushes along the bank of the river. "In an ark" is figurative language the Bible often uses to denote the security of those who have believed on the Lord Jesus Christ and are safe in Him. If mothers today would take the precaution to know that their children were safe in the keeping of Him who died to save them, before launching them forth into the world, they would not only give to the world better sons and daughters, but would save themselves untold heartache and suffering.

How long this mother was permitted to care for her own son after he was found by the king's daughter, we do not know but we do know that she made splendid use of her God-given opportunity. From the simple slave home he went to live in a corrupt, licentious court, but the honor, integrity and moral purity taught him by a godly mother lived with him through the years and has become a part of the priceless heritage of every believing mother today. The God who watched over that little life, protected and trained him, will care equally for every little life entrusted to Him today.

Chattanooga News-Free Press,
Chattanooga, Tennessee

The Influence of Christian Mothers

"Honor thy father and thy mother," the Bible says, and God emphasized the importance of this particular commandment by offering a reward for obeying it; He promised "that thy days may be long upon the land which the Lord thy God giveth thee" (Exodus 20:12). Honoring motherhood means more than gifts of flowers or candy. Children honor their parents when they respect their wishes and follow their advice. To disobey them is to dishonor them.

Happy are the parents who teach their children to obey. The Bible says, "Forsake not the law of thy mother." Obviously the reference is to the law of the Lord which the faithful mothers in Israel taught to their children in infancy. If we have been blessed with such a mother let us be grateful. We can thank God if our mother not only bathed us, fed us, and clothed us, but also taught us to fear the Lord, and poured out her heart in prayer for us.

One mother, whose children had grown to be stalwart Christians, was asked the secret of her success. She replied:

"When in the morning I washed my children, I prayed that they might be cleansed by the Saviour's precious blood. When I put on their garments, I prayed that they might be arrayed in garments of salvation and in the robe of God's righteousness. When I gave them food, I prayed that they might be fed with the Bread of Life. When I started them on the road to school, I prayed that their faith might be as the shining light, that shines more and more brightly until the perfect day is come. When I put them to sleep, I prayed that they might be enfolded in the Saviour's everlasting arms."

No wonder her children were led to a saving knowledge of Christ at an early age, and adorned the doctrine of God our Saviour. The mothers of today can do no better than to follow the example of the godly mothers of yesterday. The problems they face in training children in this present world may be more numerous and more complex; but neither human nature nor the principles of godliness have changed. The Scriptures still declare that if parents will train their offspring to walk in the paths of righteousness while they are young they will be found in the straight and narrow path when they are old.

Motherhood has always been a full-time job. It requires all the love, strength, and wisdom a woman can bring to it, and it requires all the help she can get from God. If it is the most difficult task in the world, it also is the most important, and the most rewarding.

Thank God for Christian mothers. The salvation of never-dying souls shall be their crown of rejoicing in heaven.

R. C. C.

A Message to Mother

It is unmistakably clear that Mother has a greater influence upon her children than any other person. If Mother goes astray, the children are sure to follow. How important it is, then, for each mother to have the four great "MUSTS" in her life!

1. *Mother must know God*

A mother must have a personal experience with the Lord Jesus Christ in order to rear her children correctly. Mother must know how to guide and instruct her children.

There are problems of the teen-ager, also, which are not always easy to solve. If Mother knows Christ as Saviour, she is able to come to Him and receive the wisdom and knowledge necessary to answer the dilemmas of youth. Yes, it is important—vitally   important,   that

Mother receive Christ as her personal Saviour and that she surrender to Him, the Lord of her life.

2. *Mother must pray*

Every mother must know how to pray.

What an indictment against American motherhood has been given by chaplains who were in the second World War! They tell of boys wounded and dying on the battlefield, with no knowledge of God. Many times, while bending over dying lads and asking them to pray the young men would reply in agony, "I don't know how to pray. Oh, Chaplain, please help me for I do not know how to pray."

There should never be such incidents, for every boy and girl should learn how to pray while still a child, and Mother is the logical person to instruct the child to seek God at an early age. Years ago, American mothers were known to be godly women, gathering their children about them for daily prayer. Many boys and girls learned how to pray at Mother's knee. What a difference today! We have cocktail-drinking, bridge-playing, cigarette-smoking mothers who have no experience with God, and consequently they do not know how to pray; therefore, they are rearing prayerless, godless children!

3. *Mother must read, and know her Bible*

It has well been said, "The hand that rocks the cradle rules the world." From the way the world is being governed today, it would seem that the hands which rocked the cradles of some of its leaders never fingered the Word of God.

As we go back in history and look at some of the great men of our own nation, their greatness can be traced to godly Bible-reading and Bible-practicing mothers. How sad that in an hour of great world crisis, there are thousands of American mothers who know about the latest Hollywood gossip and the current Broadway hits, but who cannot recite the Lord's Prayer or quote John 3:16.

If there ever was a time in the history of America when mothers needed to study God's Word and impart the knowledge of it to their children, it is now!

When one examines present day statistics regarding juvenile delinquency in comparison with the past, it would appear that we could very well become a completely lawless nation within a decade, unless something is done quickly.

4. *Mother must set the example*

Notice how the little girl mimics Mother. If Mother wears high heels, she will slip into them also. She will stand before the mirror and use the same cosmetics. She wants to be like her mother in every way. Mother's phraseology, tones and expressions become hers at a very early age. Whatever Mother does is absolutely right in the eyes of her little daughter.

Children receive their first impressions (which become indelible) from their mothers. For this reason, Mother, your sacred obligation is to live an exemplary life both in word and deed; however, this cannot be done until you have a personal experience of salvation. How impossible it is to lead that little boy or girl aright, unless you, first, are led by the Master Himself!

RALPH MONTANUS in *Jottings*

Praying Mothers

A boy or a girl cannot get away from the earnest, prevailing prayer of a righteous mother.

Most of our young people today are two and three generations removed from any spiritual influence. I use the word influence advisedly; the dictionary defines the word "influence" as "to alter or move in respect to character; conduce; to sway or persuade a person for good; to modify or determine . . ."

A mother's life, character and habits can influence her children.

It used to be our children were in high school before they were exposed to much worldly influence, but today even in kindergarten they find four-letter, dirty words in the rest rooms. Early in the grades they are taught the theory of organic evolution. All of this should be counteracted in the home.

The tragedy is that most mothers

don't know or aren't convinced that the Genesis account of creation is positively true or that the Apostle John's account in John 1:1, "All things were made by Him and without Him was not any thing made that was made," is true also.

All of this knowledge is so necessary to give our children a firm foundation for their faith. The trend of our high school and college students today to say "God is dead" shows the lack of this early training.

What tremendous responsibilities mothers of today have. After all, we are the architects of the characters of our future generations—presidents, senators, school teachers and mothers-to-be.

A child or a young person never gets beyond the influence of his mother's prayers.

Hannah prayed for Samuel and he became a prophet and a mighty man in Israel. The mother of John Newton, the great hymn writer, prayed for him. (It must have been before he was seven because she died about that time.) John became a very wicked man, a kidnaper of slaves from Africa. In a terrible storm at sea, he was found praying, "Oh, Thou God of my dead mother, have mercy on my soul!" God did have mercy. Otherwise, he could not have written "Amazing Grace" and "Glorious Things of Thee Are Spoken." Think of the influence of the Christian mother behind the lives of Ira D. Sankey, Robert Harkness, Frances R. Havergal, George Bennard, B. D. Ackley, Fanny Crosby and countless others.

Spurgeon said, "I cannot tell how much I owe to the prayers of my good mother ... I remember her once praying, 'Now Lord, if my children go on in sin it will not be from ignorance that they perish, and my soul must bear swift witness against them at the day of judgment if they lay not hold on Christ and claim Him as their personal Saviour.' "

Christian mother, with a burden for the salvation of a boy or girl, remember the scripture, "Train up a child in the way he should go, and when he is old, he will not depart from it," and Acts 16:31, "Believe on the Lord Jesus Christ and thou shalt be saved and thy house." Put the Blood of the Lamb of God over the door posts of your home by faith, and if you have done your part, you have a right to claim the promises of God's Word even though you may not live to see the answer to your prayers.

Mother, your example is far reaching. "Do as I say, not do as I do" is not enough. You must follow through. Take your children to Sunday School. Don't just send them.

Our Heavenly Father is faithful to His Word, I know. We have four children, three girls and one son. God called our son home fifteen years ago. But his son, whom he never saw, is now fifteen and loves the Lord. Altogether we have three grandsons and five granddaughters who are all saved and actively serving the Lord in their churches.

We are very rich in the things that money cannot buy. God is no respecter of persons. What He has done for my husband and me He will do for you if you will call upon Him.

I would like to leave you with Matthew 18:11-14,

"For the Son of man is come to save that which was lost. How think ye?

"If a man have an hundred sheep, and one of them be gone astray, doth he not leave the ninety and nine, and goeth unto the mountains, and seeketh that which is gone astray.

"And if so be that he find it, verily I say unto you, he rejoiceth more of that sheep, than of the ninety and nine which went not astray. Even so it is not the will of your Father which is in heaven that one of these little ones should perish."

As the poet put it:

'Twas a sheep, not a lamb, that strayed away
In the parable Jesus told;
A grown-up sheep that had gone astray
From the ninety and nine in the fold.
Out on the hillside, out in the cold,
'Twas a sheep the Good Shepherd brought.
And why for the sheep should we earnestly long,
And as earnestly hope and pray?
Because there is danger—if they go wrong

They will lead the lambs astray.
For the lambs will follow the sheep, you
   know,
Wherever the sheep may stray;
When the sheep go wrong, it will not be
   long
Till the lambs are as wrong as they.

And so with the sheep we earnestly plead
For the sake of the lambs today;
If the lambs are lost, what a terrible cost
Some sheep will have to pay.

THELMA MYERS
in *The Log of the Good Ship Grace*

MOTHER'S DAY TOASTS

The following is a tribute to a mother and
her response to her daughter.

What Is a Mother?

What's a Mother?
   She's usually a
      mixture.
Mostly
   She's friendly, sometimes
She's
      angry. She's always full
of energy, especially when
      she's just
   written a poem
      and she wants
   you to
      read
         it.
Mothers are sometimes
   little girls.
Then they always enjoy things
   like,
   jacks,
      jump rope,
         hopscotch,
   latest fashions,
      and your
         newest boyfriend.
But then, a mother is
   a grown-up, too.
When you have a problem
   she listens
and understands.
      Usually she
      can help you . . .
But even when mother
   doesn't know the
      answer,
She knows the
      One
      who does . . .
He's her

good Friend
      and Confidant,
and so He becomes
      yours, too.
But what IS a mother?
      The answer
         is
      simple, yet
         so
      complex
She influences
      so many things:
   a decision,
      an idea,
   a feeling,
      a life . . .
but so graciously and
   thoughtfully that
      somehow
you get the feeling the idea
      was yours
   all
      along.

PAT LANCE

Prayer for a Daughter

(Reply to toast by Pat Lance's mother)

Thank you, for giving to me
This fairest gift of beauty
A daughter.

May she live each day with a knowledge
   secure
Of my constant love that will endure
Through every joy and sorrow.
For only thus will she learn to impart
This gift to others from the heart
Devotion and loyalty.
And give to me, Father, cheerfulness

That stems from an inner peacefulness
That she may know warmth and gaiety.

Let me always, Father, seek to be
An example of truth and honesty.
My motives above suspicion.
It would seem to me the simplest way
To show her the principles of fair play
And sincerity toward others.

As I seek to guide her through the years
May my full respect as a person be hers
That she may know poise and confi-
dence.
And in this way I may safely expect
She will learn the art of giving respect
To me as well as to others.

Then may our home always an altar be
Teaching devotion, and trust in Thee
Always, with thanksgiving.
For without Thee was not anything
made,
Thou art the giver of all that is good,
May she love and serve Thee forever.

NAOMI LANCE

I Remember, Mother Dear

(A teenager speaks to her mother)

Oh, I remember, Mother Dear, as far
back as I'm able,
When I was only two feet high and
couldn't reach the table,
You used to wash my dirty knees and
kiss away my tears,
And heal my hurts and fix my clothes.
You kept me all these years;
You taught me how to say my words, and
finally, when I could,
I'll bet I drove you crazy just a chatter-
ing as I would;

Oh, I remember, Mother Dear, it wasn't
long ago
That I was 'fraid when evening came,
but darkness soon would go
When you tucked me in bed at night and
bedtime stories told,
And I'm forever glad you taught my tiny
hands to fold.

Oh, I remember, Mother Dear, that time
I tried to lie,
And how you made me feel so bad I
wanted just to cry;
You've always taught me right from
wrong; your wise advice you'd give
And put good thoughts deep in my
heart; you've taught me how to
live.

Yes, I remember, Mother Dear, and as I
do, I pray
That God will make me just the girl you
dreamed I'd be today,
And may I always follow all those standards that you set
So folks will say, "She's like her Mom"—
the best praise I could get!

JOAN KALBAKKEN

I Remember, Daughter Dear

(A mother speaks to her teenage daughter)

Oh, I remember, Daughter Dear, as if it
were tonight,
The hour you came to Dad and me to
make our life so bright;
Though short on cash when you appeared, so helpless, sweet, and small,
Your smiles and hugs soon made me like
the rightest queen of all.

Oh, I remember, Daughter Dear, the
days you wore my shoes,
And klomped about the house in clothes
quite big enough to lose;
I'd grin as you would scold your dolls,
pretending you were me,
And then I'd grit my teeth and think, "A
kinder Mom I'll be!"
The first bouquet you picked for me I'll
always greatly prize,
But better than those flowers, dear—the
light within your eyes.

Oh, I remember, Daughter Dear, I'd
tuck you in at night
And listen to your special prayers and
then put out the light;
You may not know how much it helped
—it made my old heart hum,

When Dad and I would hear you ask the
    Lord to bless your Mom.
And I recall the first big date; it filled
    my heart with joy
To see you neat and happy with your
    favorite neighbor boy.
I wondered if you'd make it home at
    ten, as Dad had said,
And, oh, how proud you made us when
    you beat the clock instead;
Yes, I remember, Daughter Dear, and as
    I do, I pray
That God will keep you kind and true in
    all you do and say.

JOAN KALBAKKEN

To Mother

If I could forget all the writings' been
    written;
    If I could forget all the sayings' been
    said
That sing of the virtues of mothers of
    millions—
    The mothers of great folk both living
    and dead—
I could still write my writings, I could
    still say my say
When it comes to a-writing or talking
    today.

For the half that's been written is only a
    part
And the half that's been spoken is but a
    good start
For the virtues of millions of mothers of
    men
Are amplified, glorified, brought forth
    again
In the one little mother I'm proud to
    call mine;
A mother exceeding the finest of fine.

Thank God for my mother; thank God
    for her care;
There's "nary a twin" to her anywhere,
For graciousness, wisdom, courage and
    tact
Are hers in abundance—and that is a
    fact.
For downright good taste and a sense of
    proportion

She has what it takes—that's not a dis-
    tortion.

But for all of her virtue
    The one I like best
Is her great heart of love
    That has stood every test.
So, Mother, today as I thank God for
    you
Please know that each line of this mes-
    sage is true.

RUTH JAMES CORDING

A Toast to Mother

When we are young we cry for her,
When we are grown we go from her,
When we are old we long for her,
Tonight let us show we love her.

ORA I. CLAIRESS

To Mother and Daughter

Each daughter here deserves a toast
    As does her darling mother;
So let's just hold our glasses up
    And drink to one another.

ORA I. CLAIRESS

My Daughter

From the first time I heard your helpless cry I knew that God had given me a
challenge greater than any I had known
before. He gave to our home a child to
train, a personality to mold, a mind to
teach and little steps to guide.

Today I want you to know that my
goal for you, dear child, is that you always follow in the path of our Master,
Jesus Christ. I want you to know Him as
your Saviour. I want you to love Him
until your death so that you may have
eternal life.

And to that end I will sacrifice my
earthly possessions, my human desire for
your success or any other thing that is
within my grasp.

I pour upon you my love, remembering that God, the Father, poured His

love upon mankind through the sacrifice of His Son Jesus.

GLORIA WILLINGHAM

A Tribute

TO MOTHER

I have searched the stores for the perfect gift for Mother. Nothing seemed just right. So I sat down and asked myself: What would Mother appreciate most? And the answer came right away.

Not fancy clothes; not delicate dishes; not sterling silver, but to my mother I give a promise.

I promise that as long as I shall live I will try to give to my children and to my home the ideals of life which she has given to me. These are:

• A contented spirit—even though she did not have as much material riches as did the lady up the street;
• Ministering hands—whether the needy be family, friend or stranger;
• Willing and anxious feet—which would quickly run at the slightest call;
• A radiant and joyful heart—even in the midst of disappointment;
• Constant desire for knowledge—when her time and energy were almost exhausted;
• An appreciation and love for beauty— especially of God's great outdoors; flowers, trees, waterfalls, forests, rivers and seas;
• A sense of humor—which appealed to all who knew her;
• A tender tact—in the company of children or men in high office;
• Gracious poise—which always made her a popular member of the group whether in the home, at school or at church;
• Tender compassion and understanding —always ready to listen;
• Reverence for God—which revealed itself every day and in all decisions;
• A faithful Christian—regular in attendance to church, believing always in the greatness of our Lord.
• All these traits are interwoven with a never-dying love for Christ which has defeated any temptation, including failures, depressions, poverty and death.

Through my promise I hope to show her my love and appreciation.

GLORIA WILLINGHAM

Toasts to Mothers by Daughters

Here is a toast to mothers to whom God entrusted the difficult task of giving life to children through the shadows of death, of giving joy to children through the portion of sacrifice, and giving truth to children that they might be better partners in life for others.

Here is a toast to the mothers grown white-haired and beautiful in motherhood, whose children are themselves mothers and fathers of other children, and whose character is seen entwined in multiplied generations. The veterans of battles have no scars more honorable than the years of a good mother, and the ribbons and badges of military service have no memories like the prayers and tears of mothers. We salute you. The weight of years makes a patterned shawl upon your shoulders, the sorrows and joys of the echoing past put rainbows and stars in your eyes and the ink of blessed memory has written history of greatness upon the sacred parchment of human lives.

Here is a toast to Christian mothers in the midst of a society whose moral threads are slowly being unraveled from the pattern of life and being twisted into a meaningless knot of theory without practice. Christian mothers are the straight and shining needle in the hands of God to stitch spiritual and moral fibers into the character of boys and girls. Education can and does teach the basic elements of literacy, and legal boundaries are erected between the criminal and the law-abiding, but only homes of Christian realities can implant into mind, heart and conscience the necessity of moral truth when dishonesty would be more profitable and when none but God could prosecute. Christian mothers are not crown-wearers and officeholders, not manipulators of fortunes and directors of institutions, but they are the keys to the lives that will make tomorrow's world a blessing or a brutality, a community or a chaos, a society or a shambles. Give them a hand—God will give them a reward.

LOUIS PAUL LEHMAN

Mother

Here's a toast to the fairest,
And sweetest, and rarest
Of women who live on this earth.

She's truly a woman
Divine and yet human
Whose love is of limitless worth.

W. W. C.

BANQUET AND SERMON SEED THOUGHTS

A Tribute to Motherhood

A Mother's Influence
  Eunice (II Timothy 1:5)
A Mother's Sacrifice
  Hannah (I Samuel 1:26-28)
A Mother's Courage
  Jochebed (Exodus 2:2,3; 7:20)
A Mother's Love
  Mary at the cross
  (Luke 23:27, 28; John 19:25-27)

The Capital "P's" of Motherhood

Precept: instruction and direction.
  Bible reading
Pattern: Set the example.
  II Timothy 1:5
Prayer
Praise: a true mother will be praised.
  Proverbs 31

G. CHRISTIAN WEISS
in The Gospel Message

M-O-T-H-E-R
II Timothy 1:5

INTRODUCTION:
M-O-T-H-E-R is as old as the race, and it is significant that we have tried to s-p-e-l-l o-u-t its meaning in verse, sermon and song.

I. Is it not significant that "mother" is pronounced similarly in many different

languages? Our efforts to spell out the meaning of mother are fully justified. M—mercy and meekness; O—others, the basic concept of motherhood; T—tenderness, tears and truth; H—heart, hand and helpfulness; E—endeavors, endurance and enthusiasm; R—righteousness, reconciliation and restoration.

II. "The hand that rocks the cradle is the hand that rules the world."
A. If it is the hand held out to God for guidance, then mother will continue to be a noble word—one with influence.

FRED REEDY

Devout Mothers

  I. Sarah (Genesis 21:6)
 II. Hannah (Samuel 1:22)
III. Elisabeth (Luke 1:41)
IV. Mary (Luke 1:46)
 V. Eunice (II Timothy 1:5)

Snappy Sermon Starters

Mother Is a Jewel
Proverbs 31:10-31

"Her price is far above rubies" (vs. 10).
1. She is faithful and does her husband good (vss. 11, 12).
2. She is busy (vss. 13-15, 17, 19, 27).
3. She is thrifty (vss. 16, 24).
4. She has strength (vss. 17, 25).

5. She is unselfish (vs. 20).
6. She is religious—clothed with scarlet (vs. 21).
7. She is neat of person (vs. 22).
8. She is wise and kind (vs. 26).
9. Her worth is recognized and she is honored (vss. 28, 29, 31).

This kind of mother is a precious jewel and praised for what she is.

MABEL PEEK

Portraits of Women

1. HELPFUL women. A Hebrew slave girl (II Kings 5:2-4). Helpful women start as helpful little girls.
2. HAPPY women. Sarah (Genesis 21:6-8).
3. FEARLESS women are a blessing. Jochebed (Exodus 2:1-10), Deborah (Judges 4:4-10).
4. PRAYING women accomplish a great deal. Hannah (I Samuel 1:1-28).
5. UNDERSTANDING women. Mary of Bethany (John 12:1-8).
6. FAITHFUL women. Lois, Eunice (II Timothy 1:5; 3:15).

MABEL PEEK

The Divine Motherhood
Isaiah 66:13

INTRODUCTION:

Here is used one of the highest of human relationships to reveal God. We use other earthly relationships to describe God's love and care for us, but the thought of motherhood is perhaps most adaptable—and should certainly not be omitted. We must keep in mind, however, that God's love transcends even the love of motherhood. God's love is marked by:

I. Closest Intimacy.
   A. The child's life at its beginning especially, is a part of its mother's life.
   B. The child is supported by maternal sustenance.
   C. The child is watched over by maternal wisdom.
   D. The child is wrapped up in maternal love.
   E. Even more intimate is our relationship to God, for "we are his offspring."

II. Intense Individualism.
   A. The mother individualizes her children.
   B. God individualizes us in His dealings with us.

III. Unwearying Care.
   A. The devotion of a mother is not that of hours or days, but a full time devotion.
   B. A mother's love and devotion are not exhausted when the object of that love leaves the home.
   C. A mother never forgets her child.
   D. Even more faithful is God's love for His children.

IV. The Sacrifice of Love.
   A. All true love is sacrificial.
   B. A mother's love is especially this.

CONCLUSION:

Motherhood means a life of sacrificial, often unhonored and unrequited love, but what if that love is revealing God?

U. R. THOMAS

The Spirit of Motherhood
Proverbs 31:10-31

I. Mother's Day is a day set aside for honoring the spirit of motherhood.
   A. It is sad, but true, that some physical mothers are not worthy of the name.
   B. It is also sad that many who should remember their mothers on this day do not do so.

II. There are many women whose hearts are full of mother love who have never had children of their own.
   A. Motherhood is really more than the physical bearing of children.
   B. These women, with their spirit of love, are mothers in a spiritual sense.

III. Ministers and others may make Mother's Day difficult instead of joyful.
   A. The stress on the glory of physical motherhood and the ignoring of those whose hearts are filled with love for children but cannot bear children themselves has caused much bitterness and anguish.
   B. Some who are not physical mothers have devoted their lives to caring for other people's children or have sacrificed to care for aging loved ones.

IV. Mother's Day should reach out to include all who have the true mother spirit. This true mother spirit should live in the lives and hearts of every Christian woman.

V. Mother's Day is a day then, when children honor their mother, and when women who care for children not their own, are given a place in the world.

PEARL NEILSON

Call Her Blessed
Proverbs 31:28

Special days are set aside to do homage to great historical personages. We do well to have a special day for honoring motherhood. And it is well that this observance should center in the church. It is religion which sanctifies the home and makes motherhood sacred.

In the true Christian mother we see:

I. A Bountiful Ministry

Mother conducts a university, a clothing establishment, a laundry, a restaurant; at the same time she is police officer, health officer, truant officer. She is president of a little state called home, where she has to face all problems of economy. As president of a bank she must study how to "make ends meet," and often faces financial panics, shortages and depressions. She is God's greatest priest on earth, the most effective teacher and indispensable companion.

II. A Beautiful Maturity

"Some faces, like evening primroses, open most beautifully in the evening of life."

Such beautiful, beautiful hands!
They are growing feeble now,
For time and pain have left their mark
On hand, and heart and brow.
I've looked on hands whose form and hue
A sculptor's dream might be
Yet are those aged, wrinkled hands
Most beautiful to me.

III. A Blessed Memory

We remember her noble trinity of virtues—love devotion and humility.

These traits link humanity closely with the Divine. In memory of mother let us have a reincarnation of her virtues.

JOHN H. NESS

Flowers and Facts
Luke 8:21

Commentators have tried hard to explain away these words of Jesus. But the facts remain that when his mother and brothers sought him at the synagogue at Nazareth he turned from them and looked at the larger group. "These," he said, "are my brethren." Other words of Jesus have added to this thought. "He that loveth father and mother more than me is not worthy of me." Yet he was a good son, supporting his widowed mother and his brothers and sisters.

I. Sentimentalism of Mother's Day

There is nothing to which we pay such lip service as the idealization of Mother. On this day we wear flowers for her, if we never gave her one in her life. We weep decorously, whether we really care much for her or not. There is a fiction that the way to our hearts is to talk about our mother. "Mother, Home, Heaven" is the trinity alike of a certain type of evangelist and of the caption writer of the movies.

Yes, we are sentimental on the question of "Mother." The fact that the mother of our idealization is being forced out of existence does not seem to worry us. We sing the same songs, preach the same sermons, buy the same kind of flowers. We are sure that the home is the bulwark of liberty and the cradle of virtue, but we do nothing to preserve it.

II. Home Is a Place Where We Belong

I remember, when I was a boy, watching a dog fight. A little dog of uncertain lineage, and not built for war, sailed into the street to engage in an argument that bade fair to enlist all the canines of legal age in the neighborhood. I remember watching the little fellow as he tried out the fight for a few minutes only to turn tail and make for his own yard. I was just marking him down as a coward when he reached his front gate, stopped a minute for breath, and returned for the fray. I think he must have run home three or four times during the fight to rest for a moment and then go back with redoubled energy. . . . There are many times when I can keep on only by taking a fresh start from my own fireside. . . . That is one thing home does, and that is one thing for which most of our mothers will be remembered.

III. *The Home Is the Place for the Transmission of Culture*

There are generations of learning which are handed down from parent to children. It is hard to teach a child to speak correctly when the parents in the home use bad language. A few minutes of time in the church school will do little to help a child who has been raised in an atmosphere of cheap literature and movies. Social virtues have their start in the home. Patriotism, for example, is but home loyalty extended to a larger circle.

Present conditions are interfering with this function of the home. New sex ideas are not extolling the virtue of chastity. The ephemeral quest for happiness is a contrast to the old search for character which distinguished the makers of our land.

IV. *The Needed Message of Mother's Day*

The shedding of tears will not help much. If this day is to be nothing but a time to pay tribute to womanhood, we may as well abolish it. A woman is not necessarily an angel because she is a mother. Instead of the sentimental gush, we should do something which will help to preserve the worthwhile things in the home.

We should exalt the spiritual values which go into the fiber of the home. All the loyalty and sacrifice of which human suffering is capable have made the home. It is love, not womanhood which should be idealized. If we can do this we can make Mother's Day mean something.

UMPHREY LEE

Motherhood at Its Best
Proverbs 31:31

Qualities of true motherhood:
I. Care (in the form of love and service).
II. Comradeship.
III. Counsel.

IV. Communion With God.
V. Comfort (Isaiah 66:13).
VI. Consistency (John 19:25).

Snappy Sermon Starters

The attributes of a great lady may still be found in the old rule of the four S's:

Sincerity,
Simplicity,
Sympathy,
Serenity.

Two more S's would make her even greater:

Service,
Spirituality.

LLOYD WERTH

Children—A Heritage of the Lord

The child—our example
Matthew 18:1-4
The child—our responsibility
Matthew 18:5, 6
The child—our opportunity
Matthew 19:13-15

LLOYD WERTH

Christian Nurture of Children
Proverbs 22:6

I. Faithful and patient nurture in godliness will abide.
II. Godly example and the teaching of wisdom by adults is a first duty.
III. Essential and eternal principles give spiritual poise through life.
IV. Children are teachable, precious souls, destined for eternity.
V. Children should be happy, helpful, hopeful, reverent and generous hearted.
VI. Children should be gracious and thoughtful, and walk humbly with God.
VII. The way consists of love, courage, merciful justice and help in trial.
VIII. The way consists of forgiveness, sacrifice and knowledge divine.
IX. The way consists of deliverance from sin, goodness, purity and peace.

X. May children grow as the Christ
grew, with the grace of God upon
them.

WALTER D. MEHRLING

Train the Children
Proverbs 22:6

I. We train by example.
II. We train by precept.
III. We train by efficient teaching of
God's Word.
IV. We train by carefully planned pro-
grams of worship and service.

O.T. DEEVER

How the Christian Family Lives the
Life
Colossians 3:1, 2

1. Keep your heart (Proverbs 4:23;
James 1:27).
2. Keep your soul (Luke 9:25; Matthew
16:26).
3. Keep instruction (Proverbs 4:13;
Matthew 11:29).
4. Keep the Word of God (Luke
11:28).
5. Keep yourself pure (I Timothy 5:22;
I Corinthians 6:16-20).
6. Do all things in His name (Colossians 3:16, 17).
7. Do all things to His glory (I Corinthians 10:31).

A.B. CARRERO

The Word of God for the Family's
Every Need
Philippians 4:19

1. It furnishes the foundation for our
faith (Romans 10:17). Faith must
have a basis on which to rest (John
20:31; Acts 8:12).
2. It reveals to man the way of salvation
(Romans 1:16). The Bible is the
story of human redemption (Romans 5:12, 20, 21).
3. It is the source of spiritual light
(Psalm 119:130). Where it is
preached—light follows (Daniel 9:2;
John 5:39).

4. It is the source of spiritual life (I
Peter 1:23). Born of the Spirit—
where there is birth—life (Hebrews
4:12; Psalm 19:7).
5. It is the source of spiritual food
(Matthew 4:4). Folk know where
to go for natural food (I Peter 2:2;
Acts 11:21-24).
6. It will build believers up in righteousness (Acts 20:32). Some folk never
build up—wrong food (I Corinthians 11:30; Jude 1:20).
7. It will be the standard by which we
are judged (John 12:47, 48). Evi-
dences in the Gospels, historical record in Acts, rule for Christian living
in epistles (John 20:31; Romans 5:
17; II Peter 1:5).

C.C. MAPLE

The Family's Daily Program
II Corinthians 4:16

1. Sing daily to perform your duties
(Psalm 61:8).
2. Read the Bible each day (Nehemiah 8:18; Acts 17:11).
3. Bear your daily cross (Luke 9:23).
4. Daily blessing from the Lord
(Psalm 68:19; Lamentations 3:22,
23).
5. Daily prayers (Daniel 6:10; Psalm
5:3).
6. Calling daily upon the Lord (Psalm
86:3; 88:9).
7. Daily exhortation (Hebrews 3:13).

A.B. CARRERO

The Christian Family—One in Christ
Galatians 3:28

1. One Father (I John 3:1, 2; John
1:12).
2. One Shepherd (John 10:14-16).
3. One Master (Matthew 23:8).
4. One Faith (Ephesians 4:5).
5. One Law (Galatians 6:2).
6. One Body (I Corinthians 12:20;
Romans 12:4, 5).
7. One Hope (Ephesians 4:4).
8. One Destiny (Romans 8:17, 21).
9. One in Love (John 17:21).

A.B. CARRERO

SPECIAL MOTHER - DAUGHTER EVENTS

Mother's Day can be observed with a variety of events—from a formal banquet to a picnic or weekend conference. The choice will depend upon the type of event most appealing to both mothers and daughters, the anticipated attendance, facilities available, time most favorable to good attendance, time available to plan and engage a special speaker or talent.

The event should be special to all concerned, not just another social to attend. The planning and preparation should be as enjoyable as the event itself. And the end result should fulfill a specific purpose, provide good fun and fellowship, and be a memorable occasion for mothers and daughters.

Types of Events

The types of events which have been found to be particularly effective for observing Mother's Day are: breakfasts, brunches, luncheons, coffee hours, teas, parties, banquets, picnics, retreats, conferences.

While banquets traditionally have been more highly favored, there is a growing trend toward the other types of Mother-Daughter programs. An important consideration is available dates, since the foregoing types of observances—except banquets and parties—should be scheduled on the Saturday before Mother's Day or during a weekend in May. The most effective events are those which best "fit" the personality of the group.

Informality should be the keynote for breakfasts, brunches, coffee hours, picnics, and parties. The daughters can plan these affairs, prepare most of the food, and arrange informal programs, using "daughter talent." Parties and picnics can be planned so that mothers with small children can attend with their children.

Luncheons and teas can be a little more formal but without pretentiousness.

Daughters will find opportunities to help with almost all the preparations for these observances, including the preparation of food and planning the program. Frequently they have included a fashion show of costumes which they have made for themselves and for their mothers. Mothers appreciate events which their daughters have planned and carried out.

Weekend retreats or conferences offer special opportunities for mothers and daughters to enjoy together a time of fellowship, inspiration, fun, and serious talks between ladies of the family in the light of God's Word. Perhaps arrangements can be made for such a time at a conference center, church camp facility, college campus, or appropriate resort-area hotel. The conference or retreat can begin with a buffet supper on Friday and conclude on Saturday (retreat) or Sunday (conference) evening. Programs can be arranged for each age group, for discussions, Bible study, recreation, etc. Times like these for mother-daughter togetherness cannot be underestimated, particularly in terms of benefits to daughters.

SUCCESS TIPS

Plan early. Reserve date and place, arrange for special speaker or talent. Select menu, engage caterer or cook, or make other arrangements for food and service. Determine cost of tickets.

Choose a good theme—one that will appeal to the group for which it is planned, and that will lend itself to attractive decorations, effective program planning, and the use of available talent.

Organize working committees to handle every detail. Leave nothing to guesswork. Spread the responsibility so that many may participate, but see that no individual is overworked.

Publicize event through posters, newspaper articles, church bulletins, special announcements, invitations, and ticket selling.

Prepare decorations, including programs, favors, table arrangements, name tags (if desired), room decorations, etc. If paper goods are to be used at tables, select place mats, napkins, plates, and cups to blend with the theme.

Plan program. Provide for variety, informality, spontaneity, fun, fellowship, and inspiration. Some of the suggestions under *Ways to Observe Mother's Day* may be helpful in program planning as well as poems, recitations, dialogues, and plays found in other sections of this book. Give careful attention to timing— through specific instructions. Eliminate lengthy announcements, acknowledgements, stories, and a crowded program. Remember, too little is better than too much on a program. Do not handicap the special speaker by delaying his part in the program.

Check final arrangements. Leave nothing to guesswork. Know exactly the number of tickets sold and underwritten, specific time for each segment of the program, persons responsible for decorations, invitations, preparation and serving of food, and cleanup.

SUGGESTED THEMES

A theme usually helps to make an event more meaningful and enjoyable. It is a guide to advertising, program planning, and decorating. Select a theme in keeping with the type of observance planned and which will generate the most interest. A number of suggestions for themes are given here which have been used by various churches and organizations who enthusiastically volunteered to share them. They may be followed as presented, adapted, expanded, or used as a "springboard" to stimulate other ideas. Originating, developing, and personalizing a theme is always a rewarding experience.

The first theme suggestion is presented with more detail than the others, as an example of how to coordinate planning, develop ideas, and work out details to stimulate interest in the event and provide an effective setting for the inspirational program.

SPRING MAGIC

An atmosphere of *Spring Magic* was created long before this particular Mother-Daughter banquet took place. The posters, tickets, and invitations carried out the use of daisies and a color scheme of yellow, orange, white, and green which prevailed to the conclusion of the banquet. (The details of this spectacularly lovely banquet were shared by banquet chairman Mrs. Jean Swanson of Thousand Oaks, California.)

Invitations: Daisy designs and information were mimeographed on both sides of a pastel green sheet and the flowers hand-colored in orange, yellow, and darker green. The invitation was triple folded and sent out by permit mail.

OUTSIDE

INSIDE

Posters: These were made from light green, lightweight posterboard, size 14"x22". Orange giftwrap yarn was used to form the words SPRING MAGIC. Small orange and yellow paper flowers were pasted on after the posters were lettered.

with yellow or white fresh daisies placed in oasis—a matrix available from florists for holding floral arrangements and keeping them fresh. Matching paper plates and napkins decorated with daisies were purchased.

Nut cups were made from a petal-like base cut from yellow construction paper topped with orange and yellow tissue paper. A yellow candy cup was glued to the center.

Tickets: These were mimeographed on light green card stock, size 5½"x3¼", then the flowers and words SPRING MAGIC were colored orange.

Name Tags: A flower pot was cut from folded orange construction paper so that fold was at the bottom of the pot. A plastic daisy was placed "inside" the pot and the two sides glued together to hold the daisy in place.

Waiters: Attractive green ties with a daisy (made from iron-on materials) were worn by the men who served dinner.

Decorations: Entrance to the banquet room was converted into a fern and flower covered arbor. In the center of the room a ten-foot (in diameter) white, yellow, orange, and green canopy hung from the ceiling. A number of five gallon plants (borrowed from a local nursery) framed the circular outline on the floor to form a center "stage." Tables were arranged in spoke-like fashion from the "stage."

Tables: Avocado-colored paper tablecloths were used. Star candleholders held yellow and orange candles. Yellow and orange oval bread baskets were filled

Program Ideas: In addition to the inspirational message, the theme was carried out in music by young daughters (Flower Fairies) and by the Ascension Kitchen Band in a Medley of Songs. One group of older daughters presented a melodrama and another presented Songs of the Daisies. Mothers were honored by a recitation of *Beatitudes for Mothers* (see page 34).

Programs: These were mimeographed with a daisy design on both sides. The design showing on the outside, when folded, was colored yellow, orange, and green.

BOUQUETS FOR MOTHER

Invitation: Cut folders from construction paper in shape of floral boxes and write invitation inside.

Decorations: Place pots and baskets of greenery and flowers about the room. Hang baskets from walls and ceilings. One corner of room can be made into a flower stall displaying a variety of bouquets, with perhaps a daughter at the stall with carnations to pin on the mothers.

Tables: Use a variety of bouquets in a variety of containers. Make miniature nosegays by fastening a number of small gumdrops to green pipecleaners and pulling them through the center of a small paper doily. These can serve as favors. Place a flower garland around the base of pastel-colored candles.

Programs: Make nosegay bouquet folders by cutting a hinged circle from folded construction paper, no larger than the diameter of a five or six inch paper doily. Glue doily to front of program. Insert a cluster of plastic flowers through the center and tape on the inside. Mimeograph program, cut out, and attach inside center fold.

Program Ideas: Follow some general gardening hints or rules for growing roses and develop parallel thoughts along spiritual lines and concerning the mother-daughter relationship. Gardening hints to follow might include tender loving care, allowing time for growth, freedom from weeds, keeping plants fed, etc. Rules for growing roses might include alertness to blight, cultivate periodically, keep in the sunshine, enjoy the blossoms.

SPRING FANTASY

Invitation: Cut tulips from folded red and pink construction paper as shown in the sketch. Insert pink portion inside red after mimeographing or writing message.

Decorations: Arrange entrance like a garden path with pots of tulips on either side and some wooden shoes, if available. The room itself should reflect an enchanted atmosphere of springtime with birds here and there (live ones in cages, if possible), blossoming trees, a small water fountain with a revolving spotlight of color turned on it, clouds made from angel's hair or wisps of cotton, a moon covered with glitter. Hang assorted sizes of silver glittered stars from the ceiling with black thread. Blue and green spotlights will add to the enchantment. Place a carpet (*Magic Carpet*) where small children can sit down during the "Enchanted Hour."

Tables: Use garlands of fern or ivy with birds and flowers tucked here and there. Also use floral arrangements of spring flowers and candles—short ones which have been placed in tall, oval-shaped, pastel-colored glasses.

Programs: Enlarge the tulip invitation pattern and use for programs.

Program Ideas: Provide background music that adds to the enchanted atmosphere. If possible, arrange for marionettes to have a part in the program during the "Enchanted Hour," for the benefit of small children who may be present. Let them sit on the *Magic Carpet.* A "Magic Hour" might feature special music, and a "Dreams-Come-True Hour" could feature the inspirational speaker.

IN A JAPANESE GARDEN

Invitation: Cut out folders in shape of a Japanese lantern. If you want to make these extra fancy, cut the lanterns from black construction paper, then cut out sections from the lanterns, and paste colored tissue paper lining so it will show through black sections. Cut a lantern pattern from pastel-colored construction paper and fasten inside lantern for inscribing invitation.

Decorations: Place boughs of flowering fruit trees and strings of Japanese lanterns about the room. Use a few colorful Japanese parasols to add atmosphere, perhaps against a bamboo mat hung on the wall. If available, use small garden pagodas and figurines. If possible, build a miniature rock garden.

Tables: Use Japanese flower arrangements or ivy garlands with miniature Japanese umbrellas placed at random. These small umbrellas may also be used as nut cups when opened.

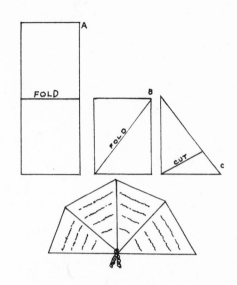

Programs: Make programs in shape of a fan. To do this, (A) fold a piece of 8½"x6" construction paper in half lengthwise and then (B) in half diagonally. (C) Measure 6" on the long side of the triangle and draw a line to the opposite center point. Cut along line. Open one fold and decorate fan as desired. Make a yarn tassel and attach to bottom of fan. Mimeograph programs, fold, and fasten inside fan.

Program Ideas: Encourage waitresses to wear Japanese dresses or kimonos. During dinner use background music which suggests an Oriental garden atmosphere. If possible, engage a missionary from Japan as a speaker.

MAY FLOWERS

Invitation: Cut a carnation from pink folded construction paper after the outside design and inside invitation have been mimeographed.

Decorations: Use ivy and flower garlands about the room, also potted plants, boughs of fruit tree blossoms, umbrellas, etc. Make groupings of garden chairs and tables, with gardening gloves and tools, packages of flower seeds, and flower pots on the tables.

Tables: Use pink candles and baskets of cut spring flowers such as iris, lilacs, daffodils, tulips, or violets. Put a pipe-cleaner handle on pastel-colored nut cups to make gay May basket favors.

Programs: Make program folders by lightly gluing pressed flowers on pastel-colored paper, then cover with Handi-wrap, gluing lightly along edges. Or, place pressed flower face down on a sheet of bathroom tissue (placed on paper bag), cover with thinned white glue. When dry, place piece of waxed paper bag), cover with thinned white iron. (Place piece of brown paper over wax paper before pressing.) Trim wax paper to fit tissue.

Program Ideas: Provide background music of birds singing, spring songs, and string ensemble. Small bouquets of flowers might be presented to the oldest mother, youngest mother, etc. (see *Ways to Observe Mother's Day*). Include the story of how Mother's Day began (see *Mother's Day*). Perhaps the program could be built around the thought of what May flowers tell about a mother's love.

SAY IT WITH FLOWERS

Poster: Mount three long-stemmed plastic roses on a poster and add announcement of the event, theme, time, place, etc.

Invitation: Obtain the appropriate forms from a telegraph office and word the invitation in the form of a floral telegram.

Decorations: Use garlands of roses on trellises borrowed or rented from a nursery or flower shop. If possible, form a rose arbor and place potted roses about the room. Use other potted plants and bouquets of flowers.

Tables: Use lace place mats with several flower stickers attached to them. Place cut flowers in runners of ivy or fern as well as in attractive containers.

Make place cards by attaching small plastic medicine bottles (with ribbon or glue) to small folded place cards. Place a small plastic flower in the bottle. If possible, use buds for daughters and open roses for mothers.

Programs: Fold small rectangular lace doilies and place colored construction pa-

per folder (with mimeographed program) inside. Place a small corsage for mothers (real or plastic flowers) on top of the programs at their places.

Program Ideas: The thought may be brought out that roses develop in three stages: the bud (the daughters), the opening bloom (mothers), and the full bloom (grandmothers). Flowers are God's expression of love to us in all stages of development, and in turn we use flowers to express our love to each other.

PIGTAILS AND APRONS

Invitations: Cut aprons from folded (at the top) gingham-checked shelf paper. Paste ribbon or yarn on inside of fold for apron ties. Glue a second apron pattern (cut from white construction paper) inside which carries written invitation.

Decorations: Use large bare tree branches with pictures of mothers and daughters tied to limbs. Tie clusters of blown-up balloons here and there around room. Also use small blackboards, slates, lunch boxes, etc.

Tables: Use gingham-checked place mats or tablecloths. Use matching paper accessories if place mats are used. Tie gingham bows on potted floral arrangements. Place a peppermint stick at the mothers' places and a lollipop at the daughters' places.

Waiters can wear checked aprons. If *waitresses* serve, they can wear checked aprons and checked hair bows.

Programs: Enlarge the pattern used for the invitations and cut from construction paper. Paste pieces of gingham cloth to the front of the programs.

Program Ideas: If each daughter present brings her baby picture, plan a baby contest, letting guests judge the most attractive baby from photographs. Also arrange a contest for the mothers and daughters who look alike. Provide prizes. The program might also include a fashion show from tots to mothers, including mother-daughter outfits. A pigtail talent show might be a special feature, also a mother-daughter chorus. The major emphasis for the devotional talk might be on the thought, "As the Twig Is Bent."

IN THE GARDEN

Invitations: These can be in the shape of a watering can, flower basket, garden gate, flower pot, or flower.

Decorations: Create a garden atmosphere with potted palms, ferns, plants, a wheelbarrow of flowers or greens, groupings of lawn furniture, miniature rock garden, birds in cages, etc.

Tables: Use potted plants with one letter on each pot so that when properly placed they spell MOTHER. Also use ivy or ferns and candles.

Packets of flower seeds can double for favors and place cards. Write names with a marking pen.

Programs: These can be in the shape of a basket, with portions of the program mimeographed on colored paper flowers which are cut out and pasted in the basket.

Waiters or *Waitresses* may wear gardening type aprons.

Program Ideas: Use background music with birds singing, water running, etc. Thoughts can be developed to show how a mother's love and care for flowers is like her love and care for her children. A flower chorus of young children can sing, dressed to resemble flowers. Perhaps there might be some love songs which are appropriate for garden scenes, or there might be a garden scene of mother-daughter chats.

FAITH OF OUR MOTHERS

Invitation: Small folders decorated with patriotic seals or a large Christian flag seal. Or, write invitation on a six-inch wide strip of paper, roll like a scroll, and tie with red ribbon.

Decorations: Use small national and Christian flags, Bibles, oil lamps, large spinning wheel, if available, and other appropriate decor. Include flowers in urns or old crockery.

Tables: Use miniature spinning wheels, small Bibles, small oil lamps, along with flower garlands or ivy. Small Christian flags might be tucked in the ivy.

Appropriate place cards can be miniature white Bibles with names inscribed in gold. A small flag placed in a nut cup of candies makes an attractive favor.

Programs: A colored patriotic church bulletin will make an appropriate program, or use a scroll as suggested for the invitation (eight inches wide).

Program Ideas: Use patriotic background music and include one number by singing waiters. A girls' chorus could sing "Faith of Our Mothers." Thoughts during the evening could center around "Our Christian Heritage" and the faith of Christian mothers down through the ages.

AROUND THE CLOCK WITH MOTHERS

Invitation: Cut round clocks from folded construction paper. Letters spelling the word MOTHER may be drawn in to make the time segments as shown in the sketch. Clock hands should point to the time of the event. Inside message may also use an acrostic spelling the word MOTHER.

MOTHER-DAUGHTER BANQUET

O ne night of the year
T he seventh of May and it's almost
H ere
E verything is planned and
R eady (Like no other!)
S et your alarm, here we go—
"AROUND THE CLOCK WITH
MOTHER"

Decorations: Use clocks of all kinds: alarm, pendulum, kitchen, radio, fancy, musical, grandfather, cuckoo, antique, etc. You might arrange an interesting display of antique pocket watches.

Tables: Use fern or ivy garlands and tuck in small hourglasses, miniature clocks, and candles.

Programs: Make in the shape of a clock, like invitation.

Program Ideas: Various hats or costumes may be worn by program participants to indicate the around-the-clock jobs of mother—chauffeur, nurse, chef, gardener, shopper, seamstress, laundress, accountant, teacher, etc. Include a Sunday-type outfit to indicate mother's spiritual interest and devotion to God as an example to her children.

LIFE TO LIFE

Invitation: Cut a folder from construction paper and decorate outside with butterfly seals.

Tickets: Use the same paper and cut out tickets, then paste on a butterfly seal.

Decorations: Cut various sizes of butterflies and place about the room on walls, as mobiles, on plants, etc. Use with floral bouquets or potted plants.

Tables: Use floral arrangements and ivy with butterflies folded and placed at random.

For favors, fold a butterfly seal in the center and glue around a pipecleaner. Fasten pipecleaner to small nut cup to form handle.

Program: Mimeograph program on inside of butterfly pattern, cut out, and decorate with glitter.

Program Ideas: Carry out the analogy of a person's relationship to Jesus Christ to the life-to-life relationship of mother and daughter.

PATTERN FOR LIVING

Poster: Picture of a mother and daughter in mother-daughter fashions, with appropriate wording.

Invitation: Portions of dress pattern cut from folded paper.

Decorations: Use regular dress patterns on the walls inscribed with appropriate Bible verses, using a felt-tip pen. (For example: I Samuel 16:7, Titus 2:7, I Corinthians 14:40, Proverbs 3:6, Philippians 3:14, II Timothy 4:7.) Additional atmosphere may be added with a few sewing baskets, hem markers, tape measures, jars of buttons, etc.

Tables: Use floral arrangements, garlands of fern or ivy with coiled tape measures, candles.

Cut place cards from lightweight cardboard in shape of a sleeve pattern and place in a gumdrop which has had a slit cut across top to hold card pattern.

Place small colored candies in nut cup for a button-box favor.

Programs: These can be made to represent a pattern. Envelopes may be designed and mimeographed, then colored and pasted together. A pattern sheet and instruction sheet can be mimeographed on 8½"x11" paper. Programs and/or menu may be printed on the pattern sketches. These two sheets may be folded and placed in the envelope.

Program Ideas: Use the word "Pattern" as a guide in planning and developing the program: Musical Patterns, Pattern for Dining, Patterns to Live By, Pattern for Spiritual Development, Pattern Finishing. There might be a modeling of fashions made by various guests, including children and teen-agers.

DOWN MEMORY LANE

Invitation: Make a folder with theme name on outside and decorated like an autograph album or a nosegay of violets.

Decorations: Place nostalgic mementos about the room: scrapbooks, family Bibles, autograph books, a jewel box, antique music box, a candy jar, miniature portraits, bundle of letters, old catalog, etc.

Tables: Decorate with oil lamps, nosegay flower arrangements, old lockets, brooches, spectacles, etc., placed among greenery.

Favors may be miniature nosegays in doilies or a peppermint stick for mothers and a licorice whip for daughters.

Programs: These may be folders decorated with pressed flowers and covered with Handi-wrap.

Program Ideas: Background music might be old 78 r.p.m. records (or gramophone, if one is available). Music might also feature a grandmothers' kitchen band or chorus, a tiny tots' chorus, an old-fashioned sing-a-long. Program features may emphasize favorites: Favorite Pastime, Favorite Family Fun (singing), Favorite Shop (malt), Favorite Time of Day (bedtime, storytime, and prayertime), Favorite Fashions, Favorite Book (Bible), etc.

PORTRAITS OF MOTHER

Poster: Feature a painter's palette with pictures of mothers cut out and pasted on ovals of color.

Invitation: Fold a piece of white paper and paste on it a silhouette of mother cut from black paper. Make a border with rickrack braid. Write invitation inside.

Decorations: Obtain all types of pictures of mothers to place about the room: velvet-framed pictures, prints of famous mothers, locket portraits mounted on a velvet background, old album photos, etc.

Tables: Use floral arrangements, miniature portraits, and candles.

Obtain, without their knowledge, pictures of mothers and daughters for place cards. Place mother's picture at daughter's place and vice versa.

Favors may be miniature paint palettes with a nutcup in the center.

Programs: These may be made in shape of a large oval-shaped locket.

Program Ideas: For a guessing game, old-time photos of mothers present may be shown with the help of an opaque projector, while guests write down names. A chalk artist may make sketches of mothers present or sketch famous mothers or Bible mothers for audience to guess. Possible topics for guest speakers: "Portraits of Bible Mothers," "Portraits of Mother's Influence."

I REMEMBER MAMA

Invitation: Place invitation inside a piece of folded red and white checked paper cut with pinking shears.

Decorations: Antique decor featuring old-fashioned albums, chairs, hall tree with old-fashioned hats, old dishes, cooking utensils, etc.

Tables: Use potted geraniums and miniature cast-iron stoves, irons, etc., placed among garlands of greens.

Favors may be made by placing nut cups on a small doily and decorating with bits of flowers and ribbons to make a hat.

Name cards may consist of favorite recipes written on one side of a 3"x5" card (handed in prior to the event so another's name can be written on the opposite side of the card).

Program: Design a cover such as that in the sketch and tuck a small plastic flower in the brim of the hat.

Program Ideas: Old-time songs may be

Remember Mama

sung by individuals or a group dressed in old-fashioned clothes. During dinner the group may view Mama's Fashions, modeled by Mama's Daughters. In a fun-time, Mama's Home Remedies may be shared. (For example: for 7-year itch, rub with sulphur and axle-grease. Other such gems may be found in books and almanacs in the library.) Program may be centered around Mama's Family Album, Mama's Daughter (singing "Sweeter as the Years Go By"), Mama's Favorite Song, Mama's Niece (an instrumental selection), Mama's Sunday School Class (a group of small girls singing), Mama's Best Friend (brief message from the Bible touching on God's love), Mama's Good-byes. Mama's Everyday Cake recipe may be shared with all: 4 C. I Kings 4:22; ½ tsp. Leviticus 2:13; 2 tsp. I Kings 10:10; 1 C. Judges 5:25 (last named item); 2 C. Jeremiah 6:20; 6 T. Isaiah 10:14; 4 T. I Samuel 14:25; 1 C. Numbers 17:8 (finely cut); 2 C. I Samuel 30:12 (last named item); 2 C. Naham 3:12; ½ C. Genesis 24:17; 3 tsp. Luke 13:21. Follow the advice in Proverbs 23:14, and you will have a good cake.

LOVE LETTERS

Invitations: Handwritten (or typewriter script) letter about the event placed in a hand-addressed envelope.

Tickets: Handwritten (and mimeographed) on 3"x5" cards in script, reminiscent of the old days.

Decorations: Tack large scrolls of shelf paper on the walls with snatches of letters to and from mother. Silhouette pictures of mothers may be mounted on the walls.

Tables: Place bundles of letters tied in ribbon, "forget-me-not" type of flower arrangements, garlands of ivy, and tall candles.

Make favors with colored feathers stuck in top of chocolate cremes (inkwells).

Program Ideas: Use songs that express love to mother. Feature a fashion show portraying "A Mother's Labor of Love" with all styles being home-sewn and models home-grown! Speakers may keep in mind the following Bible references: I John 1:4, Isaiah 50:4, and I John 1:3.

HATS AND CHATS

Invitations and Programs: Various hat shapes cut from folded construction paper with invitation or program mimeographed and fastened inside. A feather or flower may be added to the hat.

Decorations: The room may be decorated like a hat shop. Create this atmosphere with hat boxes, mirrors, hatstands of all types, children's and ladies' hats of every vintage.

Tables: Hats can be placed among greenery. To make the hats, use cottage cheese cartons and decorate with giftwrapping, feathers, and flowers. Place upside-down on a construction paper brim or lace doily.

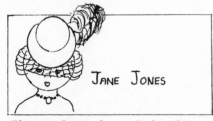

JANE JONES

Place cards can be made by gluing a button on cardboard. With colored pens and a little ingenuity, convert the button

into a face. Add a hat with a bit of net, felt, feathers, or flowers.

Program Ideas: Sunday hats—from baby bonnets to sunbonnets—may be modeled by young and old. Sing songs about hats, tell stories about hats, etc. Chats may feature the happy, serious, and spiritual chats characteristic of mothers and daughters.

MOTHER'S HANDS

Poster: Pair of lightly stuffed gloves mounted on cardboard with banquet theme and other details attractively printed.

Invitation: Hand cut from folded paper so that it is doubled when open. Attach invitation inside beginning with "We extend a hand of welcome to . . ."

Tables: Assorted floral arrangements and candles. If ceramic hands can be collected, place these with pieces of ivy here and there.

Favors can be made by gluing candy cups to open hands.

Programs: Enlarge pattern for invitation and place on folded construction paper. Mimeographed program can be fastened inside fold.

Program Ideas: Mother's hands of influence can be featured in the program in various ways: work, prayer, tenderness, encouragement, etc. Daughters might respond with ways they can use their hands.

TEA FOR TWO

Invitations: A teacup and saucer cut from folded paper with invitation inside.

Decorations: A tearoom atmosphere—display tea sets and teapots, hand-painted dishes hung on the walls, etc.

Tables: Place flower arrangements in teapots or teacups. Use napkins with teapot design. Use small toy teacups for nut cups.

Programs: Enlarge and use the teacup pattern made for invitations.

Program Ideas: A fashion parade of "Teatime Fashions Then and Now" modeled by tots, teens, mothers, and grandmothers; a "Teapot Derby" featuring a display and judging of unusual teapots, with children entering their toy teapots in a separate display. Special awards may be china teacups and saucers.

A TRIP DOWN MOTHER-DAUGHTER STREET

Invitation: A ticket inviting mothers and daughters down Mother-Daughter Street.

Decorations: Create a street atmosphere featuring various shops such as Children's Dress Shop, Malt Shop, Music Shop, Bridal Shop, etc.

Tables: Use miniature stores, houses, churches with greenery twined about them.

Assorted candy favored by children can be used in favors: jelly beans, peppermint sticks, licorice sticks, lollipops, etc.

Programs: Make a construction paper booklet cover with the words "Guide to Mother-Daughter Street." Make a separate page for each stop (planned in the program) down the street, listing the names of program participants, special features, etc.

Program Ideas: Take a trip down Mother-Daughter Street by featuring the Malt Shop for serving dinner (or tea), the Children's Dress Shop for a style show by daughters, the Music Shop for special music. Perhaps daughters could tape some special numbers ahead of time and during the program pretend they are listening to this record in the Music Shop. After a visit at the Bridal Shop, the last stop might be at the Book Shop, where the true Guide Book of life (Bible) is discussed for mothers and daughters. You might also include a scene where a young mother (seated in rocking chair) holds a tiny daughter and reads "Letter to Cynthia" (see page 197), which was originally read at a Mother-Daughter banquet at Aldrich Avenue Presbyterian Church, Minneapolis, Minnesota, where this banquet theme was originated.

OTHER BANQUET THEME SUGGESTIONS

"Mother—Queen of Our Hearts," "Hearts and Flowers," "Land of Enchantment," "Mother's Dreams," "Mother Is a Jewel," "Mothers, Memories, and Roses."

PROGRAMS, PLAYS, DIALOGUES, ETC.

Home

Choose Bible verses for the children to learn. Write each on a strip of paper to hold for group to see.

Let child discuss how verse can be practiced.

H onour thy father and thy mother (Exodus 20:12).

O bey them that have the rule over you (Hebrews 13:17).

M y mouth shall speak truth (Proverbs 8:7).

E ven a child is known by his doings (Proverbs 20:11).

Forum

Choose a panel of four to six mothers and a moderator to discuss various topics of interest to the group hearing the discussion. Such topics might be: the influence of a mother, how to help our children grow spiritually, home activities, effective family devotions.

Perhaps suggestions for topics could be submitted by the group several weeks in advance.

The Mothers Consult
(A Mothers' Day Dialogue)

(*Eight Mothers sitting in Mrs. Black's Front Room talking over their problems: Mrs. Jones, Mrs. Black, Mrs. Smith, Mrs. Tawes, Mrs. Long, Mrs. Hunt, Mrs. Brown and Mrs. Johnson.*)

MRS. JONES—Don't you think that bringing up children is a great responsibility, Mrs. Black?

MRS. BLACK—I certainly do, but I notice some people don't feel that way about it. One of my neighbors says she won't let bringing up her children tie her down. She is too busy with all her clubs to bother about her children. They just run the streets. She says she guesses they'll turn out just as well as if she wore herself out with them.

MRS. SMITH—I'm afraid your neighbor will have a sad awakening some day. The Bible says, "A child left to himself bringeth his mother to shame."

MRS. TAWES—What's that you said, Mrs. Smith?

MRS. SMITH—I just quoted the verse in the Bible which says, "A child left to himself bringeth his mother to shame."

MRS. TAWES—I never knew that was in the Bible, but I'm sure it's true.

MRS. LONG—The thing that discourages me is that we can try our best to bring our children up right, and yet there's no telling how they'll turn out.

MRS. HUNT—I don't agree with you, Mrs. Long, because if we are Christian mothers we have a Bible promise to stand on.

MRS. LONG—What do you mean, Mrs. Hunt?

MRS. HUNT—The Bible says, "Train up a child in the way he should go and when he is old he will not depart from it."

MRS. BROWN—Is that in the Bible, Mrs. Hunt? I would like to see it. (*Mrs. Hunt finds Proverbs 22:6 and shows it to Mrs. Brown who reads it aloud and then says*) I never knew that was in the Bible! It surely sounds encouraging.

MRS. JOHNSON—I suppose that's true because it's in the Bible, but I knew a very good woman whose only son broke her heart. It wasn't because he didn't know better for she talked to him all the time, but he just wouldn't pay any attention to what she said.

MRS. JONES—That verse in Proverbs didn't say that if you tell a child what is right he'll turn out well. It says, "*Train* up a child in the way he should go." That means not just telling him what's right but seeing that he *does* it!

MRS. TAWES—I don't understand how you train up a child in the way he should go. You can't make children do everything that they ought to or you'd be punishing them all the time.

MRS. BLACK—I don't agree with you. Well-trained children need punishing far less than poorly trained ones. But I think I know what you mean. Some parents give so many commands it would be impossible for a child to carry them all out. A mother should give very few commands. There should be just as few "don'ts" as possible. But she must see that every command she does give is carried out.

MRS. SMITH—I know a woman who just wears herself and her children out with commands. She says, "Don't do this" and "Don't do that" so many times a day, I should think her children would become nervous wrecks. But I guess they are used to it. They don't pay any more attention to what she says than they would to a barking puppy.

MRS. LONG—I can sympathize with her though. Most of us want our children to be good and well mannered and to keep themselves clean. And they forget so fast and interrupt and get their clothes dirty. No wonder we mothers seem to be scolding all the time.

MRS. HUNT—Perhaps we bewilder our children with trying to teach them so many things at once. Take the matter of keeping their clothes clean. We want them to learn that, but still there are other things far more important, so why not let them get their play clothes dirty, and concentrate on truthfulness, obedience, reverence to God and things like that.

Mrs. Black—I agree with Mrs. Hunt. We can afford to ignore some things that we would like to see different while we train them in the things that matter most. For instance, I don't think children should be punished for getting dirty or for accidents. But they should be punished for disobedience or for lying.

Mrs. Brown—My neighbor keeps her children looking like pictures all the time but you can't believe anything they say. She spanks them for even getting a grass stain on their clothing but when she found out that Carol had told a lie, she laughed and said, "Carol's pretty cute all right."

Mrs. Johnson—I think that's awful. The poor child will grow up thinking it's worse to stain her clothes than to tell a lie.

Mrs. Tawes—Don't you think spanking children is really out of date?

Mrs. Jones—No, I don't for the Bible is not out of date and it says, "He that spareth the rod hateth his son." But I'm afraid there is some useless spanking done and that is hard for both parents and children.

Mrs. Johnson—Useless spanking! What do you mean?

Mrs. Jones—I mean this. Many parents punish a child for disobedience one day and let him get away with it the next. Children are naturally hopeful and so they do the same thing again hoping it will be a lucky day and they won't get into trouble for it. Now if a child knows that every time he disobeys or tells a lie, he will be punished, he won't do those things very often and life will be much pleasanter for both him and his parents.

Mrs. Black—You mean that just as a child learns not to touch the stove and get burned, so he can learn to avoid sins such as disobedience and lying, if they always bring punishment.

Mrs. Jones—That's it exactly. The certainty of punishment discourages wrong doing, more than occasional severity, which is really cruel.

Mrs. Long—We've been talking so much about punishment it sounds as if that was our main business as mothers. I think loving our children is quite as important.

Mrs. Smith—You're right, and indeed the reason we punish them is just because we love them. But we must show our love in many other ways too. I think listening to their ideas and answering their questions makes them feel we love and understand them.

Mrs. Brown—I certainly believe in taking time with my children. They'll grow up fast enough. Now is our chance to guide their thinking.

Mrs. Johnson—What do you ladies think about giving children work to do? I give each of mine certain little duties to do every day. I feel that it makes them take more interest in the home if they have some responsibility. But my neighbor says it's a shame to make children work. She says they'll have enough work to do by and by. Let them have a good time while they're young.

Mrs. Hunt—I am sure you are doing right, Mrs. Johnson, in giving little duties to your children. I have seen both ways tried and I am certain that children who have some work to do enjoy their free time more and make better men and women. But it is always best to go by the Bible, rather than by our own ideas or experience, so let me give you a Bible verse on this subject. "It is good for a man that he bear the yoke in his youth." This means that the discipline of work is good for the young.

Mrs. Jones—My children have work to do and I try not to give many commands but to see that all I do give are obeyed. And I'm going to start them in Sunday school, too, as soon as they are old enough.

MRS. SMITH—My dear Mrs. Jones, your oldest little girl is almost six and ready to start school, isn't she? She's been ready for Sunday school almost six years. I hope you will start taking your family at once.

MRS. JONES—I don't see any sense in taking children to Sunday school until they are old enough to go to school. They are too little to get anything out of it, and it's a bother getting them ready.

MRS. SMITH—Over and over in the Bible the Lord says to bring the little ones. In one place it even says to bring the children which have not known anything. Your children will probably understand more than you think. But even if they don't, when you bring them to Sunday school you are starting them out right.

MRS. TAWES—I had no idea the Bible gave so much advice about bringing up a family. I will have to read my Bible more after this.

MRS. LONG—I guess all of us need to read our Bibles more. There's a lot in the Bible about children that we haven't had time to talk of today.

MRS. HUNT—I am going to read my Bible more too. But there is a verse I learned a long time ago in Sunday school that has often helped me in bringing up my family.

MRS. BROWN—What is it?

MRS. HUNT—"If any of you lack wisdom let him ask of God who giveth to all men liberally and upbraideth not, and it shall be given him." I have so often been puzzled and felt I did not have wisdom enough to know just what to do. Then I have remembered that verse and asked the Lord for wisdom, and He has given it.

MRS. BROWN—What a wonderful promise! I would like to have you mark it for me in my Bible.

MRS. HUNT—I'll be glad to. It's James 1:5.

MRS. JOHNSON—Our little visit together this afternoon has helped me very much. From now on I am going to study my Bible and when I am worried and don't know what to do, I will ask the Lord for wisdom.

MRS. JONES—(Rising)—I am afraid I must be going now. The children will soon be home from school and I always try to be there when they come. But I have enjoyed our visit this afternoon. I think we have had a real Mothers' Day.

(All the rest rise and start leaving)

MRS. LONG—I think so too. Good-by everyone.

MRS. BLACK—Good-by! See you next Sunday.

Curtain

VIVIAN D. GUNDERSON
in *The Sunday School Times*

For Christian Mothers

This brief exercise may be used in a special Mother's Day program for the closing program of Sunday school, at a Mother and Daughter banquet or whenever it can best be used. Juniors and intermediates might take part in it with each participant holding up a card with the specific characteristic printed on it.

DARE as did Jochebed who defied a godless ruler that her son, Moses, might be preserved to lead his people out of bondage.

HELP as did Rebekah who welcomed Abraham's servant to her city and watered his thirsty camels.

WIN as did Rachel for whom Jacob was willing to serve fourteen years without wages.

FIGHT as did Deborah who in defense of home and native land led her people against the mighty.

HOPE as did Naomi who found comfort in her homeland after drinking the waters of affliction in an alien land.

GLEAN as did Ruth who in the fields of Boaz at Bethlehem forever dignified manual labor.

PRAY as did Hannah whose voiceless

petition was fulfilled when she became the mother of the last and greatest of the Judges.

OBEY as did the widow of Zarephath, who willingly gave of her meager store of food to feed a Prophet of the Lord and received blessings unending.

SUFFER as did Vashti who lost her throne rather than sacrifice her modesty.

REIGN as did Esther who for a mighty task at a strategic hour came to a place of honor in the kingdom of Ahasuerus.

BELIEVE as did Elisabeth who accepted the impossible, and through her son the forerunner, prepared the way for the Lord Jesus.

WORSHIP as did Anna the prophetess when she first saw the infant Lord Jesus in the Temple and knew He was to be the Redeemer.

SERVE as did Martha who provided the best at Bethany for the Saviour.

LOVE as did Mary who from her alabaster flask of precious perfume, anointed Jesus against the day of His burying.

SACRIFICE as did the widow who gave the Lord all that she owned and was remembered in His Word as an example for every Christian.

GIVE as did Dorcas who was "full of good works and almsdeeds which she did" for the fatherless and widows in their affliction.

TEACH as did Lois, who caused her son Timothy from a child to know the sacred writings which are able to make "wise unto salvation."

TRUST as did Lydia who opened her heart to the Lord and her house to the earliest Christian missionaries to the continent of Europe.

WITNESS as did Priscilla, who, with her husband and with the missionary Paul, told of the living Christ in the days of the early Church.

ELIZABETH W. SUDLOW and
E. JEAN HYSLOP
The Sunday School World

The Seven Ages of Motherhood

The majority of Mother's Day services, sermons, poems, and even commercial advertising, feature mother as middle-aged or as an elderly, white-haired woman. But motherhood begins with the young mother in her early twenties and continues on through life, during which she may be not only a mother, but a grandmother and a great-grandmother. With the passing years there come to her changing demands, needs and responsibilities as a mother. An outline for a Mother's Day service called "The Seven Ages of Motherhood" illustrates this thought.

Seven women take the parts, each woman of the age which her part represents, speaking in a five- to seven-minute talk. This program is particularly adapted to a Mothers' and Daughters' banquet or meeting.

In between the speeches, appropriate music may be used.

1. The mother of a baby daughter: She discusses heredity, education for motherhood, prenatal care, and infant care.

2. The mother of a preschool-age lassie: She speaks of the years when her little girl is past babyhood but still at home with her, and her constant companion. These are the years which, in the molding of character, many child psychologists rate as the most important in a child's life. The daughter will never out-grow the attitude of confidence and understanding established by the mother during those years, and this attitude will govern her future life relationships with her mother.

3. The mother of a little school girl: She speaks of the child's first contacts out of the family circle, and of her contacts through the grades and high school. In these years the young girl crosses the bridge from childhood to budding womanhood. Her emotional life is stirred, and she has her first public religious experiences.

As the girl leaves childhood, she sees her mother with new eyes, measures her by new standards, and, although she may think the contrary, she has a new and greater need of her mother. Mother's calm wisdom and unfailing understanding and sympathy meet a new challenge.

4. The mother of a daughter away at school: Again there is the need of a new

adjustment on the part of the mother to keep intellectual step with a modern young lady daughter. The speaker dwells on new friendships; the choice of a school; the religious life away from the home and home church; the new temptations and problems—physical, mental, and spiritual.

5. The mother of a daughter who seeks a career: The speaker discusses whether it is wiser to help her daughter to select a vocation or to leave the selection entirely to the girl. Mother love must not become a dictatorial force in the daughter's adult life. Some of the fields now open to women are mentioned.

6. The mother of a daughter who is a wife: She speaks of the daughter's choosing her life mate, of the establishment of a new home, and of being a mother to her daughter's husband.

7. The mother of a daughter with a family—a grandmother: This mother shows that when both mother and daughter have reached advanced womanhood, there may be dictatorship on either side. Grandma may be too "bossy," or daughter may think she must now manage mother; but mother and daughter, having traveled the same road of joy and sorrow, may by these common experiences be brought together in the most complete harmony and loving unity of thought and feeling of their entire lives. Such is the ideal climax in the Seven Ages of Motherhood.

LETTIE B. RITCHIE in *Church Business*

Getting Paid

CHARACTERS: Mother, Grandmother, Mary aged 13, Molly and Polly (twins of 12), Anne aged 11, Sally aged 10 and Debbie aged 8.

SCENE I—MORNING

(*The six girls are sitting in the living room watching TV.*)

MOTHER (*calling from next room*)— Hurry up, girls, and get your work done. Work before play, you know.

MARY—Oh dear, that means we've got to do the dishes again. I just hate doing dishes! Come on Sally, it's your turn to wash them.

SALLY—It is not my turn. It's yours!

POLLY—We've got to make the beds now. Hurry up, Molly.

MOLLY—Wait till I see the end of this program. I don't see why we always have to work. Some of my friends never have to do anything but have a good time.

DEBBIE—I have to weed the garden. That's the hardest of all. It's so hot out there.

ANNE—If Mother had to pay someone to do all the work we do, I guess it would take a lot of money.

MARY—You've given me an idea. Let's tell Mother we think she ought to pay us for all the work she asks us to do.

SALLY—That's a fine idea. I wouldn't mind doing the dishes if I got paid for it every time.

POLLY—Say, if Molly and I got twenty-five cents every time we made the beds, wouldn't that be great!

MOLLY—Wouldn't it though!

DEBBIE—If I got paid for weeding the garden, I could go and get an ice cream soda or a tall coke to cool off with. Pretty nice!

ANNE—Who's going to ask Mother? You ask her, Mary.

MOTHER—(*Hurrying into room*)—Girls, didn't you hear me tell you to get to work? You will never amount to anything if you do not learn to work before you play.

MARY—We are just going to work, Mother but we wanted to ask you something first.

MOTHER—Well, what is it?

MARY—We girls were talking together and we wondered if you would be willing to pay us for the work we do.

MOTHER—How do you mean?

SALLY—If you would give us twenty or twenty-five cents for everything you ask us to do we thought it would be very nice.

MOTHER—You mean you want to be paid every time you wash the dishes or sweep the floor or do anything like that.

POLLY—Yes, that's it.

MOTHER—Am I to understand that you all want to go on a business basis with me?

MOLLY—We would all like to.

MOTHER—Very well. I will have your accounts ready for you by supper time. Now hurry up and get your work done.

(Girls scatter. Curtain)

SCENE II—AFTERNOON

(Girls with comic books, records, or any kind of pleasant occupation.)

ANNE—I didn't think Mother would agree so quickly this morning.

DEBBIE—I didn't think she would either. Do you suppose she has enough money to pay us all like that?

GRANDMOTHER (Enters, knitting) — Would you girls like to hear about the time when your mother was a little girl?

MARY—Oh, yes, Grandma, we would love to hear about it. I am so glad you came to visit us. We have often asked Mother to tell us about the time she was a girl but she is always too busy.

GRANDMOTHER—When your mother was a little girl your grandfather took up a homestead in Iowa. It was a lonely place to bring up a family, but your grandfather thought it a good place to raise children. Your mother was the oldest girl, then came five boys and baby Anne.

ANNE—I knew I was named for Aunt Anne.

GRANDMOTHER—When your mother was only twelve, your grandfather died suddenly. I had to do all the farm work with the help of the boys. They did all they could, but of course they were small. With all the farm work on my hands I simply had to let Mary, your mother, work far harder than a girl of twelve should work. She had to get up at five o'clock every morning in order

to get breakfast for the whole family, and put up lunches for all who went to school. Then she had the long walk to and from school but when she got home there was supper to get, and after supper there were piles of dishes to do. Even after the younger ones went to bed, your mother had stockings to darn or other work to do till she dropped into bed worn out. Your mother had to work hard on Saturday too. Her clothes were shabby and she never had so much as a penny to spend for treats. It was all we could do to get food and clothes for the family. But your mother was almost always pleasant and cheerful and ready to make the best of things. At the same time I have always felt sorry that I was not able to give her a happier childhood.

SALLY—Poor Mother! I did not know she had had such a hard life.

GRANDMOTHER—I'm sure you girls will try to make her life easier now. You are her greatest earthly comfort. And tomorrow is Mother's Day.

(Grandmother exits)

POLLY—I had forgotten that tomorrow was Mother's Day. We must plan something especially nice for Mother.

MARY—I had forgotten about Mother's Day too. I wish we had not asked her to pay us, just before Mother's Day.

(Curtain)

SCENE III—ALL AT SUPPER TABLE

MOTHER—Each of you will find your bill under your plate. You may read them while we are waiting for father.

SALLY—Bill! Whatever does Mother mean.

ANNE—Let's read them and see. Read yours first, Sally.

SALLY (Opens hers and reads aloud)—Mine says, "You are now ten years old. You could not get as good food as you get at home for a dollar a day anywhere else. However that is all I shall charge you. Your board bill up to the present time is therefore three thousand, six hundred and fifty dollars. You have helped with the dishes or done some other duty since you were six. That has been four years. I have therefore credited you with earning twenty-five cents a day during that time. At that rate you have earned three hundred and sixty-five dollars. Subtracting that from the three thousand six hundred and fifty dollars leaves you in debt three thousand, two hundred and eighty-five dollars.

"Note: Your bill for clothing, nursing and so forth can be taken up later."

SALLY—How dreadful! I could never pay all that money. I never thought meals cost so much money. What does your paper say, Polly.

POLLY—Mine says, "You could not get a trained nurse anywhere who would give you the care your mother gave you all through that severe illness. And you could not get one who would stay on duty night and day for only ten dollars each twenty-four hours. However that is all I shall charge you. Your hospital bill was four hundred and eighty dollars. The doctor's bill was three hundred dollars. Your medicines cost twenty dollars. You required my services night and day as nurse for thirty days. At the rate of ten dollars a day your bill for nursing is three hundred dollars. The total expense of your illness was therefore eleven hundred dollars

"You are now twelve years old and have helped make beds or in some other work since you were six. At the rate of twenty-five cents a day you have earned five hundred forty-seven dollars. Subtracting that from the seven hundred leaves you five hundred fifty-three dollars in debt for your illness. After you have paid that, you can start on your board bill which is well over four thousand dollars."

POLLY—Oh, how awful! I don't think I can ever get all that paid. What does your account say, Molly?

MOLLY—Mine says, "You could not get anyone who would keep you as well dressed as I do for one hundred dollars a year. However, that is all I shall charge you. You are now twelve years old. At the rate of one hundred dollars a year, you now owe twelve hundred dollars for clothing. I shall allow you twenty-five cents a day since you were six years old for the work you have done. At that rate you have earned five hundred forty-seven dollars. Subtracting that from the twelve hundred leaves you in debt six hundred and fifty-three dollars for clothing. After you have paid that, you can start on your board bill."

MOLLY—I could never, never pay all that money! What does your paper say, Debbie?

DEBBIE—I don't want to read mine out loud. I never thought before how much money we owe you, Mother. If we worked for you all our lives, we could never pay you back for everything.

ANNE—I never thought of all the money you had to spend on us and of all the care you have given us. I don't see how any of us will ever get you paid back.

MOTHER—All of you want to go on a business basis with me and be paid for everything you do about the house, so it is only fair that I charge you for all I have done for you.

SALLY—Oh, Mother, I think going on a business basis is horrid. I think we were horrid to want to be paid for everything we do.

POLLY—Yes, we were. We never thought of how much we cost you, and all you have done for us. We were just selfish and lazy.

MOTHER—My dear children, I am not going to ask you to pay me back.

The things I have done for you
were all done for love and not for
money. What I want is that we
shall all love one another and the
Lord most and best. Then each of
you will be willing to do her share
of the work. Everybody loving and
everybody helping makes a happy
home.

MOLLY (jumping up and hugging
Mother)—We do love you, Mother, and I think we all love the Lord
too. We all love each other excepting when we're mad. I'm never
going to grumble again about having to help.

GRANDMOTHER (wiping her eyes)—I
hear your father's car in the drive-
way now.

MOTHER—I'll bring in the hot dishes
right away.

MARY—Let me help you Mother.
(Exit together)

POLLY (holding up pretty wall text,
preferably one such as "Honor thy
father and mother")—I got this
present for Mother before the store
shut. When she hangs it on the wall
it will help us girls to remember it.

MOLLY—I'm so glad you did. Let us all
help you to pay for it and let's each
write a note to tell her how much
we love her.

DEBBIE—Let's. And let's each think of
some special job we can do to
please Mother—something she has
never even asked us to do.

ANNE—We will. And I'm going to try
to think of Mother every day, not
just of myself.

GRANDMOTHER—If you are all thoughtful of your mother, it will please the
Lord who died for us and it will
help to make this home the happiest
home in the land.

SALLY—Every day is going to be Mother's Day with me after this.

(Curtain as Mother and Mary start in
with bowls)

VIVIAN D. GUNDERSON

Mothers of the Bible
(A Mother's Day Tableau)

The lines of this tableau are read by a
narrator (or narrators) standing at a
lectern before the curtains, at one side
of the stage. The lectern should be
twined with greenery and sprays of flowers (carnations are most suitable). The
narrator should wear a simple floor-
length dress or costume of ancient Greek
or Roman design.

All direct quotations should be read
from back stage over a public-address
system. Preferably a variety of men's
and women's voices should be used. The
sources of these quotations may be given
in your printed programs, if you like.
You will probably need music between
scenes to provide time for changing
characters.

Living tableau may be prepared to
illustrate each of the mothers described,
or if you prefer, use slides of each of
these Bibles scenes flashed on a screen
during the readings. For costuming the
Biblical characters see Biblical Costumes
for Church and School, by Virginia Wilk
Elicker (New York: A. S. Barnes and
Co.)

For staging these scenes two back-
drops are needed—one of sky and the
other the arch of a stone building. By
using a variety of properties with these,
you can achieve the effects you want
simply. Green branches may be stuck
into bases of green styrofoam to be
moved about for rushes and bushes.
Rocks can be made of boxes covered
with wire and papier maché.

VOICE BACKSTAGE: "All that I am, or
hope to be, I owe to my angel
mother." (Lincoln).

SECOND BACKSTAGE VOICE: "Men are
what their mothers make them."
(Emerson).

NARRATOR (In front of curtain): A
good mother is an inspiration for
all time. We recognize good mothers by their children. We know that
children are most influenced by the
teaching and example of their
mothers.

On Mother's Day we honor all mothers. We express our gratitude for their good works. We call to remembrance their outstanding qualities. What should the ideal mother be? What qualities should true motherhood express?

For the answer to this let us turn to the pages of the Bible where we find many mothers of noble character and varied experiences. And here, too, their children bear testimony to what they were.

VOICE BACKSTAGE: "Yea, I will bless her, and she shall be a mother of nations." (Genesis 17:16)
(Curtains open showing scene with Abraham and the boy, Isaac, a bundle of faggots strapped to his back, waves to his mother with a confident smile, as she bravely watches them go.)

NARRATOR: Faith, patience and constancy are the qualities best expressed by Sarah, wife of the prophet Abraham. When her husband was called by God to go out into a new land to form a new nation, she forsook home and country to stand loyally at his side all the way. Unlike Lot's wife, she did not look back with regret. A beautiful woman, she was greatly beloved by her husband. Sarah did not become a mother until late in life. Then, according to God's promise made many years before, Isaac was born to her. Mentioned in the roll of the faithful in the Book of Hebrews, Sarah lived a life of trust in God. She made mistakes as we all do, but she corrected them.

The greatest test of her faith in God must have come, like Abraham's, when he was called upon to sacrifice their beloved son of promise upon the altar. And how great must have been her joy when her son came back down the mountain with his father because God had provided another sacrifice.
(Curtains close on first tableau)

VOICE BACKSTAGE: "Come now there-fore, and I will send thee unto Pharaoh, that thou mayest bring forth my people, the children of Israel, out of Egypt" (Exodus 3:10)
(Curtains open on second tableau showing Pharaoh's daughter discovering Moses in the bullrushes. Miriam, sister of Moses, should be hiding in the rushes at the forefront of the scene and Jochebed, his mother, farther back.)

NARRATOR: Fearless perseverance, wisdom and ingenuity characterized Jochebed, the mother of three fine children—Moses, Aaron and Miriam. From her these children must have gained the qualities they displayed as they played their various parts in freeing the children of Israel from bondage of the Egyptians. Most outstanding of the three was Moses, lawgiver, statesman and leader, through whom God was to give mankind the Ten Commandments. Aaron who was Moses' spokesman at Pharaoh's court became the first high priest. Miriam was a prophetess and also played an important role.

Although her name is mentioned only twice in the Bible, Jochebed is a picture of courageous motherhood. At the time that Moses was born, Pharaoh had decreed that all sons of the Hebrews should be killed at birth. What skill it must have taken to keep her baby from being discovered for three months! Then, when she could hide him no longer, she had a new idea.

She would make an ark of bulrushes and leave the baby where Pharaoh's own daughter might discover it when she came to the water to bathe. No doubt she counted on the womanly instincts of the princess to show pity on the doomed child. Could she have hoped for a more wonderful solution to her problem than what developed? Not only did the princess decide to adopt the beautiful baby she had found and give him every advantage of the royal household, but through the timely suggestion of Miriam, Moses' sister, it was arranged that Jochebed should serve as nurse to her own baby!

(*Curtains close on second tableau.*)

VOICE BACKSTAGE: "For this child I prayed . . . as long as he liveth he shall be lent to the Lord" (I Samuel 1:27,28).

(*Curtains open on third tableau, showing Samuel with Eli beside him, and Hannah, holding out a new garment she had made and brought to him.*)

NARRATOR: Holiness, unselfishness and humility were expressed by Hannah, mother of Samuel, the little boy who heard God's voice calling him. For a long time Hannah had longed to be a mother. At last in her grief and sorrow she went into the tabernacle and prayed fervently that if God would give her a child she would give him to the Lord. Eli, the priest, talked with her and comforted her, expressing the hope God would grant her petition.

Shortly afterward her son was born. There might have been a temptation after seeing this darling baby to forget her promise or at least delay in fulfilling it, but as soon as the child could leave her, she took him to the tabernacle and presented him to God. Hannah was repaid for giving her firstborn to the Lord, for later she bore three other sons and two daughters.

But Hannah never forgot little Samuel, busy ministering before the Lord. Each year when she came with her husband to offer the yearly sacrifice, she brought Samuel a little coat which she had made and which he could wear under the linen ephod, a simple vest worn by the priests. Samuel must often have felt his mother's affection wrapping him warmly as her arms might otherwise have done, as he wore the garment into which she had stitched her love.

(*Curtains close on third tableau.*)

NARRATOR: We could tell of other mothers of the Bible—the generosity of the Widow of Zarephath who, in time of famine, fed a guest with the last of the food left for her and her son. She was repaid many times over because their supply was never exhausted.

Then there was the hospitality of the Shunamite woman who, with her husband, entertained Elisha often in their home because he was a man of God, even built him a special guest room. She had been barren but was rewarded for her kindness by the birth of a son.

WOMAN'S VOICE (BACKSTAGE): "Son why hast thou thus dealt with us? Behold, thy father and I have sought thee sorrowing."

BOY'S VOICE (BACKSTAGE): "Wist ye not that I must be about my father's business?" (Luke 2:48,49)

(*Curtains open on tableau showing Jesus in the temple discussing with the doctors. At forefront stand Joseph and Mary, entering to find him. If you prefer not to show the boy Jesus, let the scene be of Joseph and Mary searching for Him in the crowd.*)

NARRATOR: Purity and spirituality were qualities essential to Mary. How close this mother must have been to God as she received the angel's prophecy! And all during the months of waiting, what joyful expectancy must have been hers! The wonder and glory of her child's birth must have remained with her all during His childhood.

But there came a time when she could not help being impatient with Him. Like many another boy, as He began to reach out toward manhood, He became difficult for parents to understand. How, they thought, could He be so irresponsible and thoughtless as not to be ready when their caravan started for home! Three days of anxious searching, delay and inconvenience were not easy to overlook. Just as all parents, they still thought of Him as the infant He had so recently been. They could scarcely understand that already His divine mission was beginning.

So we are told that Mary and Joseph "understood not the saying which he spake unto them in the temple," but Jesus returned meekly with them to Nazareth and was obedient to them, and His mother remembered His sayings.

Later she would be with Him to see His first miracle at the wedding feast in Cana. She was with Him, too, at His crucifixion. Although Jesus' ministry was so universal He must recognize all mankind as His family and dispense with personal relationships, at the height of His greatest agony, the crucifixion, He did not forget to provide for Mary. He entrusted her to the care of His beloved disciple who from that hour took her into his own home.

(Curtains close on fourth tableau.)

NARRATOR: Finally let us turn to one unnamed Bible mother, noted not so much for her children as for the words she taught her son, King Lemuel.

(Curtains open on final scene. A modern family—mother, father, teen-age son and younger daughter and son—are seated for family worship. The father or one of the children is reading from the Bible, all look on attentively.)

VOICE BACKSTAGE: (Reads Proverbs 31:4,5,9,10,26-28,30,31).

(Curtain)

JANE KIRK

The Weavers
(A one-act play)

INSTRUCTIONS: (The background of the platform should be curtains or screens of green. At the right is a table and desk of antique design. A huge book, to denote a record book, and a large ink well with a quill pen set on the desk, along with a candle in a massive iron holder. On the other side of the platform is a loom or spinning wheel. Nearby is a small table where there is a scroll and an oriental lamp and a Bible.)

CHARACTERS:
Record Keeper (man)
Hebrew mother
Mary, mother of Jesus
Ancient Crusader mother
Modern mother
8 teenage girls
4 small boys (5 to 7 years old)
Pioneer mother

The Record Keeper wears a plain robe of dark heavy material. He sits at the desk and turns the pages of the huge book, pausing to read here and there. Teenagers are dressed in white robes, each holding an armful of yarn that is draped over the arm. Have one girl for each color of yarn mentioned. The Hebrew mother wears a colored flowing robe. Mary, the mother of Jesus in white or blue robe with a blue scarf over her head and shoulders. Ancient Crusader mother in medieval dress. Pioneer mother in homespun garb. Modern mother in modern day dress. Children to be dressed according to the time they represent.

Enter the young Hebrew mother leading a small boy by the hand, walking slowly and with uncertainty to the Record Keeper.

HEBREW MOTHER: I know not if this is the place I seek or not.

RECORD KEEPER: All mothers come here. They find here the threads that they must choose and weave.

HEBREW MOTHER: Then this is the place I seek. I shall gladly, proudly weave for my little son a garment more beautiful than any other mother has woven, for my son is loved more than any other. Ten other sons has his father, but he loves my son more than the ten. Give me, I pray, the most beautiful threads ever spun.

RECORD KEEPER: The choice must be yours. All mothers must choose. Here are the threads of beauty and righteousness, and threads of ugliness and sin.

HEBREW MOTHER: Surely no mother would choose ugliness and sin for her child!

RECORD KEEPER: If she fails to choose godliness and righteousness, she chooses the other—ugliness and sin. Every mother chooses the colors she would weave in her child's character.

HEBREW MOTHER: (approaches the holders of the threads, touching the different colors, moving from one to another.) What colors would you recommend? My son's garment must be worthy of him, and he must be worthy of the promise of Jehovah to his forefather, Abraham.

RECORD KEEPER: Well, let's look at the different colors. Red for courage; orange for faith; yellow for joy; white for purity; green for strength; blue for truth; purple for hope; and here is grey for the appearance of evil and black for sin and impurity.

HEBREW MOTHER: Red shall he have for he must be courageous, blue for he must be true to his father's line, orange for he must be a man of faith, and yellow for he must know joy.

RECORD KEEPER: His coat then, shall be one of many colors. The record is made and may the blessing of Jehovah be upon you and upon your weaving. No mother weaves only for her son but for the sons of generations to follow.

The mother leaves with the colored yarn over her arm and leading the boy. Music to express this time of sacred history should be played while the Hebrew mother comes to platform and while she leaves. The music changes to a Christmas carol while Mary enters carrying a large doll wrapped in swaddling clothes. The Record Keeper looks up and smiles as Mary enters.

MARY: I seek for my son yarn with which to weave him a garment the most perfect that any mother has ever woven.

RECORD KEEPER: The yarns are here, the choice is yours.

MARY: The thread must be spun of the softest, purest wool, free from knot or blemish. My weaving must be even, firm and perfect. I must have patience and faith, for the garment will be long in the weaving. It must last as long as his life shall last.

RECORD KEEPER: What colors will you choose for this garment? See, here is red for courage, blue for truth, yellow for joy.

MARY: (Approaches the holders of the threads looking at the colors but takes the white.) Courage shall he have; truth, purity, faith, joy. In the white there are all the virtues, I would have his garment white—all white. And it shall have no seam. A white seamless robe.

RECORD KEEPER: In the white there is courage, truth, purity, faith and joy. In the white ray of light there are all the lovely colors of the bow set in the heavens by the hand of the Lord. Your choice is good and the record is made. Blessings upon you and upon the weaving of that white seamless robe.

(As Mary leaves use as music background "The Light Of The World." This music fades into "Fairest Lord Jesus"—the Crusader hymn or "Onward Christian Solders" as the Crusader mother enters with a small boy in hand. The Record Keeper looks up from his book.)

CRUSADER MOTHER: I seek yarn for my weaving. I have a very special task. I would weave for my son a garment stronger than ever woven. The black and grey look like good sturdy yarns. (Looks at the yarn)

RECORD KEEPER: Yes they are strong but not the strength you desire for your son's character. Let me explain what the yarns represent. Red for courage; orange for faith; yellow for joy; white for purity; green for strength; blue for truth; purple for hope; also grey for the appearance of evil and black for sin.

CRUSADER MOTHER: Will you choose the colors for me?

RECORD KEEPER: Nay, the choice must be yours.

CRUSADER MOTHER: (Looks the yarn over more carefully) I am the wife of a Crusader and I hope the mother of a Crusader. I pray that my son shall follow the footsteps of his father, a knight of valor and purity. For he served in a holy purpose. I shall weave for my son a garment of purest white, and upon it I shall make a cross of red. He shall be a soldier of the cross.

RECORD KEEPER: Your choice is wise, the record is made.

(The Crusader mother leaves platform with same music. This music fades into "Faith of our Fathers" or a Mother's Day song of your choice.) Enter the Pioneer Mother dressed in homespun garb leading a small boy.

PIONEER MOTHER: May I find threads for my weaving here?

RECORD KEEPER: Threads of all colors are here ready for your choice.

PIONEER MOTHER: I am not sure that I am able to choose wisely. Will you help me choose?

RECORD KEEPER: The choice must be yours. Every mother chooses for her own child.

PIONEER MOTHER: A responsibility indeed. I wish to weave for my child a garment, a better garment than any yet made. It must be strong, and fine, it must endure. He will see hardship, meet the temptations of a new country wherein each man makes his own law. My prayer for him is that he may share in making our nation—a great and righteous nation.

RECORD KEEPER: That prayer will be answered, pioneer mother. And your weaving will be blest. What colors will you choose for this garment? Red for courage; white for purity; orange for faith; yellow for joy; green for strength; blue for truth; and purple for hope, or grey for evil and black for sin.

PIONEER MOTHER: (Approaching the holders of the threads) Red—and white—and blue. These shall be for his ensign. And for the garb in which my grandsons shall defend that ensign—the red, white and blue.

RECORD KEEPER: Courage—purity—and truth. The record of your choice is made.

(While the Pioneer Mother leaves the platform with the child a patriotic song is to be played, such as "America the Beautiful" or "My Country Tis of Thee." The modern mother enters with the small boy. The song, "Jesus Calls Us, O'er the Tumult" or "Take My Life and Let It Be" may be used as background music.)

MODERN MOTHER: I would have some weaving done, could you tell me to whom the task may be entrusted?

RECORD KEEPER: For whom is the weaving to be done?

MODERN MOTHER: My child.

RECORD KEEPER: There is just one person that I know of who would be entrusted with that important task.

MODERN MOTHER: Fine. I am glad you know of a dependable person. Please tell me his name.

RECORD KEEPER: It is you, mother, together with your husband, the father of your son. You are the ones that will weave the character and behavior of your child.

MODERN MOTHER: B . . . b . . . but—my child will soon be at school most of the day, there will be music lessons, cub scouts, little league baseball, Sunday school, church and clubs sponsored by our church. Other people and groups do these things for my child. Why can't I have someone else do my weaving.

RECORD KEEPER: This is all the more reason why you should do your own weaving in your own home. Some eighty percent of a child's hours, up to age twelve years are spent in the home, nineteen percent in school, and one percent in the church. The home holds first place and you can't expect others to weave into the character of your son what is your sacred obligation.

MODERN MOTHER: Oh, sir, I never realized the home was so important.

RECORD KEEPER: Yes indeed it is and mothers play the key role. It has been found that the influence of the home upon the child is at least thirty times as strong as that of the church and church school. Without it the church is almost helpless. With it, the church is all-powerful.

MODERN MOTHER: If what you say is true what can I do to weave and mold a greater influence in my child.

RECORD KEEPER: Well, the home teaches not so much by what it says and does, but is. Children mimic motives, likes and dislikes, more than activities. What children see in parents is much more important than what they hear. If you would have your child be a Christian, you must be one!

MODERN MOTHER: Now, what threads should I weave into my son's garment?

RECORD KEEPER: Here they are and you can choose. Red for courage; orange for faith; white for purity; yellow for joy; green for strength; blue for truth; purple for hope.

MODERN MOTHER: After talking with you, I see that my child will need all these colors of thread woven into his garment. I desire for him a stalwart Christian character which each of these threads represent. By God's grace and strength as a mother I will work diligently to see that his garment is woven sure and true.

RECORD KEEPER: Your choice of colors is good. White stands for purity of sins forgiven by accepting Jesus Christ as Savior and Lord; red for courage to fight the good fight of faith; yellow for joy he shall know in service for Christ, the church and others; blue for truth for it is truth that sets men free; orange for faith to live victoriously in the face of opposition; green for strength to win others to Christ and to overcome obstacles; and purple for the glorious hope of the soon return of Christ. Blessings on you Modern Mother as you weave your child a garment.

As the curtain is drawn an appropriate Mother's day song is to be sung by cast.

From the *Crusader*

Robbed of Mother
(A one-act play)

CHARACTERS: Dorene, age 15; Mary, age 13; Kay, age 11; Nancy, age 10; Mother.

(Girls are seated around Dorene who has just read a letter from Mother)

DORENE (*looking at envelope*)—I see this letter has been delayed on the way. But when Mother wrote it, she didn't know when she could get back. I don't see how we can live till she is home again.

MARY—If only Aunt Jessie hadn't been taken so sick!

KAY—Father said we are big enough to keep the home going without her, but I don't think he knows what a lot of work there is!

NANCY—I don't see how Mother ever gets the work done. There's washing and ironing and cooking. I don't see how she ever manages to do so much every day!

DORENE—Don't forget beds to make and dishes to wash and floors to clean. How Mother gets everything done I don't know. How does she manage to keep so pleasant and cheerful all the time?

MARY—Mother's a good manager. And she's such a good Christian too. I know that's why. She prays about everything she has to do and she trusts the Lord to help her.

KAY—Well, who's going to get supper, I'd like to know? I'm all tired out from cleaning the front room. If the rest of you would put your things away, it wouldn't take half as long.

NANCY—What about you? Before I could set the table for lunch, I had to move your books off it and I had to take your sweater off a chair back too.

DORENE—Girls, we mustn't quarrel whatever we do. It would grieve Mother if she knew it.

MARY—I've got an idea! Instead of quarreling about who leaves the most stuff around, let's decide right now that we'll each take care of our own things. I believe that would help Mother a lot.

KAY—That's a fine idea. And you know I'm just ashamed how I've fussed about having to do the dishes when Mother has been cheerfully working hard all day.

NANCY—I've done that too, but I'm not going to do it again. When Mother comes back, let's do more to help her than she asks us to do. That'll give her the surprise of her life.

DORENE—I think we've made some good resolutions. Let's go over them again so we won't forget. (1) We'll put our things away so Mother won't have to pick up after us. (2) We'll do everything she asks us to do cheerfully. (3) We'll do even more than she asks us to do. All in favor signify by saying "Aye."

GIRLS—Aye.

DORENE—That's carried then. But now who will help get supper?

MARY—I will.

NANCY—So will I. Oh here comes Mother now!

(Girls rush to meet her)

DORENE—Oh, Mother, how good it is to have you home!

MARY—How is Aunt Jessie?

MOTHER—Your Aunt Jessie is better and your cousins are shouldering the housework in a wonderful way.

KAY—That's what we're going to do. Let me take your wraps.

MARY—You must be tired. Won't you sit down and rest while Dorene and I get supper?

NANCY—Kay and I are going to do the dishes after supper. We don't want you to do any work tonight.

MOTHER—Girls—you astonish me! What's up?

DORENE—We realize more than we did how much you have done for us.

NANCY—We want to practice up for Mother's Day.

KAY—But after this we're going to put all our things away and to work cheerfully like you do.

MARY—We're going to ask the Lord's help too, like you do.

MOTHER—He will surely give it to you. What a happy home we are going to have.

DORENE—We want every day to be Mother's Day.

VIVIAN D. GUNDERSON

Two Bible Mothers
(A one-act play)

This is a short play, with only two women needed as characters: Mary, the mother of Jesus, and Elizabeth, the mother of John the Baptist.

SCENE: A room in a home in Nazareth many years ago. The room is furnished simply with water jugs and herbs beside the cooking place: a long bench in front of the window which is in the rear center, a low stool is near the left front and there is a loom near the right front where Mary sits working and humming (or could be singing one of the psalms) as the curtains open slowly. There is a knock at the door. Mary stops her weaving and goes to open the door. The time is late afternoon.

MARY: (Stepping back as she opens the door to allow her guest to enter). Ah, it is Elizabeth. (enters) It is with joy in my heart that I greet you.

ELIZABETH: Thou art very gracious, Mary. May I set my water jug here on your door step so I will not forget to fill it when I go home?

MARY: Yes, set there and rest yourself after your long walk. (Elizabeth puts her jug just inside the door and seats herself on the stool as Mary resumes her spinning.)

MARY: Is it well with thy household?

ELIZABETH: Yes, very well indeed. My

little John reads every day with the Rabbi.

MARY: He is a fine lad, so sturdy and strong.

ELIZABETH: Yes, sometimes I do fear that his very strength will be the undoing of him. Didst thou hear him when he read from the prophet Isaiah last Sabbath? The words did seem to leap from his mouth!

MARY: He did indeed thunder them forth. Perhaps when he is older, and does read the Scripture in the synagogue in such a way the people will not dare to nod.

(*The women laugh together.*)

ELIZABETH: And little Jesus, is he well?

MARY: Yes, very well, but oh, Elizabeth, the time does seem so short that I will have him with me.

ELIZABETH: Doest thou still cling to that old dream of thine?

MARY: It is not a dream. This thing I know. See, I am weaving a robe for Him that will be so beautiful that He will wear it on the day when He is proclaimed King of the Jews.

ELIZABETH: It will be a garment worthy of a King.

MARY: It will be a garment for a King. It will be beautiful beyond words; in it will be woven, not only threads of strength and beauty, but the prayers and dreams and hopes of his mother.

ELIZABETH: Mary! Thou art weeping!

MARY: Yes, every day I weep as I weave, and so it seems that mothers will ever do.

ELIZABETH: Thou shouldst not weep. Rather, thou shouldst rejoice that thou art the mother of the Promised One, if so you do believe. (*She adds the last very softly but Mary hears her.*)

MARY (*wiping her tears*): And you, Elizabeth, do you not believe also?

ELIZABETH: I do, almost, especially when I talk with you. Dost thou fear for Him, Mary?

MARY: I do not fear for Him, but for myself. Elizabeth, wilt thou pray for me that I may love enough. It will not do for me to love as other mothers do, I must love for all

time. When the crucial hour comes I must be strong. As I show courage on that day so will all mothers, through the ages yet to come.

ELIZABETH: You speak as though it would be a day of sadness. I should think it would be a day of joy.

MARY: I do not know Elizabeth. There is a brooding in my heart that seems to foretell sorrow as well as joy. Perhaps the one precedes the other. Much that is in a mother's heart cannot be put into words, but, as I weave from day to day it seems to me that I am a part of all the mothers yet to be and I must not fail. (*She leaves her loom and goes to the window.*) Come Elizabeth. (*She goes to her and kneels beside her as she talks.*)

MARY: See, Elizabeth, (*Mary gestures with the sweep of one arm*) down the years—unnumbered mothers. Dost thou not catch the eagerness of the faces? In each face I see the dream of what that mother would have her child to be. These mothers will weave garments for their sons and into the weaving will go hopes and fears and dreams, even as I weave them today into the garment of my Jesus.

ELIZABETH: What dost thou weave, Mary? Tell me of the hopes which you do broider into the pattern of the raiment for your son. Perhaps if I know it will help me to be a better mother to my little John.

MARY (*speaking almost as if in a dream*): Into the mantle for my Son, I weave first the sturdy threads of gratitude. I would have Him a thankful lad, Elizabeth.

ELIZABETH: Wouldst thou have him give thanks for difficult tasks as well as pleasant ones?

MARY: Yes, for in so doing He will grow strong and brave. Then close beside the threads of gratitude I would put the delicate ones of hope, so fragile and so lovely that many times they are not seen. But always they must be there, underlying everything He does.

ELIZABETH: The threads of hope will

speak His mission in life. Is that not what you mean?

MARY: Yes, for it would seem that every mother must dream for her son that which she would have him to be. But these dreams of hope would all be futile if it were not for another thread to gild the pattern.

ELIZABETH: And what thread is . . . ?

MARY: *Faith*, Elizabeth. You must believe that your little John will be the great preacher that will speak with power. I must have faith that my Jesus will be lifted up and draw all men unto him.

ELIZABETH: You weep, Mary.

MARY: They are not tears of sadness, rather they are tears of joy for the triumph which I see in the life of my Son.

ELIZABETH: Are there other virtues that you weave into this mantle of your making?

MARY: Yes. A poor mother I would be indeed, if I did not run through all the wool the thread of *patience*.

ELIZABETH: I must remember to weave the thread of patience into the coat of my John. Even now he does grow impatient with the Rabbi who teaches him to read from the ancient scroll.

MARY: Your John does know so well the threads of truth which you have used so wisely. May all the mothers yet to be forget not to put them into their fabric.

ELIZABETH: (*Wistfully*) Dost thou think I have done that one thing well?

MARY: Yes, that, and one more thread I see in all your weaving of the mantle of your son.

ELIZABETH: And what is that? My heart is hungry for your words of praise.

MARY: It is the strong bright thread of *courage*. I too, must use that as must all mothers who weave mantles for their sons.

ELIZABETH: Is that all?

MARY: No. There must be *forgiveness* and the *understanding heart*.

ELIZABETH: The ancient prophets do not so speak.

(*Mary turns from the window and goes toward the front of the stage and lifts the cloth which hangs from her loom. She speaks softly but very distinctly and with great conviction.*)

MARY: A new prophet shall come among you. He shall be called the Prince of Peace.

ELIZABETH (*coming toward her and putting her arms around her*): Mary, I do believe.

MARY: Go then, Elizabeth, and weave into the mantle of your son the power to proclaim tidings of great joy.

ELIZABETH: Yes, it shall be so. And love, Mary, we must weave love into the garments of our sons.

MARY: And in so doing we shall bring light and joy into the lives of millions of mothers yet to come. Look Elizabeth, the eastern sky, already it brightens. (*They turn slowly toward the window where the light is growing brighter.*)

ELIZABETH: I see them now Mary, the mothers of the world, each busy weaving the garment on her loom.

MARY: And as she weaves God grant that she may entwine into the souls of her children the threads of gratitude, hope, faith, patience, courage, forgiveness, an understanding heart, and love.

Curtain

AUTHOR UNKNOWN

Where's Mother?
(A one-act play)

CHARACTERS: Joan, age 9; Judy, age 10; Lura Lee, age 12; Cheryl, age 14; Ann, age 16; Mrs. Smith, Mrs. Jones and Mrs. Brown, neighbors; and Mother.

The Curtain opens on a deserted living room, somewhat untidy. The phone is in sight. (*Joan and Judy come hurrying in from school.*)

JOAN: Mother! Oh Mother! What do you

think happened at school today? Why, where is she?

JUDY: (*Calls*) Mother, where are you? (*Enter Lura Lee and Cheryl*)

LURA LEE: Can we go skating, Mother?

CHERYL: I'm dreadfully hungry. Can we have a sandwich first? Why, where is Mother?

JOAN: We don't know where Mother is. She always tells us if she is going to be away when we get home.

ANN: (*Coming in from school alone.*) What's the matter? Where's Mother?

JUDY: We don't know. Did Mother tell you she was going to be away?

ANN: No, she must be somewhere in the house. Mother where are you?

(*Lura Lee comes in with a note she has just found in the kitchen.*)

LURA LEE: This is awful!

ANN: (*Takes note and reads it aloud*) Dear Children: I am going to the hospital. I had to be early so I didn't get the work finished. Please get supper and make the house as neat as you can. Grandmother is coming on the evening train. Love, Mother.

ANN: Mother in the hospital! What can be the matter?

CHERYL: Maybe we'd better not go skating.

ANN: I should think not. With Mother in the hospital and Grandmother coming in a few hours. Oh, I hope Mother isn't very sick. I'd better call Father. Maybe he will know what happened. (*At phone.*) Hello Daddy. Mother isn't here. Did you know she was in the hospital? You didn't? How did we know? There was a note on the table saying that she was going to the hospital. (*Ann turns to others.*) Dad says he'll go to the hospital right away and call us from there.

(*Mrs. Jones and Mrs. Smith knock on the door.*)

JOAN: Come in. Mother's not here. She's in the hospital.

MRS. JONES: Your Mother's in the hospital! I had no idea she was sick, but I know she works too hard. I hope it wasn't a heart attack.

ANN: We don't know what was wrong but Daddy has gone to the hospital and he will call us from there as soon as he finds out how she is.

MRS. SMITH: I hope your mother gets better. She's a very good woman, I can't understand why she doesn't make you girls help her more. I've told her time and again that if I had as many girls as she does, I'd see that they did the work.

JUDY: I wish we'd helped her more.

MRS. JONES: Why don't you start now. You can have the house all nice and clean when she comes home. She won't be very strong when she returns from the hospital. If she finds you girls can get meals and keep things clean, she'll get well much faster.

CHERYL: That's just what we'll do. Good-by Mrs. Jones. (*Exit ladies*) I'm going upstairs to make the beds and see that everything's neat up there.

LURA LEE: I'm going with you. (*Exit*) (*Mrs. Brown knocks on the door.*)

JOAN: Come in, Mrs. Brown. Mother's not here. She's in the hospital.

MRS. BROWN: How dreadful! Was it an accident?

ANN: We don't know. Mother just left a note saying that she was going to the hospital and that Grandmother was coming tonight. I suppose she's coming to take care of us while Mother is ill but it seems strange and dreadful to have Mother gone.

MRS. BROWN: You poor girls. It must have been a shock. I think if she had had an accident the neighbors would have known about it. She probably just collapsed from overwork.

ANN: That's what makes us feel so badly. We haven't thought much about helping Mother. We've mostly asked her to do things for us.

MRS. BROWN: I know it. Young folks today don't seem to have many home responsibilities. But don't feel too badly. You girls do as much as the other girls in the neighborhood and as much as my grandchildren do!

JOAN: If God will just make Mother better, we're going to help her every day, aren't we Judy?

JUDY: Yes. Maybe we could get the vegetables ready for supper now. (Exit.)

MRS. BROWN: I almost forgot what I came for. I wanted to borrow your electric iron. Mine won't heat, so I can't do the ironing until my husband fixes it.

ANN: Take ours. I know Mother would lend it to you. You are always ready to help us any time.

MRS. BROWN: Thank you. I'll bake a cake for your supper too, and bring it when I return the iron. By that time you can tell me how your mother is. (Exit)

(Enter Lura Lee and Cheryl.)

ANN: I'm so glad because we must not forget that Grandmother is coming!

CHERYL: What shall we do now?

ANN: Could you girls clean the back porch and sidewalk. I'd better work here in the living room until we get the phone call from Father.

LURA LEE: We'll go to work right away but be sure to call us just as soon as you hear how mother is.

ANN: I surely will. (Exit girls—Ann starts tidying up)

(Joan and Judy come in)

JOAN: All the vegetables are fixed. The potatoes and beans are on the stove and we made a green salad.

ANN: You've done fine. I'm sure Mother would be proud of you if she were here. (Phone rings) Daddy, you say that Mother is not in the hospital? But she said she was going and she is not here! Where can she be? You're coming home right away? Oh, I'm so glad. Where can Mother be?

(Enter Mother)

MOTHER: Here I am girls.

ANN: O Mother! Aren't you sick or hurt or anything? Oh it's wonderful to have you home again and all right! Girls, come here, Mother's home!

(Enter the other four!)

LURA LEE: Oh, I'm so glad you're home. Mrs. Jones wasn't a bit surprised that you had to go to the hospital. She says you work too hard. But we are all going to help you more after this!

CHERYL: Oh, we're so happy that you're home again!

MOTHER: Wait a minute. Why are you all so excited?

JUDY: Because you had to go to the hospital. Did you have a heart attack, Mother?

MOTHER: Whatever did I put into my note to make you think I was ill? I got a phone call that you have a new cousin and that I was wanted at the hospital right away. I had to hurry to catch the bus. Your aunt almost died, but she is getting along all right now so I came home. The baby is just fine!

JOAN: Then you weren't sick or hurt or anything? Oh, I'm so glad!

JUDY: Is our new cousin a boy or girl?

MOTHER: A girl! I'm sorry I didn't manage to put into my note that I had to go to the hospital to see your Aunt Elinor, but I was frightened at the call from the hospital and in a great rush to get the bus!

ANN: I wish we had known because we have all felt dreadful since we got home from school. But I guess it's a good thing. We haven't tried to help you as we should but I believe we all will do our share of the work after this, won't we?

LURA LEE: We surely will. Oh there's Mrs. Smith coming back with our iron and a cake for supper!

CHERYL: Daddy's just coming in too! How happy he will be! All the work's done and supper's ready.

MOTHER: Thank God we are all safe and well and I thank Him too that you girls are so eager to help. It's just like Mother's Day!

LURA LEE: We want every day to be Mother's day, don't we?

ALL GIRLS: (Enthusiastically) Yes!!!

(Curtain)

VIVIAN D. GUNDERSON

A Mother's Secret and Great Faith

(A two-scene play)

CHARACTERS: Sheba, an older woman; her daughter Salome, a young mother; three young friends of Salome: Ruth, Rachel, Sarah; and a reader.

READER: It is about the year 1570 B.C. The scene is in Egypt, near the river Nile. The Israelites are enslaved by the Egyptians. But God has heard their groanings and seen their tears, and He promised to send them a deliverer.

While some of the characters in this play are fictitious, Jochebed, the mother of Moses, is real.

The characters in the first scene are Salome and her mother Sheba. They are resting at evening time after a hard day's work in the fields. They have been talking about Pharaoh's new law. This cruel ruler is worried because the Israelites are so strong and healthy and numerous. He's afraid that they might take the country away from the Egyptians. To make sure that they will not have any future soldiers, Pharaoh has recently made a law that all baby boys born to the Israelites must be killed at birth.

SCENE I

(Salome is rocking her baby. Her mother is sitting sewing near-by.)

SALOME: How thankful I am that my baby is a girl! I could not bear to have a baby of mine killed!

SHEBA: It's terrible for the king to order all baby boys killed! I don't see how any of our poor people can bear it, but what can they do?

SALOME: It's too awful to think about! Mother, Jochebed told me her secret today. I think it's wonderful how smart and brave she is to hide her baby boy in spite of the king's orders.

SHEBA: I wanted to tell you about it before, so we could pray together to the God of Israel for Jochebed and that baby, but I promised her I wouldn't tell anybody about it. If it was found out that she is hiding her baby, she as well as her baby would likely be killed.

SALOME: Jochebed says he is a very good baby and hardly ever cries. When he does, she has Miriam start the spinning wheel at once, and that drowns out the noise. But in a few months he'll be able to make more noise, and then what can she do? I tremble for Jochebed then!

SHEBA: Instead of trembling for her, let's pray for her. The God of Israel can do anything. He can protect both mother and child from our enemies. Now we must retire as we have to be up so early in the morning.

(Curtain)

SCENE 2

READER: Scene 2 takes place three months later. It is another evening, again in the home of Sheba and Salome, near the river Nile.

Curtain Opens

SALOME: I never was so nervous in my life as I've been today! Jochebed's plan seemed so daring. After caring for her baby secretly for three months, she put him in a basket among the rushes here at the river's edge where he is certain to be found!

SHEBA: Well, she couldn't hide him any longer in her home. His cries simply could not be drowned out by the noise of spinning wheel or other household tasks. But I wouldn't call her plan daring. She asked the Lord to show her what to do to save her baby. And she believes that God put the idea of putting him in a basket into her heart.

(Enter Ruth, Rachel and Sarah)

RUTH: The strangest thing happened today! Jochebed was given a new job!

RACHEL: She's the lucky one. She won't have to toil out under the hot sun now, making bricks for Pharaoh. All she has to do now is care for a baby for the princess.

SALOME: How was it that Jochebed got such a job?

SARAH: It seems that one of our people put a baby boy into a covered basket, among the rushes near the bank of the river. The princess came down to the river, and saw the basket, so sent one of her maidens to fetch it. When she opened it, she saw a baby! He was scared and began to cry. She said, "This is a beautiful child! It must be one of the Hebrew's baby boys. Well, I won't let anyone kill him. I'm going to keep him for my own!"

RUTH: Miriam happened to be playing near by where the baby was found. She stepped right up to the princess and said, "Would you like me to get you a Hebrew woman to take care of the baby for you?"

RACHEL: The princess said "Yes," and I guess Miriam ran off like an arrow to get her mother. Anyway her mother got the job, and she now has that baby in her own home! And is she happy! Indeed the whole family seems happier than I've ever seen them before.

SHEBA: I'm so glad for Jochebed. Imagine getting work like that! She'll take wonderful care of the baby, and teach him to know the true God.

SARAH: Well, we must go now! But we just had to come over and tell you because you and Jochebed have always been such good friends.

SALOME: Thank you dear friends. We must go and see Jochebed and that baby tomorrow, as soon as we are through in the brickyard.

RUTH: Oh yes, the princess named the baby Moses. Come on Rachel and Sarah. We must be at work early, you know.

(Exit the three friends.)

SHEBA: God be praised. How wonderfully He has worked things out for Jochebed! You were so wise not to tell them that it is her very own baby she's been asked to care for!

SALOME: I knew it would be safer for Jochebed if I did not tell what I know. If those girls knew, they might accidentally let out the secret, without meaning to. If trouble came to Jochebed or the baby through me, I never could forgive myself!

SHEBA: And the princess named the baby Moses! Isn't "Moses" an Egyptian word meaning "Drawn out of the water?" Well it does my heart good to know how happy Jochebed is this night. Instead of trying to hide her baby, always fearing he'll be found and killed, now she'll get paid to care for him! We know how earnestly she'll teach him about the God of Israel. I am sure that God has some great purpose for baby Moses.

(Curtain)

READER: Jochebed did indeed teach her baby about the God of Abraham, Isaac and Jacob. When Moses left her godly home to live with the Egyptian princess in the palace, he was not tempted by all the idolatry he saw, but served the true God. It was he who led about three million people out of slavery, through the Red Sea, all the way to the borders of the promised land. And he did it because of his faith in, and obedience to God. We honor Jochebed as one of the greatest of mothers, not only for her courage and ability, but for her great faith in the only true God.

VIVIAN D. GUNDERSON

Parable for Mothers

(A Shadow Tableau)

Staging: Hang a large sheet on the platform. Weight it down or fasten it tightly at the bottom so the sheet is free from wrinkles. Have one or two bright lights behind the sheet. White or colored spot-lights are very effective if available. The figures stand between the sheet and light, casting their shadows on the sheet. The audience will see just the silhouette of the figures.

Turn the lights out while the figures take their positions for each scene. The figures should stand perfectly still when the lights go on.

CHARACTERS

Reader: (An older child who can read with depth of expression.)
The Mother: (A fairly tall high-school girl.)
Small Son: (A boy 6 or 7 years old.)
Small Daughter: (A girl 4 or 5 years old.)
Grown Son: (A high-school boy).
Grown Daughter: (A high-school girl.)

Dress: The clothing should be simple. The mother should wear a shawl and a fairly long dress. Her hair might be tied back simply. The young children should dress as they would for school—a crisp cotton dress for a little girl, pants and shirt for the boy. The older children should dress in a grown-up manner—a suit for the boy, dress and high heels for the girl. Details in the clothing will not show. You may wish to experiment to determine what clothing will give the best impression of the character.

SCENE I

SHADOW TABLEAU: The young mother stands alone looking off to the right as though gazing into the distance.
READER: The young mother set her foot on the path of life. "Is the way long?" she asked. And her guide said: "Yes, and the way is hard. And you will be old before you reach the end of it. But the end will be better than the beginning." But the young mother was happy, and she would not believe that anything could be better than these years.

(Lights out)

SCENE II

SHADOW TABLEAU: The mother is shown with her two children. Show the little girl holding a flower towards her mother. The boy stoops behind the little girl as though picking a flower. The mother is slightly bent towards the children with her arms out to them.

(Lights on)

READER: So she played with her chil-dren, and gathered flowers with them along the way, and bathed with them in the clear streams; and the sun shone on them, and life was good, and the young mother cried, "Nothing will ever be lovelier than this."

(Lights out)

SCENE III

SHADOW TABLEAU: The mother is shown with her two children, one at either side. She has her shawl over them as they huddle close to her.

(Lights on)

READER: The night came, and storm, and the path was dark, and the chil-dren shook with fear and cold, and the mother drew them close and covered them with her mantle, and the children said, "Oh, mother, we are not afraid, for you are near, and no harm can come," and the mother said, "This is better than the brightness of day, for I have taught my children courage."

(Lights out)

SCENE IV

SHADOW TABLEAU: The mother is shown ahead of the two young children as they seem to fall behind her. They appear to be struggling to keep up as she has one arm out to them in encouragement.

(Lights on)

READER: And the morning came, and there was a hill ahead, and the children climbed and grew weary, and the mother was weary, but at all times she said to the children, "A little patience, and we are there."

So the children climbed, and when they reached the top, they said, "We could not have done it without you, Mother."

And the mother, when she lay down that night, looked up at the stars and said: "This is a better day than the last, for my children have learned fortitude in the face of hardness. Yesterday I gave them courage. Today I have given them strength."

(Lights out)

SCENE V

SHADOW TABLEAU: *Mother is pointing up, directing the gaze of the children to the sky. The children stand on either side of her looking up.*

(Lights on)

READER: And the next day came strange clouds which darkened the earth— clouds of war and hate and evil, and the children groped and stumbled and the mother said: "Look up. Lift your eyes to the light."

And the children looked and saw above the clouds an everlasting Glory and it guided them and brought them beyond the darkness. And that night the mother said, "This is the best day of all, for I have shown my children God."

(Lights out)

SCENE VI

SHADOW TABLEAU: *Show the mother, slightly bent with age, with the two grown children. One child on either side of her. Each holds her elbow.*

(Lights on)

READER: And the days went on, and the weeks and the months and the years, and the mother grew old and she was little and bent.

But her children were tall and strong and walked with courage. And when the way was hard they helped their mother; and when the way was rough they lifted her; and at last they came to a hill, and beyond the hill they could see a shining road and golden gates flung wide.

(Lights out)

SCENE VII

SHADOW TABLEAU: *Show the mother facing toward her children, hand raised in a farewell greeting. The children face toward her, not waving.*

(Lights on)

READER: And the mother said: "I have reached the end of my journey. And now I know that the end is better than the beginning, for my children can walk alone, and their children after them."

And the children said, "You will always walk with us, Mother, even when you have gone through the gates."

(Lights out)

SCENE VIII

SHADOW TABLEAU: *The mother stands, slightly stooped with age, as she did in Scene VI.*

(Lights on)

READER: And they stood and watched her as she went on alone, and the gates closed after her. And they said: "We cannot see her, but she is with us still. A mother like ours is more than a memory. She is a living presence."

(While lights remain on have soloist sing, "Songs My Mother Taught Me," by Dvorak, or "To My Mother," by McGimsey,)

(Lights out)

Adapted by JUNE LORD CRABTREE from a writing by TEMPLE BAILEY

RECITATIONS AND EXERCISES

Glad Welcome

Although I am small,
  I came here to say
A welcome to all
  Dear mothers today!
ALEXANDER SEYMOUR

The Best!

When I speak of mothers—
I'm at my best
'Cause I have a mother
Who tops all the rest!

I Want Everyone to Know

Mother I love you
You know I do!
But I want everyone here
To know it too!
LLOYD WERTH

God's Love

God loves the children,
  That's plain to see,
'Cause He gave mothers
  To you and me!
MARGARET N. FREEMAN

I Love Mother

(For six small children)

FIRST CHILD—
  I love Mother because all the while
  She has the sweetest, sweetest smile.
SECOND CHILD—
  I love Mother because she never gets
    mad
  Even if I am ever so bad.
THIRD CHILD—
  I love Mother because I can tell
  My troubles to her and she's always
    swell.
FOURTH CHILD—
  I love Mother because she can cook

The luscious things she gets out of
    that book.
FIFTH CHILD—
  I love my Mother because she loves
    me;
  That's a wonderful reason, don't you
    see?
SIXTH CHILD—
  I love Mother—and so much about
    her,
  I don't know how I'd get along with-
    out her.
REGA KRAMER MCCARTY

Happy Mother's Day

My wish is brief
  And to the point,
But it's loving and it's true—
  A very happy Mother's Day
To the finest Mother—You.
AUTHOR UNKNOWN

To Our Mothers

We want to tell you Mother dear,
  It makes us happy you are here;
There's something more we want to say:
  A very happy Mother's Day!

I Love You, Mother
(For a little girl)

I'm a little girl,
  But I would like to say,
(Runs to her own mother in the congre-
    gation)
I love you, Mother
  Have a wonderful day.
(Puts her arms about her mother and
    kisses her.)
PAULINE E. SPRAY

Sing Us a Song, Mother

An exercise for two small children and
one older. The older child takes the part
of the mother and may dress accordingly

and may be seated in a rocking chair.)
FIRST CHILD—

Sing us a song of Jesus, Mother,
Of how He came from Heav'n above.

SECOND CHILD—

When you have finished, sing another;
We like the songs of Jesus' love.

MOTHER—

All right, my children, come up near
And be real still so you can hear.

(Mother then sings "Tell Me the Story
of Jesus," "Jesus Loves the Little Children," or a song of her own choice.)

FIRST CHILD—

Thank you, Mother.

SECOND CHILD—

Sing another.

MOTHER—

All right, but you help me this time.
(All sing "Jesus Loves Me" or some other children's song.)

CARLTON C. BUCK

My Mummy

My mummy has the nicest hands,
So clever when she's mending,
Or putting muffins in their pans,
Or when she's baby-tending.

My mummy has the nicest eyes.
They're always soft and tender.
I'll never ever tell her lies,
To hurt her or offend her.

My mummy has the nicest lips.
She smothers me with kisses,
And even when my temper slips,
She never ever misses.

I know she loves me up and down.
That's why we are so chummy.
Of all the ladies in our town,
I'm glad that this one's Mummy.

ALVY E. FORD

Mother's Day

An exercise for eleven children. They
should carry letters which together spell
"Mother's Day." And one should carry
a blank card for the space between the
two words.)

M is for my mother
For this is Mother's Day.
O is for each other—
This is the Christian way.
T is for tidings
Of love our mothers tell.
H is for our homes
Our mothers keep so well.
E is for the echo
Of fun along the way.
R is for the rest
She needs on Mother's Day.
S is for her smile
We always like to see.
This is for the space
And in that space is me.
D is for my Daddy;
He loves Mother, too.
A is for all of us;
Now we'll soon be through.
Y is for you people
The big folks and the small.

UNISON—

And now here is a greeting:
Happy Mother's Day to all.

CARLTON C. BUCK

To Mother

Dear Mother, I am thankful
That God gave me to you!
For you are very faithful,
So kind, so brave, and true.

ALEXANDER SEYMOUR

Flowers for Mother

I never have a special day
To give flowers to my mother,
I give them to her every day
To show how much I love her.

When I sweep the kitchen floor,
Or care for baby brother,
Run on errands, or make the beds,
I'm giving flowers to mother.

It's lots of fun pretending
And to hear my mother say,
"Thank you, dear, for all the flowers
You've given me today."

CLARA RADER

For Grandma, Too

I'd a very nice thought today.
  Did it ever occur to you
Mother's Day is for our Grandma?
  For she's a mother, too.

There's another reason, as well
  Grandma rates for Mother's joys,
For she is assistant Mom
  To all of us girls and boys.

So, Grandma, we want you to know
  And we're glad of a chance to say.
That we love you very much!
  Happy, happy Mother's Day.
                          DAISY JENNEY CLAY

The Best Way
(For a small boy)

I wish I knew a way to tell
  My mother that I love her—
I guess the best way is to show
  Her how much I think of her.

If I do jobs around the house,
  I guess she's sure to know it;
And if I behave I guess that is
  The surest way to show it.
                          REGA KRAMER MCCARTY

My Mother Is Best

Good mothers are rare,
But I have been blessed,
For none can compare
With mine who is best.
                          LYDIA REGEHR

Thankful for You

Today is only one of many
Reminding me all the year through
How thankful I am for the joy
Of having a mother like you.

Only One Like You

Millions of leaves on the trees.
Millions of stars in the blue.

Millions of people all over the world
But only one Mother like you.

My Mother

My mother always seems to know
  Just what is best for me,
And when she says a thing is so,
  It's always sure to be.

Mother's Day
(for a girl)

The month of May brings happy days—
Summer's soon to follow spring,
Birds once more begin to sing,
Mother's day is on the wing,
And daughters, love and joy do bring.
                          AUTHOR UNKNOWN

Our Special Greetings

Accept our special greeting
With our loving words of praise
And the best wishes for our mothers
On this happiest of days.

Happy Greetings

Happy Greetings, Mom
God had a very happy thought
  Not many years ago
He planned for something extra nice
  A perfect gift—and so
He looked around for lovely things
  As He knows how to do
He brought them all together
  And then, Mom, He made you!
                          AUTHOR UNKNOWN

Mother's Smiles

I'm as happy as can be,
  When my mother smiles at me;
But I want to leave the town,
  When her dear face wears a frown.

Mother's smiles are heaven's sunshine
  Blessing us for tasks well done;
Mother's tears are drops of heartache
  Caused by duties that we shun.

A Wish

For the love you've given, Mother,
For your thoughtfulness, your cheer—
May your special day be rewarded
With the joys that you hold dear!

AUTHOR UNKNOWN

A Thank You Prayer

Upon this joyous Mother's Day
  I want to say a prayer
Of thankfulness to God above
  For Mother's love and care.

I know throughout this land so wide
  Are those blessed in this way
Who from their hearts are thanking God
  For Mother's love today.

MARGARET N. FREEMAN

Mom

*(An acrostic for three boys, each holding
a letter)*

FIRST BOY:
M is for the magic things
  My Mom can do, like that. (*Snaps
  fingers*)
SECOND BOY:
O is for the only way
  I know to tell her how
I appreciate the things she does,
  So, I'll just tell her now.
THIRD BOY:
M is for the many things
  My Mom sees to for me;
Kinda makes you stop and think
  Of her responsibility.
UNISON (*holding letters high*)—
M-O-M, Mom, these letters spell;
  We figured this out to say,
Mom, we think you're swell.

REGA KRAMER MCCARTY

Happy Mother's Day

With all our hearts, we wish we knew
  The right words to express
Our gratitude for all their love,
  Their care, their thoughtfulness.
But Mothers as you're hearing this

We hope that you will know
The grateful love within our hearts
  That words could never show.

AUTHOR UNKNOWN

A Word for Grandma

While we're honoring our Mothers
With our songs and words of praise,
While we tell about their kindness
And their tender, loving ways
I should like to speak of Grandma
She's a mother, too, you see
For she mothered my dear mother
As my mother mothers me!

A Mother's Day Wish

Mother dear, you're wonderful
  In everything you do—
The happiness of daily life
  Depends so much on you—
And so these special wishes
  Are not for simple things
But for love and joy and happiness
  A Mother's Day can bring!

Which Loved Best?
(for 1 boy and 2 girls)

"I love you, mother," said little John,
Then forgetting his work his cap went
  on,
And he was off to the garden swing,
Leaving his mother the wood to bring.

"I love you, mother," said little Nell,
"I love you better than tongue can tell."
Then she teased and pouted half the day,
Till mother rejoiced when she went to
  play.

"I love you, mother," said little Fan,
"Today I'll help you all I can,"
To the cradle did she softly creep.
And rock the baby till it fell asleep.

Then stepping softly, she took the
  broom,
And swept the floor and dusted the
  room.
Busy and happy all day was she,
Helpful and cheerful as a child could be.

"I love you, mother," again they said—
Three little children, going to bed.
How do you think that mother guessed
Which of them really loved her best?

JOY ALLISON

Greetings to Our Mothers

We greet you all this Mother's Day
    And extend to each our praise;
To you who've watched and guided us
    Through all our childish days.
Oh, Mother dear, you were so kind,
    So good, so sweet, so true,
That we shall try our very best
    To praise and honor you.
Oh, beautiful the love of God,
    Who sent His Son on earth;
Oh, beautiful that mother mild
    Who gave our dear Lord birth.
Oh, Mother dear, we sing to you
    Upon this happy day
And may you live to guide our steps
    Along life's rugged way.

AUTHOR UNKNOWN

My Mom
(for a girl)

I am glad that once a year
    We have set aside a day;
To show our love to Mother
    And a kind word say.

I think my Mother can't be beat
    Suppose you all think so;
But if you want to beat my Mom
    You've a long way to go.

She is the best cook
    Just take a look at me;
That's proof enough for anyone
    I'm nice and plump you see.

She gives us the best attention
    My worries, too, are hers;
And when I want a dime or two
    She says, "Dear, get my purse."

My Pop thinks she's swell
    He's very proud of her;
He really never says so
    But looks can tell I'm sure.

My Mother taught me to pray
    When I was just so small;
And told me of the Lord
    Who loves us one and all.

How can I help but love a Mother
    Who is so kind and pure;
And someday I want to be
    A mother, just like her.

VIOLA DAVIS

My Grandmother

My grandmother is not growing old,
    Of course her hair is white,
But she is young as ever
    And her eyes are clear and bright.

Her gentle face is wrinkled
    And her walk is not as fast
As it was some years ago
    In days that have long past.

Grandmother is young in spirit
    She thinks of future days,
And never forgets to give me
    Courage, faith and praise.

On Mother's Day we honor
    All mothers that is true,
But I want my dear grandmother
    To have an extra honor, too.

That is why I tell you
    How glad I am that she
Is cheerful, young, and planning
    For the days that are to be.

HELEN KITCHELL EVANS

Happy Mother's Day

God bless you, Mother!
God made you sweet and good and wise
Put love and laughter in your eyes—
God made you kindly thoughtful, fine
And best of all, He made you mine!

AUTHOR UNKNOWN

Mother's Day Wish

We think the world and all of you,
You know that, Mother dear,

But still it's nice to tell you so
When Mother's Day is here.
And then we want to make this wish
With lots of love for you,
May all the happy things of life
Be yours the whole year through.

AUTHOR UNKNOWN

Honor Her

I wear my red carnation
 Proudly, as you see—
I'm very thankful that my mother
 Is here today with me.

I'm thankful for her love,
 And for her tender way;
My carnation is to honor her
 On this glad Mother's day.

REGA KRAMER MCCARTY

Saturday Before Mother's Day

(An exercise for six children)

FIRST CHILD (quite small)—
 I picked these flowers for you
  While I played in the woods all
  day.
 (Hands Mother a bouquet of spring
    flowers)
 "I love you dearly, Mother,"
  That's what the flowers say.

SECOND CHILD (a boy)—
 I took my allowance money
  And bought new hosiery for you.
 It took 'most all day to choose them;
  I knew you'd like them, too.

THIRD CHILD (larger girl)—
 I knew Grandma was coming tomor-
  row,
  So I stayed out of the way all day.
 Jane and I made candy—
 (Hands Mother a dish of candy in a pretty
    dish and gift wrapped)
 Happy Mother's Day.

FOURTH CHILD (a girl)—
 I knew Grandma was coming tomor-
  row;
  I didn't want you sick or too tired;

So I helped you all day to get ready;
 Now, I haven't time to buy a gift or
 a flower.
I've nothing at all for you.
  (Hangs her head sadly)
 But, I love you, also, Mother—

MOTHER (breaking in)—
 And, you've certainly proved that you
 do.
  (Places arm around shoulder of girl)
 I like the flowers from Nellie,
 I appreciate my hose from Lou,
 The candy's as sweet as Polly herself
 But what would I have done without
 you?
 Some gifts are nice that cost time or
 money,
 But the gifts like yours are of real value,
 Honey,
 Given in love from the heart.

RUTH ROZELLA DICKINSON

A Wonderful Mother

God made a wonderful mother,
A mother who never grows old;
He made her smile of the sunshine,
And He molded her heart of pure gold;
In her eyes He placed bright shining
 stars,
In her cheeks, fair roses you see;
God made a wonderful mother,
And He gave that dear mother to me.

PAT O'REILLY
in Modern Maturity Magazine

A Heart of Love Is Thine

We pay tribute to our mothers
Each day of every year.
But on Mother's Day remembering
We hold you still more dear.

To mention all your charming ways
And the splendid things you've done
It would be quite impossible
Though we appreciate each one.

Your care, your thought and interest in
Our need or least desire
Guiding the way along life's path

Your goal was ever higher.

We praise you for unselfishness,
Sympathy, and Faith sublime
And understanding loyalty
A heart of love is thine.
                    BERTHA WEAKLEY CARRIER

Mother, We Love You

We know the thoughtful things you do
    So lovingly each day,
We know the comfort of your love,
    Your understanding way.

We know the help you've given us
    Times beyond recall,
And Mother's Day and every day,
    We love you for it all!
                    AUTHOR UNKNOWN

I Wonder

I wonder, Mother dear
If you really understand
That on this day and every day
I think you're really grand;
And I wonder if you realize
How dear you are to me,
How much I wish you every joy
And gladness that can be!
                    AUTHOR UNKNOWN

A Magic Word

Mother is a magic word,
    It wipes away all tears,
All thoughts of bruises, hurts and cares
    We've met throughout the years.

Mother is a magic word,
    For she can make things right
Whenever there's no hope of peace,
    When there's no help in sight.

Mother is a magic word,
    I'm sure God planned it so;
I thank Him now for this mother of
    mine—
    She's the sweetest of any I know.
                    PHYLLIS C. MICHAEL

Your Mother Love

Your mother love means gentleness
And helpful patient care;
Means faith and trust and tenderness,
And courage deep, and prayer.

Your mother love means loyalty
Devotion fine and free—
I'll thank God always, Mother dear,
For giving you to me.
                    AUTHOR UNKNOWN

There's More

When I wish you a Happy Mother's Day
    with love,
    I've something else to say, too—
The most wonderful thing that ever hap-
    pened to me
    Was having a mother like you.

The Best Mother

Today we honor mothers, and each
    knows he had the best;
But I should like to tell why mine was
    better than the rest.
With all the things she had to do, she
    still took time to hear
Our troubles, joys and problems, and to
    wipe away a tear.

And so, because she listened, I can un-
    derstand how prayers
To God are heard and answered, and to
    realize He cares!
We knew we could depend on her, and
    that's what she said she'd do;
And by her deeds she helped us see
    God's promises are true.

"And God created all the earth. . ." —it
    was her zealous preaching
That prepared us to withstand in school,
    this "evolution" teaching.
If we persisted in a lie, or other such
    offenses,
We knew that she would find us out, and
    there'd be con-se-quences!

I'm glad she made us obey—we knew
    she'd use the rod,

Which made it easier to learn obedience
    to God!
These are the reasons why my mother
    was the best I ever knew.
Yours was like that? That must be why
    you are a Christian too!
      ETHEL HOLLINGSWORTH in *Jottings*

Greetings to Mother

In your heart all joy and gladness
And the song of birds at Spring;
All the peace and true contentment
That real happiness can bring,
And for every day that follows
All life's greatest blessings, too,
That will make your pathway always
Just a Sunshine Road for you.
      AUTHOR UNKNOWN

Mothers

With gentle hands God made the
    flowers,
Fashioning them with care,
He brushed the sky with pink and gold
Leaving a sunset there;
Beautified the earth with trees;
These works and countless others . . .
But for His greatest masterpiece
God created mothers.
      LELA BERNARD

Mother's Day

I have often wondered
   As I know so many do,
Why there's just one day a year
   For Mothers such as you.

To me there is no one as true
   As you are, Mother dear,
Not for just a day or two
   But always, year after year.

You raised me to be brave and strong,
   You always understood;
You listened to my troubles
   And helped me all you could.

Now I'm grown up and on my own,
   How much I realize

That all the things you taught me then
   Were good and true and wise.

To me each day is Mother's Day,
   Not just a certain date;
And all the love and care you gave,
   I've learned to appreciate.
      RALPH WASE

Dearest One

Mother, you are wonderful
In oh, so many ways,
You're a true and lovely blessing
Sent down to share my days.

Within your sunny smile
There's a warmth and joy to see,
And within your shining eyes
Stars seem to dance for me.

How I love your laughter
And the soft tone of your voice,
If I had to choose an angel
You would be my choice.

Your care and understanding,
The countless tasks you do,
Your words of cheer and wisdom
Are typical of you.

You've given me a special love
Through all the passing years,
And hope and faith and courage
To chase my doubts and fears.

From you I learned the meaning
Of a silent holy prayer,
And when I need you, Mother,
You are always there.

Because of you my life is blessed
And it will always be . . .
You're the sweetest, dearest mother
In all the world to me.
      LA VERNE P. LARSON

Mother's Day Greetings

Since every day is Mother's Day
Within this heart of mine,
My tribute is a sweet bouquet
Of memories set in rhyme.
   Happy Mother's Day!
      MARCELLINE BRUCKER

Mother . . .

God took the fragrance of a flower. . .
The majesty of a tree. . .
The gentleness of morning dew. . .
The calm of a quiet sea. . .
The beauty of the twilight hour. . .
The soul of a starry night. . .
The laughter of the rippling brook. . .
The grace of a bird in flight. . .
The tender care of an angel. . .
The faith of the mustard seed. . .
The patience of eternity. . .
The depth of a family's need. . .
Then God fashioned from these things
A creation like no other,
And when His masterpiece was through
He called it simply. . .MOTHER.

AUTHOR UNKNOWN

To My Mother

Somehow I very seldom have
The words with which to say
That which is deep within my heart
On each and every day.

But since today is just for you
I want to tell you now
How much you really mean to me,
And yet I can't think how.

I simply don't know words enough
To make it sure and clear . . .
I guess all I can say is this,
"I love you, Mother dear."

ELIZABETH SEARLE LAMB

What Is a Mother?

How do mothers
Spend their days?
In oh, so many
Different ways. . .

They're ti-er-uppers
And dryers of tears
Holders of hands
And calmers of fears.

They're sewers and knitters,
Sweepers and cooks;
And when it's nap-time
They're readers of books.

They're chauffeurs and umpires,
Directors of plays,
And swimming instructors
On hot summer days.

They're pushers of swings
And pullers of sleds. . .
They're crooners of lullabies
When time comes for bed.

They are answerers of questions
That are asked by the score,
And inventors of games
When little ones stay indoors.

They're climbers of trees
To retrieve little boys,
Untanglers of fishing lines
And menders of toys. . .

And so to each mother
Special credit is due,
For in all the world
There's only one . . . quite like you!

GEORGIA KNEPPRETH

SONGS AND CHORUSES

Mother, Mother, I've Been Thinking

(Tune: Reuben and Rachel.)

Daughters:
MOTHER, MOTHER I've been thinking
What a sad world this would be
If I had no loving mother
To encourage and help me.

Mothers:
DAUGHTER, DAUGHTER, I've been
thinking
That with you I quite agree
If I had no loving daughter,
What a sad world this would be.
Daughters:
MOTHER, MOTHER, I am thankful

That you are my mother dear,
Leading me in heavenly pathway
Sharing in each smile and tear.
Mothers:
DAUGHTER, DAUGHTER, I am thankful
That God gave you to be mine,
And I hope my life will always
Point you to the one Divine.

Faith of Our Mothers

*(May be sung to the tune, "Faith of
Our Fathers"—* ST. CATHERINE.*)*

Faith of our mothers, living yet
In cradle song and bedtime prayer,
In nursery love and fireside lore,
Thy presence still pervades the air.
Faith of our mothers, living faith,
We will be true to thee till death.

Faith of our mothers, lavish faith,
The fount of childhood's trust and
grace,
O may thy consecration prove
The wellspring of a nobler race.
Faith of our mothers, lavish faith,
We will be true to thee till death.

Faith of our mothers, guiding faith,
For youthful longing—youthful
doubts,
How blurred our vision, blind our way,
Thy providential care without.
Faith of our mothers, guiding faith,
We will be true to thee till death.

Faith of our mothers, Christian faith,
In truth beyond our man-made
creeds,
Still serve the home and save the
church,
And breathe thy spirit through our
deeds.
Faith of our mothers, Christian faith,
We will be true to thee till death.
ARTHUR B. PATTEN

The Word that Means the World to Me:

MOTHER

When I was but a baby, long before I
learned to walk,
While lying in my cradle I would try my
best to talk.
It wasn't long before I spoke, and all the
neighbors heard;
My folks were very proud of me, for
"Mother" was the word!
Although I'll never lay a claim to fame,
I'm satisfied that I can spell this name:

"M" is for the million things she gave
me.
"O" means only that she's growing
old.
"T" is for the tears she shed to save
me.
"H" is for her heart of purest gold.
"E" is for her eyes, with love light
shining.
"R" means right, and right she'll always be.

Put them all together,
They spell "Mother"—
A word that means the world to me!
HOWARD JOHNSON
Set to music by Theodore Morse
(1915)

Tell Mother I'll Be There

I wonder how many times your heart
has been stirred—as mine has—by those
touching lines:
Tell Mother I'll be there in answer to
her prayer.
This message, blessed Saviour, to her
bear . . .
Well, here's the story behind the song.
It was written by Charles M. Fillmore,
who was born in Paris, Illinois, in 1860.
He was a Disciples of Christ minister,
and pastored in Indianapolis, Indiana,
from 1907 until his retirement in 1939.
Rev. Fillmore wrote his famous song
when he was 36 years of age. The year
was 1896. The newspapers carried the
human interest story of how President
McKinley had left by special train to
visit his dying mother. But before he
left, he sent a telegram to the physician,
which read: "TELL MOTHER I'LL BE
THERE."
When Rev. Fillmore read this telegram in the newspaper, he was struck by

the idea that it would make a good theme for a Gospel song. So he began writing: "When I was but a little boy how well I recollect how I would grieve my mother with my folly and neglect. . . ." These words were published in a small magazine, a copy of which fell into the hands of Charles M. Alexander, Dr. R. A. Torrey's famous Gospel singer. Soon he was singing it all over the world, and hard-hearted men broke down and came to the revival altars for salvation.

Log of the Good Ship Grace

Always Onward

(Tune: *Onward, Christian Soldiers*)

Onward, Christian mothers,
　We must keep at work;
Though some days are dreary,
　We must never shirk.
We will teach our children
　Love can win the fray
Onward, Christian mothers,
　We must lead the way.

Chorus:
Onward, Christian mothers,
　Always work and pray
For the peace of Jesus
　In our world today.

GRACE STONER CLARK

How Dear to Our Hearts

(Tune: *The Old Oaken Bucket*)

How dear to our hearts are the thoughts
　of our mother
　To whom on this May day we give
　honor and love,
And now we will sing of the things we
　can do here
　To help through the hours her busy
　feet move.
There's drying the dishes, and all that
　she wishes,
　To do in the days as they pass one by
　one.
Oh, dear to our hearts are the thoughts
　of our mother

On this bright May day both from Daughter and Son.

LEONORA SILL ASHTON

Special Mother's Day Chorus

(Tune: *Everybody Ought to Love Jesus*)

Everybody ought to love Mother, Mother, Mother.
She works all day, without any pay,
Everybody ought to love Mother.

Everybody ought to love Father, Father, Father.
He works and works and never never shirks.
Everybody ought to love Father.

Welcome Mothers

(Tune: *Happy Birthday*)

We greet you, our mothers
On your day of the year,
We're happy you've come
And we welcome you here.

Happy welcome to you,
Happy welcome to you,
Happy welcome dear mothers,
Happy welcome to you.

One Mother

(Tune: *One Door*)

One mother and only one,
　And she's the one who cares;
This week or next week,
　Everything she shares
Honor Mother, honor Mother
　On this happy day,
For she is my guide
　All along my way.

WILMA SHAFFER

Happy Mother's Day

(Tune: *Happy Birthday*)

Happy Mother's Day to you,
Happy Mother's Day to you,

Happy Mother's Day, dear Mother,
Happy Mother's Day to you.
(The word "Father" may be substituted for "Mother" on his day.)

Mother Loves Me

(Tune: Jesus Loves Me)

Mother loves me this I know
For she often tells me so,
She is always kind and good
And helps me do the things I should.

Yes, Mother loves me,
Yes, Mother loves me,
Yes, Mother loves me,
She often tells me so.

Dear Lord Jesus

(Tune: Praise Him, Praise Him, All Ye Little Children)

Dear Lord Jesus,
We are here to praise you
On this glad Mother's Day.
Dear Lord Jesus,
We are here to praise you
On this glad Mother's Day.

Dear Lord Jesus,
We are here to love you
On this glad Mother's Day.
Dear Lord Jesus,
We are here to love you
On this glad Mother's Day.

Dear Lord Jesus
Bless our own dear mothers
On this glad Mother's Day.
Dear Lord Jesus,
Bless our own dear mothers
On this glad Mother's Day.

MRS. OWEN STILL

Mothers, Daughters We Love You

(Tune: Reuben, Reuben)

Daughters:
Mothers, mothers, how we love you,
We are surely proud of you
Always doing something for us
Ne'er a thought of self have you.

Mothers:
Daughters, daughters, how we love you.
You have grown up staunch and true,
Loyal to our church and country
Just what we have planned for you.

All Sing:
Mothers, daughters, sing together;
There is work for both to do;
Let us ever pull together
Toward our Father to be .true.

Sing, Sing, Mothers Sing

(Tune: Row, Row, Row Your Boat)

Sing, sing, mothers sing
Sing you daughters too
The more you laugh the more you sing
The more we'll think of you.

We're Here for Fun

(Tune: Auld Lang Syne)

We're here for fun right from the start,
Pray drop your dignity,
Just laugh and sing with all your heart,
And show your loyalty,
Let other gatherings be forgot,
The best has just begun,
(Mothers): My girl is here
(Daughters): My mother's here
We're going to have fun.

Mother's Changeless Love

(Tune: The Church's One Foundation)

We thank our heavenly Father
For blessings on our way.
We lift our hearts with gladness
To greet our Mother's Day.
So many gifts have crowned us,,
They come from Heaven above.
And now our God we're praising
For mother's changeless love.

Give thanks for her example
Her faith so true and strong,
The joy that kept her singing
Though oft the way seemed long.

We thank Him for her courage
Which naught could e'er remove,
And now, our God we're praising
For Mother's changeless love.

Praise God for Mothers

(Tune: Doxology)

Praise God for Mother's gentle hands
And love we cannot understand,
Praise Him who sent us from above
The blessings of a Mother's love.

Praise God from whom all blessings flow
Praise Him all creatures here below,
Praise Him above ye Heavenly hosts,
Praise Father, Son and Holy Ghost.

Mothers, We Welcome You

(Tune: Onward Christian Soldiers)

Daughters:

Mothers that are present,
We would welcome you:
For we want to welcome
Those so kind and true.
Prayerfully you've guided
Us along the way,
And your loving care and teachings
In our hearts will stay.

Mother, dear, so good and gentle,
Understanding, too.
We would raise our voices
Thanking God for you,

Mothers:

Daughters that are present,
We would answer you:
You have brought the sunshine
Happy hours, too.
Hearts so young and tender,
Eyes so shining bright,
Daughter, dear, we're glad we're here
Side by side tonight.

Daughter, dear, so sweet and trusting,
Happy-hearted, true,
We would raise our voices,
Thanking God for you.

Mothers, Daughters

(Tune: School Days, School Days)

Mothers, mothers,
Dear and patient mothers,
Washing and sewing and cookery
Taught with disaster and misery.
What would we do without you dears
You who would wipe away our tears?
We want you to know we love you so,
The older and older we grow.

Daughters, daughters,
Dear devoted daughters,
Thank you for loving us even though
Many's the time we have failed to show
Kind understanding, sympathy;
We have expected you to be
Little angels from heav'n, but we know,
Though wilful, you're dear little girls.

A Christian Home

(Tune: Finlandia)

O give us homes built firm up-on the
    Sav-ior,
Where Christ is Head and Coun-sel-lor
    and Guide;
Where ev-'ry child is taught His love
    and fa-vor
And gives His heart to Christ, the cru-
    ci-fied:
How sweet to know that tho his foot-
    steps wa-ver
His faith-ful Lord is walk-ing by his side!

O give us homes with God-ly fa-thers,
    moth-ers,
Who al-ways place their hope and trust
    in Him;
Whose ten-der pa-tience tur-moil nev-er
    both-ers,
Whose calm and cour-age trou-ble can-
    not dim;
A home where each finds joy in serv-ing
    oth-ers,
And love still shines, tho days be dark
    and grim.

O Lord, our God, our homes are Thine
    for-ev-er!
We trust to Thee their prob-lems, toil,
    and care;

Their bonds of love no en-e-my can
    sev-er
If Thou art al-ways Lord and Mas-ter
    there:
Be Thou the cen-ter of our least en-deav-
    or—
Be Thou our Guest, our hearts and
    homes to share.

It's Fun to Have a Banquet

(Tune: *Tipperary*)

For Daughters:
Oh what fun to have a banquet,
Oh what fun for us all;
Oh what fun for all the mothers,
For the daughters, short and tall;
Good-by work and study,
Farewell toil and care,

For it's joy, real joy to have a banquet
When your mother's right there.

For Mothers:
Oh what fun to have a banquet,
Oh what fun for us all;
Oh what fun for all the mothers,
For the daughters, short and tall;
Good-by broom and dustpan,
Farewell toil and care
For it's joy, real joy to have a banquet
When your daughter's right there.

Thank You, Lord

(Tune: *Thank You, Lord*)

Thank You, Lord, for Mother so dear,
Thank You for her comfort and cheer,
Thank You, Lord, for giving to me.
My mother's love and her trust in Thee.

QUIZZES AND PUZZLES

Find the Mothers

See how many mothers of the Bible you
can name.
1. Who was the mother of Seth?
2. Who was the mother of Jabal?
3. Who was the mother of Ishmael?
4. Who was the mother of Esau?
5. Who was the mother of Reuben?
6. Who was the mother of Dan?
7. Who was the mother of Moses?
8. Who was the mother of Obed?
9. Who was the mother of Samuel?
10. Who was the mother of Timothy?

ANSWERS:
(1) Genesis 4:25 (2) Genesis 4:20 (3)
Genesis 16:15 (4) Genesis 25:20-26 (5)
Genesis 29:32 (6) Genesis 30:5,6 (7)
Exodus 6:20 (8) Ruth 4:13-17 (9) I
Samuel 1:20 (10) II Timothy 1:5
               The King's Business

Mother Bible Hunt

Connect the following with mothers of
the Bible:

1. "My soul doth magnify the Lord."
2. "Not so; but he shall be called John."
3. "I have lent him to the Lord as long as he liveth."
4. "Is it well with thee? . . . And she answered, It is well."
5. "Entreat me not to leave thee, or to return from following after thee."
6. "Take the child away, and nurse it for me. . . . And the woman took the child and nursed it."
7. She "took the child, and laid it in her bosom, and became nurse unto it."
8. The first mother in the world, called the "mother of all living."

ANSWERS
1. Mary, Luke 1:46; 2. Elisabeth, Luke 1:60; 3. Hannah, I Samuel 1:28; 4. Great woman of Shunem, II Kings 4:26; 5. Ruth, Ruth 1:16; 6. Jochebed, Exodus 2:9; 7. Naomi, Ruth 4:16; 8. Eve, Genesis 3:20.

Name These People

Since May is the month that honors

mothers and since the word mother begins with "M," let us search the Scriptures for the names of people whose name begins with "M." How many can you name?

1. M................................who sat at Jesus' feet.
2. M................................the tax collector who became a disciple.
3. M................................the last book in the Old Testament.
4. M................................the name of Aaron's sister.
5. M................................the man who led the children of Israel through the wilderness.
6. M................................the name of the oldest man that ever lived.
7. M................................the name of Lazarus' sister who served a supper for Jesus.
8. M................................the father of Samson.

ANSWERS

8. Manoah.
Miriam; 5. Moses; 6. Methuselah; 7. Martha;
1. Mary; 2. Matthew; 3. Malachi; 4.

Acrostic

M y soul doth magnify the Lord, and my spirit hath rejoiced in God my Saviour.
Luke 1:46, 47

O pen thou mine eyes, that I may behold wonderous things out of thy law.
Psalm 119:18

T rust in the Lord, and do good; so shalt thou dwell in the land, and verily thou shalt be fed.
Psalm 37:3

H im that cometh to me I will in no wise cast out.
John 6:37

E nter into his gates with thanksgiving, and into his courts with praise.
Psalm 100:4

R est in the Lord, and wait patiently for him.
Psalm 37:7

Mother's Day Acrostic

M y grace is sufficient for thee.
II Corinthians 12:9

O taste and see that the Lord is good.
Psalm 34:8

T rust in the Lord.
Psalm 37:3

H e leadeth me beside the still waters.
Psalm 23:2

E nter into his gate with thanksgiving.
Psalm 100:4

R est in the Lord.
Psalm 37:7

S erve the Lord with gladness.
Psalm 100:2

D raw nigh to God, and he will draw nigh to you.
James 4:8

A sk, and it shall be given you.
Matthew 7:7

Y e are my friend, if ye do whatsoever I command you.
John 15:14

The King's Business

Jumbled Names of Mothers of the Bible

Arrange the letters in the following words so as to spell some of the mothers of the Bible. Also name at least one child of each mother.

1. Cheebjod
2. Nahanh
3. Raash
4. Vee
5. Cieenu
6. Ayrm
7. Hebelatis
8. Celarh
9. Keerhab
10. Slio

Women of the Bible

1. God gave me a little babe
   In answer to my prayer.
   Each year I made a little coat
   For this dear boy to wear
   Who am I? (I Samuel 1:20)

   Hannah

2. My husband's name was Abraham
   And Isaac was my only son.
   We lived to be so very old
   Before our work on earth was done.
   Who am I? (Genesis 21:1-3)

   Sarah

3. My sister, Martha, made a feast
   And Jesus was our guest.
   I poured rich ointment on His feet
   Because I loved Him best.
   Who am I? (John 12:1-3)

   Mary

4. Naomi was my mother-in-law,
   She was to me most dear.
   I followed her to Bethlehem
   And married Boaz there.
   Who am I? (Ruth 1:16)

   Ruth

5. My sister's name was Rachel,
   And I was tender-eyed.
   Because I was the elder
   I first became a bride.
   Who am I? (Genesis 29:16, 17)

   Leah

INEZ GILBERT HALLAN

Mother-Daughter Bible Hunt

Several weeks before Mother's Day, ask the students to find as many names as possible of mothers and their daughters in the Bible. Bible references should be included with the answers.

This hunt could be planned as a contest between departments, classes, mothers and daughters.

Variation: This could also be used as a quiz on Sunday morning, letting students use their Bibles.

Choose The Right Mothers

Each statement is a clue to the name of a Bible mother. Find the Mother's name that matches the clue and draw a line to connect them.

1. The name of a book
   in the Bible.   Rebekah
2. Her son was one
   of Paul's helpers.   Eve
3. The mother of twins.   Eunice
4. Her son was a cousin to
   Jesus.   Ruth
5. She named the first boy.   Hannah
6. Her son lived in the
   church.   Rachel
7. Her son dreamed of angels
   going up and down a
   ladder.   Elizabeth
8. She made a special bed
   for her son.   Bathsheba
9. Her son had a beautiful
   coat.   Rebekah
10. David was the father
    of her son.   Jochebed

HANDCRAFT

Something to Make

As you think of Mother's Day I'm sure you are asking, "What can I give to Mother on her special day?" Mothers like things that are made especially for them—so why not make your mother a Mother's Day Booklet of Bible Verses?

Choose a pretty piece of construction paper for the cover of your book, white paper for the pages, enough to make six pages.

From a piece of construction paper the same color as the piece you chose for the cover, cut the letters M-O-T-H-E-R. The headlines in the daily newspaper will furnish patterns for the letters or you may use the letters from an ABC book for the patterns.

Paste one letter on each of the white pages of the book. Then write on each page a Bible verse beginning with that letter, as:

M   "My peace I give unto you: not as the world giveth, give I unto you. Let not your heart be troubled, neither let it be afraid" (John 14:27).

O   "O the depth of the riches both of the wisdom and knowledge of God! how unsearchable are his judgments, and his ways past finding out" (Romans 11:33).

T   "The eternal God is thy refuge, and underneath are the everlasting arms" (Deuteronomy 33:27).

H   "Her price is far above rubies. . .Her children arise up, and call her blessed; her husband also, and he praiseth her" (Proverbs 31:10,28).

E   "Every good gift and every perfect gift is from above, and cometh down from the Father of lights, with whom is no variableness, neither shadow of turning" (James 1:7).

R   "Rest in the Lord, and wait patiently for him" (Psalm 37:7).

When the book is completed, place all of the white pages within the cover, punch holes and tie with a ribbon or cord. A picture of flowers, cut from a magazine, would decorate the cover; or use a picture of a mother and her child.

The King's Business

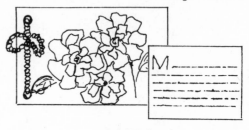

Job Ticket

Would you like to give your mother a nice gift for Mother's Day, but can't stretch your allowance far enough to buy something really nice? Here's an idea:

On a piece of paper mark off sections to look like tickets. On each one write, "Good for one dishwashing," "Good for one bedmaking," or something else that will help your mother. Then she can tear off one of these tickets whenever she needs that job done, and each one will be a gift to her.

Sunshine Magazine

Some Gifts to Make for Mother

A Breakfast Surprise

Choose a plain colored paper place mat and print across the top, "I LOVE YOU MOTHER." Choose a matching napkin and place a fresh carnation on it lengthwise when you put it next to the placemat on the breakfast table. Mother can wear the carnation to church.

A Gift Card with a Gift Promise

Cut a carnation from folded pink construction paper something like the one in the sketch. Cut a second folded carnation from white paper. Use crayons to draw in the petals on the pink carnation folder. Open the white paper and write on it a note to your mother of something special you will do for her during the week. Perhaps it will be to weed the garden, water the lawn, do the dishes, fix your own lunch, feed the pets, run errands, etc., as your special gift promise. Glue the white folder inside the pink one and put it at mother's place during breakfast on Mother's Day.

A Handy Gift

Obtain an empty facial tissue box and some pink shelf paper or contact paper. Carefully cover the tissue box with paper. If you use shelf paper, use Elmer's glue to put the paper on. Cut out several pictures of carnations from used greeting cards or seed catalogs. Paste on covered box. Collect Mother's plastic bags which may be scattered here and there in her kitchen, and place in box. Wrap gift.

Write a note and tell her that this box will fit in a kitchen drawer or cabinet and will help her in storing and finding plastic bags.

Candle Holder

Obtain one or more plain glasses and a small food warmer candle for each. Place candles in glasses. Then obtain pink or red plastic carnations or cut them from seed catalogs or greeting cards. Glue pictures or carnations to glasses or tape plastic carnations to them. Two or more of these in various sizes will make a set of candle holders for the dining room or patio.

Flower Picture For Mother

These are personalized flowers children can make for their mothers. Use white construction paper to cut out large daisies. Cut a yellow construction paper center. Then trim the corners from a recent school photo and carefully "round" it to fit inside the yellow center as shown in the sketch. Use a strip of green construction paper or a green straw for a stem.

Life-Size Greeting

A special greeting for mother may be made life size by pre-school children with a little help. Provide a piece of wrapping paper or wide shelf paper about 12 inches longer than the child is tall. Spread the paper on the floor and let the child lie on it, keeping his arms "inside" the paper. Trace around the child with a crayon. Write "Happy Mother's Day from (child's name)" on the outline. Roll the "greeting" and tie with a piece of yarn.

Greeting Cards for Mother

Children from ages 6 to 12 will enjoy designing and writing their own greeting cards, using crayons, felt-tip pens, construction paper and other materials to make the type of card they feel will please Mother. They may compose a poem-greeting or write whatever thought they wish to express.

The following show a variety of cards and messages from the hearts and hands of children.

Gift Cards

Children may design special cards to accompany a gift or telling Mother what they would like to do for her on Mother's Day or her birthday as a special love gift. Following are examples of cards children have made.

Children may use a heart shaped cookie cutter to make a gift card as shown in the sketches. The cutter is traced on a piece of folded construction paper with a crayon or colored felt-tip pen. Then the message is lettered by pen or crayon.

Potted Plant

For a pot, use an empty cheese or ice cream carton or cut off the bottom third of a milk carton. The children might even use a small terra cotta flower pot. Cover the pot with fancy wrapping paper or foil, fill it with dirt and place a spray of plastic flowers in the center. Or, fasten the flowers in the pot with a ball of clay then crumple a piece of green paper around the stem.

Twin Planters Gift

Cut off the tops of two identical plastic bottles to make planters like those in the sketch. Punch four holes in each planter. Use two pieces of yarn the same length and tie each planter to opposite ends of a wire hanger. Place plastic vines or flowers in the planters. Hang planters where Mother will enjoy them.

Extension Cord Holder

Mother will appreciate this practical gift. Cover an empty tissue roll with white or colored tissue paper or contact paper. Decorate with rick-rack braid. Slip cord in holder as shown in sketch.

Fancy Gift Soap

Select several small decals and apply to bars of toilet soap. When dry, wrap bars with Saran wrap and place in gift box.

TITLE INDEX

MOTHER, GRANDMOTHER, FATHER, PARENTS, HOME, CHILDREN, DAUGHTERS, BOYS

READINGS, DEVOTIONAL TALKS, MESSAGES, TOASTS, SERMON SEED THOUGHTS

SPECIAL MOTHER-DAUGHTER EVENTS

PROGRAMS, PLAYS, DIALOGUES, ETC.

RECITATIONS AND EXERCISES

SONGS AND CHORUSES

AUTHOR INDEX